Free Speech and Incitement in the Twenty-First Century

SUNY series in American Constitutionalism

Robert J. Spitzer, editor

Free Speech and Incitement in the Twenty-First Century

Edited by Eric T. Kasper and JoAnne Sweeny

Cover Credit: *Vision* by Joseph Vogel, 1939.
Published by State University of New York Press, Albany
© 2025 State University of New York
All rights reserved
Printed in the United States of America

No part of this book may be used or reproduced in any manner whatsoever without written permission. No part of this book may be stored in a retrieval system or transmitted in any form or by any means including electronic, electrostatic, magnetic tape, mechanical, photocopying, recording, or otherwise without the prior permission in writing of the publisher.

Links to third-party websites are provided as a convenience and for informational purposes only. They do not constitute an endorsement or an approval of any of the products, services, or opinions of the organization, companies, or individuals. SUNY Press bears no responsibility for the accuracy, legality, or content of a URL, the external website, or for that of subsequent websites.

EU GPSR Authorised Representative:
Logos Europe, 9 rue Nicolas Poussin, 17000, La Rochelle, France
contact@logoseurope.eu

For information, contact State University of New York Press, Albany, NY
www.sunypress.edu

Library of Congress Cataloging-in-Publication Data

Names: Kasper, Eric T., 1977– editor. | Sweeny, JoAnne, 1977– editor.
Title: Free speech and incitement in the twenty-first century / edited by
　Eric T. Kasper and JoAnne Sweeny.
Description: Albany : State University of New York Press, 2025. | Series:
　Suny series in american constitutionalism | Includes bibliographical
　references and index.
Identifiers: LCCN 2024042790 | ISBN 9798855802023 (hardcover) | ISBN
　9798855802047 (ebook)
Subjects: LCSH: Freedom of speech—United States. | United States—Politics
　and government—21st century. | Political crimes and offenses—Law and
　legislation—United States.
Classification: LCC KF4772 .F7394 2025 | DDC 342.7308/53—dc23/eng/20241231
LC record available at https://lccn.loc.gov/2024042790

Contents

Acknowledgments   vii
Preface

   Donald A. Downs   ix

Introduction: Advocacy, Incitement, and Imminent Lawless Action

   JoAnne Sweeny and Eric T. Kasper   1

PART I: THE THEORETICAL UNDERPINNINGS OF *BRANDENBURG*

Chapter One – Tolerating the Violent: The Liberal Egalitarian Justifications for the *Brandenburg* Test

   Adam Kunz   27

Chapter Two – Anti-Orthodoxy, Inclusion, and the Advocacy of Violence

   Timothy C. Shiell   47

Chapter Three – Free Speech, Social Justice, and *Brandenburg*

   Stephen M. Feldman   65

PART II: INCITEMENT EXTENSIONS

Chapter Four – Criminal Solicitation and Incitement as Borderline Criminal Speech: Wily Agitators and Fuzzy Lines

   Rachel E. VanLandingham   85

Chapter Five – Words Behind Walls: Examining the Line Between Incitement and Administrative Overreach in Prisons

   Shavonnie R. Carthens   105

Chapter Six – I Fought the Law, and the First Amendment Won:
How the *Brandenburg* Test Safeguards Musical Expression

    Eric T. Kasper   123

Chapter Seven – "Terrorism" and Arguments to Disregard
Brandenburg's Incitement Test

    Christina E. Wells   143

PART III: *BRANDENBURG* IN THE CONTEMPORARY ERA

Chapter Eight – Incitement on the Internet:
Rethinking First Amendment Standards in Cyberspace

    Howard Schweber and Rebecca J. Anderson   167

Chapter Nine – Incitement in Context

    JoAnne Sweeny   187

Chapter Ten – We Told You So: Why Courts Won't Hold Trump
Accountable for Incitement

    Daniel J. Canon   207

Conclusion: The Future of *Brandenburg*, Incitement, and the First Amendment

    Eric T. Kasper and JoAnne Sweeny   225

Appendix A – Brandenburg v. Ohio	241
Appendix B – Relevant US Supreme Court Rulings	247
Contributors	251
Index	255

Acknowledgments

As is the case for any book, this one has an origin story. It began as an idea after a panel presentation, titled "Fight Like Hell! Redefining Incitement in the Twenty-First Century," that took place virtually on Zoom in March 2021. Panelists included Alan Bigel, JoAnne Sweeny, and Eric T. Kasper, with Robert Pyne serving as the moderator. The panel was organized by Timothy C. Shiell and was cosponsored by the Norman Miller Center for Peace, Justice, and Public Understanding at St. Norbert College, the Menard Center for the Study of Institutions and Innovation at the University of Wisconsin–Stout, and the Menard Center for Constitutional Studies at the University of Wisconsin–Eau Claire. The panel presentation was an enlightening, spirited discussion about advocacy, incitement, free speech, and the First Amendment. We thank everyone involved with organizing, sponsoring, and participating in that panel.

After the presentations concluded for that panel, some of that evening's participants wanted to keep the conversation going. There was interest among several parties to pursue a book-length treatment about incitement, particularly if the volume could exhibit views by different experts, representing various perspectives about the First Amendment. After securing a team of interested free speech scholars, this volume eventually came to fruition. Along the way, the intellectual origins of parts of this manuscript were available elsewhere. For instance, an earlier version of chapter 6 was originally published in *Loyola of Los Angeles Entertainment Law Review* 43 (2023): 173, although chapter 6 is comprised of substantially new material and has a different focus than that much longer article.

We are grateful for those who have helped us along the way to publish this book. Notably, we are indebted to everyone at the SUNY Press who has worked to bring about this publication. In particular, we greatly thank our acquisitions editor Michael Rinella, who shepherded us through the entire process, including with peer reviews (completed by two anonymous readers) and revisions. We also thank Caitlin Bean, who oversaw the production and editing process. Similarly, we are appreciative of each writer who has contributed a chapter to this volume, as each author's unique voice has added a different perspective and caused us to think in new ways about what the First Amendment protects. We would, of course, be remiss if we did not acknowledge the generous funding for this project that was provided by the John Templeton Foundation and by the Institute for Humane Studies (grant no. IHS016528). Most importantly, we are grateful for the love and support given to us by our families.

Finally, if we have inadvertently neglected to thank anyone, we sincerely apologize. The oversight was purely accidental.

Preface

Donald A. Downs

The primary duty of every polity is to deal with the omnipresent problem of violence and lawlessness.[1] In so doing, liberal democracies must also respect the rights of citizens. This elemental tension is essential to the pursuit of criminal law and justice in nations governed by the rule of law.

This tension also underlies the most fundamental line of First Amendment cases in American constitutional law: cases that deal with the question of when the state may legally prohibit speech that poses danger to individuals or the government.[2] Simply put, it is a question of self-defense writ large: when may the state defend itself and its citizens against dangerous speech? Equally important, how may it do so? Constitutional law is concerned not only with the proper ends of state action, but also with the means to achieve those ends. It is also a question of assessing risk and reward: how much dangerous speech are we willing to permit without taking irresponsible risk?

In the wake of the social and political conflicts of the 1960s, the Supreme Court refashioned the constitutional law of civil liberties and civil rights in a decidedly liberal manner. In First Amendment jurisprudence, it limited previous "exceptions" to free speech, such as obscenity, fighting words, hate speech, libel, and commercial speech, across the board. And in *Brandenburg v. Ohio* (1969), the Court unanimously decreed a new doctrine for speech that poses a danger to social order and safety.

The *Brandenburg* test is the most protective free speech test in the world. For example, most liberal democracies interpret racial incitement broadly to include racist advocacy and rhetoric, as did US free speech jurisprudence in the years before *Brandenburg*.[3] In *Yates v. U.S.*, a 1957 case involving the Communist Party, the US Supreme Court allowed suppression of speech that directly advocates illegal action that goes beyond simply teaching or advocating revolutionary or violent ideas.[4] Before *Yates*, the famous "clear and present danger" test permitted punishment of speech that posed merely a "natural tendency" toward unlawful action.[5] *Brandenburg* significantly narrowed the kind of advocacy the state may punish. Today, advocacy and urging of illegal action is punishable only if each prong of *Brandenburg*'s three-part test is met: the speech must be (1) "directed at inciting or producing" (2) "imminent lawless action" (3) that is "likely to incite or produce such action."[6]

The US Supreme Court ultimately chose a different path from the other liberal democracies: opening the public forum and marketplace of ideas to as wide a variety of voices, including those of hate groups, as possible. As the Court wrote in *Cohen v. California* (1971), "[t]hat the air may at times seem filled with verbal cacophony is, in this sense not a sign of weakness but of strength."[7] The theory is that the cacophony of voices in a free society will ultimately sift and winnow its way to truth and good policy. More direct harms caused by real threats and direct incitements are still properly punishable, but the state must trust the citizenry to deal properly with less direct harms associated with or portended by speech.[8]

The fact that *Brandenburg* dealt with a demonstration by a Ku Klux Klan group that was replete with racist advocacy is naturally controversial, but also emblematic of the broader underlying tenets of modern First Amendment jurisprudence, which stipulate: (1) that the state must remain neutral regarding the viewpoint of speech; and (2) that the state may not suppress speech because of an undifferentiated, paternalistic fear that someone might commit an unlawful act by being exposed to it.[9]

Today *Brandenburg* is under attack on a variety of fronts, as new technologies, dangerous groups, and changing cultural sensitivities have led critics to call for its reconsideration. Let us briefly consider some arguments for and against *Brandenburg* in the twenty-first century.

The Normative Case for *Brandenburg*

The main normative argument in *Brandenburg*'s defense flows from the antipaternalism component of modern speech doctrine. A self-governing republic places ultimate power in the hands of "We the People," who are presumed, in a Kantian sense, to be moral agents who are ultimately responsible for their own actions and minds.[10] If so, then the state must not prohibit any *ideas* from being heard or read because to do so is to distrust the moral and mental responsibility of the people. Free speech philosopher Alexander Meiklejohn wrote that the right of listeners is the most important free speech right, and that "[t]o be afraid of ideas, any idea, is to be unfit for self-government."[11]

The definition of *imminence* varies, but it typically means "about to occur," or "in the present moment," or that the speech is directly tied to illegal action.[12] The older tests construed dangerous speech as a virtual trigger to action in a direct stimulus-response sense: S-R. *Brandenburg* places "mind" between the stimulus and the response: S-M-R. This placement respects the independent minds of listeners to reflect on the message, so any illegal action they undertake is their responsibility, not that of the speaker — unless the context of the speech is so heated and close to danger that it is irresponsible to rely on M. As Justice Brandeis wrote forty-two years before the Court finally adopted a direct incitement test in *Brandenburg*, "[i]f there be time to expose through discussion the falsehood and fallacies, to avert the evil by the processes of education, the remedy to be applied is more speech, not enforced silence."[13] Brandeis's opinion also presupposes that listeners have the courage and, crucially, the willingness to deal constructively with hard-hitting discourse and to engage in persuasive counterspeech. Civic virtue is presumed.

Another component of the modern doctrine of speech stipulates government neutrality regarding the content, and especially the viewpoint, of speech. The problem is that the government can often find a pretext or ostensibly neutral reason to punish speech that disguises its actual reason for suppression, such as undifferentiated paternalistic fear of how listeners will react, or simply because government disapproves of the message. Pre-*Brandenburg* tests for dangerous speech were insufficient to protect speech in such contexts. *Brandenburg*'s imminence test, coupled with the requirement that the harm be likely to occur, helps to "hold the government honest," as it were.

Interestingly, this is also what the imminence test does in the criminal law doctrine of self-defense.[14] Many motivations may trigger the use of deadly force, including greed, jealousy, irrational fear, anger, revenge — you name it. But the justifiable deployment of physical force must be limited to actual cases in which a person reasonably believes that he or she confronts imminent danger of great bodily harm or death. Otherwise, self-defense can become a license to kill or maim. Ditto *Brandenburg*, which allows state prohibition of dangerous speech only when the state reasonably and demonstratively believes that state intervention is necessary to prevent imminent lawlessness. The similarity in wording and logic between criminal self-defense law and the *Brandenburg* test makes sense because both tests address a similar problem: when a person, group, or the state may use force (or censorship) in the honest desire to protect themselves from danger.

The Practical Argument for *Brandenburg*

Brandenburg is also a practical test to apply. The Supreme Court adjudicates our republic's most profound principles and doctrines of public law. But judicial experience and statesmanship also obligate the Court to create tests that are subject to being applied in a politically neutral and consistent manner. In addition, the Court also considers judicial capacity, lest it and lower courts get overrun with cases or uncertainty.[15] *Brandenburg*'s test fulfills this obligation, especially compared to previous doctrine regarding dangerous speech, because its terms and application are narrowly defined and similar to long-standing self-defense logic. It has therefore withstood the test of time.[16]

Brandenburg Reconsidered

Critics accuse *Brandenburg* of being outmoded for several reasons. The most relevant argument for our purposes is that racist and other hateful rhetoric contribute in a causative way to the spread of prejudice-inspired crime.[17] This problem is magnified with the rise of social media that facilitates the formation of hate groups, helps the coordination of dangerous action, and influences impressionable and already biased minds. Indeed, some mass shooters and terrorist actions have been motivated by the hateful rants of online chatrooms and advocacies.[18] Beyond these connections, abusers use social media and the internet to "mob," harass, and intimidate people, although they stop short of threatening them in legal terms. These concerns about racist and similar forms of hate are real and need to be taken seriously.

Above and beyond the claims regarding causation, scholars and other commentators point out that racist and hateful rhetoric cause hurt and anxiety in individuals in the targeted groups.[19] The central question for our purposes is what impact these critiques should have on the status of *Brandenburg*. Overturning *Brandenburg* in favor of a less protective test would raise some of the concerns discussed above, to which we could add that the question of causation is considerably more complicated than is often assumed. For example, the pre–World War II period often witnessed as much anti-Semitic rhetoric in France as in Germany, yet Nazism did not take over the government in France until Hitler did by force in 1940.[20] Germany witnessed a host of distinctive problems, including those associated with economic chaos, postwar anger, and political and cultural disarray that were crucial causative factors in Hitler's rise to power.[21] Scholarly works have also delineated the inefficiency and unintended consequences of punishing hateful rhetoric, as opposed to direct incitement and threats, including the way in which such punitiveness might actually exacerbate that what it hopes to thwart.[22]

In contemplating reform, we should consider two things: first, that *Brandenburg* and the modern doctrine of speech do allow punishment for real threats, illegal incitement, and speech that is itself a component of criminal action; second, that the state has many other tools for combating the harms posed by dangerous and discriminatory rhetoric. These include such measures as government counterspeech, proper government surveillance, and forthright punishment of those who actually commit acts prohibited by law.

The Supreme Court went through trial and error over the course of many decades before it settled on a test for dangerous speech that is amenable to principled application and keeping the government honest. Any consideration of reform needs to keep these important points in mind.[23]

Notes

1. See, for example, Douglas C. North et al., *Violence and Social Orders: A Conceptual Framework for Interpreting Recorded Human History* (Cambridge University Press, 2009).
2. Most casebooks on the First Amendment begin with a treatment of this line of cases because of its fundamentality to the most important question in free speech jurisprudence.
3. See, for example, Louis Greenspan and Cyrill Levitt, eds., *Under the Shadow of Weimar: Democracy, Law, and Racial Incitement in Six Countries* (Praeger, 1993).
4. Yates v. U.S., 354 U.S. 298 (1957).
5. See Schenck v. U.S., 249 U.S. 47 (1919); Debs v. US., 249 U.S. 211 (1919). See also David Rabban, *Free Speech in Its Forgotten Years* (Cambridge University Press, 1997).
6. Brandenburg v. Ohio, 395 U.S. 444 (1969), 447.
7. Cohen v. California, 403 U.S. 15 (1971), 25.
8. On threats see, for example, Virginia v. Black, 538 U.S. 343 (2003).
9. See, for example, Laurence Tribe, *American Constitutional Law* (Foundation Press, 2000), chapter 12.
10. On the Kantian basis of constitutional principles, see Hadley Arkes, *The Philosopher in the City* (Princeton University Press, 1981).
11. Alexander Meiklejohn, "Free Speech and Its Relation to Self-Government," in *Political Freedom: The Constitutional Powers of the People* (Oxford University Press, 1965), 27–28.
12. Speech that is part and parcel of crime, as in criminal conspiracy and solicitation, also falls outside of Brandenburg's protection. See, for example, Kent Greenawalt, *Speech, Crime, and the Uses of Language* (Oxford University Press, 1989).
13. Whitney California, 274 U.S. 357 (1927), 377.
14. On how the imminence test holds claimants honest in self-defense cases, see George Fletcher, *A Crime of Self-Defense: Bernard Goetz and the Law* (Free Press, 1988).
15. See, for example, Andrew Coan, *Rationing the Constitution: How Judicial Capacity Shapes Supreme Court Decision-Making* (Cambridge University Press, 2019).
16. For example, advocacy — short of incitement — of positions linked to terrorism after 9/11 was protected in academic freedom cases according to an exhaustive report by the American Association of University Professors (AAUP). And cases upholding verdicts in criminal and civil court have involved either direct incitements or speech that was instructional or part and parcel of criminal action. One case involved inciting an angry mob in front of a jail to "assassinate" the sheriff with a chant: "Two, Four, Six, Eight! Who Shall we assassinate? Deputy Sheriff, and the whole bunch of

you!" Matthews v. State, So. 2d 1066 (1978). Another case dealt with a website that interacted with viewers while advocating the murder of abortion doctors. Planned Parenthood v. American Coalition of Life Activists, 290 F.3d 1058 (2002).
17. See, for example, Alexander Tsesis, *Destructive Messages: How Hate Speech Paves the Way for Harmful Social Movements* (NYU Press, 2002).
18. See, for example, "How Social Media Companies Could Be Complicit in Incitement to Genocide," 21 *Chicago Journal of International Law*, 83 (2020–2021).
19. See, for example, Jeremy Waldron, The Harm in Hate Speech (Harvard University Press, 2012).
20. See, for example, Anuj Desai, Anuj C. Desai, "Attacking Brandenburg with History: Does the Long-Term Harm of Biased Speech Justify a Criminal Statute Suppressing it?," *Federal Communications and Law Journal* 55: 353–94 (2003).
21. See, for example, Benjamin Carter Heit, *The Death of Democracy: Hitler's Rise to Power and the Downfall of the Weimar Republic* (Henry Holt, 2018).
22. See, for example, Nadine Strossen, *Hate: Why We Should Resist It with Free Speech, Not Censorship* (Oxford University Press, 2018).
23. See, for example, Greg Lukianoff and Jonathan Haidt, *The Coddling of the American Mind: How Good Intentions and Bad Ideas Are Setting Up a Generation for Failure* (Penguin Books, 2018).

Introduction

Advocacy, Incitement, and Imminent Lawless Action

JoAnne Sweeny and Eric T. Kasper

The freedom of speech is a fundamental right that is enshrined in the US Constitution, and the US Supreme Court has long recognized its vital importance. This First Amendment freedom is integral to the marketplace of ideas, helping to foster the search for truth through sifting and winnowing in discussion and debate. As put by the US Supreme Court in *Gertz v. Robert Welch, Inc.* (1974), "[u]nder the First Amendment there is no such thing as a false idea. However pernicious an opinion may seem, we depend for its correction not on the conscience of judges and juries but on the competition of other ideas."[1] Similarly, freedom of speech is important to the functioning of our democracy, so that we can express views on candidates for public office and advocate for the policies of our preferences. As explained by the Supreme Court in *New York Times Co. v. Sullivan* (1964), under the First Amendment we have "a profound national commitment to the principle that debate on public issues should be uninhibited, robust, and wide-open," which includes even "vehement, caustic, and sometimes unpleasantly sharp attacks on government and public officials."[2] Freedom of speech is also a part of our individual autonomy to live our lives freely as we see fit. According to the Supreme Court in *Wooley v. Maynard* (1977), "[t]he right to speak and the right to refrain from speaking are complementary components of the broader concept of individual freedom of mind."[3]

In particular, the US Supreme Court has found that the First Amendment protects speech even if some people strongly disagree with it and do not want it to be said. In *Texas v. Johnson* (1989), the Supreme Court declared the following: "If there is a bedrock principle underlying the First Amendment, it is that the government may not prohibit the expression of an idea simply because society finds the idea itself offensive or disagreeable."[4] Put another way more recently in *Mahanoy Area School District v. B.L.* (2021), "[o]ur representative democracy only works if we protect the 'marketplace of ideas.' This free exchange facilitates an informed public opinion, which, when transmitted to lawmakers, helps produce laws that reflect the People's will. That protection must include the protection of unpopular ideas, for popular ideas have less need for protection."[5]

Reflecting the capacity for speakers to use their rights to advocate for malevolent ends, the Supreme Court in *Snyder v. Phelps* (2011) opined the following:

"Speech is powerful. It can stir people to action, move them to tears of both joy and sorrow, and . . . inflict great pain. On the facts before us, we cannot react to that pain by punishing the speaker. As a Nation we have chosen a different course — to protect even hurtful speech on public issues to ensure that we do not stifle public debate."[6] For these reasons, the Supreme Court explained in *McCutcheon v. FEC* (2014) — a case finding First Amendment protection for campaign contributions — that "[m]oney in politics may at times seem repugnant to some, but so too does much of what the First Amendment vigorously protects. If the First Amendment protects flag burning, funeral protests, and Nazi parades — despite the profound offense such spectacles cause — it surely protects political campaign speech despite popular opposition."[7]

As robust as our First Amendment protections for free speech are in the United States today, the Constitution does not protect one's right to say whatever one wants, wherever one wants, however one wants, at all times. For instance, while there is a strong right to protest in traditional public forums, there may be legitimate content and viewpoint neutral regulations of the time, place, and manner of expression, such as when a municipality enacts noise limits or requires street parades to be limited to certain times of day.[8]

Likewise, public school students' free speech rights are protected until the point where they materially and substantially disrupt educational activities. Public employees remain free from reprimands at their jobs if they speak as private citizens on matters of public concern, but only if that expression is not outweighed by legitimate efficiency and effectiveness concerns of the government. Finally, and most notably for our purposes, there are a small number of narrowly defined categories of speech that are wholly outside of First Amendment protection; these include true threats, defamation, obscenity, child pornography, fraud, and speech integral to criminal conduct.[9]

Incitement to imminent lawless action is another category of speech that is outside of First Amendment protection. In short, today incitement is defined as a person intentionally provoking an audience to engage in illegal or violent action that is likely to, or will, occur imminently. During earlier periods in US history, advocacy — without immediate threats of violence — was found by the US Supreme Court to be outside of the First Amendment's protection. The Supreme Court has heard more incitement cases (thus giving it more opportunities to develop its incitement doctrine), during more tumultuous periods in our nation's history, as those are the times when speakers are more likely to use vitriolic rhetoric to advocate for radical ideas. As we will detail below, the Supreme Court began examining First Amendment protections for advocacy in the early twentieth century and first formulated a test for incitement at the end of World War I. The Supreme Court subsequently reformulated that test through times of labor strife, and during the Cold War, the civil rights movement, and at the height of protests against the Vietnam War. These reformulations culminated in a test announced by the Supreme Court in *Brandenburg v. Ohio* (1969).

Since the 1970s, incitement doctrine has remained largely unchanged by the Supreme Court and, as such, has received relatively little academic or media attention until recently. Since the late 2010s, however, public rhetoric has again become more caustic, and our politics have become more tumultuous, with violence at political rallies, armed protests around Confederate statues, social unrest associated with demonstrations against police, and an attack on the US Capitol. This has led to new incitement cases in the lower courts and an opportunity to examine how incitement is defined and applied. Some contemporary examples will help to better understand the questions raised when courts define the line between protected free speech and unprotected incitement.

Take, for instance, January 6, 2021, when a violent mob attack occurred at the US Capitol. This attack disrupted the counting of Electoral College votes and led to the evacuation of Vice President Mike Pence and members of Congress from the House and Senate chambers. The events that day caused a stoppage to the official proceedings peacefully transferring the power of the presidency and, in the process, many people illegally entered the Capitol, used dangerous weapons against law enforcement, and committed assaults, disruptive behavior, obstruction, and theft. Five people died from injuries sustained at the Capitol that day. By the fall of 2024, more than 1,000 people had been convicted of, or had pleaded guilty to, at least one crime committed at the Capitol.[10]

Clearly, those who engaged in violence and other illegal acts at the Capitol on January 6, 2021, can face — and have been facing — criminal liability. But the attack was preceded by rallying in Washington, DC, which included President Donald Trump speaking to a crowd at the Ellipse, pronouncing the lines, "You'll never take back our country with weakness," and "We fight. We fight like hell. And if you don't fight like hell, you're not going to have a country anymore."[11] Several other Trump supporters spoke at the Ellipse, including Rudy Giuliani, who advocated for "trial by combat."[12]

Were President Trump and the other speakers at the Ellipse protected by the First Amendment? Multiple Capitol rioters have stated that they believed they were acting under Trump's orders.[13] One of Trump's supporters in the 2020 election, Senator Ted Cruz, remarked the day after the Capitol attack that "yesterday in particular, the President's language and rhetoric crossed the line and it was reckless."[14] Senator Mitch McConnell, then–Senate majority leader, remarked: "The mob was fed lies. They were provoked by the President and other powerful people."[15] Acting Secretary of Defense Christopher Miller, a Trump appointee, rhetorically asked and answered the following: "Would anybody have marched on the Capitol, and tried to overrun the Capitol, without the President's speech? I think it's pretty much definitive that wouldn't have happened."[16] Given these connections between President Trump's speech and the Capitol rioters, does the First Amendment permit him to be prosecuted criminally or sued civilly, or does the First Amendment protect his speech? These are complex legal questions.

Notably, President Trump's speech at the Ellipse also contained the following lines: "I know that everyone here will soon be marching over to the Capitol building to *peacefully* and patriotically make your voices heard," and "We're going to walk down to the Capitol, and we're going to cheer on our brave senators and congressmen and -women."[17] Do statements like this negate any possible liability by President Trump in his speech and provide him with First Amendment protection? Does his intent matter? Does the amount of lawlessness that occurred matter? Does the location or timing of his speech matter, if some of the rioters were already at the Capitol, a mile away from the Ellipse, when he uttered those words? How does the overall context of the speech matter, including what President Trump said in the days leading up to January 6, 2021?

Consider, for example, one of the most emphasized lines in President Trump's speech, "fight like hell." Upon the death of author Barbara Ehrenreich in 2022, her son, Ben Ehrenreich stated the following: "She was never much for thoughts and prayers, but you can honor her memory by loving one another, and by fighting like hell."[18] The use of very similar language did not result in widespread calls for censorship or condemnation, so was there a significant difference between that statement and the one issued on January 6, 2021?

President Trump was not the only politician who communicated messages that would have been received by the Capitol rioters before they stormed the building on January 6, 2021. Senator Josh Hawley spoke symbolically to the crowd outside the Capitol that day by raising his fist in solidarity with those present, something later characterized by a member of the Select Committee to Investigate the January 6th Attack on the United States Capitol as a move that "riled up the crowd," making it more difficult for officers to hold back the throng outside the building.[19] However, this form of nonverbal communication has not led to any lawsuits or significant calls for Hawley to be charged with inciting anyone who attacked the Capitol that day. Is President Trump's speech different from Senator Hawley's gesture? If so, how?

In the days leading up to January 6, 2021, Representative Louie Gohmert was part of a lawsuit asking a federal court to expand the authority of the vice president at the time, Mike Pence, to refuse to certify the results of the 2020 presidential election. When the US Court of Appeals dismissed that lawsuit on January 2, 2021, Representative Gohmert stated of the court's decision: "Essentially, the ruling would be 'You have to go to the streets and be as violent as antifa, BLM.'"[20] This followed comments by Representative Gohmert in November 2020 that Trump's supporters should contemplate a "revolution," like the coup that occurred in Egypt in 2013; according to Gohmert, "[i]f they can do that there, think of what we can do here."[21] Although a congressional censure resolution was introduced against Representative Gohmert for his comments, that resolution never came to a vote,[22] and no legal action has been taken against him. Should these comments be protected by the First Amendment, because they preceded the relevant January 6 violence by days or weeks? How close in time to violence can speech be before it can be understood as inciting that violence?

We can also look at statements of politicians unconnected to the events of January 6, 2021. Consider how, on April 17, 2021, toward the end of Derek Chauvin's criminal trial for murdering George Floyd (of which Chauvin was ultimately convicted), Congresswoman Maxine Waters stated to the media in Brooklyn Park, Minnesota, that if there was a not guilty verdict in the case, "[w]e've got to stay on the street and we've got to get more active, we've got to get more confrontational, we've got to make sure that they know we mean business." The judge presiding over Chauvin's trial called those comments "disrespectful to the rule of law," but he refused to declare a mistrial in the case because the jury was instructed to refrain from watching the news and because "a congresswoman's opinion really doesn't matter a whole lot" in determining an outcome in the case. Why did the judge find that such comments did not affect the trial, and at what point could a politician's comments unduly affect how a court decides a case so that they are no longer protected by the First Amendment?[23]

For yet another example, one can turn to comments made by Senator Chuck Schumer on March 4, 2020, to a crowd gathered outside the Supreme Court building, as the justices were hearing oral arguments in an abortion case: "I want to tell you Gorsuch, I want to tell you Kavanaugh — you have released the whirlwind, and you will pay the price. You won't know what hit you if you go forward with these awful decisions." Chief Justice John Roberts responded by asserting that "Justices know that criticism comes with the territory, but threatening statements of this sort from the highest levels of government are not only inappropriate, they are dangerous." Nevertheless, no legal action was taken against Senator Schumer, and Chief Justice Roberts concluded that "[a]ll members of the court will continue to do their job, without fear or favor, from whatever quarter." At what point would statements using this type of rhetoric go beyond the protections of the First Amendment?[24]

More recently, in a private phone call to donors on July 8, 2024, President Joe Biden tried to reassure listeners that he was staying in the 2024 presidential race after demands from various quarters that he drop out after a poor debate performance. During the call, Biden uttered the following: "I have one job, and that's to beat Donald Trump. I'm absolutely certain I'm the best person to be able to do that. So, we're done talking about the debate. It's time to put Trump in a bull's-eye." Five days later at a campaign rally in Pennsylvania, a gunman attempted to assassinate Donald Trump, resulting in Trump being struck in the ear, with one rally attendee being fatally shot and others wounded. Following the assassination attempt, several members of Congress — including Representative Mike Collins, Senator Marsha Blackburn, and Representative Lauren Boebert — issued public comments condemning President Biden's "bull's-eye" remark. Particularly, Representative Collins made comparisons to January 6: "after an attempted assassination of President Trump, the same people who wanted him prosecuted for telling his supporters to peacefully march to the Capitol on January 6 are not calling for President Biden's prosecution after he said it was time to put President Trump in the bull's-eye after their debate."[25] Was President Biden's comment protected by the First Amendment?

At different points in United States history, different legal questions have been asked to determine if a speaker was criminally or civilly liable for the actions of that speaker's listeners or readers. This is because the US Supreme Court's interpretation of what the First Amendment protects for speakers in these situations has changed over time. Although those protections have grown substantially over the last century, that growth has not been linear, and there are questions that have arisen in recent decades about the incitement test and its application.

Since 1791, the First Amendment has commanded that "Congress shall make no law . . . abridging the freedom of speech, or of the press." Before the beginning of the twentieth century, there were very few US Supreme Court cases interpreting the constitutional protection for free expression generally, and there were virtually none directly touching on the question of advocacy of substantial political change or illegal behavior. This is true for several reasons. First, Congress did not pass much legislation that restricted expression for the first century of the First Amendment's existence, the only major exceptions being the 1798 Sedition Act (which expired in 1801) and various laws passed in the 1870s that banned obscenity, restricted what can be sent through the mail, and limited the speech of aliens. Second, it was also not until the 1870s that Congress passed legislation giving the Supreme Court general federal question jurisdiction, meaning that many early federal cases involving expressive questions were not eligible for Supreme Court review. Third, it was not until 1925 that the Supreme Court incorporated the Free Speech Clause of the First Amendment in *Gitlow v. New York*, making it applicable to the states through the Due Process Clause of the Fourteenth Amendment, so before that time there was relatively little state action affecting expression that the Supreme Court could have reviewed.[26]

One of the earliest Supreme Court cases outlining the constitutional protections for advocacy of controversial ideas was *United States ex rel. Turner v. Williams* (1904). John Turner was a British national who was deported from the United States due to his possession of anarchist literature. The Supreme Court found no constitutional protection for advocacy of anarchy: "Even if Turner . . . only regarded the absence of government as a political ideal, yet when he sought to attain it by advocating [a] universal strike . . . we cannot say that the inference was unjustifiable either that he contemplated the ultimate realization of his ideal by the use of force, or that his speeches were incitements to that end." Put another way, the Supreme Court ruled that even if "the word 'anarchists' should be interpreted as including aliens whose anarchistic views are professed as those of political philosophers innocent of evil intent," Congress still had the power to exclude such persons, as Congress could determine that "the tendency of the general exploitation of such views is so dangerous to the public weal that aliens who hold and advocate them would be undesirable additions to our population." Thus, Congress had the power to deport persons advocating such political philosophies.[27]

Similarly, in *Patterson v. Colorado* (1907), the US Supreme Court upheld a contempt conviction against Thomas Patterson for articles and a political cartoon he published that were critical of decisions of the Colorado Supreme Court that related to a gubernatorial election and a state constitutional amendment. These matters were scheduled to have a rehearing in the state's supreme court, and Patterson's contempt conviction was based on the conclusion that his publication could interfere with the court's ruling.[28] In other words, Patterson's contempt conviction was premised on the idea that his publication might incite people to intimidate justices of the state supreme court. The US Supreme Court did not say if the First Amendment applied to state governments, ruling that the justices would leave "undecided the question whether there is to be found in the Fourteenth Amendment a prohibition similar to that in the First." However, even if the First Amendment limited state powers, the Supreme Court in *Patterson* found that it limited merely prior restraints (not punishments after one spoke or published). Speaking of the constitutional protection for free expression, the Supreme Court announced that "the main purpose of such constitutional provisions is to prevent all such previous restraints upon publications . . . , and they do not prevent the subsequent punishment of such as may be deemed contrary to the public welfare." If the speech would tend to create bad outcomes, government could criminalize it, and in this case, the Supreme Court found that Patterson's publication was not protected because it "would tend to obstruct the administration of justice." Such an understanding of expression protected relatively little speech.[29]

The protection for advocacy had not improved when the Supreme Court decided *Fox v. Washington* (1915). At issue was a magazine article titled, "The Nude and the Prudes," which alleged a group of "prudes" infiltrated a group of nude sunbathers and then alerted police, who made several arrests. Jay Fox's article promoted both nudism and a boycott of businesses owned by the "prudes" who snitched on the sunbathers. However, Fox was then convicted of a state law that prohibited "advocating, encouraging or inciting, or having a tendency to encourage or incite the commission of any crime, breach of the peace or act of violence, or which shall tend to encourage or advocate disrespect for law or for any court or courts of justice." Would the Supreme Court find that advocating for nudism and a business boycott constituted protected speech? The answer in *Fox* was "no." According to the Supreme Court, the law at issue was applied constitutionally because "the article encourages and incites a persistence in what we must assume would be a breach of the state laws against indecent exposure."[30]

A different way of thinking about First Amendment protections for advocacy of illegal behavior emerged in *Schenck v. United States* (1919). Socialist leader Charles Schenck was convicted of violating the Espionage Act of 1917, which prohibited attempts at obstructing military recruitment. Schenck mailed a pamphlet to draft-eligible persons that reprinted the text of the Thirteenth Amendment (which bans slavery and involuntary servitude, except upon conviction for a crime) and alleged "conscription was despotism in its worst form and a monstrous wrong against humanity in the interest of Wall Street's chosen few." The Supreme Court unanimously upheld Schenck's conviction. Justice Oliver Wendell Holmes Jr. wrote for the justices, devising a new test for speech that advocates action, the clear and present danger test: "The question in every case is whether the words used are used in such circumstances and are of such a nature as to create a clear and present danger that they will bring about the substantive evils that Congress has a right to prevent." Justice Holmes provided a hypothetical situation to explain how not all expression is protected by the First Amendment: "The most stringent protection of free speech would not protect a man in falsely shouting fire in a theatre and causing a panic." Using the test, Holmes upheld Schenck's conviction, reasoning how if Schenck sent these leaflets he must have intended for them "to have some effect," with the logical conclusion that the desired effect was to influence draftees not to report for duty.[31]

Although *Schenck*'s clear and present danger test in theory was more protective of expression than previous Supreme Court decisions, in practice it upheld a criminal conviction for mere advocacy of political and economic philosophy that opposed government policy.[32] Indeed, the Supreme Court cited no evidence that a single draftee failed to report for duty after reading Schenck's pamphlet. Furthermore, *Schenck* introduced in American constitutional law the problematic analogy of a lack of protection for falsely shouting fire in a crowded theater. In Schenck's case, was there really a theoretical "fire," in the dangers posed by the war, of which he was trying to warn his readers? Even if there was no "fire" in this sense, did Schenck actually believe that there was one, and, if so, should he be punished for such advocacy? Within one week of *Schenck*, the Supreme Court issued unanimous decisions upholding convictions for giving a speech advocating for draft resistance, publishing newspaper articles disapproving of US involvement in World War I, and giving a speech promoting socialism and condemning militarism.[33] In a variety of cases, the Supreme Court had interpreted the First Amendment to allow government to criminalize any advocacy it could thinly claim caused any purported clear and present danger.

Justice Holmes began to rethink his approach to the criminalization of advocacy several months later when he dissented in *Abrams v. United States* (1919). Anarchist Jacob Abrams distributed leaflets advocating for a general strike to hinder United States war efforts. The leaflets decried American military involvement in World War I and the Russian Revolution, criticizing President Woodrow Wilson specifically (calling him "shameful" and "cowardly") and capitalism generally. Like Schenck, Abrams was convicted of violating the Espionage Act, and the Supreme Court upheld his conviction. A 7 to 2 majority found that instead of "an attempt to bring about a change of administration by candid discussion," the "language of these circulars was obviously intended to provoke and to encourage resistance to the United States in the war." More specifically, the majority found that "the plain purpose of their propaganda was to excite, at the supreme crisis of the war, disaffection, sedition, riots, and, as they hoped, revolution, in this country."[34] Thus, a majority of justices found no First Amendment protection for this leaflet.

In *Abrams*, Justice Holmes dissented, joined by Justice Louis Brandeis. And this dissent would eventually change the course of American free speech jurisprudence. According to Holmes, there was no threat of any real, direct harm to the United States and its war effort, as the case involved merely "a silly leaflet by an unknown man." As explained by Holmes, unless there is real, direct harm caused by the speech, it should be protected, because, "[t]o allow opposition by speech seems to indicate that you think the speech impotent, as when a man says that he has squared the circle, or that you do not care whole-heartedly for the result, or that you doubt either your power or your premises." Instead, on questions of opinion, history has shown that many opinions suppressed in the past were later found to be true, as Holmes described that "men have realized that time has upset many fighting faiths." Holmes advocated that "the ultimate good desired is better reached by free trade in ideas . . . the best test of truth is the power of the thought to get itself accepted in the competition of the market." Because we cannot know with certainty what is true and what the "right" answer is, the First Amendment requires these ideas to compete against each other, allowing everyone to speak, and listen, to others. Holmes believed that expression must be protected unless the following conditions are met: "We should be eternally vigilant against attempts to check the expression of opinions that we loathe and believe to be fraught with death, unless they so imminently threaten immediate interference with the lawful and pressing purposes of the law that an immediate check is required to save the country." For Holmes, only an imminent or immediate threat of lawlessness caused by speech was a reason to suppress it, and these "silly" leaflets were not going to lead to any such harm.[35]

Holmes's approach in *Abrams* would have protected much more expression than the jurisprudence used by the majority of the Supreme Court or even Holmes's *Schenck* opinion earlier in 1919.[36] Yet, as compelling as Holmes was, among his colleagues it convinced only Justice Brandeis. For the next decade, those two justices remained in dissent in free speech cases where a majority of justices upheld convictions for advocating ideas. In *Pierce v. United States* (1920) another Espionage Act conviction was sustained by the Supreme Court, in this case for producing a pamphlet titled "The Price We Pay," which, like the circulars at issue in *Schenck* and *Abrams*, criticized American involvement in World War I, tying its promotion to what the pamphlet characterized as war profiteering capitalists. The majority in *Pierce* found that since a jury could determine that the pamphlet at issue had "a tendency to cause insubordination, disloyalty, and refusal of duty in the military and naval forces of the United States,"[37] the First Amendment did not protect it.

Brandeis wrote a dissent in *Pierce*, joined by Holmes, finding that the cause of United States involvement in the war was the real issue of discussion in the pamphlet, and that the government did not have a monopoly on truth on that subject: "statements like that here charged to be false are in essence matters of opinion and judgment, not matters of fact to be determined by a jury . . . All the alleged false statements were an interpretation and discussion of public facts of public interest." For Brandeis, Pierce was "striv[ing] for better conditions through new legislation and new institutions . . . by argument to fellow citizens," meaning it was unconstitutional to interpret such efforts "as criminal incitement to disobey the existing law."[38]

The Supreme Court's aversion to protecting advocacy continued in *Gilbert v. Minnesota* (1920). At issue was a state sedition law making it a crime to advocate or teach that one should not enlist in the military. Joseph Gilbert was convicted for claiming that the World War I draft was aimed at conscripting the working class, and that the United States was "stampeded into this war by newspaper rot to pull England's chestnuts out of the fire for her." The Supreme Court sustained his conviction, finding that "Gilbert's speech . . . was not an advocacy of policies or a censure of actions that a citizen had the right to make," concluding instead that "every word that he uttered in denunciation of the war was false, was deliberate misrepresentation of the motives which impelled it, and the objects for which it was prosecuted."[39] Justice Brandeis dissented in *Gilbert*, arguing that Minnesota's sedition act "relates to the teaching of the doctrine of pacifism and the legislature in effect proscribes it for all time," meaning that it "aims to prevent not acts but beliefs."[40] Nevertheless, Gilbert's prison sentence remained in place.

Protections for advocacy did not improve as the 1920s progressed. Perhaps the least protective free speech decision from the Supreme Court during the decade was *Gitlow v. New York* (1925). Benjamin Gitlow was convicted for violating a New York anti-anarchy law, which banned advocating, advising, or teaching that the government should be forcibly overthrown. Gitlow, a socialist, had distributed "The Left Wing Manifesto," which, as described by the Supreme Court, stated, "the necessity of accomplishing the 'Communist Revolution' by a militant and 'revolutionary Socialism,' based on 'the class struggle' and mobilizing the 'power of the proletariat in action,' through mass industrial revolts developing into mass political strikes and 'revolutionary mass action.'" The justices upheld Gitlow's conviction, finding that government may punish speech "if its natural tendency and probable effect was to bring about the substantive evil which the legislative body might prevent." Known as the bad tendency test, this approach was much less protective than the clear and present danger test or what Holmes advocated in his *Abrams* dissent.

Writing for the majority in *Gitlow*, Justice Edward Sanford provided a fire-based analogy to explain the bad tendency test: "A single revolutionary spark may kindle a fire that, smouldering for a time, may burst into a sweeping and destructive conflagration. It cannot be said that the State is acting arbitrarily or unreasonably when in the exercise of its judgment as to the measures necessary to protect the public peace and safety, it seeks to extinguish the spark without waiting until it has enkindled the flame or blazed into the conflagration." With the *Gitlow* ruling, the government could punish expression that had merely a tendency to lead to danger, not just in the immediate moment but significantly into the future as well.[41]

The *Gitlow* decision was a major step backward compared to the clear and present danger test, and Justice Holmes seized on this in a dissent joined by Justice Brandeis: "It is said that this manifesto was more than a theory, that it was an incitement. Every idea is an incitement." Holmes argued that ideas cause us to think, and rethink, what we know about the world. Holmes continued: "there was no present danger of an attempt to overthrow the government by force on the part of the admittedly small minority who shared the defendant's views," so the speech at issue should have been protected. Adding to his concern about immediacy in *Abrams*, Holmes in *Gitlow* showed the importance of emphasizing the likelihood of illegality resulting from speech, and in this case that likelihood was nil.[42]

Although the opinion of the Court in *Gitlow* was highly problematic, there was one positive that came from the case: the Supreme Court incorporated the First Amendment's freedom of speech protection, meaning that whatever was protected would now be shielded from abridgement by the states, not just the federal government.[43]

The Supreme Court's refusal to protect advocacy continued in *Whitney v. California* (1927). Charlotte Whitney was convicted of violating a state syndicalism law (which banned organizing an association that advocates or teaches unlawful acts of force to accomplish a change in industrial ownership or to effect political change) for her efforts in establishing the California Communist Labor Party. The Supreme Court upheld that conviction, again using the bad tendency test: "a State . . . may punish those who abuse this freedom [of speech] by utterances . . . tending to incite to crime, disturb the public peace, or endanger the foundations of organized government and threaten its overthrow by unlawful means." The majority explained that the state's determination that expression advocating such illegality "must be given great weight. Every presumption is to be indulged in favor of the validity of the statute."[44]

Justice Brandeis wrote separately to explain the fault in providing such deference to the government. He began by providing his preferred standard, that speech should be protected unless it "would produce, or is intended to produce, a clear and imminent danger of some substantive evil which the State constitutionally may seek to prevent." Brandeis argued this approach was required by the First Amendment because "[t]hose who won our independence believed that the final end of the State was to make men free to develop their faculties; and that in its government the deliberative forces should prevail over the arbitrary." Opining further about the Founders, Brandeis explained that "[t]hey believed that freedom to think as you will and to speak as you think are means indispensable to the discovery and spread of political truth; that without free speech and assembly discussion would be futile." Brandeis elaborated on how "[f]ear of serious injury cannot alone justify suppression of free speech and assembly," because, historically, "[m]en feared witches and burnt women."

For those reasons, Brandeis outlined, specifically, the narrow type of situation when advocacy could be restricted: "To justify suppression of free speech there must be reasonable ground to fear that serious evil will result if free speech is practiced. There must be reasonable ground to believe that the danger apprehended is imminent [and] that the evil to be prevented is a serious one." Brandeis clarified that even if one advocates for something illegal that is "reprehensible morally," that "is not a justification for denying free speech where the advocacy falls short of incitement and there is nothing to indicate that the advocacy would be immediately acted on." As persuasive as this protection was to find truth and protect deliberative democracy, only Justice Holmes joined the opinion.[45]

Although it might have looked like the Supreme Court was always going to defer to the government's power to punish advocacy it deemed could tend toward bad outcomes, things began to change in the 1930s. Under the leadership of Chief Justice Charles Evans Hughes, a majority of justices started to move toward the Holmes–Brandeis approach to expression. For instance, *De Jonge v. Oregon* (1937) involved another state syndicalism conviction, this time for Dirk De Jonge's Communist Party meeting speech where he criticized police violence against striking union members. De Jonge did not advocate for any violence. Chief Justice Hughes wrote for a unanimous Supreme Court overturning his conviction, reasoning how although "rights may be abused by using speech or press or assembly in order to incite to violence and crime," and the "people through their legislatures may protect themselves against that abuse," this was not a reason to overly restrict speech. As Hughes further wrote for the justices, the "greater the importance of safeguarding the community from incitements to the overthrow of our institutions by force and violence, the more imperative is the need to preserve inviolate the constitutional rights of free speech . . . to maintain the opportunity for free political discussion."[46]

The Supreme Court explicitly moved back to the clear and present danger test in *Herndon v. Lowry* (1937). The case involved a conviction for violating Georgia's syndicalism law. Communist Party organizer Angelo Herndon distributed literature trying to recruit new members and advocating for a communist government. A 5 to 4 Supreme Court overturned this conviction by citing *Schenck*, finding that under the state law, "the judge and jury trying an alleged offender cannot appraise the circumstances and character of the defendant's utterances or activities as begetting a clear and present danger of forcible obstruction of a particular state function." The Supreme Court affirmed that the "power of a state to abridge freedom of speech and of assembly is the exception rather than the rule," and any "limitation upon individual liberty must have appropriate relation to the safety of the state."[47]

The Supreme Court's use of the clear and present danger test was also exhibited in *Thornhill v. Alabama* (1940), which overturned labor leader Byron Thornhill's conviction for picketing a business. As explained by Justice Frank Murphy, "no clear and present danger of destruction of life or property, or invasion of the right of privacy, or breach of the peace can be thought to be inherent in the activities of every person who approaches the premises of an employer and publicizes the facts of a labor dispute involving the latter." Instead, the justices in an 8 to 1 decision reasoned that "picketing . . . may enlighten the public on the nature and causes of a labor dispute. The safeguarding of these means is essential to the securing of an informed and educated public opinion with respect to a matter which is of public concern."[48]

Similarly, *Bridges v. California* (1941) saw the Supreme Court reverse two contempt of court convictions, one for a labor leader who telegrammed the US Secretary of Labor that a strike would be forthcoming if a state court ruled against the union, and another for newspapers that printed the text of the telegram and issued editorials about it. For a 5 to 4 Supreme Court, Justice Hugo Black opined that the First Amendment "must be taken as a command of the broadest scope that explicit language, read in the context of a liberty-loving society, will allow." Black's opinion used the clear and present danger test, while also making it evident that the Supreme Court was rejecting the bad tendency test: "In accordance with what we have said on the 'clear and present danger' cases, neither 'inherent tendency' nor 'reasonable tendency' is enough to justify a restriction of free expression." Instead, Black explained, "the 'clear and present danger' language of the *Schenck* case has afforded practical guidance in a great variety of cases in which the scope of constitutional protections of freedom of expression was in issue."[49]

The emphasis on speech needing to be immediately connected to violence was also a part of the Court's jurisprudence in *Milk Wagon Drivers Union v. Meadowmoor Dairies* (1941), a case that shows the inconsistency among the justices during this period. The case reviewed an injunction in Illinois barring truck driver labor union picketing, due to violence in Chicago. As described by Justice Felix Frankfurter in the opinion of the Court, the case involved picketing that was "enmeshed with contemporaneously violent conduct." Frankfurter emphasized how "free speech in the future cannot be forfeited because of dissociated acts of past violence," but he sustained the injunction because of the "[e]ntanglement with violence" that existed in this case.[50]

That connection, temporally, between the picketing and the violence in *Milk Wagon Drivers Union* was not nearly close enough for Justice Black in dissent, though. Black explained that there was not an "imminent, clear and present danger as to justify an abridgment of the rights of freedom of speech and the press."[51] Indeed, the majority did not emphasize that the connection between speech and illegality needed to be "imminent" or "present."

Still, as the United States entered World War II, the opposite effect occurred on the Supreme Court compared to World War I, with the justices adopting a more protective approach to advocacy during the latter conflict. This was clearest in *Hartzel v. United States* (1944), where the justices reversed an Espionage Act conviction. Elmer Hartzel mailed pamphlets criticizing the US government and advocating American withdrawal from the war; the pamphlets were also anti-Semitic and promoted a race war in the United States. Justice Murphy wrote for a 5 to 4 Supreme Court, using *Schenck*'s clear and present danger test. As explained by Murphy, Hartzel's pamphlets were *not* specifically intended to cause insubordination in the military; rather, the literature was best characterized as "vicious and unreasoning attacks on one of our military allies, flagrant appeals to false and sinister racial theories and gross libels of the President." Murphy clarified that such ideas are "odious," particularly when expressed during a war, but he also affirmed that "an American citizen has the right to discuss these matters either by temperate reasoning or by immoderate and vicious invective." Thus, the restrictions on advocacy that the justices had upheld in World War I were now being struck down, using the clear and present danger test. The Supreme Court no longer accepted thinly veiled allegations that disfavored opinions needed to be criminally punished because they could lead to violence.[52]

The justices reaffirmed that advocacy was protected unless it creates a true clear and present danger in *Thomas v. Collins* (1945), where a 5 to 4 majority overturned an injunction against a labor leader that had prevented him from speaking at a union meeting. Justice Wiley Rutledge expressed the opinion of the Court, explaining that "any attempt to restrict those liberties must be justified by clear public interest, threatened not doubtfully or remotely, but by clear and present danger." Rutledge emphasized "the preferred place given in our scheme to the great, the indispensable, democratic freedoms secured by the First Amendment." Indeed, freedom of speech, particularly political advocacy, needs strong protection because it is integral to sustaining democracy itself. This case involved what Rutledge characterized as an "assembly [that] was entirely peaceable," meaning that a "restriction so destructive of the right of public discussion, without greater or more imminent danger to the public interest than existed in this case, is incompatible with the freedoms secured by the First Amendment."[53]

At the end of World War II, it appeared that advocacy, including advocacy questioning the heart of our political order, was fully protected by the test that Justice Holmes had originally devised in *Schenck*. Justices by the 1940s had interpreted that test to be as protective as Holmes and Brandeis promoted in their dissents and concurrences in the 1920s. However, a storm was gathering that would fundamentally alter the Supreme Court's approach to the First Amendment during the Cold War. Some of the most important advocacy/incitement cases in the 1940s — including *Bridges*, *Hartzel*, and *Thomas* — were closely divided 5 to 4 decisions. Any personnel change could drive the Supreme

Court's jurisprudence in a different direction. Justice Robert Jackson, one of the Supreme Court's most prominent civil libertarians in the early 1940s, took leave from the Supreme Court at the end of World War II to serve as American prosecutor at the Nuremburg trials; what he learned there about the rise of the Nazis in Germany and what he observed of Soviet officials controlling their lawyers and judges led him to rethink his free speech jurisprudence when he returned to the Court in 1946. In 1949, disaster struck, with two of the justices most protective of expressive rights — Rutledge and Murphy — dying in office, and their successors were less protective of free speech. Not much time passed before the clear and present danger test started to be reconsidered by a new Supreme Court majority, rendering it unrecognizable.[54]

This change in approach to advocacy became clear in *Dennis v. United States* (1951). A 6 to 2 Supreme Court sustained the convictions of Communist Party leaders under the Smith Act, which criminalized the advocating, advising, or teaching that it is a duty or even desirable to overthrow the US government by force or violence. Writing for the Supreme Court, Chief Justice Vinson declared that "the societal value of speech must, on occasion, be subordinated to other values and considerations." The test Vinson used bore some resemblance to the classic clear and present danger test, but something had changed: "In this case we are squarely presented with the application of the 'clear and present danger' test, and must decide what that phrase imports. . . . In each case [courts] must ask whether the gravity of the 'evil,' discounted by its *improbability*, justifies such invasion of free speech as is necessary to avoid the danger." While Vinson expressed approval for the clear and present danger test, it was applied more as a clear and *probable* danger test, emphasizing the gravity of the evil to be prevented.[55]

Vinson easily found that the danger (violent overthrow of the government) was substantial, and he concluded that speech advocating such violence could be punished in situations far short of imminence, as "the words [of the test] cannot mean that before the Government may act, it must wait until the putsch is about to be executed, the plans have been laid and the signal is awaited. If Government is aware that a group aiming at its overthrow is attempting to indoctrinate its members and to commit them to a course whereby they will strike when the leaders feel the circumstances permit, action by the Government is required."[56] Consequently, *Dennis* distorted the clear and present danger test to permit prosecutions against political dissenters.[57] Nevertheless, to a certain extent the *Dennis* Court was doing what Holmes arguably had done in *Schenck*, as the test was applied to uphold a conviction for simple advocacy in that case too.

In dissent, Justice Black in *Dennis* decried the majority's reformulation of the constitutional test for advocacy, because Dennis and his codefendants "were not charged with an attempt to overthrow the Government. They were not charged with overt acts of any kind designed to overthrow the Government. They were not even charged with saying anything or writing anything designed to overthrow the Government. The charge was that they agreed to assemble and to talk and publish certain ideas at a later date." For Black, "this is a virulent form of prior censorship of speech and press."[58]

Justice Douglas also found fault in the majority's decision in *Dennis*, complaining in dissent that "to support a finding of clear and present danger it must be shown either that immediate serious violence was to be expected or was advocated, or that the past conduct furnished reason to believe that such advocacy was then contemplated." As explained by Douglas, the record of the case, though, "contains no evidence whatsoever showing that the acts charged viz., the teaching of the Soviet theory of revolution with the hope that it will be realized, have created any clear and present danger to the Nation."[59]

From this nadir, where the malleability of the clear and present danger test was again exposed, it took the Supreme Court several years to build back free speech protections. As the 1950s progressed, Chief Justice Earl Warren and Justice William Brennan joined the Supreme Court, helping to eventually revise the test for advocacy and incitement to be more protective of expression. This path became noticeable in *Yates v. United States* (1957). Oleta Yates and thirteen codefendants were convicted of violating the same Smith Act used to prosecute Dennis. These defendants, like Dennis, were leaders in the Communist Party, and their convictions related to organizing, advocating, and teaching about an overthrow of the government through a communist revolution. A six-justice majority in *Yates* overturned these convictions or ordered new trials, interpreting the Smith Act *not* to prohibit "advocacy and teaching of forcible overthrow as an abstract principle, divorced from any effort to instigate action to that end, so long as such advocacy or teaching is engaged in with evil intent."[60] Thus, the justices drew a distinction between advocacy of abstract doctrine (protected by the First Amendment) and direct advocacy of action (outside of First Amendment protection).

This continued in *Noto v. United States* (1961), which overturned the Smith Act conviction of John Noto, a Communist Party official. The Supreme Court reasoned that "the mere abstract teaching of Communist theory, including the teaching of the moral propriety or even moral necessity for a resort to force and violence, is not the same as preparing a group for violent action and steeling it to such action." The justices held that "there must be some substantial direct or circumstantial evidence of a call to violence now or in the future."[61]

Neither *Yates* nor *Noto* used the clear and present danger test. The justices were protecting more expression than was the case with *Dennis*, but the Supreme Court did not clarify what test it would use to measure protections of advocacy under the First Amendment. So how could one know if one's speech would be considered protected abstract advocacy or something prosecutable? Even in *Noto*, the Court phrased the matter in terms of a call to violence at some time "in the future," making it, potentially, less protective than the clear and present danger test.

These issues were resolved in *Brandenburg v. Ohio* (1969). The case involved a state syndicalism conviction against Ku Klux Klan (KKK) leader Clarence Brandenburg, who organized a rally at a farm in Hamilton County, Ohio. Twelve KKK members in white robes and hoods, some of whom brandished firearms, gathered at this rally, which included a cross burning. Brandenburg spoke at the rally, using anti-Semitic and racist language, decrying desegregation efforts of the federal government. Notably, Brandenburg's speech included the following line: "We're not a revengent [*sic*] organization, but if our President, our Congress, our Supreme Court, continues to suppress the white, Caucasian race, it's possible that there might have to be some revengeance [*sic*] taken." A short *per curiam* opinion of the Court unanimously overturned Brandenburg's conviction, stating a new test for incitement: "the constitutional guarantees of free speech and free press do not permit a State to forbid or proscribe advocacy of the use of force or of law violation except where such advocacy is directed to inciting or producing imminent lawless action and is likely to incite or produce such action." The Supreme Court found the syndicalism law at issue punished "mere advocacy," and was thus unconstitutional.[62]

Interpreting the meaning of the *Brandenburg* test — and whether there should be any changes to that test — will constitute much of what the succeeding chapters in this volume discuss. In short, the test is quite protective of expression and requires three elements to be present for speech to fall outside of First Amendment protection: (1) the speaker must have intent to, and (2) the speaker's expression must be likely to, (3) incite imminent lawless action.[63]

Brandenburg overturned *Whitney v. California*,[64] a case that used the bad tendency test to uphold a conviction for syndicalism. As Justice Black pointed out in a concurrence, *Brandenburg* also "does not indicate any agreement on the Court's part with the 'clear and present danger' doctrine."[65] Justice Douglas was happy to see what might be the end of the *Schenck-Dennis* line of tests, concurring in *Brandenburg* that "I see no place in the regime of the First Amendment for any 'clear and present danger' test, whether strict and tight as some would make it, or free-wheeling as the Court in *Dennis* rephrased it."[66] Given how much the Supreme Court had switched from one test for incitement to another between 1919 and 1969, it was not evident at the time that the justices were coalescing around a test for imminent lawless action in *Brandenburg*. But in the more than half century since 1969, the Court has remained true to this standard, burying not just the bad tendency test but all iterations of the clear and present danger test. No longer was "mere advocacy" punishable. The approach advocated by Holmes in *Abrams* and Brandeis in *Whitney* — that speech should be protected unless it is likely to cause imminent harm — was finally the law of the land.

Questions remained, though, about some meaning of the language in *Brandenburg*. For example, what constitutes "imminence" in this test? The Supreme Court clarified that a few years later in *Hess v. Indiana* (1973). Gregory Hess participated in an anti–Vietnam War protest at Indiana University. Around

100 to 150 protestors, including Hess, were demonstrating on a public street. Law enforcement officers began moving the protestors off the street. Hess then told the sheriff either, "We'll take the fucking street later," or "We'll take the fucking street again." Hess was arrested and convicted of disorderly conduct. The Supreme Court overturned Hess's conviction, finding a lack of imminence, and perhaps even a lack of intending to incite others: "At best . . . the statement could be taken as counsel for present moderation; at worst, it amounted to nothing more than advocacy of illegal action at some indefinite future time. This is not sufficient to permit the State to punish Hess' speech. . . . Since the uncontroverted evidence showed that Hess' statement was not directed to any person or group of persons, it cannot be said that he was advocating, in the normal sense, any action." As the Supreme Court clarified, Hess's speech could not be punished because it merely "had a tendency to lead to violence." *Hess* helped to solidify *Brandenburg* as precedent and clarify that "imminent" really means something is happening or is about to happen in the immediate future.[67]

The question about imminence was also at issue in *NAACP v. Claiborne Hardware Co.* (1982). The case arose out of an NAACP-led boycott of white-owned businesses in Claiborne County, Mississippi, from 1966 to 1970. The boycott attempted to pressure elected officials to desegregate public institutions, including public schools. During the boycott, the National Association for the Advancement of Colored People (NAACP) field secretary Charles Evers delivered speeches that sought to persuade African Americans to hold to the boycott. In one speech, Evers stated that "any 'uncle toms' who broke the boycott would 'have their necks broken' by their own people." In another speech, Evers proclaimed that if someone broke the boycott, "You needn't go calling the sheriff, he can't help you none. . . . He ain't going to offer to sleep with none of us men, I can tell you that." In another speech, Evers proclaimed, "If we catch any of you going in any of them racist stores, we're gonna break your damn neck." Some boycott breakers suffered physical violence or property damage.[68]

The Supreme Court unanimously found Evers's speech to be constitutionally protected. Although the justices were forthright that the "First Amendment does not protect violence," they also concluded that the "emotionally charged rhetoric of Charles Evers' speeches did not transcend the bounds of protected speech set forth in *Brandenburg*." Even though "strong language was used," the Supreme Court found that Evers's speeches were "an impassioned plea for black citizens to unify, to support and respect each other, and to realize the political and economic power available to them." Since the relevant violence occurred "weeks or months" after one speech, and did not occur after Evers's other speeches, he was protected by the First Amendment. The *Claiborne Hardware* opinion concluded by summing up its approach to advocacy since *Brandenburg*: "Strong and effective extemporaneous rhetoric cannot be nicely channeled in purely dulcet phrases. An advocate must be free to stimulate his audience with spontaneous and emotional appeals for unity and action in a common cause. When such appeals do not incite lawless action, they must be regarded as protected speech."[69]

Claiborne Hardware, decided in 1982, was the Supreme Court's last decision where a majority directly applied *Brandenburg* to a case to determine the line between protected advocacy and unprotected incitement. This raises questions about the meaning of the test today, although the contemporary Supreme Court appears to be committed to it. Indeed, a Westlaw search reveals that as of July 2024, the justices have cited *Brandenburg* in opinions in thirty-seven cases since *Claiborne Hardware*, showing its continuing significance, particularly with regard to pure speech.

Government officials have long sought to suppress advocacy they dislike. The Supreme Court, until *Brandenburg*, struggled to consistently articulate when advocacy is protected by the First Amendment. Since *Brandenburg*, the Supreme Court has remained consistent in the use of an imminent lawless action standard for incitement. But what questions remain for *Brandenburg* over four decades after the Supreme Court's last incitement case? Given societal and technological changes, should the *Brandenburg* test remain the incitement standard, or is a modification in order?

Our authors tackle these and other questions in the pages that follow. The first three chapters constitute a part titled "The Theoretical Underpinnings of *Brandenburg*." Adam Kunz's chapter, "Tolerating the Violent," uses political philosophy to argue that *Brandenburg* should remain the Supreme Court's standard for incitement because it promotes both liberty and equity. Timothy C. Shiell's "Anti-Orthodoxy, Inclusion, and the Advocacy of Violence" examines the philosophical foundations of *Brandenburg*, finding that it remains an important decision to protect dissenters and ensure constitutional protection for historically marginalized groups. Stephen M. Feldman's "Free Speech, Social Justice, and *Brandenburg*" disagrees with that analysis, claiming that the Supreme Court's incitement doctrine and free expression doctrine generally — both now and historically — have served to protect politically powerful groups at the expense of societal outsiders and minorities.

Next, we have several chapters exploring "Incitement Extensions," that look at different contexts where the *Brandenburg* test has been used, particularly in the lower courts. Rachel E. VanLandingham's "Criminal Solicitation and Incitement as Borderline Criminal Speech" sheds light on the use of *Brandenburg* in cases involving criminal solicitation. Shavonnie R. Carthens's "Words behind Walls" investigates the censorship of reading materials in America's prisons under the guise of "incitement" after *Brandenburg*. Eric T. Kasper's "I Fought the Law, and the First Amendment Won," explores court cases where musical artists' expression has been challenged as alleged incitement, arguing that the *Brandenburg* test is essential to the protection of music, particularly to safeguard the expression of dissenting viewpoints and the songs of artists who are political minorities. Christina E. Wells's "'Terrorism' and Arguments to Disregard *Brandenburg*'s Incitement Test" supports maintaining this test as it stands, including in terrorism cases, lest we revisit the Supreme Court's past mistakes that weakened the constitutional protection for advocacy.

Our final substantive chapters engage in the meaning of *"Brandenburg* in the Contemporary Era." Howard Schweber and Rebecca J. Anderson's "Incitement on the Internet" questions the application of *Brandenburg* to speech online (due to the different temporal and geographical concerns it raises compared to speech in person) and proposes what they call a modest redrafting of the test. JoAnne Sweeny's "Incitement in Context" explains that courts need to focus more on the context of speech, rather than just the actual words used by a speaker, to properly delineate protected expression from incitement. Daniel J. Canon's "We Told You So" shows how it is imperative for the survival of democracy for courts to properly guard the line between incitement and political speech. The volume's conclusion then ties past and present considerations together to examine the future of *Brandenburg*, providing a point-counterpoint analysis of *Brandenburg* and its applications.

This book examines questions about incitement in greater detail than any other contemporary manuscript. In the spirit of the First Amendment, our authors exhibit for you multiple — and at times competing — viewpoints on *Brandenburg*, including the ultimate question of whether the Supreme Court should continue to adhere to it, modify it, or replace it with something else. All of these authors agree that protecting the freedom of expression is vital to our society and is a constitutional imperative. Our disagreements over the details of the *Brandenburg* test demonstrate the complexities of advocacy and incitement.

Incitement presents a tension between two fundamental interests: the freedom of speech and the government's obligation to protect public safety. *Brandenburg* seeks to maximize the ability of people to speak their minds while minimizing violence. When the test for incitement is not set correctly, it can lead (and has led) to people going to jail for advocating for basic political policy change (including laborers' rights and civil rights), or, on the other extreme, a speaker being protected in encouraging followers to engage in violence, with the potential for property damage, physical injuries, and death. On both sides, the stakes are incredibly high.

Notes

1. Gertz v. Robert Welch, Inc., 418 U.S. 323, 339–40 (1974).
2. New York Times Co. v. Sullivan, 376 U.S. 254, 270 (1964).
3. Wooley v. Maynard, 430 U.S. 705, 714 (1977) (internal quotation omitted).
4. Texas v. Johnson, 491 U.S. 397, 414 (1989).
5. Mahanoy Area School District v. B. L., 594 U.S. 180 (2021).
6. Snyder v. Phelps, 562 U.S. 443, 460–61 (2011).
7. McCutcheon v. Federal Election Commission, 572 U.S. 185, 191 (2014).
8. Kevin F. O'Neill, "A First Amendment Compass: Navigating the Speech Clause with a Five-Step Analytical Framework a Five-Step Analytical Framework," *Southwestern University Law Review* 29 (2000): 223–300.
9. See Eric T. Kasper, "Free Speech, Social Media, and Public Universities: How the First Amendment Limits University Sanctions for Online Expression and Empowers Students, Staff, and Faculty," *Mitchell Hamline Law Review* 48 (2022): 407–66.
10. Lauren Leatherby et al., "How a Presidential Rally Turned Into a Capitol Rampage," *New York Times*, last modified January 12, 2021, https://www.nytimes.com/interactive/2021/01/12/us/capitol-mob-timeline.html; Jack Healy, "These Are the 5 People Who Died in the Capitol Riot," *New York Times*, January 11, 2021, https://www.nytimes.com/2021/01/11/us/who-died-in-capitol-building-attack.html; "Capitol Riots Timeline: What Happened on 6 January 2021?," BBC, last modified June 10, 2022, https://www.bbc.com/news/world-us-canada-56004916; Alanna Durkin Richer, "Explainer: Hundreds Charged with Crimes in Capitol Attack," Associated Press, last modified June 7, 2022, https://apnews.com/article/capitol-siege-merrick-garland-government-and-politics-conspiracy-crime-c2e427dc0fa16077d7fb98c06e61149f; Alanna Durkin Richer and Michael Kunzelman, "Hundreds of Convictions, But a Major Mystery Is Still Unsolved 3 Years after the Jan. 6 Capitol Riot," Associated Press, last modified January 5, 2024, https://apnews.com/article/capitol-riot-jan-6-criminal-cases-anniversary-bf436efe760751b1356f937e55bedaa; Scott Pelley, "U.S. Attorney Explains Jan. 6 Capitol Riot Prosecutions," CBS News, September 15, 2024, https://www.cbsnews.com/news/us-attorney-explains-jan-6-capitol-riot-prosecutions-60-minutes-transcript/.
11. Brian Naylor, "Read Trump's Jan. 6 Speech, a Key Part of Impeachment Trial," NPR, last modified February 10, 2021, https://www.npr.org/2021/02/10/966396848/read-trumps-jan-6-speech-a-key-part-of-impeachment-trial.
12. Kevin A. Johnson and Craig R. Smith, *Fear and the First Amendment: Controversial Cases of the Roberts Court* (University of Alabama Press, 2024), 2, 5.

13 Olivia Rubin, Alexander Mallin, and Alex Hosenball, "'Because President Trump Said To': Over a Dozen Capitol Rioters Say they Were Following Trump's Guidance," ABC News, last modified February 9, 2021, https://abcnews.go.com/US/president-trump-dozen-capitol-rioters-trumps-guidance/story?id=75757601.
14 Tom Abrahams, "Sen. Ted Cruz Tells Why He Still Opposed Biden's Electoral Win in ABC13 Exclusive," ABC 13, January 7, 2021, https://abc13.com/ted-cruz-dc-riots-did-cause-interview-riot/9443987/.
15 "McConnell Says Jan. 6 Capitol Attack Was 'Provoked' by Trump and Others in Power," PBS, January 19, 2021, https://www.pbs.org/newshour/politics/mcconnell-says-jan-6-capitol-attack-was-provoked-by-trump-and-others-in-power.
16 Ryan Pickrell, "Trump's Own Pentagon Chief Says Rioters Wouldn't Have Stormed the Capitol if It Hadn't Been for the President's Speech," *Business Insider*, March 11, 2021, https://www.businessinsider.com/trumps-pentagon-chief-presidential-speech-capitol-riots-responsibility-2021-3.
17 Naylor, "Read Trump's Jan. 6 Speech" (emphasis added).
18 Ed Pilkington, "Barbara Ehrenreich, Author Who Resisted Injustice, Dies Aged 81," *Guardian*, September 2, 2022, https://www.theguardian.com/books/2022/sep/02/barbara-ehrenreich-author-dies-nickel-and-dimed.
19 Zoë Richards, "Josh Hawley Seen Fleeing Pro-Trump Mob He 'Riled up' with Fist Salute in Newly Released Jan. 6 Footage," NBC News, July 21, 2022, https://www.nbcnews.com/politics/congress/josh-hawley-seen-fleeing-trump-mob-riled-newly-released-jan-6-footage-rcna39490.
20 John Bowden, "Gohmert Talks of Violence in Streets after His Lawsuit Is Dismissed," *The Hill*, January 3, 2021, https://thehill.com/homenews/house/532407-gohmert-talks-of-violence-in-streets-after-his-lawsuit-is-dismissed/.
21 Michael Kranish, Karoun Demirjian, and Devlin Barrett, "Democrats Demand Investigation of Whether Republicans in Congress Aided Capitol Rioters," *Washington Post*, January 13, 2021, https://www.washingtonpost.com/national-security/republicans-capitol-rioters/2021/01/13/9737a336-55e2-11eb-a931-5b162d0d033d_story.html.
22 See Condemning and Censuring Representative Louie Gohmert of Texas, H.Res.19, 117th Congress (2021), available at https://www.congress.gov/bill/117th-congress/house-resolution/19/text?format=txt&r=4&s=1.
23 Barbara Sprunt, "Judge Denies Mistrial Request over Rep. Waters' 'Confrontational' Comment," NPR, April 19, 2021, https://www.npr.org/sections/trial-over-killing-of-george-floyd/2021/04/19/988884471/judge-denies-mistrial-request-over-rep-waters-confrontational-comment.
24 Jan Wolfe and Lawrence Hurley, "U.S. Chief Justice Slams Schumer for 'Dangerous' Comment on Justices in Abortion Case," Reuters, March

25 4, 2020, https://www.reuters.com/article/us-usa-court-abortion-scene/us-chief-justice-slams-schumer-for-dangerous-comment-on-justices-in-abortion-case-idUSKBN20R2KX.
25 Rachel Looker, "Republicans Accuse Biden of Inciting Trump Shooting," BBC, July 14, 2024, https://www.bbc.com/news/articles/cw0y9xljv2yo.
26 Michael T. Gibson, "The Supreme Court and Freedom of Expression from 1791 to 1917," *Fordham Law Review* 55 (1986): 263–333, 271, 268; Gitlow v. New York, 268 U.S. 652, 666 (1925) ("freedom of speech and of the press — which are protected by the First Amendment from abridgment by Congress — are among the fundamental personal rights and 'liberties' protected by the due process clause of the Fourteenth Amendment from impairment by the States").
27 United States ex rel. Turner v. Williams, 194 U.S. 279, 294 (1904).
28 Michael Kent Curtis, Free Speech, *"The People's Darling Privilege": Struggles for Freedom of Expression in American History* (Duke University Press, 2000), 387.
29 Patterson v. Colorado, 205 U.S. 454, 462 (1907) (internal citations and quotations omitted).
30 Fox v. Washington, 236 U.S. 273, 275–77 (1915).
31 Schenck v. United States, 249 U.S. 47, 50–51, 52, 51 (1919).
32 See Christina E. Wells, "Fear and Loathing in Constitutional Decision-Making," *Wisconsin Law Review* 2005 (2005): 115–223, 152n218.
33 Sugarman v. United States, 249 U.S. 182 (1919); Frohwerk v. United States, 249 U.S. 204 (1919); Debs v. United States, 249 U.S. 211 (1919).
34 Abrams v. United States, 250 U.S. 616, 621–22, 624, 623 (1919).
35 Abrams, 250 U.S. at 628, 630 (Holmes, J., dissenting).
36 See Stephen M. Feldman, "Free Speech, World War I, and Republican Democracy: The Internal and External Holmes," *First Amendment Law Review* 6 (2008): 192–251, 236.
37 Pierce v. United States, 252 U.S. 239, 249 (1920).
38 Pierce, 252 U.S. at 269, 273 (Brandeis, J., dissenting).
39 Gilbert v. Minnesota, 254 U.S. 325, 327, 333 (1920).
40 Gilbert, 254 U.S. at 334, 335 (Brandeis, J., dissenting).
41 Gitlow v. New York, 268 U.S. 652, 657–58, 671, 669 (1925).
42 Gitlow, 268 U.S. at 673 (Holmes, J., dissenting).
43 Gitlow, 268 U.S. at 666 ("For present purposes we may and do assume that freedom of speech and of the press — which are protected by the First Amendment from abridgment by Congress — are among the fundamental personal rights and 'liberties' protected by the due process clause of the Fourteenth Amendment from impairment by the States").
44 Whitney v. California, 274 U.S. 357, 371 (1927).
45 Whitney, 274 U.S. at 373, 375, 376 (Brandeis, J., concurring).
46 De Jonge v. Oregon, 299 U.S. 353, 364–65 (1937).
47 Herndon v. Lowry, 301 U.S. 242, 261, 258 (1937).

48   Thornhill v. Alabama, 310 U.S. 88, 105, 104 (1940).
49   Bridges v. California, 314 U.S. 252, 263, 273, 262 (1941).
50   Milk Wagon Drivers Union v. Meadowmoor Dairies, 312 U.S. 287, 292, 296, 297 (1941).
51   Milk Wagon Drivers Union, 312 U.S. at 313 (Black, J., dissenting).
52   Hartzel v. United States, 322 U.S. 680, 687, 689 (1944).
53   Thomas v. Collins, 323 U.S. 516, 530, 536–37 (1945).
54   Noah Feldman, *Scorpions: The Battles and Triumphs of FDR's Great Supreme Court Justices* (Twelve, 2010), 349–50; Linda C. Gugin and James E. St. Claire, *Sherman Minton: New Deal Senator, Cold War Justice* (Indiana Historical Society Press, 1997), 223; David Alistair Yalof, *Pursuit of Justices: Presidential Politics and the Selection of Supreme Court Nominees* (University of Chicago Press, 1999), 35.
55   Dennis v. United States, 341 U.S. 494, 503, 508–10 (1951); Michael P. Downey, "The Jeffersonian Myth in Supreme Court Sedition Jurisprudence," *Washington University Law Quarterly* 76 (1998): 683–720, 708–9.
56   Dennis, 341 U.S. at 509.
57   Christina E. Wells, "Fear and Loathing in Constitutional Decision-Making," *Wisconsin Law Review* 2005 (2005): 115–223, 152n218.
58   Dennis, 341 U.S. at 579 (Black, J., dissenting).
59   Dennis, 341 U.S. at 586, 587 (Douglas, J., dissenting).
60   Yates v. United States, 354 U.S. 298, 318 (1957).
61   Noto v. United States, 367 U.S. 290, 297–98 (1961).
62   Brandenburg v. Ohio, 395 U.S. 444, 446, 447, 449 (1969).
63   Emerson J. Sykes, "In Defense of Brandenburg: The ACLU and Incitement Doctrine in 1919, 1969, and 2019," *Brooklyn Law Review* 85 (2019): 15–36, 24–27.
64   Brandenburg, 395 U.S. at 449.
65   Brandenburg, 395 U.S. at 450 (Black, J., concurring).
66   Brandenburg, 395 U.S. at 454 (Douglas, J., concurring).
67   Hess v. Indiana, 414 U.S. 105, 107, 108–9 (1973).
68   NAACP v. Claiborne Hardware Co., 458 U.S. 886, 900n28, 938–39, 902 (1982).
69   Claiborne Hardware Co., 916, 928.

PART I:
THE THEORETICAL UNDERPINNINGS OF *BRANDENBURG*

Chapter One

Tolerating the Violent

The Liberal Egalitarian Justifications for the *Brandenburg* Test

Adam Kunz

During a course I taught on tolerance, I witnessed an interaction between two students that I continue to replay in my mind whenever the topic of free speech comes up. The discussion centered on empathy and understanding as necessary factors in behaving with tolerance; our focal point was the writing of Montaigne in *The Essays*, specifically in his essays "On Affectionate Relationships" and "On Cruelty." The students led the conversation, and eventually, the topic drifted toward the question of whether a person of one identity background could ever truly empathize with someone of a different identity. Specifically, a student asked whether a white, heterosexual, cis-gendered male could ever experience empathy for people of other races, sexualities, and genders. At one point, one student — a white, hetero, cis-gendered male — raised his hand and made the case that he felt he *could* understand other people of different identities because he shares humanity with them. He said, "I would never be able to empathize with something like a rock or an object. But I can understand what it's like to be human and try to feel what another human feels." Another student, a nonbinary person of color, raised their hand and said, "I am deeply offended that he would compare people like me to rocks."

The room immediately fell silent as students exchanged glances with one another. I turned to the previous student and asked him if he would like to clarify. Nervously, he denied that he compared them or anyone to an object and that his point was exactly the opposite. The second student responded: "It doesn't matter what you said. I know what I heard. And I don't have to tolerate that violence." I wrapped up the discussion shortly thereafter, and the course proceeded without issue for the remainder of the semester. But the irony of that moment in a course on tolerance and during a discussion on understanding one another has never left me.

What are the boundaries between tolerance and the advocacy of violent ideas? What constitutes violence in the first place? What should a society expect of its citizens when it comes to understanding one another and engendering tolerance? How do these subjects fit within the broader scope of a political system? These are classic questions for political theory to address. And in the United States, the judiciary has made efforts — at least from a constitutional vantage point — to answer these questions through free speech case law. Enter the *Brandenburg* test. Much ink has been spilled on this test, including in this volume. Indeed, scholars have talked about it more than courts have.[1] This literature often analyzes the test through the lens of jurisprudence and the efficacy of the test as a judicial doctrine.[2] All of this commentary is, of course, useful for academics and students alike in making sense of one of the United States' most important free speech exceptions. However, I believe it will also prove helpful to make a full-throated defense of *Brandenburg* through one philosophical tradition: liberal egalitarianism.

In this chapter, I will first define what I mean by liberal egalitarianism. As the audience for this volume is likely a diverse set of readers coming from a variety of backgrounds, I feel it necessary to explain what liberal egalitarianism is, what its goals are, and who its critics are before turning to my defense of *Brandenburg*. For lay readers, I hope this will be a helpful introduction, but even for the most seasoned political theorist, I hope this background will clearly establish the approach I have adopted. Next, I will show how liberal egalitarianism resolves a seeming antinomy between two important political values — liberty and equity — by synergizing them into the metavalue of justice. Drawing on the liberal egalitarian conception of tolerance and its assumption that citizens should be able to exercise their freedom of conscience, I will show that liberty and equity are simply two sides of the same fundamental commitment that a liberal egalitarian system envisions for a tolerant society. Using this background, I will then turn to exploring how the *Brandenburg* test neatly fits within the liberal egalitarian conception of tolerance using both theoretical analysis and recent examples from case law. In doing so, I will showcase how the *Brandenburg* test factors are simply restatements of liberal egalitarian tolerance in one specific area — free speech. Finally, I will propose some lessons that I believe *Brandenburg* offers to liberal egalitarian political theory and calls to action for further development. Ultimately, the goal of this chapter is to complement the analysis of this volume's other contributors.

Background on Liberal Egalitarianism

Liberal egalitarianism is a major development in twentieth-century political theory aimed at balancing liberty with equitable distributions of primary social and economic goods. While a full account of liberal egalitarianism is beyond the scope of this chapter, it is necessary to establish its primary features.[3] I will start with the basic, fundamental principles of the theory.

The Fundamentals of Liberal Egalitarianism

Liberal egalitarianism, as the name suggests, bears two primary features that distinguish it from other contemporary political theories. On the one hand, it is a quintessential liberal theory; it is grounded in the Enlightenment emphasis on persons over communities, institutions over force, and human flourishing over tradition. Like its counterpart, classical liberalism, liberal egalitarianism holds to the following tenets: (1) that the best life is one that individual humans choose for themselves through their own theory of the good; (2) that humans have rights that cannot be taken away but which can be voluntarily relinquished; (3) that justice is the first principle of politics and the touchstone for resolving claims of right in individuals' pursuit of the good; (4) that just political, social, and economic institutions are necessary for preserving individuals' space within which to act; and (5) that it is rational and reasonable, and therefore legitimate, for individuals to consent to state action that preserves justice and just institutions.

On this account, liberal egalitarianism bears the influences of Jean-Jacques Rousseau, John Locke, and Immanuel Kant, with primary contemporary writers being John Rawls and Ronald Dworkin.

On the other hand, liberal egalitarianism is a theory of equity. Unlike classical liberalism, liberal egalitarianism defines justice in a particular way. Political, social, and economic institutions are to be arranged to minimize social inequalities and compensate for natural inequalities. Insofar as social and natural inequalities exist among individuals, where they can be eliminated or mitigated, they should be — provided that the method for doing so is consistent with the other goals of liberal egalitarianism. In other words, liberal egalitarianism claims that an individual cannot *truly* have the freedom to pursue their own theories of the good (Tenet 1 above) unless political, social, and economic institutions remove or diminish arbitrary disadvantages that society or nature has assigned to that individual. While this significantly oversimplifies the distinction, it is helpful to think of classical liberalism as "liberty — full stop" and liberal egalitarianism as "liberty consistent with equity."[4]

The primary goal then of liberal egalitarianism is to create a political arrangement in which persons exercise their freedom within action spaces that do not infringe on the action spaces of others. Under ideal theory, individuals would be free to pursue their justice-consistent conceptions of the good with as little state interference as possible. In reality, conflicts will always exist across these action spaces; whether it is tensions in religious beliefs (or nonbeliefs), economic competition, or something as simple as moving from one place to another, free persons will come into conflict. For this reason, liberal egalitarianism adopts the practice of other forms of liberalism by requiring vigorous public law through constitutions, legislation, administration, and judicial enforcement of criminal and civil laws. Through transparent and accessible political participation, individuals can help shape public laws to maximize the possibility of reducing interpersonal and interorganizational conflict. Because this is its primary goal, liberal egalitarianism is similar to other social contractarian theories in that it focuses on institutional design over the character or commitments of individual citizens.[5]

Liberal egalitarianism has been attacked on all sides of the political theoretical spectrum. On the one hand, it has been attacked on its right by theories that give even greater priority to liberty than liberal egalitarianism. For example, classical liberals disagree that the definition of justice should extend to (or at least as far as) liberal egalitarianism's focus on arbitrary disadvantages. The disagreement tends to be over the degree to which social and natural disadvantages truly stand in the way of an individual's pursuit of their theory of the good. While classical liberals agree that extreme disadvantages (such as natural disasters, severe disabilities, and overt racism) should be addressed, they often disagree that more subtle disadvantages should be within the purview of the state to address (such as generational poverty, lack of education, access to healthcare, implicit bias, and so forth).[6] Nevertheless, classical and egalitarian liberals accept the notion of a neutral state and recognize that, in instituting justice, a vigorous source of law backed by state power is essential to protect liberty. Libertarianism goes even further than classical liberalism by insisting that individual rights are violated when the state addresses *any* disadvantage unless all the individuals involved in the state action voluntarily consent to the resolution.[7] In the eyes of libertarians, both classical and egalitarian liberals violate liberty by permitting too much of a paternalistic state. These critiques are often conceptualized as disagreements from the "theoretical right."

On the other hand, theories such as multiculturalism (including its predecessor, communitarianism), Marxism, and feminism take a variety of different approaches that have the same flavor. All three argue that liberal egalitarianism does not go far enough in addressing inequalities by emphasizing historically white, capitalist, or male ideas like constitutionalism or justice. In some instances, such as Marxism or versions of multiculturalism, these theories argue that an individual's freedom to pursue any conception of the good is shortsighted, as there is only one conception of the good the state should seek to instill in citizens — communal production of goods, in the case of Marxism, or group-specific heritage, in the case of multiculturalism. In other cases, these theories would replace justice as the primary political principle with some other principle, such as diversity, care ethics, or the collective ownership of the means of production. These critiques are often loosely conceptualized as disagreements from the "theoretical left."[8]

It is far beyond the scope of this chapter to account for every detail of liberal egalitarianism and its debates with other political theories. However, the foregoing analysis serves two purposes in the present context. First, it provides a groundwork for situating the *Brandenburg* test as a liberal egalitarian form of jurisprudence. In defending that claim later in the chapter, I will regularly refer to the hallmarks of liberal egalitarianism discussed above. As readers explore the details of liberal egalitarianism, I believe this discussion will serve as a fruitful roadmap to such an investigation. Second, it provides a helpful orientation to defend the *Brandenburg* test against criticism from multiple angles. Although, as I explain in the final section, the *Brandenburg* test is not flawless, it is a helpful facet of a public law that champions the individual pursuit of conceptions of the good. Insofar as the debates in political theory are about trade-offs between different values that a society might adopt, this section should help show what liberal egalitarianism prioritizes — and what its critics believe should be prioritized instead.

As to this second point, liberal egalitarianism has high aspirations for its values, producing a seemingly paradoxical commitment to supposedly inconsistent goals. However, rather than being at odds with one another, there is a way to resolve this antinomy through the unique form of tolerance that liberal egalitarianism embraces. This resolution can be illustrated in many ways, but the *Brandenburg* test is a helpful one, as I explore below. Before turning to that discussion, it is important to understand the antinomy at the heart of liberal egalitarianism and hinted at in the above discussion.

The Antinomy and Metavalue Within Liberal Egalitarianism

Based on the brief summary I present above, a critical analysis can uncover a tension in values espoused by liberal egalitarianism. On the one hand, a truly liberal theory that prioritizes liberty to the exclusion of other values would not be preoccupied with whether institutions and policies happen to function unless they strengthen liberty. For example, one could not criticize libertarianism on the grounds that it creates a less equitable society for citizens; provided that such citizens have maximum liberty, the political theory is satisfied. There is a similar problem for egalitarian theories insofar as they elevate equity above other values. For example, some versions of Marxism hold that communal ownership of the means of production is best judged according to whether citizens have similar life chances and equal claims over an abundance of resources. As before, it would not be much of a criticism of this kind of Marxism to claim that its citizens will enjoy less liberty.

However, liberal egalitarianism seeks to do both at once. It is true that the Rawlsian articulation of liberal egalitarianism lexically prioritizes liberty; under

Rawls's rubric, conflicts between institutions and policies are to be resolved in favor of the one that better adheres to the Liberty Principle and respects a scheme of basic civil liberties. In that sense, it would appear that liberal egalitarianism tips in favor of liberty.[9] But Rawlsian liberal egalitarianism is not the only form of such a theory — many of which refine this prioritization of liberty.[10] And even under Rawls's statement of the Liberty Principle, liberty is defined in egalitarian terms: "Each person has an *equal right* to a fully adequate scheme of *equal basic liberties* which is compatible with a similar scheme of liberties *for all*" (emphasis added). Under this definition, liberty does not necessarily mean "my liberty to the exclusion of others," but rather, "my liberty consistent with a corresponding liberty for others." In other words, even where liberty receives special treatment under liberal egalitarianism, it is in terms of equitable treatment: similarly situated individuals are treated similarly under the law.[11]

But how can liberal egalitarianism do both at once? Are not these values mutually exclusive or, at best, values that cannot be given identical weight? This controversy cannot be fully resolved in this chapter, but I argue that at least one element of liberal egalitarianism illustrates why there is not really any antinomy between these two values. The liberal egalitarian conception of tolerance demonstrates a practical example of how these two values can be consistent with, if not mutually supportive of, one another.

Liberal egalitarian tolerance has two components: (1) *Full Exercise Component*. Citizens acting through institutions and public law must tolerate the right of fellow citizens to fully exercise their freedom of conscience, and (2) *Limitation Component*. Citizens have a right to exercise their freedom of conscience provided that it does not: (a) clearly and substantially jeopardize the essential function of public order (*public order undermining*) or (b) self-defeatingly undermine the scheme of equal basic liberties for all (*scheme of equal liberty undermining*).

The first component is an articulation of one civil liberty — freedom of conscience —that fits within the scheme of equal basic liberties. Liberal egalitarian writers generally agree that this includes concepts like freedom of religion, academic freedom, a free press, and, most importantly, for the present purpose, freedom of speech. The first component contains both a positive right and a negative duty: on the one hand, one is free to exercise their freedom of conscience with presumptively wide latitude, while, on the other hand, that same citizen is under a duty to support institutions and laws that grant that same latitude to other citizens. As Rawls points out, this is rooted in the contractarian nature of liberal egalitarianism.[12]

The second component provides two specific limitations to the liberty of conscience, each of which is aimed at preserving the system that gives life to the liberty in the first place. Citizens acting through the state are justified in limiting freedom of conscience when doing so would resolve a clear and substantial threat to public order. What that might look like depends greatly on the emergent circumstances, but it at least means situations in which public law itself is threatened by exercise of the liberty. Similarly, this liberty may also be limited where the individual exercises the liberty so as to undermine the very right to have this liberty in the first place. This highly specific conception of the "intolerant speaker" refers to those situations in which one exercises their freedom of conscience to actively destroy the scheme of equal basic liberties that would normally give the speaker the freedom to do so. In both instances, these limitations are about preserving the action spaces of individuals to pursue their conceptions of the good; rather than define the *content* of conscience, citizens acting through the state define the *procedural landscape* for the exercise of conscience.

Both liberty and equity are at the heart of the liberal egalitarian version of tolerance in at least two ways. First and foremost, this version of tolerance assumes the free exercise of a right (liberty) working in tandem with reciprocal allowance for others to likewise freely exercise that right (equity). Rather than being at odds with one another, liberty and equity serve as synergizing forces: one's liberty is only fully secure when it is situated in a space where others can expect to exercise their liberty as well, which in turn should generate the ability to vigorously exercise that liberty. Second, and relatedly, this definition of tolerance employs a kind of "metavalue" that subsumes both liberty and equity, namely, the value of supporting the justice project at the heart of liberal egalitarianism. To put it another way, if vigorous liberty is the thesis and equity is its antithesis, the two are reconciled when synthesized as a commitment to justice. Thus, the seeming antinomy between the two values is nothing more than an expression of justice in two particular contexts.

At least in the United States, liberal egalitarianism is the most useful lens through which to view the American legal project. From a historical perspective, many of leaders in the Founding Era recognized the need to balance liberty and equity as twin priorities of the state. In this era, we can find defenses for ideas such as the need for representative government, promotion of liberal education, and a vigorous bill of rights as being consistent with the need for an insulated judiciary, equal applicability of the rule of law, and political offices open to individuals regardless of status.[13] The founding generation of the United States wrestled with the synthesis of liberty and equity. Moreover, liberal egalitarianism can help make sense of political discourse today. No matter the topic — wage slavery, environmental conservation, foreign policy, education, social justice, and so forth — there is a constant undercurrent of finding the tolerant line between the freedom of the individual to self-govern and the need for equitable treatment. If every other theory I have discussed solves the liberty/equity paradox by embracing one value over the other, liberal egalitarianism's reconciliation of the two is a useful frame for US law and politics.

Situating *Brandenburg* Within Liberal Egalitarianism

Up to this point, this discussion has been purely theoretical. While my goal has not been to unpack every nuance of liberal egalitarianism, I have offered an articulation of its primary features, goals, and interlocutors to lay the groundwork for the discussion of liberal egalitarian tolerance. I then used liberal egalitarian tolerance to illustrate and resolve a seeming contradiction within the theory. I now turn to using the *Brandenburg* test as a practical exemplar of the underlying theory at work. In doing so, I wish to first defend *Brandenburg* as founded in liberal egalitarian theory by showing how it embraces the metavalue described above. In doing so, I will also offer real-world examples of the *Brandenburg* test in operation. In the following section, I will then turn a critical eye to *Brandenburg* and present some thoughts on how it might be improved to further the liberal egalitarian project.

Brandenburg's Embrace of the Liberal Egalitarian Metavalue

The *Brandenburg* test provides that the state may prohibit speech only if that speech is "directed to inciting or producing imminent lawless action and likely to incite or produce such action."[14] In looking at the test through the lens of liberal egalitarianism, it should be noted that the test is specific to speech; while liberal egalitarian tolerance covers the full gamut of the freedom of conscience, the *Brandenburg* test is focused on only one component of this freedom the public expression of one's conscience in the marketplace of ideas. It is also worth noting that the test is purely negative in that nothing about *Brandenburg* tells individual citizens how to behave. As I have argued above, liberal egalitarian tolerance gives citizens both the privilege to exercise freedom of conscience as well as the duty to protect it for others. In that sense, the *Brandenburg* test is purely a device for constraining how citizens acting through the state can police one instantiation of the freedom of conscience. Thus, one should be cautious in asking *Brandenburg* to do too much from a political theory perspective.

Nevertheless, the authors of *Brandenburg* were arguably working in a liberal egalitarian tradition when they crafted the test. *Brandenburg* captures the essence of liberal egalitarian tolerance in a number of ways. First, and perhaps most obviously, the *Brandenburg* test is highly deferential to speech. As has been discussed throughout this volume, it is often difficult for the state to overcome the hurdle placed in front of speech by the *Brandenburg* test. As US history has shown, speech that advocates for provocative and, at times, violent behavior can itself accomplish the goals of liberal egalitarianism. For example, calls for violence during the American Revolution and abolitionist speeches in the run-up to the Civil War are clear examples of language that led to bloody, catastrophic violence, which in turn produced improvements to liberty and equity. Calls for various forms of violence during the civil rights era are similar examples. Yet, liberal egalitarian tolerance is equally deferential to the use of liberty; such tolerance cares less about the content of speech and more about the right to determine that content. Additionally, this deference is consistent with the liberal egalitarian purpose I describe above, which is to give citizens sufficient action space to pursue their own conceptions of the good. It may be true that some conceptions of the good espouse quasi-lawless behavior. But liberal egalitarianism would prefer that these conceptions be addressed by competing conceptions through the exercise of others' freedom of conscience rather than through state action.

Second, the test's factors are jurisprudential articulations of the Limitation Components that I describe above. As the test makes clear, citizens acting through the state are not permitted to prohibit speech except in cases of imminent and likely lawless action. This overlaps with the Public Order Limitation Component of liberal egalitarian tolerance that contains the negative proscription against using the freedom of conscience to substantially undermine order. Insofar as public law is a tool for preserving political order among citizens, speech that advocates imminent and likely actions that violate public law would violate both *Brandenburg* and liberal egalitarian tolerance. But perhaps less obvious, under *Brandenburg*, such imminent and likely lawless action would potentially fall within the Scheme Undermining Limitation Component of liberal egalitarian tolerance. Speech that advocates for imminent and likely lawless action is carving out for itself special treatment that it does not grant to competing speech. Speakers who wish to see anything short of such lawless action would have their own liberty curtailed by the success of the lawless advocate. This self-defeating lack of reciprocity falls squarely within one of liberal egalitarian tolerance's prohibitions. In other words, *Brandenburg*'s limiting principles are simply restatements of liberal egalitarian tolerance directed toward government action.

All of this shows *Brandenburg*'s commitment to the liberal egalitarian metavalue of justice in a very specific way. As I explained above, justice in the liberal egalitarian tradition is a political and social arrangement that affords wide latitude for conceptions of the good while minimizing arbitrary disadvantages assigned by nature and society. Although the *Brandenburg* test is specific to constitutional law and a protection against state action, its policy implications are that individuals are free to pursue their conceptions of the good, not only free from state action but free from arbitrariness. A speaker who is born in a social or economic condition that disadvantages them among their fellow citizens will find in the *Brandenburg* test a powerful equalizing, if not very specific, right — the right to be radical, provocative, perhaps even violently revolutionary, without fear of being silenced by the more powerful. *Brandenburg* is not directed at economic or social status; those subjects are beyond the scope of free speech jurisprudence. But *Brandenburg* does ensure that a speaker can engage with the status quo with the most powerful rhetorical tools available, regardless of their standing within the political community. This is exactly the synergistic relationship between liberty and equity that liberal egalitarianism envisions in its conception of justice.

Two Real-World Illustrations

To further illustrate the liberal egalitarian foundation of the *Brandenburg* test, consider two examples. In the first case, the city of Dearborn, Michigan, hosted its annual Arab International Festival in June 2012 to celebrate the rich Arab heritage in the community. The event was the largest organization of its kind in the United States and drew a substantial crowd of more than 300,000 people over the course of three days. Each year, various religious groups applied to participate in the festival, including Christian evangelical groups that proselytized by roaming the crowd of attendees.[15]

In the year prior to the events at issue, a group called the "Bible Believers," led by a man named "Israel," had attended the festival and attempted to preach to listeners. According to the Court, "[t]he quintessential attribute of the Bible Believers' message was intolerance, principally proclaiming that Mohammed was a false prophet who lied to them and that Muslims would be damned to hell if they failed to repent by rejecting Islam." Their language led to physical altercations with festival attendees and one arrest of the Bible Believers by Wayne County law enforcement. When asked to explain why he and his group engaged in this sort of activity, Israel claimed that "due to his sincerely held religious beliefs he was required 'to try and convert non-believers, and call sinners to repent.'"[16]

The Bible Believers returned in 2012, this time alerting county law enforcement, through counsel, that they planned to proselytize and would be prepared to take whatever legal action would be necessary if they were silenced again. The county responded, saying that law enforcement was under a duty under state and local ordinances to hold criminally liable anyone who "incite[s] riotous behavior or otherwise disturb[s] the peace." The county argued that "law enforcement personnel are not required 'to defend the right of a speaker to address a hostile audience . . . when to do so would unreasonably subject them to violent retaliation" and that they may "remove the speaker for his own protection" if necessary.[17]

During the festival, the Bible Believers walked among the crowd with banners and T-shirts that said, among other things, "Islam is a Religion of Blood and Murder" and "Turn or Burn." One member of the group carried a severed pig's head on a spike because, according to Israel, "it would 'keep the Muslims at bay since 'unfortunately, they are kind of petrified of that animal.'"

Another member told the crowd that Muhammad was "a false prophet" and "a pedophile." The reaction of the crowd began to turn hostile. A group of teenagers that grew in size as time passed began heckling the Bible Believers and throwing bottles and trash at the speakers. Law enforcement intervened to tell the speakers to stop using a megaphone and to push the crowd back. When law enforcement moved on, the crowd again turned hostile, and Israel was hit by flying debris, causing a small laceration. Eventually, law enforcement returned and asked the Bible Believers to disband. Israel refused to do so unless law enforcement put him under arrest or cited him. After conferring with counsel for the county, law enforcement informed Israel that he and his group would be cited for disorderly conduct if they did not leave immediately. The Bible Believers ultimately left, with Israel saying, "I would assume 200 angry Muslim children throwing bottles is more of a threat than a few guys with signs." They were subsequently detained and issued a citation by eight officers as they drove away from the festival because, according to law enforcement, they had removed the license plate from their vehicle prior to departing. Only one teenage member of the crowd was cited for throwing debris.[18]

The Bible Believers sued the county under federal law, claiming deprivation of their civil liberties.[19] Among other claims, the Bible Believers' complaint alleged that their free speech rights were violated when the county removed them from the festival under threat of citation. The parties filed cross-motions for summary judgment, and the District Court for the Eastern District of Michigan granted the county's motion dismissing the Bible Believer's claims. On appeal before the Sixth Circuit Court of Appeals, the Bible Believers argued that the lower Court had incorrectly applied the *Brandenburg* test to the case. When a split panel affirmed the lower Court's decision, the Bible Believers petitioned for and were granted an *en banc* rehearing.[20]

The Sixth Circuit reversed the decision of the lower court and found in favor of the Bible Believers for a variety of reasons, including *Brandenburg* grounds. After recounting the test's factors, the Court held that, while the Bible Believer's "speech advocated for their Christian beliefs and for harboring contempt for Islam," there were no "references to violence or lawlessness" in their speech. While phrases like "Islam is a religion of blood and murder" and "Turn or burn" were certainly designed to be provocative and offensive, they did not "advocate for, encourage, condone, or even embrace imminent violence or lawlessness." Moreover, nothing in the speaker's actions indicated that "they intended imminent lawlessness to ensue." "Quite to the contrary, the Bible Believers contacted Wayne County prior to their visit, requesting that the WCSO keep the public at bay so that the Bible Believers could "engage in their peaceful expression." Both the words and the conduct of the speakers gave no indication that there was an intent on the part of the Bible Believers to engender violence. According to the Sixth Circuit, "[t]he Bible Believers did not ask their audience to rise up in arms and fight for their beliefs, let alone request that they hurl bottles and other garbage upon the Bible Believers' heads."[21]

Now, contrast this case with a second case about a highly controversial event that has consumed US discourse for nearly two years: the speech given by President Donald Trump on January 6, 2021, the day on which conservative supporters of Trump breached the US Capitol. As of this writing, the investigation into what Trump did, said, and knew during the rally and prior to the subsequent riot is still ongoing. However, at least one federal district court, the District Court for the District of Columbia, has taken up the question of whether or not Trump's comments survive under the *Brandenburg* test.[22] In the case, a group of members of the House of Representatives sued Trump and a number of other participants in the January 6th rally under the Ku Klux Klan Act of 1871.[23] The Act protects officers of the US government, including congresspersons, from "conspir[acy] to prevent, by force, intimidation, or threat," their holding said office. The plaintiffs argued, among other things, that Trump's language and the effect it had on the rioters did just that.[24] Trump moved to dismiss the complaint on a variety of grounds, including that his language was protected speech under the First Amendment's Free Speech Clause.[25] In doing so, Trump argued that the *Brandenburg* test was not met and his inflammatory language had not created imminent, likely lawless action.[26]

In ruling on the matter, the District Court noted the dearth of cases applying *Brandenburg* but concluded, based on scholarly commentary and the few holdings of the Supreme Court, that the "key to the *Brandenburg* exception is incitement."[27] Moreover, the Court held that there is a subjective component of *Brandenburg*: the speaker has to intend or know that their speech is likely to incite imminent lawless action. The court then summarized Trump's statements as follows: "'[W]e fight. We fight like hell, and if you don't fight like hell, you're not going to have a country anymore,' and '[W]e're going to try to and give [weak Republicans] the kind of pride and boldness that they need to take back our country,' immediately before exhorting rally-goers to 'walk down Pennsylvania Avenue.'"[28]

Viewing these statements in their most favorable light, the District Court held that, at least for purposes of surviving a motion to dismiss, the statements were plausibly words of incitement that did not survive under *Brandenburg*. This was true for a few reasons. First, the District Court noted, the context of the language mattered: Trump and his advisers had spent weeks creating an "air of distrust" around the 2020 presidential election results, Trump knew that his supporters had made threats against elected officials prior to the rally, and Trump and his advisers had actively monitored social media for calls for violence. Moreover, the District Court found that Trump's speech was rife with references to a "stolen" or "rigged" election, President Joe Biden's being an "illegitimate President," and the need for Trump's supporters to "take back their country." Indeed, the District Court pointed out that one former Trump aide had predicted that "there will be violence on January 6th because the President himself encourages it." Given this context, the Court also dismissed Trump's arguments that his audience misinterpreted his language or that he was only doing what other elected officials on the political left were doing. Ultimately, the Court denied Trump's motion to dismiss on *Brandenburg* grounds.[29]

Putting aside whether the courts in these cases "got it right," the liberal egalitarian conception of tolerance at the heart of *Brandenburg* offers some insight into the different results. First, in both cases, the courts are deferential to speech. The Sixth Circuit in *Bible Believers* assumed that, in cases of conflict, the draw goes to the individual speaker and not the state. Similarly, while the District Court in *Thompson* ultimately ruled against the speaker, it did so against the backdrop that the hurdle is enormously high for a speaker to be held liable; much of the analysis turns on intent and context, a fact that counts in favor of the speaker. Second, the Limitation Components of liberal egalitarian tolerance are at the forefront of each court's analysis. The threat of peaceful, however provocative, evangelical speakers at a festival in Dearborn, Michigan, is in stark contrast to the calls for action by a sitting president at a rally in Washington, DC, the ostensible purpose of which is to call an election into question. The threats to public order are markedly different from one another. Likewise, in the *Bible Believers* case, the scheme of equal liberties is hardly threatened; just as the speakers claimed for themselves the right to voice their conscience, nothing in their conduct suggested that they would deny an equal right to others to disagree. Meanwhile, in the *Thompson* case, Trump's language is explicitly designed to silence others and to undermine the political institutions that allow citizens to express their conscience in the first place.

But even more so, these two cases highlight the very essence of liberal egalitarianism's message to its critics. For example, a key difference is that speakers in *Bible Believers* were not in agreement with their audience; their language walks the line to fighting words or other unprotected categories of public speech. In the *Thompson* case, on the other hand, Trump was speaking to the audience to advocate violence against a shared enemy. The requirements of liberal tolerance depend greatly on the broader speaking context. But on an even more philosophical level, where the theoretical right and theoretical left critics debate with it on the scope of liberty and equity, liberal egalitarianism makes the bold declaration that every citizen is afforded the right to pursue their conception of the good in free action spaces, provided that doing so is consistent with an equal right for others. Both cases adhere to this metavalue of justice by reading the *Brandenburg* test as a license for speakers and their listeners to pursue their own conceptions. In *Thompson*, nothing was preventing Trump from advocating his political ideas, however provocative they were. It was when he encouraged a group of supporters that he knew to be armed to march on the US Capitol that he ceased to adhere to a justice-centered political arrangement. As the District Court in *Thompson* hints, liberty and equality were at their lowest ebb when Trump stepped to the lectern. Meanwhile, the Sixth Circuit in *Bible Believers* recognized that the point of *Brandenburg*, like all of free speech jurisprudence, is to leave it to citizens to develop their *own* ideas without commandeering the power of the state to silence their critics: "Diversity, in viewpoints and among cultures, is not always easy. An inability or a general unwillingness to understand new or differing points of view may breed fear, distrust, and even loathing. But it is the function of speech to free men from the bondage of irrational fears."[30] This is quite literally the upshot of liberal egalitarian tolerance. One would be hard-pressed to find two recent cases that better illustrate the theoretical foundations of *Brandenburg*.

Aspirations and Possibilities Beyond *Brandenburg*

Throughout this chapter, I have taken the position that the *Brandenburg* test is perfectly consistent with liberal egalitarianism; it accomplishes the main goals of liberal egalitarianism in the very specific case of speech while adhering to the values at the heart of the theory, namely, liberty, equity, and the metavalue of justice. When it comes to a case involving violent, provocative expression of ideas, the *Brandenburg* test makes up a necessary component of the public law scaffolding that liberal egalitarianism requires. At the same time, there are important lessons to be drawn from *Brandenburg* that go beyond the highly specific cases of advocacy for lawless behavior. True, when it comes to the potential criminal prosecution of speakers, *Brandenburg*'s urgency in preventing state-sanctioned chilling of speakers is justified. But beyond those cases, there are new boundaries that *Brandenburg*-esque innovations might explore within the liberal egalitarian tradition.

First, it is important to reiterate that liberal egalitarianism is primarily concerned with the freedom of conscience — not just speech. As I explain above, liberal egalitarianism assumes that individuals will pursue their conceptions of the good in their private and public life using the full range of human faculties. Speech is only one outward expression of inner beliefs, and it often implies advocacy, statement of opinion, and dialogue. But conscience involves much more than speech. As I have hinted above, the exercise of one's conscience can include any of the following: beliefs or nonbeliefs in religion and spirituality; academic inquiry; decision-making about personal life plans such as family, career, hobbies, and so forth; the choice of media to consume, not just the creation or exchange of it; the internal development of ideas about politics and society — just to name a few things. Indeed, the freedom of conscience may be thought of as the developmental aspect of one's conception of the good; without this freedom, a person could never select and pursue their chosen conception.[31]

A truly liberal egalitarian freedom of conscience could take lessons from the *Brandenburg* test beyond the context of criminal punishment for speech. Reframed in this way, liberal egalitarianism might include a principle similar to the test's factors: "Citizens acting as citizens have the right to exercise their freedom of conscience, provided that in so doing they do not produce imminent and likely lawless action." This would capture the necessary components of the liberal egalitarian definition of tolerance while presenting them as privileges exercised by citizens rather than proscriptions against behavior. Of course, it is too much to suggest that this principle would carry with it a mechanism like judicial enforcement. But this principle would inform the practices and policies of institutions, organizations, and individual citizens.

Second, *Brandenburg* invites policy makers and citizens to think carefully about what constitutes "lawless" behavior. The test itself assumes that there is a corpus of law that has been publicly and transparently delineated. But this simply begs the question of what those laws capture in the first place. Liberal egalitarianism, as I explained above, focuses on public order as a test for what does not necessarily have to be tolerated by a society. Set against one another, *Brandenburg* and liberal egalitarian tolerance ask us to consider: does what we define as lawlessness truly overlap with what we consider to be threats to order? Insofar as citizens can simply redefine unlawful behavior to be "things we just do not like," the *Brandenburg* test may prove to be a useless protection for speakers, and liberal egalitarian tolerance may be meaningless. Take, for example, the "unlawful" behavior in *Church of Lukumi Babalu Aye, Inc. v. City of Hialeah*: the ritual sacrifice of animals by followers of Santeria. The City of Hialeah had passed legislation banning such practices while at the same time remaining silent about the slaughter of animals for other purposes, such as factory farming. Although the case was ultimately resolved on Free Exercise Clause grounds, imagine the scenario in which an advocate of Santeria encouraged listeners to conduct sacrificial rituals during a meeting of adherents. Down the street, a meeting of barbecue aficionados has come together with a culinary expert who is advocating for a particular method of slaughtering animals for cooking. Put aside the religious issue, and it is not too difficult to see how a community's definition of "unlawful" can lead to arbitrary and inconsistent results. The Santeria advocate would run afoul of *Brandenburg* for advocating unlawfulness, but the barbecue expert would not. Thus, *Brandenburg* invites introspection: if we embrace the general commitment of *Brandenburg* to permitting speech that we find frightening, then the onus is on us as citizens to carefully consider what lines our society will not permit to be crossed. Unironically, this introspection has an egalitarian capacity for change; behavior that we deem "unlawful" now but which does nothing to undermine public order in the slightest should no longer be marginalized and criminalized. Without specifying what those behaviors might be, it's not hard to hazard a guess that some communities of citizens will find themselves less stigmatized and threatened. In short, critical application of *Brandenburg* might be a very helpful tool for liberal egalitarian development.

Third, if *Brandenburg* can be situated in the liberal egalitarian tradition, as I have argued, then it is on safe footing against critiques from what I have referred to as the theoretical right and left. It is a constant refrain in contemporary lay discourse to lament the speech of others while carving out unique rights for oneself. Spend an hour or so on a social media platform populated by otherwise intelligent people, and it will not be long before one encounters the hypocrisy of speech: I deserve my right to speak, while you do not. This smacks of the sort of theoretical left position I described above; the in-group, communitarian desire to give my tribe special treatment over that of others runs across the US political spectrum. At the same time, one will also encounter an arrogant and uninformed refrain that free speech is unrestricted, unregulated, and unchecked — that there are no limits to what one can say in the United States. This elevation of liberty above any practical needs or theoretical values is precisely the sort of critique that would come from the theoretical right. But the liberal egalitarian position espoused by the *Brandenburg* test charts a course between the claims of liberty and equity; neither is speech unlimited nor is it limited to one group over another. Instead, the liberal egalitarianism at the heart of *Brandenburg* makes a clear statement to would-be participants in the marketplace of ideas: say what you will and be prepared to encounter ideas you do not like, but do not look to the coercive power of the state to protect you short of specific limits.

Finally, *Brandenburg* exposes the need for a rich set of public institutions that inculcate civil discourse in citizens. Public schools, open media, community-based forums, a free and open internet, and real access to representatives by lay citizens would be good starting points for engendering civil discourse in the public. *Brandenburg* assumes that citizens may present and encounter provocative ideas that are potentially offensive or advocate violent behavior; as the examples above illustrate, a cross-section of listeners will often find themselves feeling uncomfortable with the speech anticipated by *Brandenburg*. But while the test prepares *the state* with principles for when it may or may not act, it does nothing to prepare *citizens* with similar principles for when they may act on offensive speech, whether that be through political participation or simply engagement with ideas. In other words, *Brandenburg* has written the check, but there remains the need for funds from which to draw.

This fact provides urgency for the realization of other parts of liberal egalitarianism. The theory assumes that a truly just society provides space within which to act and resources to do so, including education. If *Brandenburg* envisions a world in which speakers can present speech that a large portion of the population will find difficult to accept, then it also envisions that those speakers will be prepared to follow the definition of tolerance laid out by liberal egalitarianism. In doing so, *Brandenburg* is jurisprudence for ideal conditions. However, it should go without saying that, at least in the United States, we have taken some steps toward such ideal conditions while having significant ground yet to cover. In Rawlsian terms, we have begun implementing liberty, made some inroads with regard to fair equality of opportunity, and have done next to nothing to create a more egalitarian economy that benefits the least advantaged (and, in some ways, have actually done the opposite). *Brandenburg* should provide a wake-up call for those liberal egalitarians who wish to see a theoretical world come to life, as at least free speech jurisprudence seems to assume that this process is already well underway.

Conclusion

I have endeavored to take a unique approach to the *Brandenburg* test from a political theory perspective. I have drawn on the principles of liberal egalitarianism, showing what it is, why it matters, and how it has been criticized. I have also rooted *Brandenburg* within this philosophical position, showing through both theory and examples how *Brandenburg* adheres to the values of liberty and equity. In doing so, I have also shown that the test captures the metavalue of liberal egalitarian justice. Finally, I have presented ideas for further development prompted by this analysis of the test. Without a doubt, *Brandenburg* has been and will continue to be an important facet of US free speech law. That is abundantly clear in the jurisprudential and legal debates that occur around the topic, some of which are presented in this volume. But *Brandenburg* is an important focal point for political theory, and especially so for those of us working in the liberal egalitarian tradition. One who would truly be committed to the synergy between liberty and equity would do well to wrestle with the implications of *Brandenburg*.

Notes

1. A quick search of the doctrine in Westlaw reveals almost 6,000 articles on the subject, while the number of cases that give it more than a marginal discussion is around 500.
2. Marc Rohr, "Grand Illusion? The Brandenburg Test and Speech that Encourages or Facilitates Criminal Acts," *Willamette Law Review* 38 (2002): 1–92; Thomas E. Crocco, "Comment: Inciting Terrorism on the Internet: An Application of Brandenburg to Terrorist Websites," *Saint Louis University Public Law Review* 23 (2004): 451–84.
3. For the primary accounts of liberal egalitarianism, see John Rawls, *A Theory of Justice*: rev. ed. (Harvard University Press, 1999); Ronald Dworkin, *Sovereign Virtue: The Theory and Practice of Equality* (Harvard University Press, 2000).
4. For a thorough distillation of these concepts, see Will Kymlicka, "Liberal Equality," *Contemporary Political Philosophy* (Oxford University Press, 2002).
5. Rawls, *A Theory of Justice*, 347–50.
6. For the clearest articulation of the classical liberal position, see Friedrich A. Hayek, *Law Legislation and Liberty*, vol. 2, *The Mirage of Social Justice* (University of Chicago Press, 1976).
7. Robert Nozick, *Anarchy, State, and Utopia* (Basic Books, 1974).
8. For the communitarian critique, see Michael Sandel, *Liberalism and the Limits of Justice* (Cambridge University Press, 1982); Charles Taylor, *Philosophy and the Human Sciences: Philosophical Papers* (Cambridge University Press, 1985). For the multiculturalist critique, see Ian Shapiro and Will Kymlicka (eds.), *Ethnicity and Group Rights: NOMOS 39* (New York University Press, 1997). For the feminist critique, see Catherine MacKinnon, *Feminism Unmodified: Discourses on Life and Law* (Harvard University Press, 1987), Carol Gilligan, *In a Different Voice: Psychological Theory and Women's Development* (Harvard University Press, 1982).
9. Rawls, *A Theory of Justice*, 214–15, 476–78.
10. Ronald Dworkin, *Taking Rights Seriously* (Harvard University Press, 1977), 262–65.
11. Rawls, *A Theory of Justice*, 53, 266, 476–78.
12. Rawls, *A Theory of Justice*, 186.
13. See, for example, John Adams, "Thoughts on Government," in *American Political Thought*, ed. Keith E. Whittingon (Oxford University Press, 2017).
14. Brandenburg v. Ohio, 395 U.S. 444, 447 (1969).
15. Bible Believers v. Wayne County, Mich., 805 F.3d 228 (6th Cir. 2015).
16. Bible Believers at 236.
17. Bible Believers at 236–37.

18 Bible Believers at 238–41.
19 See 42 U.S.C. § 1983.
20 Bible Believers at 241–42.
21 Bible Believers at 244–46.
22 See Thompson v. Trump, 590 F.Supp.3d 46 (D.D.C. Feb. 18, 2022).
23 42 U.S.C. § 1985(1).
24 Thompson at 62.
25 Thompson at 69.
26 Thompson at 111.
27 Thompson at 112.
28 Thompson at 114.
29 Thompson at 115–17.
30 Bible Believers at 233–34 (internal citations and quotations omitted).
31 For this broad definition of freedom of conscience in liberal egalitarian terms, see Rafael Domingo, "Restoring Freedom of Conscience," *Journal of Law and Religion* 30:2 (June 2015).

Chapter Two

Anti-Orthodoxy, Inclusion, and the Advocacy of Violence

Timothy C. Shiell

Brandenburg v. Ohio, 395 U.S. 444 (1969), was a landmark decision distinguishing constitutionally protected abstract advocacy of violence from constitutionally unprotected intentional incitement to imminent lawless action. Even though *Brandenburg* overturned the conviction of a Ku Klux Klan leader advocating the possibility of violence, this chapter argues that the decision is rooted in the normative imperative to protect criticism of orthodoxy by equality-minded historically marginalized and oppressed people, and it continues to play that role.

The argument proceeds in three stages. The first section explains how the reciprocal values of anti-orthodoxy and inclusion were central to the creation and justification of robust expressive rights. The second section extends that discussion to the legal status of the advocacy of violence up to and including the *Brandenburg* decision. The final section addresses the role of dissent and inclusion in *Brandenburg* and how the incitement test continues to protect the dissent and inclusion of those advocating greater equality.

The Relationship of Anti-Orthodoxy and Inclusion to Expressive Rights

Nan Hunter introduces the values of anti-orthodoxy and inclusion to resolve the "expression-equality conundrum."[1] She acknowledges that expressive rights can be and are exercised in ways that conflict with progress in equality but maintains that robust expressive rights and progress in equality are not fundamentally at odds. Rather, they are inseparably connected due to their mutual commitment to protecting dissent and increasing inclusion. For example, the extension of freedom of expression, assembly, and association to the LGBT community played a critical role in attaining greater equality for them.[2] This does not mean that LGBT gains were inevitable, uncontested, or permanent;

but it does mean that in the absence of expressive rights the LGBT community would still be "the love that dare not speak its name" as it remains in countries that continue to criminalize LGBT expression.

To be sure, Hunter's view that expressive rights and equality are inseparable is not new. Consider, for example, Justice Thurgood Marshall.[3] Marshall won 29 of 32 history-making decisions defending civil rights as a lawyer with the National Association for the Advancement of Colored People (NAACP) and Legal Defense Fund from 1934 to 1961, and as an associate justice of the US Supreme Court from 1967 to 1991 participated in 165 free speech decisions insisting that "constitutional liberties contained a strong equality component and that liberty and equality properly understood complemented each other,"[4] and "sweeping speech protection was necessary to ensure that the voice of the politically weak and despised was heard."[5] Rather, Hunter's insight is to introduce anti-orthodoxy and inclusion to support the inseparability thesis. These mutually reinforcing values help show the connection between expression and equality is not a historical quirk limited to a particular country or era.

Modern expressive rights in the United States developed primarily in Supreme Court decisions concerning the dissents of labor activists, civil rights activists, and Jehovah's Witnesses during the mid-twentieth century. Consider some landmark decisions. The Supreme Court incorporated the free speech and press clauses in *Gitlow v. New York*, 268 U.S. 652 (1925), a case involving socialist politician and journalist Benjamin Gitlow. The court first struck down a state restriction on free speech in *Stromberg v. California*, 283 U.S. 359 (1931), a case involving a Young Communist League summer camp worker. The Court first used the clear and present danger test to protect expression in *Herndon v. Lowry*, 301 U.S. 242 (1937), a case involving a Black communist labor organizer. The free assembly and petition clauses were incorporated in *De Jonge v. Oregon*, 299 U.S. 353 (1937), a case concerning a speech during a communist labor meeting protesting police shootings and raids targeting striking workers. Between 1939 and 1950, the Jehovah's Witnesses won fourteen Supreme Court cases protecting their door-to-door and street evangelizing. Most notably, *Cantwell v. Connecticut*, 310 U.S. 296 (1940), incorporated the free exercise clause and *West Virginia v. Barnette*, 319 U.S. 624 (1943), produced a "fixed star" in the constitutional "constellation" in rejecting government compelled speech in matters of belief and opinion. Academic freedom was recognized in *Sweezy v. New Hampshire*, 354 U.S. 234 (1957), a decision protecting Marxist economist and activist Paul Sweezy. The court recognized freedom of expressive association in *NAACP v. Alabama*, 357 U.S. 449 (1958), a decision protecting NAACP members from government and private harassment and retribution. Modern free press and libel law regarding public officials was created in the *New York Times v. Sullivan*, 376 U.S. 254 (1964) decision protecting civil rights advocacy. *Brown v. Louisiana*, 383 U.S. 131 (1965), held peaceful civil rights sit-ins were protected expression under the First Amendment. The extension of First Amendment rights to public school students in *Tinker v. Des*

Moines, 393 U.S. 503 (1969), took its "material and substantial disruption" test from a lower court's decision protecting student civil rights protest.[6] *Healy v. James*, 408 U.S. 169 (1972), extended First Amendment protection to public-higher-education students in a case involving the antiestablishment Students for a Democratic Society. These decisions are the tip of the iceberg, and later decisions have continued to protect anti-orthodox expression.[7]

The integral role anti-orthodoxy and inclusion play in the link between expressive rights and greater equality also is demonstrated in Jacob Mchangama's masterful history of free speech in a global context. The pursuit of expressive rights full of "epic struggles, setbacks, false starts and enormous sacrifices" has been waged worldwide by and for heterodox and excluded groups and individuals seeking liberty and equality.[8] People resisting, for example, government imposition of Catholicism in Europe, Protestantism in the United States, or Islam in Muslim-dominated countries. Abolitionists demanding an end to slavery. Indigenous peoples seeking self-government free from colonial masters. The list is long, and Mchangama's nearly 400 pages do not exhaust it.

Anti-orthodoxy and inclusion also are central to the three major justifications for expressive rights, namely, the pursuit of truth, democratic self-government, and individual autonomy and self-realization. These justifications are routinely invoked in the historic, global struggle for expressive rights as well as in decisions of the Supreme Court.

To paraphrase the English philosopher John Stuart Mill, the search for truth requires robust expressive rights for three reasons.[9] First, we are all fallible humans who have some false beliefs. Having epistemic humility enables us to allow, even encourage, those who have contrary views to correct our errors. Second, knowledge is often partial rather than complete. We should allow, even encourage, diverse viewpoints as these contesting perspectives correct errors, fill gaps, and produce new knowledge. Finally, exposure to false views is necessary to keep the justification and vibrancy of the truth alive. When truth becomes dogma, it shrivels into a hollow truism unable to defend itself from attack.

The truth justification for free speech and the related "marketplace of ideas" metaphor, despite limitations,[10] is routinely invoked by the Supreme Court. Including heterodox beliefs and believers in an environment of open inquiry is part and parcel of a fruitful social and educational milieu producing critical thinkers, innovation, and truth. Overbroad and unduly vague as well as content and viewpoint biased government restrictions on expression handicap our ability and opportunities to think critically and creatively. Increasing who is permitted to express ideas (inclusion) and what ideas they may express (anti-orthodoxy) are essential to expressive rights and truth-seeking.

The idea that expressive rights are essential to democratic self-government also has ancient roots and has become more popular as more people demand and enact democratic forms of government and more inclusive democracies evolve. In the United States, Alexander Meiklejohn was a major contributor to this strain of thought.[11] This is not to say every democracy has or should have the same set of expressive rights or that they are or should be equally robust.[12] The democracy of ancient Athens had a constricted idea of who could be a citizen and what their rights were, yet it recognized *isegoria*, the equal right of citizens to participate in public debate in the democratic assembly, and *parrhesia*, the license to say what one pleased, how and when one pleased, and to whom.[13] Mchangama describes how religious conflicts across Europe that caused horrific violence and repression also led to the twin demands for free speech and democracy that eventually bore fruit.[14] Indeed, National Coalition Against Censorship (NCAC) executive director Christopher Finan argues that free speech saved American democracy in his analysis of free speech and democratic social and political change.[15] European colonial powers enforced severe restrictions on expression in an attempt to control indigenous populations but resistance to their oppressive rule produced more free speech and democracy in many former colonies.

Expressive rights are essential to democracy by contributing to an informed and active citizenry, government transparency and accountability, tolerance, and other important features of a pluralistic democracy. These fade into the shadows when heterodox and marginalized groups and individuals are silenced and excluded from democratic debate and processes. Indeed, the right to vote, the essence of democracy, is tantamount to an expressive right.[16] Extending the right to vote to unpropertied men, non-Protestants, men of color, women, and citizens aged eighteen to twenty contributed to a more inclusive and stronger democracy.

The more recent autonomy/self-realization justification has many supporters.[17] Developing autonomy and reaching one's potential require both speaking and listening; thus, expressive rights exist not only to protect speakers but also listeners. They are "two sides of the same coin," as Justice Thurgood Marshall put it.[18] For example, *Martin v. City of Struthers*, 319 U.S. 141 (1943), protected the right to distribute religious materials door-to-door since the First Amendment "necessarily protects the right to receive it." *Thomas v. Collins*, 323 U.S. 516 (1945), struck down a Texas law requiring union officials to obtain an organizer's card before soliciting members in part due to the right of listeners to hear what they had to say. *Virginia State Board of Pharmacy v. Virginia Citizens Consumer Council*, 425 U.S. 748 (1976), struck down a state law prohibiting pharmacists from advertising prices of prescription drugs based on a consumer's interest in knowing the costs of medications. Autonomy and self-realization require interaction with diverse viewpoints, including unpopular, controversial, and "divisive" ones. Living in a bubble makes for puppets and pawns of orthodoxy.

To be sure, expressive rights protect anti-egalitarian expression too. The idea that government should protect the speaker from the mob rather than allow the mob to silence the speaker (the heckler's veto doctrine) in *Terminiello v. Chicago*, 337 U.S. 1 (1949), protected a rant attacking Jews, President Roosevelt and his wife, communists, and others that caused a riot. Frank Collin's small group of Nazis did not march in Skokie, Illinois, in 1977, but courts upheld their right to do so.[19] *R.A.V. v. St. Paul*, 505 U.S. 377 (1992) struck down the city's Bias-Motivated Crime Ordinance reversing the conviction of a racist cross-burner. *Forsyth County v. Nationalist Movement*, 505 U.S. 123 (1992), upheld a racist group's challenge to a policing fee ordinance. The rights to free speech and assembly enabled white supremacists to march to "Unite the Right" in Charlottesville, Virginia, in 2017, which led to mayhem and murder.[20] Robust expressive rights do not guarantee victory for greater equality. Nothing guarantees progress in equality. Inseparability is not invincibility. The point — well understood by civil rights icons like Eleanor Holmes Norton, Thurgood Marshall, Pauline Murray, and Rev. Fred Shuttlesworth — is that progress in equality has greater opportunity with robust expressive rights.

Anti-Orthodoxy, Inclusion, and First Amendment Decisions on the Advocacy of Violence

Anti-orthodoxy and inclusion also are central to Supreme Court decisions regarding the advocacy of violence. We begin with some historical background to set the stage.

From the ratification of the Bill of Rights in 1791 to the early twentieth century, freedom of expression existed primarily as a "darling privilege," not an enforceable legal right.[21] Three factors contributed to this. First, the "bad tendency" test adopted from English common law was used to determine the legality of expression. Still in use in *Whitney v. California*, 274 U.S. 357 (1927), the court held that government may punish "utterances inimical to the public welfare, tending to incite crime, disturb the public peace, or endanger the foundations of organized government and threaten its overthrow by unlawful means." Expressions whose risk of violence or lawlessness was remote in time or purely conjectural were punishable. Criticism and insults directed at government officials were punishable.[22] Second, prosecutions often invoked seditious libel laws that partisans used to punish critics and political opponents. Indeed, truth was not a defense against seditious libel — it was an aggravating factor — until jury nullification became prevalent following the 1733 Zenger trial,[23] and it became law in the nineteenth century. Federalists enacted and used the 1798 Sedition Act to persecute Jeffersonian Republicans; Jeffersonians used state sedition laws to persecute Federalists. A third reason free speech was more a privilege than a legal right was *Barron v. Baltimore*, 32 U.S. 243 (1833), holding that the Bill of Rights applied to actions of the federal government, not state government. State governments were free to censor expression according to their own constitutions and statutes and later decisions allowed state governments to ignore private suppression of and even violence against unpopular expression.[24] Antebellum abolitionists were persecuted in Southern states by law and in Northern states by mob violence.[25] Labor activists endured government and private suppression from the mid-1880s into the twentieth century.[26] During World War I, pervasive hostility to unpopular expression resulted, with few exceptions, in judicial decisions upholding federal and state censorship of antiwar expression as mild as claiming "it's a rich man's war."[27]

The first hint of change was *Patterson v. Colorado*, 205 U.S.454 (1907). Although the court upheld a contempt citation against Thomas Patterson, a former United States senator and owner of the *Denver Times* and the *Rocky Mountain News*, for criticizing a Colorado Supreme Court decision, it was the first time the court heard a case involving state censorship and two justices dissented. Writing for the majority, Justice Oliver Wendell Holmes Jr. noted the First Amendment did not apply to state government, and even if it did, the free press clause only prohibited prior restraint of the press, not punishment for expression that had a "bad" tendency.

There was no progress in *Fox v. Washington*, 236 U.S. 273 (1915) and *Mutual Film Corp v. Ohio*, 236 U.S. 230 (1915). Both upheld state restrictions, lacked dissenting opinions, and ignored First Amendment concerns. *Fox* upheld a Washington law used to punish an advocate of nude bathing for a published article titled "The Nude and the Prudes." *Mutual Film* upheld Ohio's requirement that films be approved by a censorship board because films were not speech; they were commercial enterprises no different than "circuses and other sideshow spectacles."

The court's rulings in World War I federal Espionage Act cases continued to short shrift First Amendment concerns; however, there was a notable judicial innovation and dissents. The cases typically involved an immigrant socialist, communist, or anarchist criticizing the country's involvement in the war and the military draft instituted to support the war. The court upheld the conviction in every case except one.[28] Although the court upheld the convictions in *Schenck v. United States*, 249 U.S. 47 (1919), Justice Holmes introduced the clear and present danger test, which offered a more speech protective test than the bad tendency test and was invoked in a series of famous dissents by Holmes and Justice Louis Brandeis supporting expressive rights.[29]

The Holmes–Brandeis defense of robust expressive rights did not win a majority on the court until 1931's *Stromberg v. California* (state "red flag" ban was overbroad) and *Near v. Minnesota* (state law banning "malicious, scandalous and defamatory" publications was an unconstitutional prior restraint of the press). The clear and present danger test finally was applied to protect expression in the 1937 *Herndon* decision overturning the inciting insurrection conviction of a Black communist and was used in some later cases to protect expression.[30]

The growth of labor activism and unions[31] prompted anti-union government officials, private companies, and vigilantes to develop many strategies to suppress them.[32] In the late 1910s, states began enacting criminal syndicalism laws outlawing the advocacy of violence and criminality to achieve labor objectives. Karl Marx and others believed peaceful transition to communism was possible through class struggle in democracies such as the United States; but they also believed workers had a right to revolt when their goal was not attainable through peaceful methods.[33] Dale Mineshima–Lowe notes the result was "[d]uring the 1910s and 1920s, authorities arrested thousands of people for advocating views and opinions that differed from or opposed those of the government. In many cases — despite these views and opinions being expressed in peaceful protests and organized meetings — hundreds were tried, convicted, and sent to prison under the criminal syndicalism laws of more than 20 states and territories."[34]

After World War I, the Court began to address appeals of criminal syndicalism convictions. This section addresses a few major cases. Before addressing the cases, it is useful to distinguish two axes resulting in four standards. One axis is incitement to violence versus abstract advocacy of violence. The other axis is present/imminent violence versus distant/potential danger.[35]

Table 2.1. Categories of Incitement

	Intentional Incitement	Abstract Advocacy
Present/Imminent	1	2
Distant/Potential	3	4

(1) The most speech protective standard (1) requires intentional incitement to lawless action plus present/imminent violence. This test sets a high bar, limiting government censorship to, for example, a speaker at a rally outside a courthouse who demands an angry and armed mob immediately attack the courthouse and its occupants and lynch a defendant on trial therein. (2) The second most protective standard requires present/imminent violence but extends censorship to abstract advocacy of violence. An example might be a labor leader at a work strike distributing copies of the *Communist Manifesto* to angry picketers outside the workplace. The two other less protective standards drop the present/imminent violence requirement and permit suppression of expression that poses a speculative risk. Still, (3) requiring the potential future danger arise from intentional incitement is more speech protective than (4) allowing censorship for abstract advocacy. For example, under (4), but not (3), the *Communist Manifesto* could be banned from publication or possession.

In *Gitlow v. New York* (1925) the Court continued its use of the bad tendency test in upholding a law banning socialist publications endorsing the potential of future violence or criminality to achieve socialist goals. The decision was not based on the "clear and present danger" test (as the court claimed) but rather on the "bad tendency" test and the least protective standard (4). The majority acknowledged the manifesto had no effect and was unlikely to have any effect. It was illegal due solely to the Court's opinion (unsupported by any evidence) that this was a "spark" whose "natural tendency" was to "endanger" and "threaten" the foundations of organized government. And, as Justice Oliver Wendell Holmes Jr. noted in his dissent, there was "no present danger of an attempt to overthrow the government by force" and "every idea is an incitement." In effect the decision allowed government to punish abstract advocacy that posed any risk of future violence or criminality no matter how remote in time or how unlikely the risk.

Fiske v. Kansas, 274 U.S. 380 (1927) raised the bar a notch. The Court held that the speaker had to have the intent to endorse violence or criminal means as opposed to merely possessing literature endorsing violent or criminal means to achieve political and economic change. Since the state's prosecution of Harold Fiske rested solely on his possession of Wobbly literature and failed to demonstrate any intent on his part, Fiske's conviction was vacated.[36] Thus, the decision clearly rejected *Whitney*'s use of standard (4); however, it did not require that the danger be imminent, and so is consistent with standard (3).

The *Fiske* intent requirement combined with the *Schenk* clear and present danger test to overturn Angelo Herndon's conviction for inciting insurrection in *Herndon v. Lowry* (1937).[37] His "incitement" consisted of possessing communist literature in his home and attempting to recruit workers to the Communist Party. The Court found the law overbroad and void for vagueness. Moreover, the state failed to show Herndon had the requisite intent. The ruling in effect limited government censorship to (1) and (2), that is, to expression that was intended to directly incite or abstractly advocate violence and posed a clear and present danger or was imminent.

The Court retreated from the *Herndon* standard when a "Red Scare" gripped the country. With the Cold War against communist Soviet Union and China and their proxies escalating, the Court upheld the 1940 Smith Act convictions of leaders of the American Communist Party in *Dennis v. United States*, 341 U.S. 494 (1951). The Smith Act made it a crime to "knowingly or willfully advocate, abet, advise, or teach the duty, necessity, desirability, or propriety of over-throwing . . . the government of the United States by force or violence." In its decision, the Court invented the "gravity of evil" test: although a violent revolution was quite unlikely, the expression was not protected because of the tremendous evil resulting if did happen. In effect, the Court reverted to a *Gitlow*-like position allowing censorship of (1) through (4) so long as the potential evil was thought by judges to be great enough. This included (as noted in Justice Douglas's dissent) upholding convictions for merely reading and discussing books by communist authors.

Yates v. United States, 354 U.S. 298 (1957) returned the situation to a *Herndon*-like position in striking down the Smith Act convictions of fourteen Communist Party officials by applying the clear and present danger test and distinguishing "actual advocacy to action" from "mere belief." Soon after, *Noto v. United States* (1961) "signaled the turning point when requirements of proximity and likelihood became part of the consensus opinion."[38]

Brandenburg v. Ohio (1969) completed the Court's evolution toward robust protection for abstract advocacy of violence or criminality. Barely four pages, the *per curiam* decision held that "the constitutional guarantees of free speech and free press do not permit a State to forbid or proscribe advocacy of the use of force or of law violation except where such advocacy is directed to inciting or producing imminent lawless action and is likely to incite or produce such action." The speaker must have the intent to incite violence or criminality, the violence or criminality must be imminent, and the violence or criminality must be likely. Clarence Brandenburg's conviction under Ohio's criminal syndicalism statute was struck down since his advocacy lacked intent to incite and lacked imminence. The decision rendered unenforceable similar laws in twenty other states.

The decision explicitly rejected the bad tendency test, but it did not address the clear and present danger test. However, concurrences by Justices Douglas and Hugo Black stated the clear and present danger test should have no place in the interpretation of the First Amendment. Later decisions confirmed the incitement test had replaced the clear and present danger test. The 1972 ruling in *Healy v. James* found the radical student organization Students for a Democratic Society (SDS) was entitled to university recognition even though the national SDS had a philosophy of violence and disruption. *Hess v. Indiana*, 414 U.S. 105 (1973) struck down a disorderly conduct conviction for stating during a street protest, "We'll take back the fucking street [later or again]," after police ordered protesters to disperse. Further decisions have led to a system described by Stephen Gey as "guaranteeing virtually absolute protection of free speech within the realm of political advocacy."[39]

The overall trend expanding protection for abstract advocacy from *Gitlow* in 1925 to *Brandenburg* in 1969 tracks closely with the Supreme Court's overall expansion of expressive rights. All First Amendment clauses were incorporated, the doctrines of overbreadth and void for vagueness were frequently used to strike down expressive restrictions, content and viewpoint neutrality gained prominence, and expressive conduct — not merely verbal speech — was constitutionally protected.[40] Anti-orthodoxy and inclusion continued to play an important role. *Senn v. Tile Layers Protection Union*, 301 U.S. 468 (1937) upheld a state law allowing peaceful labor picketing. *Schneider v. New Jersey*, 308 U.S. 147 (1939) struck down laws requiring a government permit to distribute literature because they allowed officials to issue permits in an arbitrary and viewpoint biased manner privileging orthodox views. Similarly, *Hague v. CIO*, 307 U.S. 496 (1939), struck down a Jersey City ordinance used to ban labor meetings and distribution of literature. *Marsh v. Alabama*, 326 U.S. 501 (1946), provided First Amendment protection to a Jehovah's Witness distribution of religious literature in a "company town." *Burstyn v. Wilson*, 343 U.S. 495 (1952) (reversing *Mutual Film v. Ohio* [1915]), extended First Amendment protection to films.

Federal and state "Comstock Laws" severely limiting sex-related expression (including medical expression such as anatomy textbooks) were overturned in *Roth v. United States*, 354 U.S. 476 (1957). and later decisions ruling that sexual expression can have constitutionally protected social, political, or artistic value. *Talley v. California*, 362 U.S. 60 (1960) protected anonymous leaflets urging boycotts of racist businesses. *Stanley v. Georgia*, 394 U.S. 557 (1969), struck down state laws banning the private possession of obscene materials in the home. *Street v. New York*, 394 U.S. 576 (1969) overturned Sidney Street's flag desecration conviction for burning a flag to protest the shooting of civil rights activist James Meredith. *Cohen v. California*, 403 U.S. 15 (1971), held Paul Robert Cohen's jacket declaring "Fuck the Draft" worn in a Los Angeles courthouse was protected expression. *Police Department of Chicago v. Mosley*, 408 U.S. 92 (1972), protected Earl Mosley's picketing a school for racial discrimination since "the First Amendment means that government has no power to restrict expression because of its message, its ideas, its subject matter, or its content." A dramatically more protective speech regime existed by the late 1960s than at any earlier stage in American history, a regime built on increasing inclusion of heterodox expression.

Brandenburg, Anti-Orthodoxy, and Inclusion

We now address two final questions. *Brandenburg* was rooted in anti-orthodoxy and inclusion, but are these in the *Brandenburg* decision itself? Second, how, if at all, does *Brandenburg* promote or protect the struggle for greater equality?

Unsurprisingly, "anti-orthodoxy" and "inclusion" are not explicitly mentioned in *Brandenburg*. However, they are implicit via the precedents cited. Most of the precedents cited are discussed above (in order of appearance in the opinion: *Whitney*, *Fiske*, *Dennis*, *Noto*, *Herndon*, *Yates*, *De Jonge*, and *Stromberg*). Further precedents cited also involve anti-orthodoxy and inclusion. *Bond v. Floyd*, 385 U.S. 116 (1966) upheld elected African American Julian Bond's right to hold office despite his criticism of Vietnam War. *United States v. Robel*, 389 U.S. 258 (1967), held that freedom of association protects a Communist Party member's job at defense facility. *Keyishian v. Board of Regents*, 385 U.S. 589 (1967) ruled that states cannot prohibit employees from being members of the Communist Party. *Elfbrandt v. Russell*, 384 U.S. 11 (1966), struck down an Arizona law requiring state employees to sign a loyalty oath as a violation of freedom of association. *Baggett v. Bullitt*, 377 U.S. 360 (1964), struck down Washington State laws requiring loyalty oath as violations of free association and free speech.

Anti-orthodoxy and inclusion also are evident in Justice Douglas's concurring opinion. Douglas insisted *Brandenburg*'s incitement test must replace the clear and present danger test. Why? "When one reads the opinions closely and sees when and how the 'clear and present danger' test has been applied, great misgivings are aroused. First, the threats were often loud but always puny and made serious only by *judges so wedded to the status quo* that critical analysis made them nervous. Second, the *test was so twisted and perverted* in *Dennis* as to make the trial . . . an all-out political trial which was part and parcel of the cold war that has eroded substantial parts of the First Amendment" (emphasis added).[41] Douglas adds a series of cases to support his point.[42]

The idea that judges wedded to orthodoxy and exclusion twist and pervert free speech principles is supported by numerous historical and legal analyses, and the problem is not limited to the judicial branch. The executive and legislative branches as well as private organizations engage in partisan subversion of free speech principles. Leonard Levy's *Legacy of Suppression* (1960) and *Emergence of a Free Press* (1985) broke new ground in detailing censorship and suppression in the colonial era and early years of the United States. David Rabban's *Free Speech in Its Forgotten Years: 1870–1920* (1997) describes the exclusion of heterodox expression during the late nineteenth and early twentieth centuries. Nat Hentoff's *Free Speech for Me — But Not for Thee* (1992) describes the perpetual attempts of the political left and political right to suppress the other side through legal or extralegal methods. More recently, my own *Campus Hate Speech on Trial* (2009) describes how hundreds of public universities and colleges sought to punish student and faculty speech they opposed through "hate speech codes" that courts consistently struck down for overbreadth and vagueness.

Both the political right and left continue to seek to exclude and silence opponents and ideas they disagree with. For example, UCLA School of Law's CRT Forward Tracking Project (2022)[43] found 495 attempts by conservatives at the local, state, and federal levels to ban critical race theory or "divisive concepts." Attempts were made in every state except Delaware, and approximately 200 proposals were adopted. PEN America, a nonprofit organization defending free expression through the advancement of literature and human rights since 1922, has tracked 1,600 book bans or restrictions in public schools and libraries across the country initiated by conservatives mostly targeting books addressing LGBT issues, with about 95 percent of the attempts subverting existing policy or procedure.[44] The political left engages in censorship too,[45] seeking to remove art and cancel other expression and speakers (both historical and contemporary) thought to be offensive or harmful.[46] Both the left and the right seek to censor culture[47] and manipulate k–12 school textbooks to reflect their view of history and the future.[48] In the face of unrelenting partisan attacks on expressive rights, a high bar for censorship is necessary if meaningful First Amendment rights to speech, press, religion, assembly, petition, association, and academic freedom are to survive.

Although *Brandenburg* is "celebrated"[49] for its commitment to robust expressive rights and "stands as one of the most well-established aspects of modern constitutional doctrine,"[50] it faces increasing scrutiny and criticism as promoters and perpetrators of hate and violence flood the internet and social media.

Although it would be beneficial for the Supreme Court to provide greater guidance on how imminent and how likely the violence must be to be unprotected, we do well to keep in mind that weakening expressive rights during "emergencies" or "crises" opens the door to partisans censoring political opponents. For example, American Civil Liberties Union (ACLU) attorney Emerson Sykes discusses his experience working with African nations, describing how violent events in Rwanda and Tanzania led to speech bans that subsequently have been used by authoritarian governments to censor political and social opponents.[51]

Mchangama discusses internet and social media problems and solutions in a chapter titled "The Internet and the Future of Free Speech," arguing that recent empirical studies show increasing government censorship is more likely to increase the problems, rather than reduce them.[52] In discussing the Canadian scene, Stefan Braun notes that "[h]ate laws tend to become whatever those with power to threaten or enforce it think it is in the particular circumstances. In practice it may be stretched, narrowed, even redefined . . . without a single word [of the law] being changed."[53] The Foundation for Individual Rights and Expression (FIRE) has fought back against a frightening number of "red light" and "yellow light" polices in higher education and cases in which heterodox faculty and student online expression is punished or investigated that come nowhere near to meeting *Brandenburg*'s requirements or any other category of unprotected expression.[54]

In response to those on the political left who call for weakening expressive rights to suppress anti-egalitarian expression,[55] it should be noted robust speech protections, including the incitement doctrine, are more valuable to unpopular and marginalized expression than to privileged and mainstream expression since the government typically most protects the status quo and the powerful while using speech restrictions and the police power to target those demanding equality. Sykes notes the nation's "limited interpretation of incitement has given a broad array of social movements the freedom to breathe" and provides two progressive examples. His first example is *NAACP v. Claiborne Hardware, Inc.*, 458 U.S. 886 (1982), protecting a civil rights business boycott. His second example is *Dakota Rural Action v. Noem*, 416 F. Supp. 3d 874 (D.S.D. 2019), striking down South Dakota's riot-boosting law targeting indigenous, environmental, and civil rights protestors opposing the Keystone XL pipeline.

Moreover, law enforcement too often targets egalitarian expression. For example, peaceful protests demanding racial equality frequently are often confronted by hostile police, whereas white supremacist protests are not.[56] BLM protests in 2020, despite 93 percent of the recorded 7,750 being peaceful,[57] inspired conservative legislators in thirty-three states to redefine or broaden antiriot statues to squelch those demanding racial equality.[58] From 1956 to 1971, the FBI Counter-Intelligence Program covertly and illegally surveilled, infiltrated, discredited, and disrupted egalitarian movements and abuse of enforcement authority against Black dissenters continues through the Black Identity Extremists designation.[59] Expanding the ability and authority of government to censor and suppress expression through law or enforcement will only make it even more difficult for egalitarians to dissent against the status quo.

Conclusion

Brandenburg is part of a long line of decisions creating and enforcing expressive rights that protect the struggle for greater equality in principle and in practice. Although the expressive rights that *Brandenburg* and other decisions protect also protect to anti-egalitarian expression, robust expressive rights are more essential for egalitarians because egalitarians have been and continue to be more heterodox and excluded. As Sykes notes: "The powerful will always be more successful at vindicating their rights. But incitement doctrine, and free speech more generally, has been a demonstrably vital tool for all social movements in the United States, including progressive messages that challenge state and corporate power."[60] When people insist (correctly) that egalitarian and antiegalitarian expression are not morally equivalent, we must remember content and viewpoint neutrality are crucial to the protection of egalitarian expression. Extending the long arm of the law to ban every immoral expression requires overbroad and unduly vague laws that will be enforced more to the detriment of egalitarian expression than current narrowly tailored policies are. Not only is this self-defeating for egalitarians, it undermines the quest for truth, democratic self-governance, and autonomy and self-realization.

Notes

The author thanks Eric Kasper, JoAnne Sweeney, Bob Zeidel, and people at the 2022 Civil Liberty Symposium hosted by the Menard Center for the Study of Institutions and Innovation at University of Wisconsin–Stout for their comments and criticisms.

1. Nan Hunter, "Escaping the Expression-Equality Conundrum: Toward Anti-Orthodoxy and Inclusion," *Ohio State Law Journal* 61, (2000): 1671.
2. See Carlos Ball, *The First Amendment and LGBT Equality: A Contentious History* (Harvard University Press, 2019), and Dale Carpenter, "Born in Dissent: Free Speech and Gay Rights," *Southern Methodist University Law Review* 72 (2019): 375.
3. See Kenneth L. Karst, "Justice Marshall and the First Amendment," *National Black Law Journal* 6 (1978): 26; David L. Hudson Jr., "Justice Thurgood Marshall, Great Defender of First Amendment Free-Speech Rights for the Powerless," *Howard Human and Civil Rights Law Review* 2 (2017–2018): 167; and Judge Lynn Adelman, "The Glorious Jurisprudence of Thurgood Marshall," *Harvard Law & Policy Review* 7 (2013): 113.
4. Adelman, "Glorious Jurisprudence of Marshall," 129.
5. Smith and Burrell, Justice Thurgood Marshall," 462.
6. Burnside v. Byars, 363 F. 2d 744 (5th Cir. 1966).
7. A few examples. Brown v. Socialist Workers '74 Campaign Committee, 459 U.S. 87 (1982), shielded donors and recipients of funds from compelled disclosure. NAACP v. Claiborne Hardware, 458 U.S. 886 (1982), protected a civil rights economic boycott. Texas v. Johnson, 491 U.S. 397 (1989), protected flag burning as political protest. Matal v. Tam, 582 U.S. 218 (2017), protected an Asian-American musical group's trademark use of "the Slants."
8. Jacob Mchangama, *Free Speech: A History from Socrates to Social Media* (Basic Books, 2022).
9. John Stuart Mill, *On Liberty*, available at https://www.gutenberg.org/files/34901/34901-h/34901-h.htm.
10. See, for example, Paul H. Brietzke, "How and Why the Marketplace of Ideas Fails," *Valparaiso University Law Review* 31 (Summer 1997): 951; Stanley Ingber, "The Marketplace of Ideas: A Legitimizing Myth," *Duke Law Journal* 1 (Feb. 1984); and Daniel E. Ho and Frederick Schauer, "Testing the Marketplace of Ideas," *New York University Law Review* 90 (Oct. 2015): 1160.
11. Alexander Meiklejohn, *Free Speech and Its Relation to Self-Government* (Harper, 1948).
12. See Ronald J. Krotoszynski Jr., *The First Amendment in Cross-Cultural Perspective: A Comparative Legal Analysis of the Freedom of Speech* (New York University Press, 2006).

13   Teresa Bejan, "The Two Clashing Meanings of 'Free Speech,'" *The Atlantic*, December 2, 2017, https://www.theatlantic.com/politics/archive/2017/12/two-concepts-of-freedom-of-speech/546791/.
14   Mchangama, *Free Speech*, 35–231.
15   Christopher M. Finan, *How Free Speech Saved Democracy* (Steerforth Press/Truth to Power, 2022).
16   See, for example, Armand Derfner and J. Gerald Heber, "Voting Is Speech," *Yale Law and Policy Review* 34 (2016): 471.
17   See, for example, C. Edwin Baker, "Autonomy and Free Speech," *Constitutional Commentary* 471 (2011): 251; and Susan H. Williams, *Truth, Autonomy, and Speech: Feminist Theory and the First Amendment* (New York University Press, 2004).
18   Kleindienst v. Mandel, 408 U.S. 753, 775 (1972).
19   David Goldberger, the Jewish ACLU lawyer who defended the right of the Nazis to assemble, provides a useful review of the case: https://www.aclu.org/issues/free-speech/rights-protesters/skokie-case-how-i-came-represent-free-speech-rights-nazis.
20   The ACLU-Virginia argued the case. https://acluva.org/en/news/why-we-represented-alt-right-charlottesville. However, they did not know their client lied about his intentions and where the march would occur or that there would be significant law enforcement failures. See, for example, Dakin Andone and Chuck Johnston, "Report on Charlottesville Rally Faults Police over Planning, Failure to Protect Public," CNN, December 2, 2017, https://www.cnn.com/2017/12/01/us/charlottesville-riots-failures-review.
21   Michael Kent Curtis, *Free Speech, The People's "Darling Privilege": Struggles for Freedom of Expression in American History* (Duke University Press, 2000).
22   The fifty-one cases involving 126 defendants prosecuted under the Sedition Act of 1798 provide an apt example. Wendell Bird, *Criminal Dissent: Prosecutions under the Alien and Sedition Acts of 1798* (Harvard University Press, 2020). Another example is Patterson v. Colorado, 205 U.S. 454 (1907), upholding the conviction of a newspaper editor who lampooned Colorado judges.
23   Crown v. John Peter Zenger (1735). Zenger, editor of the *New York Weekly Journal*, was tried for criticizing New York governor William Cosby. Factually guilty under the law, the jury acquitted him anyway.
24   See Blyew v. United States, 80 U.S. 581 (1872); United States v. Harris, 106 U.S. 629 (1882); Slaughter-House Cases, 83 U.S. 36 (1873); and United States v. Cruikshank, 92 U.S. 542 (1875).
25   See, for example, Curtis, Free Speech, chs. 6–13.
26   David Rabban, Free Speech in Its Forgotten Years (Cambridge University Press, 1997); Laura Weinrib, *The Taming of Free Speech: America's Civil Liberties Compromise* (Harvard University Press, 2016); and Getman, Supreme Court on Unions.

27 For example, federal actions were taken against 105 people in Wisconsin. The most frequent words prosecuted were "It's a rich man's war." John D. Stevens, "When Sedition Laws were Enforced: Wisconsin in World War I," *Wisconsin Academy of Sciences, Arts and Letters* 58 (1970). See also Geoffrey Stone, *Perilous Times: Free Speech in Wartime from the Sedition Act of 1798 to the War on Terrorism* (W. W. Norton, 2004).

28 The exception was Wisconsin socialist publisher and politician Victor Berger. The Supreme Court overturned his conviction in Berger v. United States, 255 U.S. 22 (1921), due to prejudicial conduct by Judge Kennesaw Mountain Landis.

29 See, for example, Abrams v. United States, 250 U.S. 616 (1919); Gitlow v. New York, 268 U.S. 652 (1925); and United States v. Schwimmer, 279 U.S. 644 (1929).

30 See, for example, Thornhill v. Alabama, 310 U.S. 88 (1940), Taylor v. Mississippi, 319 U.S. 583 (1943), Hartzel v. United States, 322 U.S. 680 (1944); Thomas v. Collins, 323 U.S. 516 (1945), and Craig v. Harney, 331 U.S. 367 (1947).

31 "Union membership leapt from less than 500,000 in 1897 to more than 2 million in 1904. The greatest growth came in the unions of the American Federation of Labor (AFL)." John Whiteclay Chambers, *The Tyranny of Change: America in the Progressive Era, 1890–1920* (Rutgers University Press, 2000), 70.

32 Postmasters denied mailing privileges to labor publications. The Department of Justice "Palmer Raids" conducted warrantless searches and denied due process to more than 10,000 labor organizers. Wobblies were arrested for public speeches. Local governments denied labor groups permits to parade. Peaceful organizing efforts were met with violence by vigilantes, private security agents, police, National Guard, and the US Army. The Supreme Court upheld right of employers to require employees promise not to join a union and fire an employee for being a union member. Shiell, *African Americans and the First Amendment*, 28–29.

33 See, for example, Adam Schaff, "Marxist Theory on Revolution and Violence," *Journal of the History of Ideas* 34, no. 2 (Apr.–Jun. 1973), 263–70.

34 Dale Mineshima-Lowe, "Criminal Syndicalism Laws," *The First Amendment Encyclopedia* (2009), https://www.mtsu.edu/first-amendment/article/942/criminal-syndicalism-laws.

35 I adopt this framework from Staughton Lynd, "Brandenburg v. Ohio: A Speech Test for All Seasons?" *University of Chicago Law Review* 43 (1975): 151.

36 Members of the Industrial Workers of the World (IWW), founded in Chicago in 1905, were called "Wobblies." Their "free speech fights" played an important role in free speech history. See Rabban, *Free Speech*, 18, 77–78, 80–83, and 88–89.

37 Two years earlier the court had upheld his conviction on a technicality. See Shiell, African Americans and the First Amendment, 40–42.
38 Richard Ashby Wilson and Jordan Kiper, "Incitement in an Era of Populism: Updating Brandenburg after Charlottesville," *University of Pennsylvania Journal of Law and Public Affairs* 5 (2020): 55, 67.
39 Stephen Gey, "The Brandenburg Paradigm and Other First Amendments," *University of Pennsylvania Journal of Constitutional* 12 (2010): 971, 975.
40 The court also identified categories of unprotected speech such as fighting words (Chaplinsky v. New Hampshire, 315 U.S. 568 [1941]); group libel (Beauharnais v. Illinois, 343 U.S. 250 [1952]); and violations of reasonable time, place, and manner restrictions (Cox v. New Hampshire, 312 U.S. 569 [1941]).
41 Brandenburg at 454.
42 For example, the 1919 trilogy Schenk v. United States, Frohwerk v. United States, 294 U.S. 204, and Debs v. United States, 294 U.S. 211; the 1919 duo Abrams v. United States, 250 U.S. 216 and Schaefer v. United States, 251 U.S. 466; Pierce v. United States, 252 U.S. 239 (1920); Whitney v. California (1928); Gitlow v. New York (1925); Dennis v. United States (1951); Noto v. United States (1961); and Barenblatt v. United States, 360 U.S. 109 (1958).
43 https://crtforward.law.ucla.edu/.
44 https://pen.org/banned-in-the-usa/.
45 See The Editorial Board, "America Has a Free Speech Problem," *New York Times*, March 18, 2022, https://www.nytimes.com/2022/03/18/opinion/cancel-culture-free-speech-poll.html.
46 See, for example, Jonathan Zimmerman, "When Will Liberals Reclaim Free Speech?" *Wall Street Journal*, April 7, 2021, https://www.wsj.com/articles/when-will-liberals-reclaim-free-speech-11617813301.
47 See, for example, Robert Atkins and Svetlana Mintcheva (eds.), *Censoring Culture: Contemporary Threats to Free Expression* (New York: W. W. Norton, 2006).
48 Diane Ravitch, *Censorship from the Right . . . Censorship from the Left* (WestEd, 2004).
49 Susan M. Gilles, "Brandenburg v. State of Ohio: An 'Accidental,' 'Too Easy,' and 'Incomplete' Landmark Case," *Capital University Law Review* 38 (2010): 517, 520.
50 Steven G. Gey, "The Brandenburg Paradigm and Other First Amendments," *University of Pennsylvania Journal of Constitutional Law* 12 (2010): 971, 977.
51 Emerson Sykes, "In Defense of Brandenburg: The ACLU and Incitement Doctrine in 1919, 1969, and 2019," 85 *Brooklyn Law Review* 15, 35 (2019).
52 Mchangama, Free Speech, ch. 13.

53 Stefan Braun, *Democracy Off Balance: Freedom of Expression and Hate Propaganda Law in Canada* (Toronto University Press, 2004), 97.
54 https://www.thefire.org/.
55 Catharine MacKinnon proposed (in effect) reviving the bad tendency test as a tool to censor anti-egalitarian expression in *Only Words* (Harvard University Press, 1993). Cass Sunstein argues under certain conditions the clear and present danger test is defensible in "Does the Clear and Present Danger Test Survive Cost-Benefit Analysis?," *Cornell Law Review* 104 (2019): 1776. Social media focused examples include Zachary Leibowitz, "Terror on Your Timeline: Criminalizing Terrorist Incitement on Social Media through Doctrinal Shift," *Fordham Law Review* 86 (2017): 795; Justin Hyland, "Conspiracy Speech: Reimagining the First Amendment in the Age of QAnon," *Hastings Communications and Entertainment Law Journal* 44 (2021): 1; and Anna Rhoads, "Incitement and Social Media-Algorithmic Speech: Redefining Brandenburg for a Different Kind of Speech," *William & Mary Law Review* 64 (2022): 525.
56 See, for example, Justin Hansford, "The First Amendment Freedom of Assembly as a Racial Project," *Yale Law Journal Forum* 127 (2018): 685.
57 The Armed Conflict Location & Event Data Project (ACLED), https://acleddata.com/2020/09/03/demonstrations-political-violence-in-america-new-data-for-summer-2020/.
58 Following the BLM protests state policy-makers introduced at least 100 proposals in thirty-three states from June 2020 to March 2021, reducing the scope of protest rights. Nora Benavidez, James Tager, and Andy Gottlieb, "Closing Ranks: State Legislators Deepen Assaults on the Right to Protest," PEN America, https://pen.org/closing-ranks-state-legislators-deepen-assaults-on-the-right-to-protest/.
59 See, for example, Zahra N. Mian, Note, "Black Identity Extremist" or Black Dissident? How United States v. Daniels Illustrates FBI Criminalization of Black Dissent of Law Enforcement, from COINTELPRO to Black Lives Matter, *Rutgers Race and the Law Review* 21 (2020) 53; and ACLU, "Leaked FBI Documents Raise Concerns about Targeting Black People Under 'Black Identity Extremist' and Newer Labels," ACLU, August 9, 2019, https://www.aclu.org/press-releases/leaked-fbi-documents-raise-concerns-about-targeting-black-people-under-black-identi-1.
60 Sykes, "In Defense of Brandenburg," 31.

Chapter Three

Free Speech, Social Justice, and *Brandenburg*

Stephen M. Feldman

Before the Roberts Court era, which began in 2005, some commentators described the US Supreme Court as generally shielding societal outsiders and minorities from majoritarian overreaching, including in First Amendment cases.[1] Yet, at least through the 1960s, the Court's decisions on expression (speech and writing) inciting unlawful conduct contravene that historical description. Societal outsiders and minorities, in this essay, include people of color, religious minorities (especially non-Christians), immigrants, political dissidents (including socialists and communists), and others on the periphery of American society.

The question is whether *Brandenburg v. Ohio*, decided in 1969,[2] shifted the Court's approach in incitement cases to harmonize better with the historical depiction of the Court as a defender of outsiders and minorities. The answer is complex: yes, *Brandenburg* is rightly celebrated as a First Amendment landmark, articulating doctrine that, in theory, strongly protects expression, including that of outsiders and minorities.[3] But no, the implications of *Brandenburg* become obscure and protean if one digs below the surface, beyond the doctrine. In *Brandenburg* itself, the Court applied its new speech-protective First Amendment doctrine to shield expression attacking outsiders and minorities. And in a limited number of subsequent cases, the Court has inconsistently applied the doctrine. As is true with all constitutional doctrine, the *Brandenburg* doctrine is not self-executing. The justices must interpret and apply it when new cases arise.[4] And those interpretations do not necessarily result in social justice or, in other words, the protection of outsiders and minorities. In the context of this essay, social justice means concern and respect for the rights and interests of outsiders and minorities equal to that afforded to society's mainstream and powerful.[5]

History of Incitement Cases Before 1969

The Court did not explicitly address free expression under the First Amendment until 1919.[6] From that point forward, the Court decided significant incitement cases during three time periods: the World War I era; the first Red Scare; and the second Red Scare. Before 1937, the Court largely decided free-expression issues in accordance with the so-called bad tendency test, which lower courts had applied throughout the nineteenth and early twentieth centuries. Under the bad tendency test, the government could criminally punish speech or writing that had bad tendencies or likely harmful consequences.[7] As explained by Justice Joseph Story, the government could punish speakers and writers for "what is improper, mischievous, or illegal."[8] The Constitution, from this perspective, allowed government to punish expression with bad tendencies because such speech or writing supposedly undermined civic virtue and contravened the common good, central principles of republican democratic government.[9] Thus, for example, in *Updegraph v. Commonwealth*, an 1824 prosecution for blasphemy,[10] the court emphasized that "if the matter published contains any such evil tendency, it is a public wrong. An offence against the public peace may consist either of an actual breach of the peace, or doing that which tends to provoke and excite others to do it."[11] In application, the flexibility of the bad tendency test readily allowed courts (including the Supreme Court) to uphold convictions of outsiders and minorities, whose speech and writing could be deemed contrary to the common good precisely because the defendants were peripheral or opposed to mainstream culture.[12]

The World War I era cases arose from a series of Espionage Act prosecutions in which the government sought to punish individuals who criticized aspects of the nation's war effort, including the imposition of a military draft. In *Schenck v. United States*, the first Espionage Act case to reach the Supreme Court, two leaders of the Socialist Party were convicted for distributing a leaflet that opposed the draft.[13] A unanimous Court upheld the convictions, with Justice Oliver Wendell Holmes Jr., writing the opinion. In rejecting the defendants' claim that the First Amendment protected their expression, Holmes wrote: "The question in every case is whether the words used are used in such circumstances and are of such a nature as to create a clear and present danger that they will bring about the substantive evils that Congress has a right to prevent."[14] While Holmes's "clear and present danger" terminology was novel, his conclusion demonstrated that he did not intend to pronounce a new (more speech-protective) standard for delineating the scope of free expression. For Holmes (and the Court), clear and present danger meant bad tendency.[15] In fact, Holmes cited approvingly to *Patterson v. Colorado*, a 1907 case involving free-expression principles under the Fourteenth Amendment.[16] Holmes's *Patterson* opinion expressly stated that the Constitution allowed government to criminally punish expression "deemed contrary to the public welfare" — that is, contrary to the common good, in accordance with the bad tendency test.[17]

After *Schenck*, in the next Espionage Act cases, *Frohwerk v. United States*[18] and *Debs v. United States*,[19] Holmes again wrote for unanimous Courts upholding the convictions. When addressing the First Amendment issues, Holmes continued to follow bad tendency principles while disregarding his "clear and present danger" terminology. In *Frohwerk*, the defendant was convicted for editing articles in a German-language newspaper that criticized the nation's entrance into the war. Holmes reasoned: "[It] is impossible to say that it might not have been found that the circulation of the paper was in quarters where a little breath would be enough to kindle a flame and that the fact was known and relied upon by those who sent the paper out."[20] In *Debs*, which upheld the conviction of a prominent leader of the Socialist Party, Holmes more explicitly followed bad tendency principles. His opinion approved a jury instruction that presented the bad tendency test in conventional terms: The jurors, as charged, "could not find the defendant guilty for advocacy of any of his opinions unless the words used had as their natural tendency and reasonably probable effect [to violate the law]"[21]

In subsequent Espionage Act cases, the Court continued upholding convictions, but the Court's decisions were no longer unanimous. Holmes and Justice Louis Brandeis began dissenting. They argued that the Court should have applied an invigorated clear and present danger test, which would have resulted in more expansive First Amendment protections for expression.[22] In *Abrams v. United States*, the defendants were Russian-Jewish immigrants who had distributed leaflets criticizing aspects of the nation's war effort.[23] Despite Holmes's dissent, joined by Brandeis, the Court affirmed the convictions, with Justice John H. Clarke writing for the seven-justice majority. Clarke's opinion pointed out that many of the leaflets were printed in Yiddish, that the defendants were born in Russia, and that the defendants had not applied for naturalization. For Clarke and the majority, in other words, the defendants' foreignness apparently factored into the decision.[24]

The first Red Scare arose soon after World War I, in 1919 and 1920.[25] During the war and soon after, numerous states passed criminal syndicalism statutes — laws that prohibited violence or advocacy of violence as a means of accomplishing political change — and challenges to convictions under these laws began to reach the Court in mid-decade. The Court continued upholding the convictions, finding the expression unprotected, with Holmes and Brandeis refusing to join the majority opinions. In *Gitlow v. New York*,[26] decided in 1925, and *Whitney v. California*,[27] decided in 1927, the Court applied bad tendency principles, deferring to the respective state governments as they sought to punish ostensibly harmful expression. In both cases, the defendants were dissenting outsiders. New York had convicted Benjamin Gitlow for publishing *The Left Wing Manifesto* and a paper called *The Revolutionary Age*, writings the state charged as "advocating, advising and teaching . . . that organized government should be overthrown by force, violence and unlawful means."[28] California had convicted Charlotte Whitney for organizing and belonging to the Communist

Labor Party, an organization advocating criminal syndicalism, even though Whitney personally sought peaceful political change. Meanwhile, Holmes and Brandeis wrote opinions advocating for more expansive First Amendment free-expression protections pursuant to an invigorated clear and present danger test.[29] Unlike the bad tendency test, the Holmes–Brandeis clear and present danger test would constitutionally protect expression unless the government proved that the speech or writing likely produced *imminent* danger.[30]

The first "explicit" free speech win in the Supreme Court did not come until 1931,[31] with larger changes coming later in the decade.[32] In 1937, the Court repudiated republican democracy, with its emphasis on the virtuous pursuit of the common good. At that point, the Court accepted pluralist democracy, which emphasized widespread participation in the democratic arena where a plurality of values and interests could clash, leading to political negotiation and compromise.[33] For example, in *NLRB v. Jones and Laughlin Steel Corporation*, the Court upheld a statute empowering employees to form labor unions.[34] Although prior decisions suggested such a labor law would be found to favor partial or private interests (the employees) and therefore contravene the common good, the Court reasoned: "Employees have as clear a right to organize and select their representatives for lawful purposes as the [employer] has to organize its business."[35] The Court's transition from republican to pluralist democracy had enormous implications in multiple realms of constitutional jurisprudence, including free expression.[36] In fact, during the next few years, the Court upheld one free-expression claim after another, with the justices often invoking and applying the Holmes–Brandeis invigorated clear and present danger test.[37] Pluralist democracy, as the justices elaborated it, accepted diversity rather than attempting to suppress it within the confines of a culturally homogeneous common good. Free expression, therefore, did not need to be constrained to preserve "the existing order";[38] the justices had "no fear that freedom to be intellectually and spiritually diverse or even contrary will disintegrate the social organization."[39] By the 1940s, the Court was emphasizing that "[t]he vitality of civil and political institutions in our society depends on free discussion,"[40] and that a strong conception of free expression was consequently a "fixed star in our constitutional constellation."[41]

Despite the Court's generally more open and expansive approach to free expression, which extended some protections to dissenting outsiders and minorities, the justices still narrowed First Amendment protections during times of political crisis. After the end of World War II, the nation plunged into its Cold War confrontation with the Soviet Union, which soon led to the Second Red Scare. Fearing Communist infiltration and influence, the government repeatedly restricted free expression.[42] The Court acquiesced to these restrictions. For instance, in *American Communications Association v. Douds*, decided in 1950, the Supreme Court upheld a statute requiring labor union officers to sign an affidavit declaring that "he is not a member of the Communist Party or affiliated with such party."[43] In 1952, *Adler v. Board of Education of the City of New York* upheld a New York law that compelled teachers to sign affidavits swearing they did not belong to subversive organizations.[44]

The Court's most renowned anticommunist decision involving incitement was *Dennis v. United States*, decided in 1951.[45] By a six-to-two vote, *Dennis* upheld the convictions of eleven leaders of the Communist Party of the United States (CPUSA) for advocating the violent overthrow of the government. Chief Justice Frederick M. Vinson's plurality opinion invoked the clear and present danger test but he reformulated it to facilitate a judicial balancing of interests: "In each case (courts) must ask whether the gravity of the 'evil,' discounted by its improbability, justifies such invasion of free speech as is necessary to avoid the danger."[46] Consequently, although the prosecution had proven only that the defendants taught Marxist-Leninist doctrine — which would be unlikely to produce imminent danger — Vinson reasoned that the advocated evil, the violent overthrow of the government, was sufficiently grave as to outweigh any First Amendment free-expression concerns.[47] The prosecution's success in *Dennis* then prompted the government to arrest and prosecute dozens of additional CPUSA members.[48]

Brandenburg, Incitement, and Social Justice

Through much of the twentieth century, the Court allowed the government to punish dissident outsiders and minorities for ostensibly inciting or urging illegal or dangerous conduct. First Amendment protections often disintegrated when the government was pursuing immigrants, religious minorities, socialists, communists, or others on the periphery of American society. Yet, during the 1960s, the later Warren Court became increasingly protective of free expression in a variety of contexts.[49] For instance, *Tinker v. Des Moines Independent Community School District* articulated broad free-speech rights for public school students who had worn black armbands to protest the Vietnam War.[50] The Court explained: "Any departure from absolute regimentation may cause trouble. Any variation from the [societal] majority's opinion may inspire fear. . . . But our Constitution says we must take this risk, and our history says that it is this sort of hazardous freedom — this kind of openness — that is the basis of our national strength."[51] Perhaps most famously, in a case involving a newspaper advertisement soliciting support for the civil rights movement, *New York Times v. Sullivan* protected the newspaper and four black clergy from a defamation lawsuit.[52] The Court resoundingly declared its support for free expression: "[W]e consider this case against the background of a profound national commitment to the principle that debate on public issues should be uninhibited, robust, and wide-open, and that it may well include vehement, caustic, and sometimes unpleasantly sharp attacks on government and public officials."[53]

When the justices turned to the issue of speech inciting unlawful conduct, they continued in that same direction. Numerous commentators have described *Brandenburg v. Ohio*,[54] decided in 1969, as a "landmark," although the Court issued it as a *per curiam* opinion.[55] The typical *per curiam* ("by the court") or unsigned opinion summarily disposes of an insignificant case. *Brandenburg*, however, did not fit that mold. After hearing oral argument, the justices voted unanimously to protect the expression, and Chief Justice Warren assigned the opinion to Justice Abe Fortas, a liberal developing a reputation as a First Amendment expert. As expected, Fortas wrote a highly speech-protective opinion, but intervening events would prevent the Court from issuing the opinion in his name. President Lyndon B. Johnson had already nominated Fortas, his longtime confidant, to replace the retiring Warren as Chief Justice, but he would never be confirmed. The Senate confirmation hearings and investigative reporting uncovered that Fortas had accepted payments for summer teaching and for consulting — compensations that, at the time, appeared improper for a Supreme Court justice. Disgraced by the scandal, Fortas withdrew from consideration for the chief justiceship and eventually resigned from the Court. Warren then designated Justice William Brennan to finish the *Brandenburg* opinion, and Brennan adopted Fortas's draft with some minor changes. The Court issued the opinion as a *per curiam* rather than under Brennan's or Fortas's name.[56]

Brandenburg arose when Ohio convicted a Ku Klux Klan (KKK) leader, Clarence Brandenburg, "under the Ohio Criminal Syndicalism statute for 'advocat[ing] . . . the duty, necessity, or propriety of crime, sabotage, violence, or unlawful methods of terrorism as a means of accomplishing industrial or political reform.'"[57] In determining the constitutionality of this statute as applied to Brandenburg, the Court repudiated its prior doctrinal tests for determining when expression inciting unlawful conduct was outside of First Amendment protections. The Court did not use the bad tendency test or any of the versions of the clear and present danger test. Instead, the Court stated that the First Amendment does "not permit a State to forbid or proscribe advocacy of the use of force or of law violation except where such advocacy is directed to inciting or producing imminent lawless action and is likely to incite or produce such action."[58] The First Amendment, in other words, protects expression unless the speaker specifically intends to incite imminent unlawful action, and such unlawful action is likely to occur imminently. In cases involving expression inciting unlawful conduct, *Brandenburg* unquestionably articulated "the most speech-protective standard yet."[59] Equally important, the Court applied this new doctrine to protect the expression of the defendant, Brandenburg, a political pariah.

While *Brandenburg* is a doctrinal landmark, if one digs below the doctrine and immediate result — that the defendant won — then the implications of the case become far murkier. Brandenburg, a KKK leader, had invited a reporter and cameraman to attend the Klan "rally," so many of Brandenburg's actions and statements were filmed.[60] Entered as evidence at trial, the film showed hooded figures gathered around a burning cross, Brandenburg repeatedly denouncing Black and Jewish Americans with epithets, and then Brandenburg warning that "if our President, our Congress, our Supreme Court, continues to suppress the white, Caucasian race, it's possible that there might have to be some revengeance taken."[61] Therefore, pursuant to the facts of the case, the Court articulated the *Brandenburg* doctrinal test in protection of malicious hate speech directed against racial and religious minorities and in support of white, Christian nationalism.[62]

Unfortunately, *Brandenburg* is not anomalous. If one examines free-expression cases beyond the context of incitement, one discovers that numerous celebrated free-speech victories came at the expense of outsiders and minorities. For example, in *Cantwell v. Connecticut*, a renowned hostile-audience case decided in 1940, the Court held that the First Amendment protected the expression of a religious outsider — Cantwell was a member of the Jehovah's Witnesses — even though Cantwell had "incensed" passing pedestrians.[63] The pedestrians, however, were Roman Catholics, and Cantwell's speech specifically assailed the Catholic Church — it is important to remember that, despite the current political alliance of Protestant evangelicals and Catholics, Protestant anti-Catholicism was strong and widespread for centuries, including in the United States.[64] In other words, while Cantwell can be understood to extend constitutional protection to a religious minority (the Jehovah's Witnesses), the decision came at the expense of another religious minority or outgroup (Roman Catholics). Another case, decided three years later, involved a similar dynamic: *Murdock v. Pennsylvania* invalidated an ordinance requiring individuals to pay a license fee before they could distribute literature and solicit contributions.[65] The defendant-speakers, once again Jehovah's Witnesses, had knocked on doors, "including those of devout Catholics on Palm Sunday morning," and declared that the Church was a "whore" and that "the paying over of money to a priest" was a "great racket."[66]

A comparison of two post–World War II hostile-audience cases suggests how the identity of targeted groups might influence the Court's application of the First Amendment. In *Terminiello v. Chicago*, decided in 1949, the Court held that the conviction of a Catholic priest for disorderly conduct violated the First Amendment.[67] The defendant, though, had condemned "atheistic, communistic Jewish or Zionist Jews" and claimed that Jewish doctors had performed atrocities on Germans.[68] The defendant said: "Do you wonder they were persecuted in other countries?"[69] He then declared that "we want them to go back where they came from."[70] Audience members were moved to exclaim, "'Kill the Jews,' 'Dirty kikes,'" and "'the Jews are all killers, murderers. If we don't kill them first, they will kill us.'"[71] Thus, in *Terminiello*, we again find the Court protecting the speech of a religious outsider (a Catholic priest) but at the expense of a non-Christian minority (Jewish people). Another hostile-audience case, decided two years later, reached a distinctly different result. In *Feiner v. New York*,[72] the defendant was a college student who had spoken to a racially mixed crowd of seventy-five to eighty white and Black Americans gathered together on a sidewalk in Syracuse, New York. He had encouraged the audience to attend a meeting of the Young Progressives of America, protested the city's cancelation of a permit for a prior meeting, and made derogatory remarks about "President Truman, the American Legion, the Mayor of Syracuse, and other local political officials."[73] The Court held that the First Amendment did not protect this speech because it created a clear and present danger, although the evidence showed only that "[t]he crowd was restless and there was some pushing, shoving and milling around."[74] The justices seemed especially worried that Feiner had urged Black Americans to "rise up in arms and fight for equal rights."[75] Yet, witnesses had sworn that Feiner had instead encouraged his listeners to "rise up and fight for their rights by going arm in arm to the [Young Progressives meeting], black and white alike."[76] Thus, in similar hostile-audience situations, *Terminiello* protected inflammatory anti-Semitic speech, while *Feiner* upheld the punishment of speech criticizing public officials and encouraging Black Americans to take political action.

Incitement Cases After *Brandenburg*

The Court has not decided many incitement cases after *Brandenburg*. Two cases, *NAACP v. Claiborne Hardware Co.*,[77] and *Holder v. Humanitarian Law Project*,[78] decided decades apart, illustrate the varied implications of *Brandenburg*. *Claiborne Hardware*, decided in 1982, arose from an NAACP boycott of white merchants in the area of Port Gibson, Mississippi. The boycott, seeking greater racial equality and justice, began in 1966 and stretched over multiple years, with several of the merchants filing suit in state court in 1969, to recover their losses and enjoin further boycotting. The case was complex, with a trial lasting eight months and testimony from 144 witnesses. The Mississippi Supreme Court upheld a common-law tort judgment for damages in favor of the merchants.[79] The US Supreme Court reversed on multiple issues, including a free-speech issue based on *Brandenburg*.

Charles Evers, the field secretary of the NAACP in Mississippi, was instrumental in organizing the boycott. He also made speeches that generally threatened boycott violators with disciplinary punishment. For instance, he stated: "'If we catch any of you going in any of them racist stores, we're gonna break your damn neck.'"[80] Then, at various times in the future, several boycott violators were specifically threatened (not by Evers), sometimes suffering property damage, such as having a brick thrown through a windshield.[81]

The question was whether Evers's statements constituted incitement outside First Amendment protections. In resolving this issue, the Court emphasized "that mere advocacy of the use of force or violence does not remove speech from the protection of the First Amendment."[82] Rather, speech encouraging or inciting violence remains constitutionally protected unless it satisfies the *Brandenburg* doctrine; the Court quoted the test from *Brandenburg*.[83] In other words, the state needed to prove that Evers had specifically intended to incite imminent unlawful action and that such unlawful action had been likely to occur imminently.

Based on its application of the *Brandenburg* doctrine, the Court concluded that the First Amendment constitutionally protected Evers's statements. While the Court did not explicitly hold that speech inciting violence is constitutionally protected unless actual violence occurs imminently, it did suggest that the lack of such actual imminent violence is probative. That is, in this case, because acts of violence did not occur until "weeks or months after" Evers's statements,[84] the state had failed to satisfy the *Brandenburg* double-imminence requirement — first, Evers must have intended to produce imminent unlawful action, *and* second, such action must have been likely to occur imminently.

Claiborne Hardware illustrates the Court interpreting and applying the *Brandenburg* test in a rigorous fashion. Contrary to the state court decision in the case, the Court did not waver from the strong free-expression stance articulated in *Brandenburg*. Significantly, the Court in *Claiborne Hardware* protected the expression of Evers and the NAACP boycotters, prototypical racial outsiders in American society. Yet, one should not overstate the implications of this decision. By the time the Court decided *Claiborne Hardware*, mainstream white American society had largely accepted the legitimacy of the civil rights movement (though not substantive racial equality and justice). For instance, President Ronald Reagan would soon sign a bill, in 1983, establishing a national holiday in honor of Dr. Martin Luther King Jr.[85] The Court's decision therefore harmonized with generally positive views of civil rights protests. If the Court had decided this case in an earlier era, such as the 1950s or early to mid-1960s, the justices might have reached a different conclusion.

A free-expression case, decided in 1966, arising from a civil rights protest, demonstrates this point. In *Adderley v. Florida*, 200 students marched from their college to a jail to protest the prior arrests of other student-civil-rights protestors.[86] The Court upheld the convictions of the marchers for trespassing on jail premises, with a majority opinion written by Justice Hugo Black, renowned as a free-speech absolutist.[87] In prior opinions, Black had argued that the First Amendment mandated a formal rule prohibiting all government restrictions of expression.[88] Free speech, to him, was inviolable — at least in theory. Yet, in *Adderley*, Black reasoned that the state could apply its general trespass law to punish the protestors' *conduct* — despite their political message.[89] Although the jailhouse seemed to be the perfect location for this particular civil rights protest — given the incarceration of the prior student-civil-rights protestors[90] — Black skirted the First Amendment issue by emphasizing the marchers' conduct rather than their expression.

While *Adderley* did not involve incitement, the *Adderley* Court's reasoning presaged the decision in *Holder v. Humanitarian Law Project*, an incitement case decided in 2010.[91] *Humanitarian Law Project* must be understood in the post-9/11, antiterrorism context. The plaintiffs were United States citizens and organizations challenging the constitutionality of a statute that prohibited providing material support or resources to certain designated foreign-terrorist organizations. Like *Claiborne Hardware*, *Humanitarian Law Project* was a complex case; the litigation stretched over twelve years.[92] The Secretary of State had designated "the Kurdistan Workers' Party (also known as the Partiya Karkeran Kurdistan, or PKK) and the Liberation Tigers of Tamil Eelam (LTTE)" as foreign terrorist organizations, although the two organizations engaged in humanitarian and political activities as well as terrorism.[93] The plaintiffs wanted to contribute to the PKK and the LTTE in support of their peaceful, nonviolent, and nonterrorist activities. Pursuant to the statutory prohibition, the government blocked these contributions. The plaintiffs claimed this government action violated multiple constitutional protections, including free expression.

The Court held in favor of the government. The dissent, written by Justice Stephen Breyer and joined by Justices Ruth Bader Ginsburg and Sonia Sotomayor, argued that the case raised an incitement issue. "[The] plaintiffs seek to advocate peaceful, lawful action to secure political ends; and they seek to teach others how to do the same," Breyer wrote.[94] "No one contends that the plaintiffs' speech to these organizations can be prohibited as incitement under *Brandenburg*."[95] Even if the plaintiffs' contributions, insofar as they constituted speech, supported or incited illegal terrorist conduct, the government should have needed to prove that this speech was specifically intended to produce imminent unlawful action and that such unlawful action had been likely to occur imminently. Given the lack of proof of imminence, the First Amendment should have constitutionally protected the plaintiffs' contributions (speech).[96]

The Court majority, however, skirted this issue, not even citing or discussing *Brandenburg*. The Court did not go so far as to claim that the case involved solely conduct and not speech, as Justice Black had reasoned in *Adderley*. Instead, the Court acknowledged that the plaintiffs "want to speak to the PKK and LTTE, and whether they may do so under [the statute] depends on what they say."[97] Insofar as the statute prohibited the plaintiffs' conduct, that conduct was "communicating a message."[98] Yet, the Court reasoned that the plaintiffs' "material support to the PKK and LTTE in the form of speech" could not be "meaningfully" segregated from the terrorist organizations' violent activities.[99] Congress, according to the Court, had reasonably found that "[foreign] organizations that engage in terrorist activity are so tainted by their criminal conduct that any contribution to such an organization facilitates that conduct."[100]

Consequently, while the Court did not label the plaintiffs' contributions to be pure conduct, the result was the same. Because, according to the Court, the plaintiffs' contributions (speech) could not be adequately isolated or separated from the PKK's and LTTE's violent activities, the government could restrict the expression without satisfying the *Brandenburg* test. The government did not need to prove the plaintiffs' intentions or the likelihood of imminent unlawful conduct. Ultimately, then, *Humanitarian Law Project* allowed the government to restrict the expression of outsiders — or at least those who wished to support outsiders — despite the First Amendment and *Brandenburg*.[101]

Conclusion

In one important respect, the Court's incitement decisions are similar to other free-expression decisions, which in turn are similar to other constitutional decisions. The "haves" usually come out ahead while societal outsiders and minorities typically lose.[102] In other words, the Court seldom seems intent on protecting or promoting social justice. As political scientists have shown in empirical studies, the Court rarely protects outsiders from majoritarian overreaching. In the words of Robert Dahl, "It would appear to be somewhat naive to assume that the Supreme Court either would or could play the role of Galahad."[103] Instead, the Court typically acts as an integral "part of the dominant national alliance," deciding in harmony with the interests and values of that dominant political alliance or regime.[104] In short, the Court rarely departs too far from the political mainstream.[105]

When it comes to free expression, this pattern — the haves winning and the have-nots losing — has held true from the early years of the republic through today. In the 1830s, Alexis de Tocqueville recognized that societal outsiders risked social and legal punishments if they expressed dissident views. An individual was free to speak or write if the expression remained within the broad mainstream of culture and opinion, but individuals venturing outside those parameters were often severely punished. "In America the majority raises formidable barriers around the liberty of opinion," Tocqueville wrote.[106] "[W]ithin these barriers an author may write what he pleases, but woe to him if he goes beyond them."[107] Nowadays, the Roberts Court in free-expression cases continues to favor the wealthy and mainstream at the expense of outsiders and minorities. Corporations and Christians have consistently won cases involving free expression.[108] Meanwhile, free-expression losers have included people of color,[109] religious minorities,[110] prisoners,[111] public employee unions,[112] and those seeking an equal voice in democratic government.[113]

The Court's incitement decisions throughout history fit this pattern. Before the Court decided *Brandenburg*, societal outsiders consistently lost free expression cases involving incitement of unlawful conduct. Likewise, long after *Brandenburg*, *Humanitarian Law Project* held against those who wanted to express support for the peaceful activities of terrorist organizations. When outsiders or minorities have won incitement and other free-expression cases, their interests and values have typically converged or overlapped with those of the mainstream or wealthy.[114] For example, in *Claiborne Hardware*, the Court's decision for the NAACP accorded with the then-widespread approval of the civil rights movement. In *Brandenburg* itself, the Court protected white, Christian hate speech targeting Jewish and Black Americans.

If incitement cases arise in the near future, one should not expect the Roberts Court to deviate from these historical practices. The justices do not generally seem concerned with social justice.[115] Despite *Brandenburg*, the haves will likely win and the have-nots will likely lose. In those rare cases when outsiders or minorities win, their interests and values will have converged with the mainstream or wealthy. What, then, can be done? If arguing before the Roberts Court, societal outsiders and minorities might increase their chances for victory by arguing for broad principles that encompass their interests and values — as well as the interests and values of the mainstream and wealthy.[116] Otherwise, outsiders and minorities might do best by seeking support from other institutions.

Notes

1. Richard Kluger, *Simple Justice: The History of* Brown v. Board of Education *and Black America's Struggle for Equality* (Knopf, 1976), 710.
2. Brandenburg v. Ohio, 395 U.S. 444 (1969).
3. Geoffrey R. Stone, *Perilous Times: Free Speech in Wartime from the Sedition Act of 1798 to the War on Terrorism* (W. W. Norton, 2004), 522.
4. Stephen M. Feldman, *Pack the Court! A Defense of Supreme Court Expansion* (Temple University Press, 2021), 79–94.
5. Jeremy Waldron, *The Harm in Hate Speech* (Harvard University Press, 2012), 65–104 (discussing justice, a well-ordered society, and hate speech).
6. Stephen M. Feldman, *Free Expression and Democracy in America: A History* (University of Chicago Press, 2008), 241–90.
7. Feldman, *Free Expression*, 111–15.
8. Joseph Story, *Commentaries on the Constitution of the United States*, vol. 3 (Hilliard, Gray, 1833), 736.
9. Knowles v. United States, 170 F. 409 (8th Cir. 1909); Updegraph v. Commonwealth, 11 Serg. & Rawle 394 (Pa. 1824); Commonwealth v. Morris, 3 Va. 176 (1811).
10. 11 Serg. & Rawle 394 (Pa. 1824).
11. Updegraph, 11 Serg. & Rawle at 406.
12. Feldman, *Free Expression*, 209–40.
13. 249 U.S. 47 (1919).
14. Schenck, 249 U.S. at 52.
15. Feldman, *Free Expression*, 260–64.
16. 205 U.S. 454 (1907).
17. Patterson, 205 U.S. at 462.
18. 249 U.S. 204 (1919).
19. 249 U.S. 211 (1919).
20. Frohwerk, 249 U.S. at 209.
21. Debs, 249 U.S. at 216. The jury instruction continued by suggesting that the defendant needed to specifically intend to cause harm — a requirement that many courts added. Nevertheless, under the doctrine of constructive intent, the courts typically reasoned that a defendant was presumed to have intended the natural and probable consequences of his or her statements. If a defendant's expression was found to have bad tendencies, then the defendant's criminal intent would be inferred. Shaffer v. United States, 255 F. 886 (9th Cir. 1919).
22. Feldman, *Free Expression*, 275–81.
23. 250 U.S. 616 (1919).
24. Abrams, 250 U.S. at 617–18.
25. Feldman, *Free Expression*, 285–90.
26. 268 U.S. 652 (1925).

27 274 U.S. 357 (1927).
28 Gitlow, 268 U.S. at 655.
29 Gitlow, 268 U.S. at 672–73 (Holmes, J., dissenting); Whitney, 274 U.S. at 377–78 (Brandeis, J., concurring in judgment).
30 Feldman, *Free Expression*, 383–86.
31 Harry Kalven, A Worthy Tradition: Freedom of Speech in America (Harper & Row, 1988), 167.
32 Stromberg v. California, 283 U.S. 359 (1931). In an earlier case that seemed to raise free-speech issues, the Court upheld the defendant's claim to constitutionally protected liberty, but the opinion focused exclusively on due process and did not discuss free expression. Fiske v. Kansas, 274 U.S. 380, 386–87 (1927).
33 Feldman, *Free Expression*, 349–82.
34 301 U.S. 1 (1937).
35 Jones & Laughlin Steel, 301 U.S. at 33.
36 Howard Gillman, *The Constitution Besieged: The Rise and Demise of Lochner Era Police Powers Jurisprudence* (Duke University Press, 1993); Michael J. Sandel, *Democracy's Discontent: America in Search of a Public Philosophy* (Belknap Press, 1996), 200, 250–71.
37 Bridges v. California, 314 U.S. 252, 263 (1941) (discussing clear and present danger); Thornhill v. Alabama, 310 U.S. 88, 105 (1940) (holding that labor picketing is protected free speech; discussing clear and present danger); Schneider v. State, 308 U.S. 147 (1939) (invalidiating conviction for distributing handbills); Hague v. C.I.O., 307 U.S. 496 (1939) (upholding right of unions to organize in streets).
38 West Virginia State Board of Ed. v. Barnette, 319 U.S. 624, 642 (1943).
39 Barnette, 319 U.S. at 641.
40 Terminiello v. Chicago, 337 U.S. 1, 4 (1949).
41 Barnette, 319 U.S. at 642.
42 Feldman, *Free Expression*, 431–50.
43 American Communications Association v. Douds, 339 U.S. 382, 396, 402–3, 412 (1950) (upholding provision of Taft-Hartley Act).
44 342 U.S. 485 (1952).
45 341 U.S. 494 (1951).
46 Dennis, 341 U.S. at 510. Vinson quoted from Judge Learned Hand's lower court opinion in Dennis. United States v. Dennis, 183 F.2d 201, 212 (2d Cir. 1950).
47 Dennis, 341 U.S. at 508–11.
48 Robert Justin Goldstein, *Political Repression in Modern America from 1870 to 1976* (University of Illinois Press, 2001), 332–33.
49 Lucas A. Powe, *The Warren Court and American Politics* (Belknap Press, 2000), 303–35.
50 393 U.S. 503 (1969).
51 Tinker, 393 U.S. at 508–9.

52 376 U.S. 254 (1964).
53 *New York Times*, 376 U.S. at 270.
54 395 U.S. 444 (1969).
55 Stone, *Perilous Times: Free Speech*, 522; Thomas L. Tedford, *Freedom of Speech in the United States* (Strata, 1997), 66–69.
56 Bernard Schwartz, *Decision: How the Supreme Court Decides Cases* (Oxford University Press, 1996), 172–74; Laura Kalman, Abe Fortas a Biography (Yale University Press, 1990), 319–78.
57 Brandenburg, 395 U.S. at 444–45.
58 Brandenburg, 395 U.S. at 447.
59 Stone, *Perilous Times: Free Speech*, 522.
60 Brandenburg, 395 U.S. at 445.
61 Brandenburg, 395 U.S. at 444–47.
62 Stephen M. Feldman, "White Christian Nationalism Enters the Political Mainstream: Implications for the Roberts Court and Religious Freedom," *Seton Hall Law Review* 53 (2023): 667.
63 310 U.S. 296, 303 (1940).
64 Sydney E. Ahlstrom, *A Religious History of the American People* (Yale University Press, 1972), 7, 53, 853–54, 1006–7, 1090; Feldman, *Free Expression*, 39–40, 170, 294–95, 304.
65 319 U.S. 105 (1943).
66 Douglas v. City of Jeannette, 319 U.S. 167, 167, 171, 180 (1943) (Douglas 2) (Jackson, J., dissenting from Murdock); see Near v. Minnesota, 283 U.S. 697, 703-04 (1931) (protecting the publication of anti-Semitic articles).
67 337 U.S. 1 (1949).
68 Terminiello, 337 U.S. at 20 (Jackson, J., dissenting).
69 Terminiello, 337 U.S. at 20 (Jackson, J., dissenting).
70 Terminiello, 337 U.S. at 21 (Jackson, J., dissenting).
71 Terminiello, 337 U.S. at 22 (Jackson, J., dissenting).
72 340 U.S. 315 (1951).
73 Feiner, 340 U.S. at 317.
74 Feiner, 340 U.S. at 317, 320.
75 Feiner, 340 U.S. at 317.
76 Feiner, 340 U.S. at 324 and n5 (Black, J., dissenting).
77 458 U.S. 886 (1982).
78 561 U.S. 1 (2010).
79 Claiborne Hardware Co., 458 U.S. at 889–902.
80 Claiborne Hardware Co., 458 U.S. at 902.
81 Claiborne Hardware Co., 458 U.S. at 904–6.
82 Claiborne Hardware Co., 458 U.S. at 927.
83 Claiborne Hardware Co., 458 U.S. at 928.
84 Claiborne Hardware Co., 458 U.S. at 928.

85 James T. Patterson, *Restless Giant: The United States from Watergate to Bush v. Gore* (Oxford University Press, 2005), 15–17, 170–71.
86 385 U.S. 39 (1966).
87 Bernard Schwartz, *A History of the Supreme Court* (Oxford University Press, 1993), 283.
88 Konigsberg v. State Bar of California, 366 U.S. 36, 60–71 (1961) (Black, J., dissenting).
89 Adderley, 385 U.S. at 46–48.
90 Adderley, 385 U.S. at 49–50, 54 (Douglas, J., dissenting).
91 561 U.S. 1 (2010).
92 Humanitarian Law Project, 561 U.S. at 14.
93 Humanitarian Law Project, 561 U.S. at 9.
94 Humanitarian Law Project, 561 U.S. at 44 (Breyer, J., dissenting).
95 Humanitarian Law Project, 561 U.S. at 44 (Breyer, J., dissenting).
96 Humanitarian Law Project, 561 U.S. at 43–44, 51 (Breyer, J., dissenting).
97 Humanitarian Law Project, 561 U.S. at 27.
98 Humanitarian Law Project, 561 U.S. at 28.
99 Humanitarian Law Project, 561 U.S. at 28–29.
100 Humanitarian Law Project, 561 U.S. at 29.
101 Humanitarian Law Project, 561 U.S. at 25–33.
102 Marc Galanter, "Why the 'Haves' Come Out Ahead: Speculations on the Limits of Legal Change," *Law and Society Review* 9 (1974): 95.
103 Robert A. Dahl, "Decision-Making in a Democracy: The Supreme Court as a National Policy-Maker," *Journal of Public Law* 6 (1957): 284; Keith E. Whittington, *Political Foundations of Judicial Supremacy: The Presidency, the Supreme Court, and Constitutional Leadership in U.S. History* (Princeton University Press, 2007), 42–45.
104 Dahl, "Decision-Making in a Democracy: The Supreme Court as a National Policy-Maker," 293.
105 Terri Peretti, "Constructing the State Action Doctrine, 1940–1990," *Law and Social Inquiry* 35 (2010): 275.
106 Alexis de Tocqueville, *Democracy in America*, vol. 1, The Henry Reeve text as revised by Francis Bowen et al. (Vintage Books, 1990), 264.
107 Tocqueville, *Democracy in America*, 264.
108 Citizens United v. Federal Election Commission, 558 U.S. 310 (2010) (invalidating restrictions on corporate campaign spending). Many religious-freedom cases also involve free expression. For example, Masterpiece Cakeshop, Ltd. v. Colorado C.R. Comm'n, 138 S. Ct. 1719, 1723–24 (2018). To be sure, some Roberts Court decisions appear to depart from the Court's generally conservative conclusions. With many of those cases, though, a close examination reveals an underlying conservative explanation. Feldman, *Pack the Court*, 161–69. Moreover, in an occasional early Roberts Court decision, the Court reached a progressive or liberal conclusion because the moderately conservative Anthony

Kennedy voted with the progressive rather than the conservative justices — for example, Christian Legal Society v. Martinez, 591 U.S. 661 (2010) (upholding a school policy preventing the Christian Legal Society from discriminating against LGBTQ individuals).

109 Manhattan Community Access Corporation v. Halleck, 139 S. Ct. 1921, 1927 (2019) (invoking the state action doctrine to defeat free-speech claim of television producers focusing on East Harlem, a predominantly Hispanic and Black neighborhood in New York City).

110 Pleasant Grove City v. Summum, 555 U.S. 460 (2009) (holding against free-expression claim of Summum, a minority religious group, which sought to display a monument in a public park).

111 Beard v. Banks, 548 U.S. 521 (2006) (severely limiting prisoner access to written materials and photographs).

112 Janus v. Am. Fed'n of State, Cty., & Mun. Employees, Council 31, 138 S. Ct. 2448 (2018) (holding that workers cannot be forced to pay union fees related solely to collective bargaining representation even though the workers benefit from the representation); Knox v. Service Employees International Union, 132 S. Ct. 2277 (2012) (holding that public employee union could not impose a special assessment fee to support political advocacy even if union members could opt out).

113 For example, Rucho v. Common Cause, 139 S. Ct. 2484 (2019) (holding that constitutionality of extreme political gerrymandering was nonjusticiable political question).

114 For example, Martin v. City of Struthers, was a free-expression case (though not an incitement case) where a religious minority won because of a convergence of interests. 319 U.S. 141 (1943). Martin invalidated an ordinance proscribing door-to-door distributions of written materials as applied to a Jehovah's Witness. In concluding that the ordinance violated the First Amendment, the Court stressed that the Witnesses' method of disseminating information, going door-to-door, resonated with mainstream practices. Martin v. City of Struthers at 145–47.

115 Feldman, *Pack the Court*, 121–69 (discussing the Robert Court's conservatism).

116 Stephen M. Feldman, "Religious Minorities and the First Amendment: The History, the Doctrine, and the Future," 6 *University of Pennsylvania Journal of Constitutional Law* 222 (2003) (detailing how American Jewish organizations successfully — and unsuccessfully — argued to the Supreme Court during the post–World War II era).

PART II:
INCITEMENT EXTENSIONS

Chapter Four

Criminal Solicitation and Incitement as Borderline Criminal Speech

Wily Agitators and Fuzzy Lines

Rachel E. VanLandingham

The Rich and Complicated Arena of Criminal Speech

The thickets of First Amendment expressive theory and jurisprudence have long been thorny. Even so, the conceptual interplay among the quintessential speech crime of solicitation of criminality, its cousin criminal incitement of lawlessness, and noncriminal advocacy of lawlessness, is particularly dense. This chapter highlights boundaries and intersections associated with these activities to magnify the criminal dividing line. While solicitation and incitement were historically viewed as one common law crime that generally prohibits urging another to commit a felony — some criminal codes continue to use incite and solicit interchangeably — this chapter distinguishes them based on distinctions made by the Supreme Court.

Solicitation in this chapter refers to the crime of (1) asking, ordering, encouraging, etcetera (some states use the term *inciting*) another to commit crime X (this urging is the required act), with (2) the intent that the other person actually commit crime X (meaning that the speaker isn't simply kidding with their request). In contrast, whereas criminal incitement, like solicitation, also requires that the speaker urge lawlessness with the intent that the urged criminality be committed, incitement additionally requires a reasonable likelihood of imminent lawlessness following said advocacy.[1] There is no such likelihood or imminency requirement for solicitation.

For example, the crime of solicitation of murder does not require that there be a reasonable likelihood that such a request will result in an imminent murder. Indeed, there may not even be a reasonable likelihood such murder will ever be carried out. It is the words themselves coupled with the intent that the target crime of murder be committed by the person solicited (the solicitee) that constitutes solicitation of murder. Solicitation thus criminalizes speech that is related to, but not always or even necessarily instrumental to, a distinct criminal act (here, murder). The speech itself, coupled with the requisite desire that the target crime be committed by the person solicited, is criminal even when the urged crime never occurs, and even when it never *could* occur (such as when the solicitee is an undercover agent).

Despite solicitation's broad sweep, some advocacy of criminality that in many respects looks like plain old solicitation of crime is protected from prosecution by the First Amendment. Incitement's additional likelihood and imminency requirements pop up in some circumstances in which lawlessness is urged, thus protecting that speech from criminal prosecution if not met. This chapter's simple goal is to try and identify those "some circumstances" that trigger these hurdles' sudden appearance. As discussed below, these hurdles seemingly appear when the advocacy in question is to a collective versus an individual, and when there is a political context to the speech (that is, the speech is associated with classically protected expression versus simply manifesting a desire to advance a criminal act). However, this context is not always clear, and the justifications for the hurdles' materialization seem shallowly planted.

The circumstances requiring these high hurdles, thus separating incitement from solicitation and thereby making it harder for the government to punish said speech, are vitally important to discern not simply because the speech advocating illegality itself is protected from prosecution if the hurdles of reasonable likelihood of imminent lawlessness are present and not cleared. What seems even more important is that if plain old vanilla solicitation to commit a crime is found (in circumstances in which the hurdles are not required), or incitement to criminality is found (when the hurdles are both required plus cleared), *and* the urged criminality actually occurs, the person who solicited or incited the target crime *is criminally liable for the target crime that is committed by the person incited/solicited.* This criminal responsibility for the crimes committed by third parties results from the theory of accomplice liability. It makes actors who assist with another's crimes — by providing physical assistance, such as by acting as a lookout during a robbery, or by providing psychological assistance, such as by encouraging or requesting someone else commit a crime — guilty of the target crime the actor assisted (as long as the speaker intended the encouraged crime's commission).

Incitement's distinction from solicitation is fascinating, revealing that that speech dealing with unlawful action by others is sometimes protected, and therefore does not make the speaker liable for others' crimes. Solicitation and incitement are similar in that the speaker will be shielded from criminal liability by proving that they lacked the intent that any urged crime actually be committed. The much thornier question asks for greater clarity regarding the circumstances requiring incitement's high hurdles of reasonable likelihood of imminent lawlessness. If required, these hurdles must be cleared before the speaker is criminally responsible for their listeners' crimes. That is, when is an agitator criminally responsible for the crimes their listeners commit, versus not criminally liable for those crimes because of the lack of reasonable likelihood of imminent lawlessness when she was agitating?

This question has deep political and historical roots in the United States, given its history of persecuting, through criminal prosecution, political and ideological opponents through offenses such as sedition crimes, syndicalism laws, and common law incitement. My ancestor was a victim of such abuse (the similar last name plus striking resemblance to my father made my family's claim that we were related highly believable to ten-year-old me when studying this claimed ancestor in my Ohio elementary school history books). Clement Laird Vallandigham, an Ohio politician and lawyer, was convicted in 1863 by a hastily assembled military commission (despite being a civilian, and despite courthouses remaining open), for violating a Union general's order prohibiting criticism of the government during the Civil War. Vallandigham's conviction, approved by President Lincoln himself, was for a public speech given in Dayton, Ohio, in which Vallandigham criticized the Civil War while defending states' supposed rights to allow slavery. Vallandigham claimed that the Civil War was "a war for the purpose of crushing out liberty and erecting a despotism" and that "the sooner the people should inform the minions of usurped power, that they would not submit to such restrictions upon their liberties, the better"; the Union Army claimed that such "opinions and sentiments he well knew did aid, comfort, and encourage those in arms against the Government, and could but induce in his hearers a distrust of their own Government, sympathy for those in arms against it, and a disposition to resist the laws of the land."[2] After conviction, President Lincoln banished Vallandigham from the country, and even used Vallandigham's military prosecution to publicly rationalize the criminalization of speech that is only obliquely related to potential future illegality. Because of this family history — and because I've taught criminal law for years after practicing it at the military trial and appellate levels, and because I served in military uniform for over two decades to help protect Americans' right to criticize their government — I am continually fascinated by historical and current speech crimes, and the murky boundaries surrounding so-called dangerous speech..

Additionally, in the immediate aftermath of the January 6, 2021 insurrection at the Capitol, I was quick to wonder (along with many fellow Americans) whether then-President Trump was criminally responsible for the numerous acts of outrageous violence committed by hundreds that day — liable thanks to his speech seemingly urging said violence. Or was Trump, like my ancestor Clement, simply a "wily agitator" (President Lincoln's moniker for

Vallandigham), shielded from liability for his followers' subsequent criminal acts? It is quite possible that Trump's speech is indeed constitutionally protected because the modern Supreme Court, long after Vallandigham's conviction and banishment, erected high hurdles that snap into place to protect advocacy of illegality, notably in certain political contexts that lack individual requests of criminality.

I write this chapter not to determine whether Trump was a wily agitator whose speech is protected, versus a criminal inciter thus liable for violence his followers engaged in on January 6, but to provide food for thought for others to wrestle with this question. I also write this chapter to suggest to fellow criminal law professors that they inject more constitutional law into their criminal law courses and use speech crimes such as solicitation and incitement to do so. While law school courses, particularly the first year, are extremely siloed from one another by topic, real life and law are full of intersections of many doctrinal legal areas. Speech crimes, including solicitation and the related theory of accomplice liability, provide rich opportunities to explore such overlap.

While other speech crimes, such as true threats, also raise serious constitutional issues, my focus here is on the interplay among solicitation, incitement, accomplice liability, and protected advocacy. This narrow focus flows from my long-standing interest in incitement law, and because the inchoate nature of these crimes (versus true threats, for example) provides an additional interesting layer. The term *inchoate* means incomplete, and in criminal law typically refers to the common law crimes of conspiracy, attempts, and solicitation. The incomplete nature refers to their relationship with another crime; each of these crimes is charged in relation to a separate substantive offense. For example, solicitation by itself isn't typically a crime — solicitation to commit crime X, such as solicitation to commit murder, is an offense (similarly, the other inchoate crimes related to murder would be attempted murder and conspiracy to commit murder).

All three inchoate offenses are preventative in that they provide a basis for criminality to attach (and a legal basis to incapacitate the offender) *prior* to the commission of the more serious crime to which they are linked. Better to stop a murder in its attempt before it is completed; better yet, it is preferable to stop a murder before it is even attempted by interrupting it when it is solicited, given how close the prohibited harm (death) may be when trying to stop it at the attempt stage. These inchoate crimes carry no causation component, as there is no result they must cause (otherwise, such offenses wouldn't be inchoate, instead we would have the completed target crime). If someone solicits someone else to commit murder, and the solicitee commits said murder, the solicitor is guilty of the murder itself through accomplice liability; the solicitation disappears as a separate crime.

The reason solicitation itself is criminal, divorced from its target crime, is because it allows law enforcement to incapacitate the offender at an early point far from the intended murder and prior even to an attempted murder. Solicitation provides the earliest basis for law enforcement to arrest someone regarding the commission of a future crime: law enforcement needs probable cause that solicitation has occurred, which is found at an earlier point than probable cause that an attempt to commit X has occurred. Thanks to solicitation's criminalization, perhaps murder is also less likely due to criminal law's deterrence effect (while murder itself is theoretically deterred by the penalization of murder, solicitation to commit murder is also deterred by its separate criminalization, and less solicitation of X should lead to less X). Finally, as explained earlier, there is no requirement that a reasonable likelihood exists that the person solicited will act on the request, whether imminently or not; the likelihood of criminality occurring due to the solicitation is irrelevant. The request alone (accompanied by the solicitor's intent that the solicitee actually commit the crime) is sufficient for conviction (unlike with criminal incitement, which additionally requires reasonable likelihood of compliance with the request).

The harm involved in the inchoate nature of solicitation and its narrower cousin of criminal incitement contrasts greatly with that involved in their fellow speech crime of true threats, thus complicating their relationship with the First Amendment. The harm is different because the speech that constitutes solicitation and incitement — advocating, commanding, urging, or requesting illegality — is not harmful in and of itself. Instead, these inchoate crimes are criminal because of their relationship to another crime; they are criminalized solely as tools of prevention designed to thwart a separate subsequent serious criminal act. True threats, on the other hand, are inherently harmful, and therefore criminal because they carry the specter of intimidation; they are a type of speech "which by their very utterance inflict injury."[3] A threat itself causes harm due to the fear it naturally produces in the person threatened. In contrast, the very words used to solicit or incite lack such inherent injury divorced from the crimes' target offenses. Solicitation's criminalization of words that by themselves do not cause inherent harm poses a greater First Amendment reconciliation challenge than the speech crime of true threats, and this reconciliation warrants greater attention.

In regard to my ancestor, President Lincoln asked, "Must I shoot a simpleminded soldier boy who deserts, while I must not touch a hair of a wily agitator who induces him to desert?"[4] While I apply the *Brandenburg* Court's rationale to find that the wily agitators' speech should be protected unless it counsels illegality that is imminently likely to occur (Vallandigham's did not), the line-drawing is not easy and should be consistently revisited in light of evolving understandings of human behavior. I disagree with President Lincoln's rationale for suppressing so-called dangerous speech not because I agree with Vallandigham's Civil War opinions, and not because I think his and similar speech is harmless. Criminalizing such speech because of speculative harm is simply not worth the suppression of valuable speech — speech that is only tenuously linked to any potential future harm. Suppression is harmful given the "political, economic and social" value of the speech at issue, expression that is necessary for pluralistic, democratic functioning as both an outlet and to reach shared understandings — and is also harmful due to the vast, vast, vast abusive tendency historically associated with the punishment of similar speech.[5] Simply put, the juice is not worth the squeeze and may exacerbate the danger such suppression was designed to avoid.[6]

The relevant foundational questions may appear basic but are far from it. They ask when and why is speech that sits on the far end of the criminality spectrum — linked to a separate crime but without any casual connection it, and involving speech that poses no inherent harm by the uttered words themselves — punishable by the state, despite the Constitution's expressive freedom inherent in the command, "Congress shall make no law . . . abridging the freedom of speech."[7] As explored in the next section, the "when" of speech criminality (turning words into crimes of solicitation or incitement) depends on the type of speech (including expressive, communicative conduct as well as words) and the context in which it was spoken. The "why" of speech criminality searches for theoretical justifications for the criminal punishment of indirect speech that is uttered quite a distance on the criminality path from the ultimate substantive crime linked to the speech at question. Justifications range from risk reduction operating through classic deterrence theory, to punishing a "dangerous personality," to prevention of other crimes by providing an early intervention point for law enforcement.[8]

The First Amendment Landscape of Speech Crimes

It is worth briefly noting the myriad ways speech is criminalized in America and generally how the Court exempts such speech from the First Amendment's protections. While "[a]s a general matter, the First Amendment means that government has no power to restrict expression because of its message, its ideas, its subject matter, or its content,"[9] it seems plain that this claim is far from true. It is abundantly clear from the following examples that indeed the government restricts quite a bit of speech exactly because of all these things, and is expressly permitted to do so by the Court's jurisprudence. The Court allows such speech restrictions based on content, message, and ideas (while minimizing that it is doing so) largely by identifying several categorical types of speech — essentially large conceptual speech buckets — that fall outside the First Amendment's shield: "Since its enactment, the First Amendment has permitted restrictions on a few historic categories of speech — including obscenity, defamation, fraud, incitement, and speech integral to criminal conduct — that 'have never been thought to raise any Constitutional problem.'"[10] The Court has added child pornography to that list,[11] and seemingly places solicitation within the "speech integral to criminal conduct" exception, finding that "[o]ffers to engage in illegal transactions are categorically excluded from First Amendment protection."[12] Incitement is broken out from this group into its own unprotected category, with the Court considering incitement as one of the "historic and traditional categories long familiar to the bar."[13] However, it is unclear whether the Court was referring to *Brandenburg* incitement, with its high hurdles not present in solicitation, or incitement under old common law as synonymous with solicitation (hence without the reasonable likelihood of imminent lawlessness element).

These buckets or categories of unprotected speech are reflected in modern criminal law, which punishes speech in ways ranging from the relatively straightforward (including criminal conduct that causes virtually no expressive heartburn), to those that are more challenging to square with theories of punishment, harm, and expressive theory. Starting with the former, it is relatively easy to see that speech can be instrumental to the commission of a crime as a form of action; it can serve as a vehicle for committing a particular crime. The Court considers such speech as integral to criminal conduct (an above-mentioned category of unprotected speech) and thus punishable for its content. Take Professor Kent Greenawalt's vivid example of a woman telling her blind hiking partner to step to the right on a trail, intending the partner to plummet to his death as he steps off the path into an abyss; in this scenario, the murderer's speech constitutes a deadly weapon in that circumstance.[14] The harmful gravamen of that crime of murder is the intentional killing of another human being, not the means by which that killing was carried out — hence the use of speech to commit said killing raises no First Amendment concerns. There is no concern that by punishing the speech used to kill someone, protected expression will be chilled. Similarly, a bank robber may hand a teller a demand note in the course of their robbery, raising no First Amendment issues by speech serving as a vehicle for criminality. The speech in such situations, while instrumental to subsequent crime commission, does not immunize the speaker from criminal liability; "[t]he first amendment does not provide a defense to a criminal charge simply because the actor uses words to carry out his illegal purpose."[15]

This unprotected category seemingly also includes the modern speech crimes of perjury, bribery and extortion; such offenses differ from the above bank teller and murder examples in that speech is not simply one method of performing each crime's *actus reus* (criminal law's terminology for the particular conduct required for the crime). Instead, speech in these crimes is the *only* way they can be committed; speech is the required *actus reus*. Other crimes that turn on expression, specifically obscenity and fraud, while conceivably fitting into the Court's loose "speech integral to criminal conduct" category, per the Court, constitute their own unprotected categories.[16] As noted by scholars such as Frederick Schauer, "there are activities that are speech acts in the ordinary sense, yet have nothing whatsoever to do with freedom of speech"[17]; and as noted by the Court, "[t]here are certain well-defined and narrowly limited classes of speech, the prevention and punishment of which has never been thought to raise any Constitutional problem."[18] Speech crimes such as fraud rarely raise First Amendment eyebrows; per the *Giboney* Court, there is no freedom of speech impairment in making conduct illegal "merely because the conduct was in part initiated, evidenced, or carried out by means of language."[19]

However, there are crimes involving speech as prohibited conduct that do raise First Amendment concerns, such as the criminalization of threats. Here, the Court has addressed constitutional concerns by finding that only "true threats" fall within the speech integral to crime categorical exception. Such criminal threats possess an objective component in that they must reasonably convey that the "speaker means to commit an act of unlawful violence," that is, a reasonable person would interpret the words at issue as threatening, regardless whether the speaker meant any listener to interpret them as such.[20] This requirement inoculates speech that a particularly sensitive person may take as threatening, but objectively is not viewed as such, and lessens the chilling effect from criminalizing threatening speech.

In 2023, the Court finally answered in the affirmative the long-standing question of whether or not true threats require a subjective component, that is, whether or not the speaker, to be convicted of conveying criminal threats, has to be aware not simply of the content of their speech (versus repeating a phrase in a foreign language which they don't understand), but also has to be aware of the threatening nature of their speech. The Court concluded that for true threats to be criminally punished, the speaker must be at least reckless with regard to the threatening nature of his or her words: "The State must show that the defendant consciously disregarded a substantial risk that his communications would be viewed as threatening violence."[21] Both components, the objective nature of the threat and the subjective mental state of the speaker, serve to lessen chilling of protected speech, such as out of fear a particularly sensitive listener will misinterpret the words uttered, or that mere jest or hyperbole may be taken as threatening. As a mental state — meaning the subjective state of mind accompanying a proscribed act that is a requisite part of almost all crimes — recklessness is less than that required for incitement and solicitation, both of which require the government to prove that the speaker intended the listener to engage in the lawlessness urged, versus merely acting recklessly with regard to the risk that the listener will take them up on their urging of criminality. As the Court noted in its 2023 true threats case, the higher mental state of intent (purposefully or knowingly), at least for incitement, is warranted because "incitement to disorder is commonly a hair's-breadth away from political 'advocacy' — and particularly from strong protests against the government and prevailing social order."[22] That is, the expression at issue in incitement treads much closer to the reasons animating the First Amendment, with the protection of political speech at its core, meaning that such speech requires the stronger protection that a higher mental state (of intent versus mere recklessness) provides.

This chapter leaves threats to the side, focusing instead on expressive conduct that is linked to substantive crime yet distinct from it, such as an agreement with another to commit a future crime (a conspiracy) as well as solicitation of illegal conduct. The agreement at the heart of the crime of conspiracy, for example, is a stand-alone crime of expression that does not depend upon the commission of the agreed-upon crime, though it is connected to a target crime by the agreement to commit it. For example, if Jack and Jill agree to commit a bank robbery the following week, with the intent that they indeed will commit said robbery, and one of them buys a gun to use in said robbery, Jack and Jill are both guilty of conspiracy to commit bank robbery even if they never attempt the actual robbery. Unlike a true threat, no one is experiencing harm by the expression of a conspiratorial agreement itself; conspiracy as a classic inchoate crime designed for prevention: "they deal with conduct that is designed to culminate in the commission of a substantive offense, but has failed in the discrete case to do so or has not yet achieved its culmination because there is something that the actor or another still must do."[23] Indeed, the Supreme Court has recognized solicitation as a type of inchoate crime, one that falls under the integral to crime exception; it is one of the "sorts of inchoate crimes — acts looking toward the commission of another crime."[24]

The following discussion in the next section highlights that incitement can be construed as a close cousin of solicitation that carries with it additional elements, and fleshes out where the line seems to at times uneasily lie between the two, and places these crimes in the general pantheon of freedom of expression. While some scholars claim that "[i]t is black-letter law that the First Amendment prohibits governmental sanctioning of speech unless that speech incites 'imminent lawless action and is likely to incite . . . such action,'" this is simply not accurate.[25] There is plenty of speech, in the form of the crime of solicitation, that requests future criminality that is not only not imminent, but indeed will never occur, yet the request is unlawful and hence punishable. As alluded to earlier and further explained in the following section, speech that encourages future crime, as long as accompanied by the requisite intent that the future crime be committed, is both sanctionable and indeed is sanctioned across the country, with no imminence or likelihood required — as the substantive crime of solicitation to commit a particulate separate offense. Hence, the Supreme Court's holding in *Brandenburg v. Ohio* that speech must be "directed to inciting or producing imminent lawless action," and "likely to incite or produce such action" before it can be criminalized is certainly not a blanket statement that covers all inducement or encouragement of crime.[26] *Brandenburg* must be appropriately contextualized, and solicitation distinguished from the incitement meant by the Court that requires the extra *Brandenburg* elements.

Criminal Solicitation

Under common law (judge-made law that developed over centuries and today is reflected in varying degrees in criminal statutes), the crime of solicitation broadly punishes requesting or urging another to commit a crime, regardless of whether the urged crime is committed, with the speaker possessing the specific intent that the person so urged commit the offense.[27] As explained in this chapter's introduction, solicitation is designed to punish speakers in situations in which their intended target crime is never attempted, never mind completed; it functions primarily as a means of early prevention, allowing law enforcement to intervene at this early stage, one quite far from commission of the intended offense. If the encouraged crime is eventually attempted or completed, solicitation as a crime falls away and the encouragement itself, even if the subsequent offense would have been committed without it, makes the solicitor liable for the urged crime as a principal through aiding and abetting (accomplice) liability.[28]

Solicitation is the most inchoate of the three traditionally considered inchoate crimes, in line with its preventive purpose: it focuses on criminalizing the most incipient action involving a third party regarding the potential commission of a separate, future crime.[29] That is, it occupies the farthest left compared to other inchoate crimes on the *actus reus* harm spectrum from the actual harm — that inherent in the target crime — that the crime of solicitation is primarily designed to prevent.[30] While there is an inherent risk involved, as "messages urging commission of a crime which are received expose individuals to invitation to crime and create a risk of criminal activity," solicitation provides the earliest point for law enforcement intervention and thus is best supported by a prevention model of criminality versus one designed to mitigate risky behavior.[31] Indeed, such a risk may not even exist, given that most states criminalize solicitation regardless of whether the intended recipient receives the communication, as long as there is conduct intended to effectively transmit the communication.

Solicitation's *actus reus* verbs of commanding, encouraging or requesting covers quite a large swath of action. As noted by scholars such as Professor Ira Robbins, the terms used by courts to describe solicitation's requisite act include, "advising, attempting to persuade another, counseling, encouraging, enticing, entreating, hiring, importuning, inciting, instigating, procuring, requesting, stimulating, and urging."[32] As another example, California's model criminal jury instructions, building off California case law, provide that "to solicit" in the California Penal Code means "to ask, entreat, implore, importune, to make petition to, to plead for, to try to obtain, or to offer or invite another to commit a crime."[33]

The Model Penal Code (a compendium of exemplary crimes with explanations first published in the 1960s in an attempt to reform and standardize American criminal law), plus many states and the military penal code, all utilize a general solicitation statute to criminalize the solicitation of any statutory offense — out of the sense that "[i]f behavior is serious enough to be classed as criminal its solicitation should be punishable"; other jurisdictions limit solicitation to particularly serious and/or violent crimes.[34] As an example of the latter, the federal criminal code's general solicitation statute only criminalizes solicitation of crimes of violence: "Whoever, with intent that another person engage in conduct constituting a felony that has as an element the use, attempted use, or threatened use of physical force against property or against the person of another in violation of the laws of the United States, and under circumstances strongly corroborative of that intent, solicits, commands, induces, or otherwise endeavors to persuade such other person to engage in such conduct, shall be imprisoned."[35]

Additionally, as mentioned above, "[t]here is no requirement that the solicitation result in action by the person solicited or even that such action seem likely at the time of solicitation," with that latter caveat relevant to the below discussion distinguishing solicitation from incitement.[36] As mentioned above, what is at times required, however, is that the intended recipient receive the intended communication. The Model Penal Code does not require such delivery, stipulating instead that, "[i]t is immaterial under Subsection (1) of this Section that the actor fails to communicate with the person he solicits to commit a crime if his conduct was designed to effect such communication."[37] As noted by the drafters of that code, "[t]he crucial manifestation of dangerousness lies in the endeavor to communicate the incriminating message to another person, it being wholly fortuitous whether the message was actually received. Liability should attach, therefore, even though the message is not received by the contemplated recipient."[38] States such as California and New Mexico disagree, requiring that the communication reach the intended recipient; however, failed delivery can constitute an attempted solicitation, if the requisite line between preparation and perpetration is crossed. (Attempt crimes require acts not of mere preparation of crime, but of perpetration of the crime, with the common law employing a host of tests to determine the line between the two concepts. Applied here, the defendant must take a substantial step to effect the transmission of their solicitation in order to be guilty of attempted solicitation in the minority jurisdictions that provide for attempted solicitations.)[39]

When discussing solicitation's required mental state, it must be noted that solicitation is the closest offense to a thought crime in modern US criminal law. While close, it is not a reviled thought crime, as it requires conduct in the form of speech in addition to the required mental state. The most fundamental principle of criminal law holds that crimes must include both an evil mind and evil hand[40] — prohibited conduct (or failure to act when a legal duty to act exists) must be committed with a blameworthy mental state — and both parts of this equation are found in the crime of solicitation. The solicitor cannot simply want someone else to commit a crime (that would be something left in the realm of thoughts, and the law does not yet criminalize mere thoughts); the solicitor must actively encourage, command, or request that someone else commit the crime they desire. While a communicative act is required, it is the solicitor's intent (their mental state) — their conscious objective that the person solicited commit, for example, the solicited murder (or larceny, or tax fraud, etcetera) — that does the heavy lifting in the crime of solicitation to delineate criminal versus noncriminal expression (though the best evidence for that mental state may indeed be the words used to carry that objective into fruition).[41]

The importance of solicitation's *mens rea*, or scienter element (the required mental state) is seen by the fact that the crime requires showing (beyond reasonable doubt) the highest level of moral blameworthiness on the mental state scale. The Model Penal Code requires the communication be made with "the purpose of promoting or facilitating" a crime; at common law and in many states today, solicitation's mental state is referred to as intent, which is met by the mental states of either purposefully or knowingly.[42] Such a stringent scienter requirement makes sense, given that solicitation's primary purpose as an inchoate offense is to provide a basis for law enforcement to intervene early enough to prevent the actual danger of the target offense — this intervention point is when "an individual's actions, though not criminal in themselves, have sufficiently manifested an intent to commit a criminal act."[43]

Criminal Solicitation Versus Incitement: Different Crimes

Incitement and solicitation were conflated throughout common law within the Anglo-American tradition; the terms were used interchangeably to describe the crime of solicitation.[44] Solicitation has long existed in the common law (judge-made law) and had little statutory existence prior to Model Penal Code's codification efforts.[45] Common law solicitations, also referred to as incitements, largely related to breach of the peace and obstruction of justice type crimes, though not exclusively.[46] Today, as explained above, all states and the federal government have some type of statutory criminal solicitation offense that criminalizes encouraging, offering, commanding or requesting another person to commit a crime, with the intent that the target crime be committed; the Court has instructed that solicitation as a criminal speech offense falls into the "speech integral to crime" category of speech that is unprotected by the First Amendment.

Beginning in the late 1960s with *Brandenburg*, the Court has distinguished the crime of incitement from that of solicitation. While placing both categorically outside the protection of the First Amendment, thus allowing them to be punished, the Court has muddied the inchoate crime waters by failing to draw bright lines between the two similar offenses.[47] Specifically, the Court has left unclear when encouragement of illegal activity, to be punishable, must only meet solicitation's two required elements of (1) an act of encouragement/ request with (2) the intent that the person so encouraged/requested carry out the encouraged crime, versus when encouragement of illegal activity must go beyond solicitation's two elements and additionally satisfy *Brandenburg*'s elements of imminence and likelihood of occurrence, in addition to intent that the incited lawlessness be committed, thus becoming the unprotected speech crime of incitement.[48]

Incitement per *Brandenburg* bears the following hallmarks:

> [T]he constitutional guarantees of free speech and free press do not permit a State to forbid or proscribe advocacy of the use of force or of law violation except where such advocacy is directed to inciting or producing imminent lawless action and is likely to incite or produce such action. As we said in *Noto v. United States*, 367 U.S. 290, 297–98 (1961), "the mere abstract teaching of the moral propriety or even moral necessity for a resort to force and violence, is not the same as preparing a group for violent action and steeling it to such action."
> . . . A statute which fails to draw this distinction impermissibly intrudes upon the freedoms guaranteed by the First and Fourteenth Amendments.[49]

Solicitation of crime, as evidenced in the above discussion, contains no requirement that the requested crime occur immediately, nor that there be a reasonable likelihood of said crime occurring; speech asking or encouraging someone else to commit a crime, accompanied by the requisite intent that the counseled crime be committed, is sufficient. As evidenced by the Court's statements in *United States v. Williams*, a 2008 case regarding a federal child pornography solicitation statute, the majority clearly considered incitement as a different crime from solicitation: "[m]any long established criminal proscriptions — such as laws against conspiracy, incitement, and solicitation — criminalize speech (commercial or not) that is intended to induce or commence illegal activities."[50] But how does one know which category a person's encouragement of crime falls into? The *Williams* Court provided no insight into that question, albeit emphasizing, citing to *Brandenburg* and *NAACP v. Claiborne Hardware Co.* for support, that, "[t]o be sure, there remains an important distinction between a proposal to engage in illegal activity and the abstract advocacy of illegality."[51] However, the Court didn't sketch the difference between a proposal and abstract advocacy; that is, when a proposal to engage in illegal activity only has to meet solicitation's act and intent elements to be punishable, versus *Brandenburg*'s more onerous test for incitement, because instead of a concrete proposal, there is ambiguous or "abstract advocacy" of illegality.

To draw the line distinguishing criminal solicitation, criminal incitement, and protected so-called advocacy from one another using the Court's rationale in *Williams*, one must ascertain the qualitative difference between the two expressive activities of advocating and proposing, with only the former requiring *Brandenburg*'s heightened requirements of imminency and likelihood of occurrence in order to be punishable. Does the *Brandenburg* qualifier "abstract" aid in this analysis? If there is no real difference between encouragement and advocacy, when does advocacy as encouragement to future criminal action qualify simply as solicitation, and when does advocacy as encouragement instead qualify as potential incitement, with the latter receiving heightened First Amendment protection through *Brandenburg*?

An answer, though not a fully satisfactory one, can be found by examining the specificity involved in solicitations versus the general nature of the advocacy speech at issue in *Brandenburg*. As best argued by First Amendment scholar Professor Eugene Volokh, "The line between protected abstract advocacy and unprotected solicitation must instead turn on specificity: solicitation should be limited to directly, specifically, and purposefully encouraging people to commit a particular crime."[52] The requirement of such narrow specificity for solicitation, with its absence triggering *Brandenburg*'s guardrails designed to protect lawful advocacy of lawlessness, can be seen in the Court's treatment of the speech at issue in cases such as *Hess v. Indiana*. In *Hess*, the appellant's loud statement that "we'll take the fucking street later" — made during an antiwar protest at a college campus as police were trying to clear the street blockaded by fellow protestors — was on its face and in that context not a specific request or encouragement to anyone in particular to commit a specific criminal act. The Court instead treated this statement as abstract advocacy to commit lawlessness, thus requiring *Brandenburg*'s reasonable likelihood, imminency and intent requirements to kick in (the intent being the same as for solicitation). The first two elements were not met, thus making his speech protected by the First Amendment. The speech in *Brandenburg* itself was similarly general (unspecific) in the acts it was advocating — it was not aimed at any one person, nor did it describe a particular crime desired for commission: "[w]e're not a revengent organization, but if our President, our Congress, our Supreme Court, continues to suppress the white, Caucasian race, it's possible that there might have to be some revengeance taken."[53]

Solicitation, in contrast and as noted earlier, is not a solo crime: it includes, for example, solicitation to commit murder, or commit bank robbery, or to commit mutiny. It is always a direct request, order, encouragement, etcetera of someone else to commit a specific separate crime, and usually of an identifiable solicitee. This specificity requirement distinguishing a proposal of criminality (solicitation) from abstract advocacy of lawlessness (triggering *Brandenburg* requirements to become punishable as incitement) runs parallel to the specificity requirement likewise required in true threats. Punishable true threats, if made with at least reckless disregard that they'll be taken as a real threat, are only those "serious expression[s] of an intent to commit an act of unlawful violence to a particular individual or group of individuals."[54] This particularity echoes the specificity required in solicitation of crime in contrast to protected abstract advocacy of lawlessness.

Yet specificity is not the sole distinguishing factor between speech that is solicitation of a crime and speech that is abstract advocacy that, to be punishable, requires *Brandenburg*'s extra elements. The Court has acknowledged that with protected abstract advocacy (and its criminal counterpart of incitement), context matters. The speech at issue that triggers *Brandenburg*'s guardrails is seemingly always uttered in a context that resonates with the values aminating the First Amendment: as mentioned earlier, this constitutional protection was designed to protect that speech necessary for healthy functioning of a pluralistic democracy. The Court has noted that, regarding incitement, that "we recognized that incitement to disorder is commonly a hair's-breadth away from political 'advocacy' — and particularly from strong protests against the government and prevailing social order."[55] The cases in which the Court has struggled with incitement's lines have all involved such contexts.

Closing Thoughts

Solicitation to commit murder, or another specific crime, can occur in a political context, or in one in which speakers are protesting hot-button social issues; such context by itself doesn't magically transform said speech into protected abstract advocacy. However, such a context plus lack of specificity regarding crime urged, and lack of particular individual(s) to whom the conduct is urged, are strong indicators of protected abstract advocacy. While such speech may be potentially harmful, the late great Professor Frederick Schauer noted that "robust free speech systems protect speech not because it is harmless, but despite the harm it may cause."[56]

Notes

1. Brandenburg v. Ohio, 395 U.S. 444, 447 (1969) (per curiam).
2. Michael Kent Curtis, "Vallandigham, and Anti-War Speech in the Civil War," *William & Mary Bill of Rights Journal* 7, no. 1, (1998): 121–22.
3. Chaplinsky v. New Hampshire, 315 U.S. 568, 572 (1942).
4. Geoffrey R. Stone, *Perilous Times: Free Speech in Wartime: From the Sedition Act of 1798 to the War on Terrorism* (W. W. Norton, 2004); see Dennis J. Hutchinson, "Lincoln the Dictator," *South Dakota Law Review* 55, no. 2 (2010): 294.
5. Kenneth Lasson, "To Stimulate, Provoke, or Incite? Hate Speech and the First Amendment," *St. Thomas Law Review* 3, no. 1 (1991): 53.
6. Eugene Volokh, "The Speech Integral to Criminal Conduct Exception," *Cornell Law Review* 101, no. 4 (2016): 986, http://scholarship.law.cornell.edu/clr/vol101/iss4/3/. ("Given that speech sometimes both constitutes advocacy of social change and helps cause illegal conduct, the question is where the rule of law calls for the line to be drawn.") [hereinafter Volokh, Speech].
7. U.S. Const. amend. I.
8. Tinker v. Des Moines Indep. Cmty. Sch. Dist., 393 U.S. 503, 508 (1969).
9. United States v. Stevens, 559 U.S. 460, 468 (2010) citing Ashcroft v. ACLU, 535 U.S. 564, 573 (2002).
10. Stevens, 559 U.S. at 468 (quoting Chaplinsky, 315 U.S. at 572).
11. New York v. Ferber, 458 U.S. 747, 761–62 (1982).
12. United States v. Williams, 553 U.S. 285, 297 (2008).
13. Stevens, 559 U.S. at 468.
14. R. Kent Greenawalt, *Speech, Crime, and the Uses of Language* (Oxford University Press, 1989), 6, 85.
15. United States v. Barnett, 667 F.2d 835, 842 (9th Cir. 1982)
16. Miller v. California, 413 U.S. 15 (1973) (establishing a three-part test for determining what materials fall into the category of obscenity, thus unprotected by the First Amendment).
17. Greenawalt, *Speech, Crime, and The Uses of Language*, 7n14 (quoting Frederick Schauer), *Free Speech: A Philosophical Enquiry* (Cambridge University Press, 1982). Chaplinsky, 315 U. S. at 571–72 (1942).
18. Chaplinsky v. New Hampshire, 315 U.S. 568, 571–72 (1942).
19. Giboney v. Empire Storage & Ice Co., 336 U.S. 490, 502, (1949).
20. Virginia v. Black, 538 U.S. 343, 359 (2003)
21. Counterman v. Colorado, 600 U.S. 66, 69 (2023).
22. Counterman, 600 U.S. at 81.
23. Model Penal Code and Commentaries, Art. 5 at 293 (1985).
24. Williams, 553 U.S. at 300.

25 Benjamin Means, "Criminal Speech and the First Amendment," *Marquette Law Review* 86, no. 3 (Winter 2002), https://scholarship.law.marquette.edu/mulr/vol86/iss3/3/.
26 Brandenburg, 395 U.S. at 447.
27 Joshua Dressler and Stephen P. Harvey, *Criminal Law Cases and Materials*, 8th ed. (West Academic Publishing, 2018), 820 ("At common law the actus reus for solicitation can take the form of inviting, requesting, commanding, hiring or encouraging another to commit a particular offense. The mens rea of solicitation encompasses (1) the intent to perform the acts constituting the solicitation and (2) the specific intent that the other person commit the solicited offense."); see Ira P. Robbins, "Double Inchoate Crimes," *Harvard Journal on Legislation* 26, no. 1 (Winter 1989) at 29, https://journals.law.harvard.edu/jol/wp-content/uploads/sites/86/2023/02/26HarvJonLegis1.pdf (defining solicitation as synonymous with incitement, in that "[s]olicitation, or incitement, is the act of trying to persuade another to commit a crime that the solicitor desires and intends to have committed").
28 For an example of accomplice liability tying a solicitor to a target crime, see Cal. Penal Code §31 (2008) ("All persons concerned in the commission of a crime, whether it be felony or misdemeanor, and whether they directly commit the act constituting the offense, or aid and abet in its commission, or, not being present, have advised and encouraged its commission, and all persons counseling, advising, or encouraging children under the age of fourteen years, or persons who are mentally incapacitated, to commit any crime, or who, by fraud, contrivance, or force, occasion the drunkenness of another for the purpose of causing him to commit any crime, or who, by threats, menaces, command, or coercion, compel another to commit any crime, are principals in any crime so committed").
29 See Larry Alexander and Kimberly D. Kessler, "Mens Rea and Inchoate Crimes," *Journal of Criminal Law & Criminology* 87, no. 4 (1996–1997): 1139 (defining inchoate crimes as those "crimes that are preliminary to bringing about the harms that are the criminal law's ultimate concerns").
30 See generally Williams, 553 U.S. at 300 (2008).
31 People v. Saephanh, 80 Cal.App.4th 451, 458–59 (2000).
32 Robbins, *Double Inchoate Crimes*, 29n27.
33 Judicial Council of California Criminal Jury Instructions No. 441 (2023) citing California decisions including People v. Gordon 47 Cal.App.3d 465, 472 1975) and People v. Phillips 70 Cal.App.2d 449, 453 (1945).
34 Model Penal Code §5.02 cmt. at 370 (1985).
35 18 U.S.C. § 373 (1994). In enacting this crime, Congress believed that "a person who makes a serious effort to induce another person to commit a crime of violence is a clearly dangerous person and that his act deserves criminal sanctions whether or not the crime of violence is

actually committed." S. Rep. No. 98-225, at 308 (1984), reprinted in 1984 U.S.C.C.A.N. (98 Stat.) 3487.
36 S. Rep. No. 98-225, at 308 (1984), reprinted in 1984 U.S.C.C.A.N. (98 Stat.) 3487.
37 Model Penal Code §5.02(2) (1985).
38 Model Penal Code §5.02 cmt. at 382 (1983).
39 State v. Cotton, 109 N.M. 769 (1990); see also Saephanh at 451 (2000) (finding that the letter soliciting deadly harm to an unborn fetus was not solicitation given that it was intercepted by prison authorities and never reached its intended recipients).
40 Morissette v. United States, 342 U.S. 246, 341–42 (1952). ("A relation between some mental element and punishment for a harmful act . . . has afforded the rational basis for a tardy and unfinished substitution of deterrence and reformation in place of retaliation and vengeance as the motivation for public prosecution.")
41 John W. Curran, "Solicitation — A Substantive Crime," *Minnesota Law Review* 17 (1933): 499, https://scholarship.law.umn.edu/mlr/1623/. ("The corpus delicti of the crime is the evil intent of the solicitor coupled with the act of solicitation.")
42 Model Penal Code §5.02 (1985) ("It is not enough for a person to be aware that his words may lead to a criminal act or even to be quite sure they will do so; it must be the actor's purpose that the crime be committed.")
43 Robbins, "Double Inchoate Crimes," 7n27 ("potential harm can be prevented, as the person's dangerousness has been manifested").
44 I. R. Scott, "The Common Law Offence of Incitement to Commit Crime," *Anglo-American Law Review* 4, no. 3, (1975): 290n1 (noting that, "where a crime is not in fact committed, those who have unsuccessfully solicited or incited another to commit it are, at common law, guilty of an indictable misdemeanor").
45 Model Penal Code §5.02 cmt. at 367 (1985).
46 See generally Curran, "Solicitation," 501n41(interestingly noting that "[a]t common law it was a crime to solicit or invoke evil spirits to cast a spell or give the evil eye.").
47 Brandenburg, 395 U.S at 444; the Court has put Brandenburg to work in only two subsequent cases of Hess v. Indiana, 414 U.S. 105, 108–9 (1973) and NAACP v. Claiborne Hardware Co., 458 U.S. 886, 927–28 (1982).
48 Williams, 553 U.S. at 298–99; see Brandenburg, 395 U.S. at 447–48 (1969).
49 Brandenburg, 395 U.S at 444.
50 Williams, 552 U.S. at 298.
51 Williams, 553 U.S. at 298–99; see Claiborne Hardware Co., 458 U.S. at 928–929 ("[f]or liability to be imposed by reason of association alone, it is necessary to establish that the group itself possessed unlawful goals and that the individual held a specific intent to further these illegal aims" and

also finding that speech must result in "imminent disorder" if it was to be unprotected by the First Amendment).
52 Brief for Professor Eugene Volokh as Amicus Curiae in Support of Neither Party at 4, United States v. Sineneng-Smith, 140 S. Ct. 1575 (2020) (No. 19-67).
53 Brandenburg, 395 U.S at 446.
54 Black, 538 U.S. at 359.
55 Counterman, 600 U.S. at 81.
56 See Frederick Schauer, "Uncoupling Free Speech," *Columbia Law Review* 92, no. 6 (1992): 1321.

Chapter Five

Words Behind Walls

Examining the Line Between Incitement and Administrative Overreach in Prisons

Shavonnie R. Carthens[1]

As of the writing of this chapter there are 158,842 people incarcerated in federal prisons across the United States,[2] and there are many more prisoners housed in state correctional facilities. America's prisons rely on the work of administrators to ensure their function, internal security, and punitive and rehabilitative purposes. To that end, wardens, and those who work under their authority, must make decisions about how to ensure that correctional aims are carried out, with both precision and efficiency.

In examining their actions in banning literature from entering the prison population there are some glaring defects, namely, the overboard censorship of literary content on the basis that such materials would impede rehabilitative aims or diminish prison security.[3] In particular, censorship actions suggest that certain categories of content are considered contraband,[4] incite violence, or diminish the security of the prison environment.[5]

Contraband in prisons is a reality, and responses to the presence of these items should be taken seriously. Books that detail how to make bombs or other weapons should be banned, but these examples are on the extreme end of the censorship spectrum. Unfortunately, other books that offer literary, historical, or political value have been excluded as well, including *Slavery by Another Name* by award winning journalist Douglas Blackmon,[6] *The New Jim Crow: Mass Incarceration in the Age of Colorblindness* by Michelle Alexander,[7] and Toni Morrison's *The Bluest Eye*.[8] I question whether these titles, or the presence of *The Autobiography of Malcolm X*[9] or *Nutrition for Dummies*,[10] would hinder a warden's ability to ensure prison safety. Will these books lead to incitement to any greater degree than James Battersby's *The Holy Book of Adolf Hitler*,[11] which has been approved in US prisons? Does a book written in a prisoners' native language mean that it is in code that may impact security?[12] If not, then these acts of censorship are overbroad, and indicative of the type of administrative overreach that strips the prison population of the guaranteed protection of freedom of speech and expression under the First Amendment.[13]

This chapter will call into question whether incarcerated individuals' rights to receive books and other literary materials are wrongfully abridged by the unjustified wielding of "incitement" as a censorship tool by prison officials. The following discussion will: (1) identify the detrimental impacts of book bans on the prison population, (2) survey the rights of the incarcerated under the First Amendment to receive information and read, (3) explore the realities of book banning as a biproduct of the use of "incitement" as a tool for overbroad censorship, (4) detail reasons why administrative censorship is an exaggerated response that goes beyond justifiable boundaries, and (5) call for enhanced procedural safeguards to address administrative overreach, and shield the First Amendment rights of the incarcerated.

Detrimental Impacts on the Prison Population

The Supreme Court has held that prisons may only lawfully ban a publication if doing so furthers a legitimate penological objective.[14] A prison inmate's rights flow to the demarcation of policies that support legitimate penological interest, but not beyond.[15] The penological interests most frequently cited by prison officials are institutional security and rehabilitation.[16] These stated interests are often in direct contention with studies that show that increased education and literacy lead to better rehabilitative outcomes.[17] Limited access to a diverse range of content hinders incarcerated people from developing a sense of self-governance, experiencing a state of self-realization, and preparing to succeed postrelease.

Cultivating self-governance skills requires that one can participate in the making of laws the govern society through participation in public discourse and debate.[18] Reading books such as *The New Jim Crow*, arms formerly incarcerated people with language needed to participate in such conversations. This is especially important for incarcerated minority populations. Of the incarcerated individuals in federal prisons 38.6 percent of them are Black.[19] Repeatedly books of interest for this incarcerated population have been targeted for censorship.[20] Books related to civil rights, criticisms of correctional institutions, and examinations of American history are frequently in the "bull's-eye" for censorship by prison wardens and their subordinates.[21] Unwarranted censorship by prison officials erects barriers between prisoners and information that is most valuable,[22] such as the identification of rights violations, including those secured by the First Amendment.

Exaggerated censorship also interferes with a prisoner's state of self-realization, which only increases due to the demoralizing aspects of the prison environment.[23] Access to information from outside of prison walls is needed to help incarcerated people acquire knowledge and skills that will give them a window into the world they will inhabit postrelease.[24] In order to wholly participate in a democratic society upon release, former inmates need to understand the ecology of their new environment, including social, political, legal, economic, and cultural changes,[25] as well as knowledge and skills that will give them a window to the world.[26] Therefore, foundational underpinnings of the First Amendment support the idea that realizing one's autonomy is important to the human experience.[27] Specifically, protecting freedom of speech and self-expression is necessary for allowing one to develop self-respect and realize autonomy in making choices for themselves.[28]

Last, one of the most effective ways to reduce recidivism[29] is through education programs, and exposure to new ideas.[30] Prison programs that focus on education, life and social skills ready incarcerated men and women to transfer that knowledge in a meaningful way following reentry into society,[31] and educational opportunities reduce health problems associated with harmful and risky lifestyles, poor housing conditions, and general social marginalization experienced by former prisoners upon re-entry.[32] Indeed, receiving an education in prison decreases the likelihood that someone will return after they are released.[33] Further, for every dollar spent educating someone in prison, taxpayers save five dollars on reduced reincarceration costs.[34] Yet, prison officials continue to indiscriminately ban books that may relieve some of the anxiety associated with adjusting within, and positively contributing to, the world following imprisonment.

Prisoners' First Amendment Right to Receive and Read Information

Protections for Speech in Prisons

Incarcerated people, as the remainder of the American population, can still claim protections provided by the First Amendment,[35] with freedom of speech and freedom of the press being among those freedoms.[36] The Supreme Court has held that these rights "encompass the right to receive information and ideas, which includes the right to read."[37] There are categories of speech that are unprotected, or less protected, with incitement to illegal activity being one of those.[38] The possibility of incitement within prisons is of greater concern than in other environments, as mentioned above. As is the case for government-controlled facilities, such as schools and military bases, prisons belong to a category of properties where courts have historically sided with the government in regulation of speech in those facilities.[39] While content-based distinctions within strata of unprotected speech must meet strict scrutiny,[40] such is not the case with speech in government institutions such as prisons.[41] The Supreme Court reasoned that in these government properties, administrators must be allowed deference in determining the type of speech that is allowed because they are in the best position to anticipate security challenges and take action to avoid or limit complications.[42] In short, prisoners do not retain rights that are inconsistent with their status as prisoners or with the legitimate penological interests of the institution.[43] Notwithstanding, even in the face of limited rights, it is well established that the First Amendment protects the right to receive information in prisons.[44]

The Supreme Court's approach to the role of prison administration in many ways mirrors the Court's approach to deference in other contexts. This deference is well established in case law[45] and through legislative action.[46] In *Chevron* the US Supreme Court held that where a federal statute is ambiguous a court should defer to the interpretation made by the relevant agency.[47] Although *Chevron* was highly criticized for its seeming contradiction of the Administrative Procedure Act,[48] and then overturned by *Loper Bright Enterprises v. Raimondo* (2024),[49] the interpretative rights and spirit of deference afforded to administrative bodies will likely continue to thrive within the prison administrative complex.[50]

Incitement, Prison Security, and Precedent

The Supreme Court's position of deference to prison wardens has manifested in several book censorship decisions.[51] In addition to case law, the law around book bans within the federal prison system derives from the enactment of Title 28, specifically 28 C.F.R. § 540.71. Section 540.71 details the extent to which prisoners may receive publications, as well as the standard by which those publications may be rejected.[52] For example, at medium- and high-security institutions soft-cover publications are allowed from the publisher, book club, or bookstore.[53] At minimum-security institutions and low-security institutions inmates are allowed to receive softcover publications (other than newspapers) from any source.[54]

The application of the clear and present danger test in prisons was explained in *Sostre v. Otis* (1971), where a federal trial court held that certain literature may pose such a clear and present danger to the security of the prison or to the rehabilitation of prisoners, which would justify censorship.[55] In *Procunier v. Martinez* (1974) the Court used the theory of judicial restraint for First Amendment challenges by federal and state inmates.[56] This case affirmed the human rights of inmates[57] but left questions regarding the concrete procedural safeguards needed to ensure that prisoners' First Amendment rights are preserved.[58] It is this refinement of procedural safeguards that is most needed. The most striking limitation of the *Procunier* decision was that the Court offered no distinct standard of review for subsequent courts to apply.[59]

Shortly thereafter, federal regulation 28 C.F.R. § 540.71 was enacted for the purpose of establishing "procedures to determine if a publication is detrimental to the security, discipline, or good order of the institution or if it might facilitate criminal activity."[60] However, decisions on which publications are accepted remain in the hands of wardens and their downlines.[61] In the language of § 540.71, there is some recognition of the need to protect the First Amendment right of incarcerated individuals. Based on the language of § 540.71 wardens, although in the power position, must act within boundaries.[62] For example, a warden can only reject a publication if it is determined that it is "detrimental to the security, good order, or discipline of the institution or if it might facilitate criminal activity."[63] Nevertheless, a warden may not reject a publication "solely because its content is religious, philosophical, political, social or sexual, or because its content is unpopular or repugnant."[64] The statute enumerates circumstances that allow for rejection, including, but not limited to, depictions of weapons or incendiary devices,[65] depictions of prison escapes,[66] books written in code,[67] or works that "depict, describes or encourages activities which may lead to the use of physical violence or group disruption."[68] These limiting provisions appear to evince an intent to prevent arbitrary book banning decisions, but the discussion below will highlight gaping holes that still allow for censorship decisions that are overbroad and extremely fluid in application.

In *Bell v. Wolfish* (1979), the Court held that prisoners, including pretrial detainees, have no constitutional right to receive packages from outside of prison walls, in light of the prison's greater interest in security and order.[69] The Court found that security officials exhibited sound discretion when applying a regulation that was "reasonably related" to security concerns.[70] Later, the Court in *Turner v. Safley* (1987) aimed to resolve confusion over the appropriate standard by stating, "When a prison regulation impinges on inmates' constitutional rights, the regulation is valid if it is reasonably related to legitimate penological interests."[71] This desire to clarify the standard resulted in a four-part test for evaluating First Amendment challenges in prisons.[72] First, the test requires that there must be a "valid, rational connection" between the prison regulation and the legitimate governmental interest put forth to justify it.[73] Second, the Court must determine whether there are alternative means of expressing the right that remain open to prison inmates.[74] Third, the Court should consider whether accommodating the asserted right would have a significant ripple effect on fellow inmates or prison staff.[75] Finally, the Court should consider that the feasibility of ready alternatives is to serve as proof of the regulations' reasonableness.[76] These factors lay the groundwork for balancing the prisoners' rights against the institution's legitimate penological interests.[77] Although *Turner* calls for a balancing of factors, when relying on *Turner* the Court has consistently deferred to legislatures and prison officials, placing a heavy weight on the rational basis approach in the first factor, rather than a true factor-balancing approach.[78]

Thornburgh v. Abbott (1989)[79] put a finer point on the *Turner* test's application to alleged violations of prisoners' fundamental rights.[80] It specifically addressed 28 C.F.R. § 54.71(b) and the ability of prison officials to reject publications as a matter of institutional security.[81] In *Thornburgh* a class of inmates and publishers brought a First Amendment claim, mounting a facial challenge to regulations as well as a challenge to the application of the regulation to forty-six specific publications rejected by the Federal Bureau of Prisons.[82] The Court found that the appropriate interpretation of the *Turner* test is whether the regulations are "reasonably related to legitimate penological interests,"[83] and noted that §54.71 includes safeguards for those outside of prisons and for prisoners as well — again highlighting that prison officials are in the best position to determine how the receipt of materials impacts the security of the prison atmosphere.[84] This standard was reinforced in *Shaw v. Murphy*, where the Court held that speech activities[85] of prisoners related to the First Amendment, would be upheld if the regulation is reasonably related to a legitimate penological interest.[86]

Incitement as a Tool for Exaggerated Censorship Responses

Evidence of Books as Contraband

Since *Turner* (1987) the Supreme Court has relied on the four-part test which ultimately balances the prisoner's rights against legitimate penological interests.[87] However, the extent of the dangers that written materials pose to penological interests is not well documented. In most jurisdictions, there is no requirement that prison wardens offer reasons for bans that only underscore the illegitimacy of a substantial number of book ban decisions. Both precedent and public outcry suggest that when prisoners are denied access to books, that denial is often linked to the content of the books themselves — not to verifiable reports that books are contraband materials that diminish prison security. A report by PEN America[88] commented on two types of book possession denials, content-based, and content-neutral book bans.

The former category where there is a fear of violence or group disruption due to the content within books relies heavily on the reader's perception. Books banned due to content may contain elements that include depictions of violence or language perceived to encourage group disruption or anti-authority attitudes or actions, racial animus or language alleged to encourage hatred.[89] Whether or not these materials pose any real threat to safety or security within prisons is based on the subjective opinion of prison officials. In these instances, the usual argument is that the content of the books themselves are the potential cause of incitement.[90] We can surmise that those wardens who limit access to these books are not doing so as a result of tested hypotheses that establish a verifiable presumption that literary content materially, or at least peripherally, degrades prison security. For example, the North Carolina American Civil Liberties Union wrote a letter urging state officials to remove *The New Jim Crow* from the banned books list in state prisons.[91] It was removed from the list a day after officials received their letter.[92]

Content-neutral book bans would result in book rejections regardless of the content. The justification in those instances is that the books may be a tool for bringing in contraband. It is this category of concern that supports the proposition that book content might excite violence because the book itself may introduce materials that create security risks within prisons.[93]

Such fears are difficult, if not impossible, to substantiate. The information that is available may be outdated or studies on the impact of materials on prison safety may not be available.[94] What is clear is that definitions of "contraband" will vary across jurisdictions. Investigators reviewed data from forty-four states and found that cell phone recoveries were particularly high in southern states, with up to one phone confiscated per three incarcerated individuals in South Carolina.[95] In addition to cell phones, there are also major issues with the dissemination of drugs and alcohol,[96] which create prison economies that decrease the security of prisons.[97] Further, drugs and alcohol can continue or help others develop substance abuse problems.[98] These are legitimate concerns, yet, when we look to research around the most common sources of contraband, and items that threaten prison security, books are not listed as posing significant dangers to prison security.[99]

If the tangential argument that books may be used to smuggle other contraband into prisons is allowed, this suggestion fails to consider how one might access literary materials without the physical medium. One glaring possibility is that technology may be used to mitigate the prospect of contraband smuggling, while preserving prison populations' access to books, magazines and other written materials. As an illustration, in 2018 the Pennsylvania Department of Corrections switched to e-books, which required that incarcerated individuals access those materials with a tablet. While the structure of Pennsylvania's system was highly problematic, because it was cost-prohibitive and highly censorial, it stands as evidence that there are ways to diminish concerns about books being the access point for contraband.

There is not compelling evidence-based information that suggests that books related to history, culture, and political structures are a major content or contraband-related[100] concern in prisons. Without this evidence, it appears that much of the censorship of prison officials is an exaggerated response, an administrative overreach that flies in the face of the First Amendment rights of incarcerated individuals.

The Reality of Book Censorship and Administrative Overreach

Prison wardens, and their reports, go beyond the action necessary to ensure prison security. There are some key markers of administrative overreach in book censorship actions in America's prisons. First, prison wardens act without an adequate review system. It is known that the number of banned materials is widespread due to the Supreme Court's policy of prison deference.[101] Unchecked deference in these systems is created by the decision-making powers resting solely in the hands of the warden (or the warden's downline), and this decision-making, absent procedural safeguards, allows for constitutional violations.[102] There is no clear system within prisons for evaluating the potential for a book or piece of literature to incite violence within the prison population or disturb the security of prisons. Censorship decisions go largely unchallenged, in part, because the Supreme Court grants wardens, and prison employees, a wide deference in determining which books should be approved and their decisions are overwhelmingly upheld.[103]

Second, a related matter is that the prison population faces several administrative barriers in seeking judicial review of these decisions. Although case law provides a foundation that allows for administrative overreach sparked by unchecked deference, these cases do not stand alone in propping up unjust censorship. The holding in *Turner*,[104] coupled with the Prison Litigation Reform Act's (PLRA) requirement of exhaustion,[105] has made it extremely difficult for prisoners to seek remedy through the courts. According to the PLRA, prisoners must exhaust all remedies before filing a First Amendment claim.[106] Many people incarcerated in prisons may not exhaust the administrative process; cutting them off from redress through the courts.[107] Meeting the exhaustion requirement can be cost prohibitive. In Kansas, if a prisoner wants to challenge a book ban, they must pay to ship a copy of the rejected book to the Kansas Department of Corrections headquarters.[108] Assuming that this individual is able to exhaust administrative appeals, if he does not see success at the administrative level, only then may he bring a First Amendment challenge in the courts.

Third, another alarming characteristic of book censorship practices is that unchecked deference contradicts the intolerance the Supreme Court has for prior restraints. Prior restraints are detrimental and have traditionally been viewed as indicative of anti–First Amendment actions.[109] Simply put, a prior restraint is "an administrative or judicial order that prevents particular communication from occurring."[110] The function of book bans aligns with this definition and is analogous to a licensing scheme. Book banning systems in prisons, such as within the federal system under §54.71, blocks the receipt of pieces of literature before a prisoner has an opportunity to read them. The Court said that systems of prior restraints of expression come with a heavy presumption against constitutionality.[111] Prison wardens have not overcome this presumption and are not required to do so because they enjoy judicial deference.

Arguing that administrative action constitutes an unconstitutional prior restraint may seem to be a stretch, but current book banning practices are a dangerous biproduct of unfettered administrative deference. A limitation of speech without knowledge of content or impact is likely to cover a greater swath of speech without access to procedural review. The Supreme Court frowned on prior restraints as a particularly disturbing form of speech regulation because of such broad impact.[112] In this case, the broad impact is that books, and other forms of literature, that could aid in security and rehabilitation never reach prisoners. A prisoner may never read children's the book titled *My Daddy Is in Jail* by Janet M. Bender,[113] Dante Alighieri's *Inferno*,[114] *To Kill a Mockingbird* by Harper Lee,[115] or Alice Walker's *The Color Purple*.[116]

As a fourth characteristic of book censorship, the categorical limitation on expression also limits the opportunity for public appraisal and analysis.[117] Public appraisal is of utmost importance in the case of book censorship. Some of the compelling critiques of prison banning decisions have occurred due to public outcry and advocacy. Of note were the public protestations that forced the hands of prison wardens to restore access to *Uncle Tom's Cabin* by Harriet Beecher Stowe.[118]

Potential Solutions and Procedural Safeguards

It is natural to think of solutions to the problem of book censorship and prison administrative overreach. Although the Supreme Court clarified the standard of review in *Turner*,[119] there is a deference created by the law, and administrative hurdles[120] that ensure prisoners are rarely successful in challenging book bans. This is due to the "reasonableness" standard, which is an easily manageable standard for prison officials to satisfy.[121] As a remedy, the most immediate thought for many scholars is to change the standard of review to one that requires a more heightened level of scrutiny.[122] This remedy would require a significant shift in the Court's application of the *Turner*[123] standard, or the application of "rational basis with a bite."[124] This position argues that by the nature of the prisoner classification their constitutional rights have been abridged; therefore, to abridge those rights to an even greater extent requires a heightened level of scrutiny.[125] I am also interested in how a new standard might emerge in light of the Supreme Court's decision in *Counterman v. Colorado*.[126] When reviewing whether a book ban decision was a justified use of discretion, in response to concerns of incitement to violence, the Court might be informed by whether the book's language poses a "true threat" to prison security and safety. Perhaps a review of censorship decisions, which looks to the speaker's conscious disregard that their words might harm another,[127] might add color to determinations of whether prisoner administrators' book banning decisions are constitutional.

Ultimately, I agree that the standard needs revision, but I think that such a modification is not probable. Beyond looking for the Supreme Court to change course, I think more ground-level action is needed to address the drawbacks of unregulated administrative deference through fortified procedural safeguards that could bring consistency and transparency to the book banning process. A large part of the battle for access to information begins with a revision of the review process, and a removal of the systemic barriers that make challenging book ban decisions insurmountable.

The first barrier is a lack of transparency regarding how censorship policies are implemented or reviewed.[128] It is difficult to track censorship practices, and the true range of unjust censorship practices may be unknown. In fact, many state corrections systems do not publicly report the list of acceptable publications.[129] Only Pennsylvania and Washington State publish their banned books list online, and Florida currently leads the nation with the most banned books.[130] However, nonprofit organizations have been able to obtain book ban lists and information through interviews with incarcerated people and formal requests to the prison system.[131] Even among states that are more forthcoming with information, they can only disclose their lists as the result of Freedom of Information Act (FOIA) requests from the media or prisoners' rights organizations.[132]

Additionally, a second systemic issue is that book banning decisions are inconsistent. The process for banning books varies from prison system to prison system. Policies may be created on the institution level, meaning that books allowed at one facility may be banned at another facility.[133] These various policies create overlapping types of censorship, as there may be policies that are only institution-specific, as well as differing state or federal censorship policies.[134] Due to the level of deference given to prison officials, they can usually find some way to link a book's rejection to security interests, no matter how tenuous that connection may be.[135]

There are several ways to procedurally address transparency and consistency. Book banning processes could be more transparent through revisions to policies that govern prison operations. Such revisions would help to guard against arbitrary decisions. Even requiring prison officials to identify the reason why a title is censored due to incitement creates a level of accountability that is absent from the current system. Training review staff on the historical, cultural, or political significance of certain materials would be beneficial as well.

As a more ordered approach to solidifying procedural safeguards, I would call for the creation of federal and state prison censorship commissions, that operate outside of the corrections system. The commissions would oversee access to information issues including, but not limited to, review of book banning decisions. This commission would follow the model exemplified in censorship boards that allow prior review of movies before they are released into the community.[136] Due to the need to make more timely decisions in the prison environment, review of banning decisions could immediately be escalated to the commission for review.

The commission would hold administrative hearings when a prisoner claims she was denied access to materials due to some misapplication of the *Turner* standard or an unsupported claim that the material had potential to "incite violence." The incarcerated claimant would be able to file an "access to information claim" with the commission from the outset. However, a claimant who is unsuccessful before the commission would still have an opportunity to file a claim in a court of law alleging First Amendment violations.

To address the potential for bias and conflicts of interest, the commission would operate independent of any bureau of prisons and be an objective arbiter during ban review proceedings, while appreciating the need for administrative decision making in lieu of immediate litigation. Moreover, the commission would have members who represent diverse ranges of experiences and knowledge regarding the books — their literary, educational, rehabilitative merits, as well as the potential implications of information not being available to the prison population. This commission panel of course would also consider any possible threat posed to administrator's ability to maintain safety and security within the prison population. It is also imperative that the commission include a representative(s) who appreciates the role that racial bias plays in some banning decisions, and members should be vetted on a rolling basis to determine conflicts of interest that might influence their decision making. Finally, the commission would have an outreach and education arm that is responsible for overseeing the training of prison administration and staff.

Conclusion

Despite evidence that reading, and prison education programs, reduce recidivism and help former incarcerated citizens thrive upon release,[137] prison officials continue to use their power to deny incarcerated people access to books and other reading materials. The role of the prisoner administrator is undoubtedly challenging in that they must ensure safety in prisons for prisoners, staff, and members of the public. While they should be afforded discretion to determine how to best carry out their duties, acting without accountability for violating First Amendment rights is unacceptable. Behind the armor provided by legal precedent prison officials claim that the censorship of literature is necessary to ensure the security of prisons and further rehabilitation efforts, but this is often done in a way that is overbroad. The most troubling aspect of book censorship in prisons is that administrative overreach, justified by fears of "incitement to violence," is largely unsubstantiated. Through their decisions to ban literature, without evidence that these works would pose a significant security risk, prison officials are violating the First Amendment, and incarcerated individuals suffer, owing to the inability to access knowledge and participate in the public discourse afforded to all Americans.

On a societal level the entire United States population suffers because we are deprived of the contributions to public discourse that are never fully realized once these individuals are reintegrated into the free population. Additional procedural safeguards are needed to strike a balance between the charge to prison administrators to secure penal institutions and protecting incarcerated individuals' right to receive and read information of literary, social, historical, and political significance.

Notes

1. Assistant professor of law, University of Kentucky, J. David Rosenberg College of Law. I would like to thank those who have reviewed and provided helpful feedback that influenced my work on this chapter, especially: Cassie Chambers Armstrong, Daniel J. Canon, Eric Kasper, Ariana Levinson, Kelly Meurer, Sara Ochs, Cedric Merlin Powell, Christopher "CJ" Ryan, JoAnne Sweeny, and members of the Lutie A. Lytle Collective.
2. "Agency Report," Federal Bureau of Prisons, accessed October 25, 2024. https://www.bop.gov/about/agency/.
3. Procunier v. Martinez, 416 U.S. 396, 404–15 (1974); Turner v. Safley. 482 U.S. 78 (1987).
4. Bell v. Wolfish, 441 U.S. 520 (1979).
5. Procunier, 404–15.
6. "Melvin v. Thomas: Prison Ban on "Slavery by Another Name" Equal Justice Institute, accessed April 2, 2022, https://eji.org/cases/melvin-v-thomas/; Alicia Bianco, "Prisoners Fundamental Right to Read: Courts Should Ensure that Rational Basis Is Truly Rational,"*Roger Williams University Law Review* 21 (2016): 1–44.
7. "The New Jim Crow," The Marshall Project, accessed April 24, 2023, https://www.themarshallproject.org/records/5217-the-new-jim-crow.
8. Lee Gains, "Who Should Decide What Books Are Allowed in Prison?," NPR, accessed February 22, 2023, https://www.npr.org/2020/02/22/806966584/who-should-decide-what-books-are-allowed-in-prison.
9. Malcolm X and Alex Haley, *The Autobiography of Malcolm X* (Ballantine Books, 1965).
10. Nazish Dholakia, "The Cruel Practice of Banning Books in Prison," Vera, April 4, 2022, https://www.vera.org/news/the-cruel-practice-of-banning-books-behind-bars.
11. Gaines, "Who Should Decide What Books?"
12. Bianco, "Prisoners Fundamental Right to Read," 12–13.
13. U.S. Const. amend. I; Martin v. Struthers, 319 U.S. 141, 143, 147 (1943) (holding that the freedom of individuals to receive and distribute information is key to preserving a free society).
14. Bianco, "Prisoners Fundamental Right to Read," 22.
15. Megan McDonald, "Thornburgh v. Abbott: Slamming the Prison Gates on Constitutional Rights," *Pepperdine Law Review* (1990).
16. Bianco, "Prisoners Fundamental Right to Read," 22.
17. James S. Vacca, "Educated Prisons Are Less Likely to Return to Prison," *Journal of Correctional Education*, December 2004.
18. Franciska Coleman, "They Should Be Fired: The Social Regulation of Free Speech in the U.S.," University of Wisconsin Legal Studies, Research Paper No. 1597, *First Amendment Law Review* 16 (2017).

19 "Inmate Race," Bureau of Federal Prisons, accessed January 30, 2024, https://www.bop.gov/about/statistics/statistics_inmate_race.jsp.
20 Lois M. Davis, "Evaluating the Effectiveness of Correctional Education: A Meta-Analysis of Programs That Provide Education to Incarcerated Adults," Rand Corporation, 2013.
21 "Literature Locked Up: How Prison Book Restrict Policies Constitute the National's Largest Book Ban," PEN America, accessed March 21, 2022, https://pen.org/wp-content/uploads/2019/09/literature-locked-up-report-9.24.19.pdf.
22 Bianco, "Prisoners Fundamental Right to Read."
23 "Prisoners' Right to Read: An Interpretation of the Library Bill of Rights," American Library Association, America Library Association, accessed January 28, 2024. https://www.ala.org/advocacy/intfreedom/librarybill/interpretations/prisonersrightoread.
24 "Prisoners' Rights," American Library Association.
25 "Prisoners' Rights," American Library Association.
26 "Prisoners' Rights," American Library Association.
27 David A. J. Richards, "Free Speech and Obscenity Law: Toward A Moral Theory of the First Amendment," *University of Pennsylvania Law Review* 45 (1974): 62–63.
28 Coleman, "They Should Be Fired: The Social Regulation of Free Speech in the U.S." (citing Martin Redish, "The Value of Free Speech," *University of Pennsylvania Law Review* 591 (1982): 625–26.
29 Lois M. Davis, "Evaluating the Effectiveness of Correctional Education: A Meta-Analysis of Programs That Provide Education to Incarcerated Adults," Rand Corporation (2013).
30 Kate Cauley, "Banned Books Behind Bars: Prototyping a Data Repository to Combat Arbitrary Censorship Practices in U.S. Prisons," *MDPI Humanities* 9 (2020).
31 Daniel M. Blumberg and Dawn A. Griffin, "Family Connections: The Importance of Prison Reading Programs for Incarcerated Parents and Their Children," *Journal of Offender Rehabilitation* 52 (2013): 254–69.
32 Anna Pekala-Wojciechowska et al., "Mental and Physical Health Problems as Conditions of Ex-Prisoner Re-Entry," *International Journal of Environmental Research and Public Health* (2021).
33 Gaines, "Who Should Decide."
34 Gaines, "Who Should Decide."
35 U.S. Const. amend. I.
36 U.S. Const. amend. I.
37 Griswald v. Connecticut, 381 U.S. 479, 482 (1965) (citing Martin v. Struthers, 319 U.S. 141, 143, 147).
38 United States v. Stevens, 559 U.S. 460, 468–69 (2010).
39 Erwin Chemerinsky, *Constitutional Law: Principles and Policies* (Aspen Publishing, 2019), 1256.

40 R.A.V. v. City of St. Paul, 505 U.S. 377, 380 (1992) (citing Chaplinsky v. New Hampshire, 315 U.S. 568 572 [1942]).
41 Jones v. North Carolina Prisoners' Labor Union, 433 U.S. 119, 125 (1977) (citing Pell v. Procunier, 417 U.S. 817, 822 [1074]).
42 Turner v. Safley, 482 U.S. 78, 81 (1987).
43 Jones, 433 U.S. at 129.
44 Procunier, 416 U.S. 396 at 405.
45 Chevron U.S.A., Inc. v. NRDC, 467 U.S. 837 (1984).
46 Administrative Procedure Act. 5 U.S.C. § 551 et seq. (1946).
47 Administrative Procedure Act.
48 Blake Emerson, "'Policy in the Administrative Procedure Act: Implications for Delegation, Deference, and Democracy," *Chicago Kent Law Review* (February 2022).
49 Loper Bright Enterprises v. Raimondo, 144 S. Ct. 2244 (2024).
50 In Nat'l Cable & Telecomms. Ass'n v. Brand X Internet Servs., the Court noted the history of administrative deference offered to administrative agencies. 545 U.S. 967, 1014–15 (2005); United States v. Mead, 533 U.S. 218 (2001); City of Arlington v. FCC, 133 S. Ct. 1863, 1874–75 (2013).
51 Pell v. Procunier, 417 U.S. 817 (1974); Bell v. Wolfish, 441 U.S. 520 (1979); Thornburgh v. Abbott, 490 U.S. 401, 403 (1989); Shaw v. Murphey, 532 U.S. 223 (2001); Beard v. Banks, 548 U.S. 521 (2006).
52 28 C. F. R. § 540.71.
53 28 C.F.R. § 540.71 (a)(2).
54 28 C.F.R. § 540.71 (a)(3). The function of this section is similar to other statutory prison provisions.
55 Sostre v. Otis, 330 F. Supp. 941 (1971).
56 Procunier, 416 U.S. at 405.
57 Procunier.
58 Cauley, "Banned Books Behind Bars," 2–3.
59 Bianco, "Prisoners Fundamental Right to Read," 15.
60 "Program Report," Federal Bureau of Prisons, accessed August 28, 2022, https://www.bop.gov/policy/progstat/5266_011.pdf.
61 28 C.F.R. § 540.71(b).
62 28 C.F.R. § 540.71(b).
63 28 C.F.R. § 540.71(b).
64 28 C.F.R. § 540.71(b).
65 28 C.F.R. § 540.71(b)(1).
66 28 C.F.R. § 540.71(b)(2).
67 28 C.F.R. § 540.71(b)(4).
68 28 C.F.R. § 540.71(b)(5).
69 John W. Palmer, *Constitutional Rights of Prisoners* (Routledge, 2010), chap. 5.
70 Bell, 441 U.S. 520 at 582, 588–89.
71 Turner, 482 U.S. 78 at 89.

72 Turner, 482 U.S. 78.
73 Turner, 482 U.S. 78; Block v. Rutherford, 468 U.S. 576 (1984).
74 Jones v. North Carolina Prisoners' Union, 433 U.S. 119 (1977).
75 Turner, 482 U.S. 78 at 90.
76 Turner, 482 U.S. 78 at 90.
77 Bianco, "Prisoners Fundamental Right to Read," 42.
78 Bianco, "Prisoners Fundamental Right to Read," 42.
79 Thornburgh v. Abbott, 490 U.S., 401, 403 (1989).
80 Thornburgh v. Abbott, 401, 403.
81 28 C.F.R. § 540.71 (b) (1).
82 Thornburgh, 490 U.S. at 403.
83 Thornburgh (citing Turner, 482 U.S. at 89).
84 Thornburgh, 490 U.S. at 407; Procunier v. Martinez 416 U.S. 396 (1974); Pell v. Procunier, 416 U.S. 396 (1974).
85 Shaw v. Murphy, 532 U.S. 223, 227, 231 (2001).
86 Shaw, 532 U.S. 223; Beard v. Banks, 548 U.S. 521 (2006); Clay Calvert and Justin B. Hayes, "To Defer or Not to Defer? Deference and Its Differential Impact on First Amendment Rights in the Roberts Court," *Case Western Reserve Law Review* 63, no. 13 (2012): 43–48.
87 Turner, 482 U.S. 78 at 89.
88 "About Us," PEN America, accessed August 12, 2022.
89 Cauley, "Banned Books Behind Bars," 5.
90 Beard v. Banks, 548 U.S. 521 (2006).
91 Amanda Magnus and Frank Stasio, "North Carolina Audits the List of Banned Books in Prisons," WUNC 91.5, January 25, 2018, https://www.wunc.org/show/the-state-of-things/2018-01-26/north-carolina-audits-the-list-of-banned-books-in-prisons; "Disapproved Publications Report," North Carolina Department of Public Safety, January 23, 2018, chrome-extension://efaidnbmnnnibpcajpcglclefindmkaj/http://media2.newsobserver.com/content/media/2018/1/23/BannedBookList.pdf.
92 Magnus and Stacio, "North Carolina Audits the List of Banned Books in Prisons."
93 Cauley, "Banned Books Behind Bars," 3, 9.
94 Bryce Peterson, Megan Kizzort, KiDeuk Kim, and Rochisha Shukla, "Prison Contraband: Prevalence, Impacts, and Interdiction Strategies," *Corrections* (April 2021).
95 Matt Riley, "Southern Prisons Have a Cellphone Smuggling Problem," NBC News, September 30, 2017, https://www.nbcnews.com/news/corrections/southern-prisonshave-smuggled-cellphone-problem-n790251.
96 Bryce Peterson et al., "Prison Contraband."
97 Bryce Peterson et al., "Prison Contraband."
98 Bryce Peterson et al., "Prison Contraband."
99 Rochisha Shukla, Bryce E. Peterson, and KiDeuk Kim, "Contraband and Interdiction Strategies in Correctional Facilities," *Urban Institute*,

February 2021, 2, 12, https://www.urban.org/sites/default/files/publication/103619/contraband-and-interdiction-strategies-in-correctional-facilities_0.pdf.
100 Rochisha Shukla et al., "Contraband and Interdiction Strategies."
101 Cauley, "Banned Books Behind Bars," 4.
102 28 C.F.R. § 540.71(b).
103 Turner v. Safley, 482 U.S. 78 (1987); Battle v. Anderson, 376 F. Supp. 402 (E.D. Okla. 1974).
104 Battle v. Anderson, 376 F. Supp. 402.
105 42 U.S.C. § 1997(e).
106 42 U.S.C. § 1997(e)(a).
107 "Melvin v. Thomas: Prison Ban on "Slavery by Another Name" Equal Justice Institute, accessed April 2, 2022, https://eji.org/cases/melvin-v-thomas/.
108 "Melvin v. Thomas: Prison Ban."
109 Chemerinsky, *Constitutional Law*, chap. 11.
110 Chemerinsky, *Constitutional Law*, chap. 11.
111 Chemerinsky, *Constitutional Law*, chap. 11; Organization for a Better Austin v. Keefe, 402 U.S. 415, 419 (1971).
112 Thomas Emerson, *The System of Freedom of Expression* (Random House Trade, 1970).
113 "Literature Locked Up: How Prison Book Restrict Policies Constitute the National's Largest Book Ban," PEN America, accessed March 21, 2022, https://pen.org/wp-content/uploads/2019/09/literature-locked-up-report-9.24.19.pdf.
114 Bianco, "Prisoners Right to Read," 14.
115 "Literature Locked Up," PEN America.
116 "Books Behind Bars: The Right to Read in Prison," National Coalition against Censorship, accessed September 19, 2022, https://ncac.org/news/books-behind-bars-the-right-to-read-in-prison.
117 Chemerinsky, *Constitutional Law*, chap. 11.
118 Peter Nickeas, "'It's the Racial Stuff': Illinois Prison Banned, Removed Books on Black History and Empowerment from Inmate Education Program," *Chicago Tribune*, August 15, 2019, https://www.chicagotribune.com/news/ct-illinois-prison-books-removed-inmate-education-20190815-6xlrmfwmovdxnbc3ohvsx6edgu-story.html.
119 Turner, 482 U.S. at 81.
120 42 U.S.C. § 1997(e).
121 Turner, 482 U.S. at 82.
122 Bianco, "Prisoners Fundamental Right to Read."
123 Turner, 482 U.S. at 82.
124 Bianco, "Prisoners Fundamental Right to Read," 21–26. Alicia Bianco argues that an enhanced rational basis review should be applied to prisoners' First Amendment rights challenges.

125 Bianco, "Prisoners Fundamental Right to Read."
126 Counterman v. Colorado, 600 U.S. 66 (2023).
127 Counterman v. Colorado, 600 U.S. 66.
128 "Literature Locked Up: How Prison Book Restrict Policies Constitute the National's Largest Book Ban," PEN America, accessed March 21, 2022, https://pen.org/wp-content/uploads/2019/09/literature-locked-up-report-9.24.19.pdf.
129 "Literature Locked Up."
130 Jo Ellen Knott, "Florida Tops the Nation for Number of Book Bans in Prisons," Prison Legal News, accessed on January 18, 2024, https://www.prisonlegalnews.org/news/2023/feb/2/florida-tops-nation-number-books-banned-prisons/.
131 "Literature Locked Up."
132 "Literature Locked Up."
133 "Literature Locked Up."
134 "Literature Locked Up."
135 "Literature Locked Up."
136 Heller v. New York, 413 U.S. 483 (1973); Maryland v. Macon, 472 U.S. 463 (1985). These cases speak to the allowance of censorship boards to screen movies prior to their release.
137 "Literature Locked Up."

Chapter Six

I Fought the Law, and the First Amendment Won

How the *Brandenburg* Test Safeguards Musical Expression

Eric T. Kasper

"Beginnings"

Government attempts to restrict music, and punish musicians for their alleged incitement, are nothing new. The Supreme Court described in *Ward v. Rock against Racism* (1989) that "[m]usic is one of the oldest forms of human expression. From Plato's discourse in the Republic to the totalitarian state in our own times, rulers have known its capacity to appeal to the intellect and to the emotions, and have censored musical compositions to serve the needs of the state. The Constitution prohibits any like attempts in our own legal order."[1] The Supreme Court in *Ward* failed to account for examples of domestic music censorship, but its accounts of the age-old attempts to censor music and its protected status in the United States by the 1980s were both historically accurate. Incitement precedents like *Brandenburg v. Ohio* (1969) and *Hess v. Indiana* (1973) — along with decisions finding implicit or explicit protection for music like *Southeastern Promotions, Ltd. v. Conrad* (1975) and *Ward* — ensure that the First Amendment prevents government restrictions on music because of the viewpoint expressed, even if music advocates that people take ill-advised or illegal action. These precedents have benefited both musical artists and their listeners over the last several decades. Musicians have long been fighting the law to protect their craft, and in this fight against censorship, the First Amendment should continue to win on behalf of those artists.

"It's the Same Old Song"

Ward's reference to Plato recalls his *Republic*, written in the fourth century BCE. Plato used Socrates as a character to describe how music's "rhythm and harmony . . . insinuate themselves into the inmost part of the soul and most vigorously lay hold of it in bringing grace with them." In Plato's view, music influences human development and behavior: one who is "properly reared on rhythm and harmony would have the sharpest sense for what's been left out and what isn't a fine product of craft or what isn't a fine product of nature." Thus, Plato wanted government to control music, stating, "overseers of the city" should ensure that "there must be no innovation in . . . music contrary to the established order." Plato thought the government must "supervise . . . the poets and compel them to impress the image of the good disposition on their poems." Plato advocated that musicians (whom he also referred to as poets) be limited in their ability to provoke people into thinking inappropriate thoughts and taking unacceptable actions.[2]

After Plato, governments frequently censored music, often under the guise that it could incite people to act unsuitably, as cover for the officials' desires to silence artists whose views were deemed immoral or seditious. During China's Han dynasty (202 BCE to 120 CE), a music bureau reviewed songs to judge their utility to the regime.[3] Eighth-century Frankish kings Pepin the Short and Charlemagne stifled local liturgical traditions to culturally unify Western Europe.[4] After William the Conqueror defeated England in 1066, his replacement of ecclesiastical officials led to suppression of some religious music in the country.[5] In the Middle Ages, clergy in Europe banned the playing of the tritone interval because of its supposed association with the Devil.[6] In the sixteenth century, England prohibited the printing of ballads, out of concern that they might improperly "instruct" people, particularly "the youth of the realm."[7] In the 1800s, censors in Italian city-states ruled on what themes were permitted in publicly performed operas.[8]

Ward's report of music censorship in "the totalitarian state in our own times" was not hyperbole. Nazi Germany was the most extreme example. The Third Reich banned what officials deemed "degenerate" music, including that by Jewish and Black artists, with Jewish musicians first prohibited from composing and later forced into concentration camps. As one scholarly work put it, "the Nazis' most insidious form of music censorship was genocide."[9]

Musicians in Russia have experienced much censorship over the last century. In the 1920s, the Soviet Union put bans on religious music and jazz music. In the 1930s, music had to contain socialist themes to avoid censure. After World War II, formalistic music was banned for alleged "decadent Western influences." Restrictions on classical music were eased after Joseph Stalin died, but bans on recording or performing foreign music — chiefly Western rock songs — continued into the 1980s. Although glasnost and the ensuing fall of communism led to musical freedom in Russia in the 1990s, in the twenty-first century under Vladimir Putin the country has resumed censorship, especially of artists critical of the state. In 2012, three members of Pussy Riot were convicted of "hooliganism" for performing music condemning Putin and the Russian Orthodox Church. Recent concerts by other performers have been shut down for allegedly promoting illegal behavior, including as it relates to drug use, suicide, and "gay propaganda." In 2024, the Ministry of Culture for the Russian republic of Chechnya announced that to "conform to the Chechen mentality and sense of rhythm," songs would be banned there unless they had a tempo of 80 to 116 beats per minute.[10]

China also has a long history of music censorship. The communist revolution in the 1950s to 1960s led to sanctioning artists whose music was deemed adverse to Communist Party values, with some artists being exiled to labor camps. China's contemporary restrictions include constraining which foreign artists can perform concerts, curbing domestic access to online music, and jailing Tibetan artists who criticize state policy. In the twenty-first century, artists who have had their concerts canceled or placed under strict restrictions by the Ministry of Culture include Harry Connick Jr., Björk, and Oasis. China has limited performances of religious music in recent decades.[11]

There are many other governments — particularly authoritarian and totalitarian regimes — that have censored modern music. In Francisco Franco's fascist Spain, officials altered lyrics and banned performances, forcing some musicians into exile. In the 1950s, Egypt banned rock 'n' roll. In the 1960s, Indonesia forbade the playing of Beatles' songs, and North Korea began banning all music from abroad. In the 1970s, Chile banned radio broadcasts of unapproved songs and even killed leftist musicians; South Africa barred approximately 120 albums and singles (including those that opposed apartheid); the Serbian republic in Yugoslavia imposed a major tax on music deemed to be "Šund" (art trash); Taiwan banned protest songs that could promote positive sentiment toward China; and Cambodia's Khmer Rouge banned concerts and recordings of popular music. In the 1980s, Iran closed music schools and forced popular musicians, particularly women, into exile, with only songs promoting the revolution and Islam permitted to be performed. In the 1990s, the Taliban in Afghanistan prohibited all musical performances, including at funerals and weddings. In addition to the ongoing music censorship today in regimes like China, North Korea, and Russia, Myanmar recently executed a pro-democracy musician.[12]

As much as *Ward* proclaimed that the First Amendment bans musical censorship in the United States, censorship of allegedly subversive or dangerous music has occurred in the United States, even if it was never as common or severe as the previous illustrations from other countries. In the Antebellum South, states forbade enslaved persons from using drums when playing music, reasoning that they could transmit messages during a slave revolt. In the Reconstruction South, performance of Confederate war songs was prohibited, presumably because they could encourage another rebellion. In the 1920s, Cleveland banned jazz music in dance halls, classifying it as "vulgar" and "noisy." The FBI put Billie Holiday under surveillance after she released the antilynching song "Strange Fruit" in 1939. In the late 1940s and early 1950s, Paul Robeson's statements critical of racism led to him being banned from performing by multiple city governments. The US State Department revoked Robeson's passport (prohibiting him from performing overseas), a decision that was sustained when challenged in federal court.[13]

By the 1950s, censorship efforts in the United States took other forms. In South Carolina, ordinances restricted popular music from being played on jukeboxes on Sundays or within hearing distance of a church. The New Jersey Division of Alcohol Control and Order revoked alcohol licenses from bars unless they removed objectional records from jukeboxes. Congress conducted repeated investigations out of concerns that rock music might incite young people to engage in undesirable behavior. Senate committees held hearings on, or issued reports alleging, that rock music caused juvenile crime. One congressional bill would have mandated government review of lyrics before songs could be broadcast on the air or sold commercially. When Pete Seeger declined to testify before the House Un-American Activities Committee on communism in music, he was cited with, and convicted of, contempt of Congress; the conviction was overturned on appeal, but not based on the First Amendment. Elvis Presley was threatened with arrests in multiple states if he danced on stage while singing. Gene Vincent was convicted on lewdness charges in Virginia for singing the song "Lotta Lovin.'" Both Presley and Vincent were censored due to their performances potentially provoking sexual activity among young people.[14]

Censorship efforts against music escalated in the 1960s and early 1970s, especially against artists criticizing the government or allegedly encouraging illegal behavior or immoral acts. The FBI kept files and surveilled various artists, including Phil Ochs and Bob Dylan, due to their opposition to the Vietnam War. After Indiana Governor Matthew Welsh declared concern that the Kingsmen's "Louie, Louie" might contain obscene lyrics, the Federal Communications Commission (FCC), the Postal Service, and the FBI investigated the song. After a 1965 Rolling Stones performance, the mayor of Cleveland banned rock concerts in the city. Police in Kansas City in 1966 stopped James Brown from performing because of allegedly lewd dancing. The Doors' Jim Morrison was convicted of disturbing the peace in Connecticut when he used profanity to criticize police brutality during a 1967 show, and he was convicted of indecent exposure and profanity in Florida for actions and remarks he gave during a 1969 show. Janis Joplin was convicted of "vulgar and indecent language" for yelling at police, "Don't fuck with those people," during a concert song in Tampa in 1969. Ohio Governor James Rhodes — incensed at Neil Young's song "Ohio," which denounced President Richard Nixon for the 1970 Kent State Shootings — instructed (without success) that radio stations not play the song. In 1971, the FCC threatened radio broadcasters with nonrenewal of licenses if they played songs promoting illegal drug use; in 1973 a federal appellate court upheld against a First Amendment challenge the FCC's actions. That same year, the Senate held a hearing on rock music encouraging illegal drug use. Censorship of music that advocated what authorities believed were immoral or illegal deeds was on the rise.[15]

"Here Comes the Judge"

As censorship efforts against musical artists were escalating in the United States, the Supreme Court signaled a new approach to incitement in *Brandenburg v. Ohio* (1969) and *Hess v. Indiana* (1973). These cases caused a ripple effect that eventually enhanced protections of advocacy in music. Clarence Brandenburg was a Ku Klux Klan leader convicted of violating an Ohio law barring advocacy of violence to achieve political or industrial reform. As has been explored at length in this volume, Brandenburg spoke at a Klan rally where he advocated what he called "revengent" action against the Supreme Court, Congress, and the president for their efforts on civil rights. In *Brandenburg*, the justices proclaimed the following test for incitement: "The constitutional guarantees of free speech and free press do not permit a State to forbid or proscribe advocacy of the use of force or of law violation except where such advocacy is directed to inciting or producing imminent lawless action and is likely to incite or produce such action." The decision explained, "mere abstract teaching . . . of the moral propriety or even moral necessity for a resort to force and violence" is protected, even as preparing others for actual violence is not. For advocacy of violence to be punishable under the First Amendment, the following must be met after *Brandenburg*: (1) the speaker must intend to incite others, (2) the speaker's words must be likely to incite others, and (3) the lawless action advocated must be imminent.[16]

Hess clarified the meaning of the *Brandenburg* test. In *Hess*, the justices reversed a war protestor's conviction for stating to police clearing the street, "We'll take the fucking street later." Hess was not advocating *imminent* lawlessness, so the Supreme Court found that his speech was protected: "At best . . . the statement could be taken as counsel for present moderation; at worst, it amounted to nothing more than advocacy of illegal action at some indefinite future time."[17] *NAACP v. Claiborne Hardware Co.* (1982) later emphasized the need to find imminence, holding that physical assaults that occurred weeks or months after "politically charged rhetoric" advocating violence fell short of *Brandenburg*'s imminence requirement.[18]

The door to lower courts applying *Brandenburg* to song lyrics was opened by the Supreme Court finding First Amendment protections for music. In *Southeastern Promotions v. Conrad* (1975), the Board of Directors for a municipal auditorium refused to let a company book the facility to put on the musical *Hair*, due to the play's irreverence and nudity. The Supreme Court found that this violated the First Amendment, writing how musical theater performances should be thought of like pure speech: "Only if we were to conclude that live drama is unprotected by the First Amendment — or subject to a totally different standard from that applied to other forms of expression — could we possibly find no prior restraint here." The justices reasoned that theater and musical performances are expressive: "By its nature, theater usually is the acting out — or *singing* out — of the written word, and frequently mixes speech with live action or conduct . . . that is no reason to hold theater subject to a drastically different standard."[19]

Although *Hair* was controversial for more than its songs, the opinion in *Southeastern Promotions* implied that music is protected by the Constitution.[20] Similarly, in *Schad v. Mount Ephraim* (1981) the Supreme Court reasoned that "live entertainment, such as *musical* and dramatic works fall within the First Amendment guarantee."[21] This protection was made explicit in *Ward* in 1989. *Ward* involved a challenge to New York City regulations mandating that acts at the Central Park band shell use city-provided sound technicians and amplification equipment. The Supreme Court upheld those requirements (to protect residents from excessive noise). In doing so, the *Ward* Court boldly concluded that "[m]usic, as a form of expression and communication, is protected under the First Amendment." The *Ward* Court applied the same standard to regulations of musical expression that are used for the spoken word.[22]

"Let the Music Play"

The reasoning in *Southeastern Promotions*, *Schad*, and *Ward* would lead lower courts to apply the Supreme Court's First Amendment incitement jurisprudence to musical expression, including using the *Brandenburg* test when evaluating if music is constitutionally protected. This started in the lower courts around the same time as the *Ward* decision.

The California Court of Appeals decision *McCollum v. CBS* (1988) was the first appellate decision to apply Supreme Court incitement precedents to music. The case arose out of a tragic set of facts: John McCollum took his life with a handgun on the same day he was listening to Ozzy Osbourne's album, *Blizzard of Ozz*. The album's song "Suicide Solution" contains lyrics advising the listener to obtain a gun and shoot it. McCollum's parents sued Osbourne and CBS Records, arguing that Osbourne's music caused their son's suicide. The case was dismissed by a trial judge, a decision that was affirmed by the California Court of Appeals. As explained by the Court of Appeals, "artistic expressions such as the music and lyrics here involved" are "generally to be accorded protection under the First Amendment." The court referenced *Schad* for the proposition that "First Amendment guarantees of freedom of speech and expression extend to all artistic and literary expression, [including] music." The court clarified that "the freedom of speech guaranteed by the First Amendment is not absolute," and cited *Brandenburg* for the prospect that "speech which is directed to inciting or producing imminent lawless action, and which is likely to incite or produce such action, is outside the scope of First Amendment protection." The court also cited *Hess* to conclude that "[s]peech directed to action at some indefinite time in the future will not satisfy this test."[23]

The *McCollum* court utilized *Brandenburg* and *Hess*, concluding that there was no intent or likelihood of lawless conduct incited by "Suicide Solution": "Apart from the 'unintelligible' lyrics . . . to which John admittedly was not even listening at the time of his death, there is nothing in any of Osbourne's songs which could be characterized as a command to an immediate suicidal act." The lyrics failed to "command anyone to any concrete action at any specific time, much less immediately" and can instead "easily be viewed as a poetic device." The court explained, "the lyrics sung by Osbourne may well express a philosophical view that suicide is an acceptable alternative to a life that has become unendurable — an idea which, however unorthodox, has a long intellectual tradition." The "argument that speech may be punished on the ground it has a tendency to lead to suicide or other violence is precisely the doctrine rejected by the Supreme Court in *Hess v. Indiana*." The court reasoned that "[n]o rational person would or could . . . mistake musical lyrics and poetry for literal commands or directives to immediate action. To do so would indulge a fiction which neither common sense nor the First Amendment will permit." For the court, "it is simply not acceptable to a free and democratic society to impose a duty upon performing artists to limit and restrict their creativity in order to avoid the dissemination of ideas in artistic speech which may adversely affect emotionally troubled individuals."[24]

Incitement via subliminal messages was alleged in *Vance v. Judas Priest* (1990), a case decided the year after *Ward*. Like *McCollum*, this case began with a youth suicide. Raymond Belknap and James Vance each took a turn at shooting himself with a sawed-off shotgun, with both eventually dying from their gunshots. The parents of both teenagers filed a lawsuit against Judas Priest, alleging that the band's 1978 *Stained Class* album's song, "Better by You, Better Than Me" contained a subliminal message of "Do It" that caused the two boys to shoot themselves. Although a Nevada trial judge, Jerry Carr Whitehead, determined that the plaintiffs established that the subliminal words "Do It" were present in the song below the level of conscious awareness, he also found that they were not placed there by the band intentionally. Although Judge Whitehead noted that "the constitutional issues raised by the use of subliminal communication are so entirely different than those raised by the use of supraliminal music lyrics," if only supraliminal lyrics were at issue in the case, "the Court would follow the incitement standard in *Brandenburg* and hold that the lyrics were protected speech." Ignoring questions about subliminal messages, which raise issues never addressed by the Supreme Court, Judge Whitehead continued the practice of applying *Brandenburg* to musical lyrics that are alleged to have incited lawlessness. The way *Vance* was decided also ensured that the song was protected speech, with Judge Whitehead finding no incitement.[25]

Waller v. Osborne (1991) began similar to *McCollum*, with Michael Waller killing himself with a gun after listening to Ozzy Osbourne's "Suicide Solution." Waller's parents sued Osborne and CBS Records. The Wallers claimed the song's lyrics caused their son's death and (like the *Vance* plaintiffs) that the song contained subliminal messages that led to their son's death. In *Waller*, US District Judge Duross Fitzpatrick issued a summary judgment for Osbourne and CBS. Before exploring the relevant First Amendment case law, Judge Fitzpatrick first explained that the plaintiffs' experts failed to establish that the song contained any subliminal messages, going so far as to reason that those experts could not even agree over how to define "subliminal."[26]

Judge Fitzpatrick relied on *Schad* to conclude that musical "entertainment represents a type of speech that is generally afforded first amendment constitutional protection." This extends to "notes, rhythms, tones, and lyrics." Like the *McCollum* court, Judge Fitzpatrick in *Waller* stressed how "first amendment protection that shields those who produce, perform, and distribute music is not however absolute," including if it "incites imminent lawless activity." Judge Fitzpatrick cited *Brandenburg* and *Hess* to explain that the inquiry focuses "on the imminence of the threat." Using *Brandenburg* and *Hess*, Judge Fitzpatrick determined that the song was not inciteful: "There is no indication whatsoever that defendants' music was directed toward any particular person or group of persons. Moreover, there is no evidence that defendants' music was intended to produce acts of suicide, and likely to cause *imminent* acts of suicide; nor could one rationally infer such a meaning from the lyrics." Judge Fitzpatrick characterized Osbourne's lyrics "as asserting in a philosophical sense that suicide may be a viable option one should consider in certain circumstances," and "an abstract discussion of the moral propriety or even moral necessity for a resort to suicide," which "is not the same as indicating to someone that he should commit suicide and encouraging him to take such action." Like *McCollum*, *Waller* applied *Brandenburg* to find Osbourne's music had First Amendment protection.[27]

The preceding cases from the 1980s and 1990s raised incitement issues in the context of listeners dying by suicide. Another question raised during this time was whether listeners were incited by lyrics to commit violence against others, particularly police. These incidents generated public controversy, but most did not result in criminal prosecutions or civil suits. For instance, in 1989, N.W.A.'s album *Straight Outta Compton* included the song "Fuck tha Police," with lyrics describing a sniper and the killing of Los Angeles police officers. The song's release caused an FBI agent, Milt Ahlerich, to pen a letter to N.W.A.'s record company, claiming that the song "encourages violence" against police, with Ahlerich insinuating he was writing for the FBI: "I wanted you to be aware of the FBI's position relative to this song and its message." Although police in Detroit once halted N.W.A. from performing the song live, no band members were arrested for incitement related to the song, and no other official law enforcement action was taken against the band for their music. Similarly, Body Count's "Cop Killer" was controversial for advocating for killing law enforcement officers when released in 1992, including with lyrics that used profanity and referred to police officers in derogatory ways. However, no civil or criminal cases attempted to stop the song's distribution.[28]

Like N.W.A. and Body Count, rapper Shawn Thomas, known professionally as C-Bo, was accused of incitement. Thomas was arrested in 1998, due to allegations that his song "Deadly Game," which criticized California's three-strikes-and-you're-out law, promoted "violence against law enforcement" violating the terms of his parole. Some of the lyrics at issue in "Deadly Game" encouraged the shooting of law enforcement during a traffic stop. Revocation of Thomas's parole posed concerns that he may have been targeted for expressing political views, but he was later released, with the only punishment imposed for failing a drug test.[29] Although there were insinuations among some law enforcement and others that songs like this were not protected because of their advocacy of violence, the Supreme Court's interpretation of the First Amendment to protect music (and lower court applications of the *Brandenburg* test to music), resulted in progressively fewer cases being filed to restrict the ideas advocated in songs.

One exception to this 1990s trend of cases not even being filed against alleged musical incitement was *Davidson v. Time Warner* (1997), although that case was ultimately dismissed. At issue were two songs on Tupac Shakur's album, *2Pacalypse Now*: (1) "Trapped" described the shooting of police who were chasing after the shooter, and (2) "Souja's Story" referred to Rodney King when describing the shooting of a police officer during a traffic stop. *2Pacalypse Now* played on the radio of a car driven by Ronald Howard when he was stopped by Texas State Trooper Bill Davidson in 1992. During the stop, Howard shot and killed Davidson. Howard claimed at his criminal trial that the album caused him to shoot Davidson, but this claim failed, and Howard was sentenced to death. Davidson's next of kin sued Shakur and the distributors of his album, making similar claims to Howard, that the album incited violence against police.[30]

US District Judge John Rainey ruled for the defendants, averring that the album, "as music, receives full First Amendment protection." Judge Rainey cited *Ward*, recognizing that "musical expression, like other forms of entertainment, is a matter of First Amendment concern" and is protected even if "the music takes an unpopular or even dangerous viewpoint." Like other courts asked to decide these questions by the 1980s, Judge Rainey identified the pertinent issue, that "there are categories of speech that receive no constitutional protection," including "words likely to produce imminent lawless action (incitement)." Judge Rainey cited *Brandenburg* and *Hess*, outlining the inquiry: "To restrain *2Pacalypse Now* in this case, the Court must find the recording (1) was directed or intended toward the goal of producing imminent lawless conduct and (2) was likely to produce such imminent illegal conduct."[31]

Applying *Brandenburg* to the case, Judge Rainey found no evidence of incitement. First, on the question if Shakur *intended* to incite violence against police, Judge Rainey reasoned thusly: "Calling ones music revolutionary does not, by itself, mean that Shakur intended his music to produce imminent lawless conduct. At worst, Shakur's intent was to cause violence some time after the listener considered Shakur's message. The First Amendment protects such advocacy." Second, even if Shakur *intended* to incite violence, Judge Rainey explained why such an outcome was not *likely*: "The Davidsons are the first to claim that *2Pacalypse Now* caused illegal conduct, three years after the recording *2Pacalypse Now* and after more than 400,000 sales of the album. The Davidsons argue that, because Howard shot Officer Davidson while listening to *2Pacalypse Now*, that Davidson was killed *because* Howard was listening to *2Pacalypse Now* . . . it is far more likely that Howard, a gang member driving a stolen automobile, feared his arrest and shot officer Davidson to avoid capture." Third, Judge Rainey addressed the issue of *imminence*: "The Davidsons face the difficulty of arguing that *2Pacalypse Now* caused imminent violence when Howard lashed out after listening to recorded music, not a live performance. Shakur's music, however, was not overtly directed at Howard. . . . Considering Howard allegedly was 'addicted' to rap music . . . and that he had not lashed out against peace officers from the beginning of his 'addiction' until his murder of Officer Davidson, the Court cannot conclude that *2Pacalypse Now* was likely to cause imminent lawless conduct." Put bluntly by Judge Rainey, "[a]t best, the recording reveals that weak-willed individuals may be influenced by Shakur's work. . . . The Defendants cannot be responsible for determining the mental condition of each and every potential listener." In *Davidson*, another court found constitutional protection for musical lyrics (following *Southeastern Productions* and *Ward*) that advocate illegality, with the court analyzing the protection according to *Brandenburg* and *Hess*.[32]

As uncomfortable as lyrics advocating violence can be, if *Brandenburg* protects pure speech (without accompanying music), then consistency demands that these recorded lyrics are protected as well. Like the words uttered by Clarence Brandenburg, lyrics in "Fuck tha Police," "Cop Killer," "Dangerous Game," "Trapped," and "Soulja's Story" advocated violence in ways that were critical of the existing political order, the major difference being that these artists were criticizing racism rather than promoting it like Brandenburg was. If Brandenburg's speech was protected, then these artists' lyrics should be protected too. Furthermore, generalized lyrics in songs are almost always provocative artistic expressions that are not meant to be literally taken as calls to violence.[33] This is the case with the songs by Shakur, Body Count, and N.W.A., as their music depicts a violent story told by the singer in the first person, rather than directly calling anyone to commit acts of violence. Those songs may make abhorrent violence seem appealing, and one has every right to criticize and condemn them, but they do not meet the legal definition of incitement. As reasoned by the Texas Court of Criminal Appeals in *Hart v. State* (2024), "[h]olding song lyrics to their literal meaning would lead to the following conclusions: Freddie Mercury 'killed a man,' Bob Marley 'shot the sheriff,' Macy Gray 'committed murder and . . . got away,' the band formerly known as the Dixie Chicks killed Earl, and classically, Johnny Cash 'shot a man just to watch him die.' These are conclusions we cannot accept outside of some other evidence demonstrating the lyrics are something more than fiction."[34] Applying *Brandenburg* ensures that songs like these, and countless others, are protected artistic expression. Indeed, what these songs depict artistically should be protected like the violent elements to a plot in a film, another medium of expression that the Court has long held is shielded by the First Amendment.[35]

Cases applying *Brandenburg* to music are not restricted to those that require lyrical analysis of recorded music. *Brandenburg* has protected artists in concert and those using music at live events. In *Matarazzo v. Aerosmith Productions* (1989), the plaintiff filed a lawsuit after being struck in the nose by another fan at a 1986 Aerosmith concert at Madison Square Garden. According to the complaint, "Aerosmith's music encourages violence and the group's concerts attract 'crazies' who are particularly drawn to this type of message." The claims were dismissed. US District Judge Mary Johnson Lowe cited *Brandenburg* and *McCollum* as relevant precedents. Quoting *McCollum*, Jude Lowe in *Matarazzo* explained how *McCollum* "dismissed the action concluding that 'nothing in any of Osbourne's songs could be characterized as a command to an immediate suicidal act.'" Judge Lowe stated, "It is clear that plaintiffs' similar claim against Warner would not survive a summary judgement motion in this Court."[36]

No legal action was ever attempted against the Red Hot Chili Peppers after they played the Jimi Hendrix song "Fire" at Woodstock '99, even though raging bonfires burned on the grounds of the music festival during and after the band played the song. On the final night of Woodstock '99, victims of the 1999 Columbine school shooting were being honored in a vigil via the distribution of thousands of candles to the crowd. Those candles were then used to start fires, with looting and violence following. Many crowd members were upset on the final night of the festival after several days of experiencing a heat wave, high food and drink prices, and inapt sanitation services. Insufficient security during the festival failed to prevent violent crimes, including sexual assaults.[37]

One could argue the crowd was more likely than most to engage in arson if told — in the moment — to start fires, given their general state of disgruntlement at the organizers and the fact that many of them already possessed lit candles. Thus, elements of *Brandenburg* related to imminence and likelihood could plausibly be met. However, Red Hot Chili Peppers' lead singer Anthony Kiedis offered a credible reason why the band did not possess *Brandenburg*'s requisite *intent* to incite arson. As explained by Kiedis, when they arrived on the final day of the festival, the band had not "heard any reports about people getting abused or raped or anything like that. It just seemed to us like another big rock festival." Lacking knowledge of the crowd's infuriation, the band was not aware that their song choice could spark conflagration. Kiedis also explained that Janie Hendrix, sister of Jimi Hendrix, a star of the original Woodstock in 1969, asked the band to play a song in tribute to the famed rocker, who was not otherwise being recognized in any major way by the 1999 festival. Thus, Kiedis claimed that the band chose the song "Fire," "not because there were fires raging, but as a palliative for poor Jimi's sister." Although Kiedis recalled seeing at least one fire in the audience when taking the stage, he explained that the band had "been through tons of festivals where bonfires had been started, so this one didn't seem out of the ordinary." Kiedis admitted that the band "should have paid closer attention . . . and not been so isolated from the fan's point of view," but he provided evidence that the band had no intent to incite lawlessness, thus protecting their playing of "Fire" under *Brandenburg*.[38]

Frank Torries and Tricia Boudoin, the owner and employee, respectively, of Skate Zone, a skating rink in New Iberia, Louisiana, filed a federal lawsuit in *Torries v. Hebert* (2000). Skate Zone hosted evening rap dance parties, with many youths in attendance. This included youths from New Iberia, but many were from Franklin, a high school rival of New Iberia. Youths from Franklin were driven there in a bus by Ernest Sikes. One night, some of the youths displayed gang signs, which caused Sikes to ask the disc jockey to announce that the Franklin bus would soon leave. Some of the youths then became physically violent. Boudoin later called the Iberia Sheriff's department for help. Property damage occurred to a vehicle in the parking lot. Members of the sheriff's department eventually seized CDs of songs that had been played that evening, due to concerns that the music "contained explicit language which promoted violence and incited the teenagers at the Skate Zone to become entangled in fights." Torries demanded the return of the CDs. Torries and Boudoin were arrested for playing music that evening, so they sought a federal court injunction against the sheriff's department to halt any prosecution of them for playing the music at issue. US District Judge Tucker Melancon granted that injunction.[39]

Judge Melancon's ruling in *Torries* cited *Brandenburg* and *Hess*, recounting the elements of the *Brandenburg* test. Judge Melancon emphasized how "[i]n *Brandenburg*, the Supreme Court specifically addressed the distinction between speech containing offensive messages — which is protected under the First Amendment — and speech directly inducing others to engage in violent action, which is not." Examining the facts in *Torries*, Judge Melancon found that "[a]lthough persons could differ as to whether the music at issue is offensive, it clearly is not directed at inciting and producing imminent lawless action." The music was played directly preceding the violence, but a group rivalry existed among the patrons, and Sikes had made an announcement about the Franklin bus leaving, which, in the words of Judge Melancon, is what "provoked the situation." After reviewing the facts, "the only conclusion the Court can make with confidence is that the 'gangster rap' music did not in and of itself incite imminent lawless action under *Brandenburg*." Overzealous prosecution related to music was stopped in *Torries*, following the Supreme Court's requirements in *Brandenburg*.[40]

Courts have also used *Brandenburg* and its progeny to draw the line between protected speech and incitement for statements given by a musical artist at a live concert. *Stricklin v. Stefani* (2018) involved facts very different from the other court cases above. Lisa Stricklin attended a Gwen Stefani concert at the PNC Music Pavilion in Charlotte, North Carolina, in 2016. As described by US District Judge Robert Conrad, in the pavilion "[t]here are approximately 8,614 reserved theatre-style seats ('reserved area') closer to the performance stage and approximately 10,154 available spaces in the lawn seating area farther from the stage ('lawn')." Roughly twenty minutes into her performance, Stefani stated to the crowd, "I'm just going to talk to the security guards for one second. If anyone wants to come down a little closer so I can see you a little better, just come on down, I don't think anyone's going to care, like just fill it in." A crowd of fans from the lawn area rushed to the reserved area to get closer to the stage. Within minutes of Stefani's announcement, Stricklin, seated in the reserved area, was trampled by the crowd and pushed into a wall. Stricklin suffered a broken leg, requiring surgery.[41]

In *Stricklin*, Judge Conrad ruled that the First Amendment did not immunize Stefani from civil liability. Judge Conrad identified that "incitement to riot" is not protected by the First Amendment. He reviewed Stefani's comments, interpreting them as "intended to prompt action." Stefani argued that *McCollum* — which itself used the *Brandenburg* test — protected her comments, even claiming that her words were closely connected to her music, in that her statements "were made solely to enhance the feel and experience of her music at her concert." However, Judge Conrad drew important distinctions between this case and *McCollum*: "First, *McCollum* involved substantive lyrics — not concert directions — which could be seen as triggering fundamental principles of First Amendment protection." Second, Judge Conrad explained how, "unlike the *McCollum* plaintiff who was physically and temporarily distant from the artist and musical performance at issue, [Stricklin] was in the same time and place as Stefani when Stefani invited the audience to come forward" during a live performance. For Judge Conrad, "Stefani issued an in-person invitation to thousands of people in a stadium-like arena to come forward toward the stage. And Stefani's announcement, unlike the lyrics in *McCollum*, was intended to produce immediate action and was likely to bring that action about. Therefore . . . Stefani could have anticipated the reaction that her statement would prompt: thousands of people, many of whom were consuming alcohol, to descend toward the stage immediately."[42]

Ultimately, Judge Conrad discussed all three parts of the *Brandenburg* test. He surmised Stefani's intent (she wanted thousands of people to move forward in a crowded stadium); he explained how people were likely to react to Stefani's statement (they were her fans, and many had consumed alcohol); and he described how the action by the crowd took place immediately after Stefani's statement. The only portion of *Brandenburg* that Judge Conrad did not explicitly discuss was whether the fans' actions were lawless, but that was self-evident, as Stefani was telling fans to take seats they had not legally purchased at the venue. Thus, Stefani's concert speech met the requirements of incitement under *Brandenburg*. Her expression was quite unlike the cases above involving lyrics by Ozzy Osbourne, Judas Priest, N.W.A., Body Count, Tupac Shakur, Aerosmith, the Red Hot Chili Peppers, and the artists whose songs played at the Skate Zone. Indeed, as summarized by Judge Conrad, "Stefani's in-person invitation weighs more toward a statement prompting immediate and likely action than one promoting artistic expression and the free exchange of ideas (i.e., one meriting First Amendment protection)."[43]

"Listen to the Music"

Governments have long attempted to censor music due to alleged encouragement of illicit conduct, including violence, sexual activity, or drug use. Before Supreme Court precedents were used to apply *Brandenburg* to music, music censorship was increasing in the United States, but that is not the case today. Nevertheless, after decades of Supreme Court decisions finding protections for music and lower courts applying *Brandenburg* to music, a 2023 Freedom Forum survey revealed, incredibly, that just 54 percent of Americans knew that the First Amendment even protects music![44] At the very least, this is an educational failure regarding the Supreme Court's decisions. Even more to the point, it could be a harbinger of things to come if courts do not continue to be zealous in their protection of songs, applying *Brandenburg* to protect offensive music short of incitement, regardless of the viewpoint a song expresses.

Judge Fitzpatrick explained in *Waller* what Supreme Court precedent concludes: The First Amendment protects "music irrespective of whether it constitutes aberrant, unpopular, and even revolutionary music."[45] Judge Rainey in *Davidson* explained that we protect what may be offensive to some, even if it advocates violence, for the greater good. After articulating his personal disgust at the songs on Shakur's *2Pacalypse Now* album, Judge Rainey opined how "the First Amendment became part of the Constitution because the Crown sought to suppress the Framers' own rebellious, sometimes violent views. Thus, although the Court cannot recommend *2Pacalypse Now* to anyone, it will not strip Shakur's free speech rights."[46] Judge Melancon in *Torries* echoed this point; after commenting how he would never personally expose children to the music played at the Skate Zone, "under the Constitution which established the Republic in which we live, it is not the musical likes or dislikes of this United States District Judge, nor the individual musical tastes of the Sheriff of Iberia Parish, that can or should be allowed to establish the boundaries of the First Amendment."[47]

Indeed, applying *Brandenburg* to music ensures the First Amendment protects the right to compose, sing, distribute, and listen to music the same as it does for other expression. To return to Judge Rainey in *Davidson*, if *Brandenburg* did not protect as much music as it did, there would be a chilling effect on musical expression: "This self-censorship not only would affect broadcasters, who would be chilled into producing only the most mundane, least emotional material. This self-censorship would also prevent listeners from accessing important social commentary, not just the violent and aesthetically questionable *2Pacalypse Now*. The public, like Mr. Shakur, has the right to access social, aesthetic, moral, and other ideas and experiences."[48] Without that protection, government could deem fit for prosecution music that questions the prevailing order, or we risk civil suits censoring those songs. Before *Brandenburg* was applied to music, songs questioning the status quo were challenged, including the expression of Jim Morrison and Phil Ochs. After *Brandenburg*, the music of controversial rockers like Ozzy Osbourne and Judas Priest were targeted for suppression for their boundary-pushing expression; likewise, songs by hip-hop artists like Tupac Shakur that criticized police were under attack. Applying *Brandenburg* to music ensured that such efforts would be unsuccessful in court.

Furthermore, the race of the artists and their audiences are sometimes part of the calculus of suppression. Judge Rainey in *Davidson* spoke to this point, explaining how the plaintiffs in the case argued that *2Pacalypse Now* did not deserve constitutional protection because it "is directed to the violent black 'gangsta' subculture in general." Judge Rainey refused to rule that such music could be denied First Amendment protection and reasoned that "to hold otherwise would remove constitutional protection from speech directed to marginalized groups."[49]

As noted above, before *Brandenburg*, minority artists, particularly African Americans, were targeted by censors. Enslaved persons in the 1800s were stripped of all rights — including musical expression. Restrictions were put on jazz halls in the early 1900s due to that genre's association with Black artists, and this continued with other forms of music developed by African Americans, including rock and rap. A Houston Juvenile Delinquency and Crime Commission targeted Black artists when trying to restrict airplay on local radio stations in the 1950s. Censorship efforts targeted Billie Holiday, Paul Robeson, and James Brown. But since *Brandenburg*, the music of N.W.A., Tupac Shakur, and Shawn Thomas has found protection in the courts. That would not have been the case before *Brandenburg* was applied to music.[50]

To ensure that cultural and political expression through music remains protected, regardless of the viewpoint being expressed, and to ensure that artists who are political minorities are not targeted by those in power, *Brandenburg* must remain as protective as it has been, and it must continue to be applied to musical expression. Music censorship in the United States never approached what has been documented in some other regimes around the globe historically or today, but that is because our courts have held firm to *Brandenburg*. When it comes to protecting musical expression and the *Brandenburg* test, the Supreme Court would do well to listen to the lyrics of Tom Petty's famous song, "I Won't Back Down."

Notes

1. 491 U.S. 781, 790 (internal citations omitted).
2. Plato, *The Republic of Plato*, trans. Alan Bloom (Basic Books, 2016), 80, 101.
3. Arnold Perris, "Music as Propaganda: Art at the Command of Doctrine in the People's Republic of China," *Ethnomusicology* 27 (1983): 1–28, 12.
4. Luisa Nardini, "In the Quest of Gallican Remnants in Gregorian Manuscripts: Archaisms in the Masses for the Holy Cross in Aquitanian Chant Books" in *The Oxford Handbook of Music Censorship*, ed. Patricia Hall (Oxford University Press, 2018), 7–37, 7.
5. Alejandro Enrique Planchart, "The English Kyrie," in The *Oxford Handbook of Music Censorship*, ed. Patricia Hall, 39–67, 47–48.
6. Cecilio J. Novillo, "Government," in *The SAGE International Encyclopedia of Music and Culture*, vol. 3, ed. Janet Sturman (SAGE Publications, 2019), 3, 1026–29, 1028.
7. Martin Cloonan, *Banned!: Censorship of Popular Music in Britain, 1967–92* (Arena, 1996), 11.
8. Francesco Izzo, "'Years in Prison': Giuseppe Verdi and Censorship in Pre-Unification Italy," in *The Oxford Handbook of Music Censorship*, ed. Patricia Hall, 237–57, 239–40.
9. Marie Korpe, Ole Reitov, and Martin Cloonan, "Music Censorship from Plato to the Present," in *Music and Manipulation: On the Social Uses and Social Control of Music*, eds. Steven Brown and Ulrik Volgsten (Berghahn Books, 2006), 239–63, 251–53.
10. See Barbara Makanowitzky, "Music to Serve the State," *Russian Review* 24 (1965): 266–77, 266–67; Korpe, Reitov, and Cloonan, 254–55; Dustin Koenig, "Pussy Riot and the First Amendment: Consequences for the Rule of Law in Russia," *New York University Law Review* 89 (2014): 666–99, 667–68; "Russia: Censorship of Younger Generation's Music," Human Rights Watch, last modified February 28, 2019, https://www.hrw.org/news/2019/02/28/russia-censorship-younger-generations-music#; Eric T. Kasper, "Explicit Lyrics: The First Amendment Free Speech Rulings that Have Protected against Music Censorship in the United States," *Loyola of Los Angeles Entertainment Law Review* 43 (2023): 173–246, 180–81, 84; Rachel Treisman, "Chechnya Is Banning Music that's Too Fast or Slow: These Songs Wouldn't Make the Cut," *NPR*, April 9, 2024, https://www.npr.org/2024/04/09/1243632570/chechnya-music-ban-bpm.
11. Hon-Lun Yang, "Curb that Enticing Tone: Music Censorship in the PRC," in *The Oxford Handbook of Music Censorship*, ed. Patricia Hall, 453–74, 456, 461–63, 467; David Pimentel, "The Blues and the Rule of Law: Musical Expressions of the Failure of Justice," *Loyola Law Review* 67 (2020): 191–222, 217.

12 See Novillo, "Government," 3: 1028; Peter Blecha, *Taboo Tunes: A History of Banned Bands and Censored Songs* (Backbeat Books, 2004), 5; Christine Feldman-Barrett, *A Women's History of the Beatles* (Bloomsbury Academic, 2021), 48; Jemayel Khawaja, "North Korea's Secret Weapon Is Terrible Synth Pop," *Vice*, last modified July 10, 2017, https://www.vice.com/en/article/7x9x8d/north-koreas-secret-weapon-is-terrible-synth-pop; Paula Thorrington Cronovich, "Out of the Blackout and into the Light: How the Arts Survived Pinochet's Dictatorship," *Iberoamericana* 13 (2013): 119–37, 120, 125; Michael Drewett, "Exploring Transitions in Popular Music: Censorship from Apartheid to Post-Apartheid South Africa," in *The Oxford Handbook of Music Censorship*, ed. Patricia Hall, 593–621, 595; Ana Hofmann, "Micronarratives of Music and (Self-)Censorship in Socialist Yugoslavia," in *The Oxford Handbook of Music Censorship*, ed. Patricia Hall, 259–73, 262–73; Nancy Guy, "Popular Music as a Barometer of Political Change," in *The Oxford Handbook of Music Censorship*, ed. Patricia Hall, 275–302, 279; Stephen Mamula, "Starting from Nowhere? Popular Music in Cambodia After the Khmer Rouge," *Asian Music* 39 (2008): 26–41, 30; Amenah Youssefzadeh, "Veiled Voices: Music and Censorship in Post-Revolutionary Iran," in *The Oxford Handbook of Music Censorship*, ed. Patricia Hall, 657–74, 661; John Street, "'Fight the Power': The Politics of Music and the Music of Politics," *Government and Opposition* 38 (2003): 113–30, 119–20; Hannah Beech, "Phyo Zeya Thaw, Burmese Pro-democracy Rapper, 41, Is Executed," *New York Times*, July 27, 2022, https://www.nytimes.com/2022/07/27/world/asia/27phyo-zeya-thaw-dead.html?referringSource=articleShare; Kasper, "Explicit Lyrics," 182–84.

13 See Mark Knowles, *Tap Roots: An Early History of Tap Dancing* (McFarland, 2002), 39; Patricia L. Dooley, *Freedom of Speech: Reflections in Art and Popular Culture* (ABC-CLIO, 2017), 54; Ralph G. Giordano, *Satan in the Dance Hall: Rev. John Roach Straton, Social Dancing, and Morality in 1920s New York City* (Scarecrow Press, 2008), 80; Blecha, *Taboo Tunes*, 143–48; Darlene Clark Hein, "Paul Robeson's Impact on History," in *Paul Robeson: The Great Forerunner*, ed. Freedomways (International, 1998), 142–49, 147; Kasper, "Explicit Lyrics," 184–87.

14 See Eric Nuzum, *Parental Advisory: Music Censorship in America* (Perennial, 2001), 214, 216, 221–22; Minna Bromberg and Gary Alan Fine, "Resurrecting the Red: Pete Seeger and the Purification of Difficult Reputations," *Social Forces* 80 (2002): 1135–55, 1140–41; Christopher Gair, *The American Counterculture* (Edinburgh University Press, 2007), 32; Blecha, *Taboo Tunes*, 96; Kasper, "Explicit Lyrics," 187–89.

15 See "Rocker Jim Morrison Arrested this Day in New Haven," *New Haven Register*, December 9, 2019, https://www.nhregister.com/news/article/Rocker-Jim-Morrison-arrested-this-day-in-New-Haven-14892565.php; Dave Itzkoff, "Jim Morrison Is Candidate for Pardon in '69 Arrest," *New*

York Times, November 16, 2010, https://www.nytimes.com/2010/11/17/us/17crist.html; Gabrielle Calise, "How Janis Joplin Was Arrested in Tampa 50 Years Ago," *Tampa Bay Times*, November 14, 2019, https://www.tampabay.com/news/tampa/2019/11/14/how-janis-joplin-was-arrested-in-tampa-50-years-ago/; Will Higgins, "That Time Indiana Teens Ratted Out Dirty 'Louie Louie' Lyrics, and the FBI Got Involved," *Indianapolis Star*, January 2, 2019, https://www.indystar.com/story/entertainment/2019/01/02/kingsmen-louie-louie-richard-berry-song-lyrics-dirty-version-fbi-investigation-indiana-teens/2240339002/; In Re Licensee Responsibility to Review Records before Their Broadcast, 28 F.C.C.2d 409, 409 (1971); Yale Broadcasting Co. v. F.C.C., 478 F.2d 594, 595 (D.C. Cir. 1973); Blecha, *Taboo Tunes*, 151, 154, 158; Nuzum, *Parental Advisory*, 145–47, 154, 224; Kasper, "Explicit Lyrics," 189–92.

16 Brandenburg v. Ohio, 395 U.S. 444, 444–46, 448–49 (1969).
17 Hess v. Indiana, 414 U.S. 105, 107–9 (1973).
18 See NAACP v. Claiborne Hardware Co., 458 U.S. 886, 900n28, 902, 910, 928 (1982).
19 Southeastern Promotions, Ltd. v. Conrad, 420 U.S. 546, 557–58 (1975) (emphasis added).
20 Alan K. Chen, "Instrumental Music and the First Amendment," *Hastings Law Journal* 66 (2015): 381–442, 392.
21 Schad v. Borough of Mount Ephraim, 452 U.S. 61, 65 (1981) (emphasis added).
22 Ward, 491 U.S. at 790, 791.
23 McCollum v. CBS, Inc., 202 Cal. App. 3d 989, 993–1000 (1988).
24 McCollum, 202 Cal. App. 3d at 1001–2, 1005–6.
25 Judas Priest v. Second Judicial District Court of State of Nevada, 104 Nev. 424, 425 (1988); Vance v. Judas Priest, 1990 WL 130920, at *8–14, *22 (Nev. Dist. Ct. Aug. 24, 1990).
26 Waller v. Osborne, 763 F. Supp. 1144, 1145-49 (M.D. Ga. 1991).
27 Waller, 763 F. Supp. at 1150–51 and n10.
28 See Peter Hart, "Straight Outta Compton's Censorship Lesson," National Coalition Against Censorship, August 25, 2015, https://ncac.org/news/blog/straight-outta-comptons-censorship-lesson; Bryan J. McCann, *The Mark of Criminality: Rhetoric, Race, and Gangsta Rap in the War-on-Crime Era* (University of Alabama Press, 2017), 54; Mathieu Deflem, "Popular Culture and Social Control: The Moral Panic on Music Labeling," *American Journal of Criminal Justice* 45 (2019): 16–17.
29 Anita M. Samuels, "Comebacks, Rap Smashes Spark R&B," *Billboard*, Dec. 26, 1998, at 36.
30 Davidson v. Time Warner, Inc., 1997 WL 405907, at *1 (S.D. Tex. Mar. 31, 1997).
31 Davidson, 1997 WL 405907, at *12, *15–16, *20.
32 Davidson, 1997 WL 405907, at *20–22.

33 Lissa Skitolsky, *Hip-Hop as Philosophical Text and Testimony: Can I Get a Witness?* (Lexington Books, 2020), 3–4.
34 Hart v. State, No. PD-0677-22, slip op. at 17 (Tex. Crim. App. May 8, 2024).
35 See Joseph Burstyn, Inc. v. Wilson, 343 U.S. 495 (1952).
36 Matarazzo v. Aerosmith Productions, 1989 WL 140322, at *1–3 (S.D.N.Y. Nov. 16, 1989).
37 Molli Mitchell, "What Went Wrong at Woodstock '99? 'Perfect Cocktail of Unfortunate Events,'" *Newsweek*, August 5, 2022, https://www.newsweek.com/what-happened-woodstock-1999-limp-bizkit-riots-director-1731258.
38 Brian Ives, "Anthony Kiedis: Why Red Hot Chili Peppers Played 'Fire' at Woodstock '99," WMMR, August 9, 2022, https://wmmr.com/2022/08/09/anthony-kiedis-why-red-hot-chili-peppers-played-fire-at-woodstock-99/.
39 Torries v. Hebert, 111 F. Supp. 2d 806, 810-13 (W.D. La. 2000).
40 Torries, 111 F. Supp. 2d at 819–20.
41 Stricklin v. Stefani, 358 F. Supp. 3d 516, 522–23 (W.D.N.C. 2018).
42 Stricklin, 358 F. Supp. 3d at 527–29.
43 Stricklin, 358 F. Supp. 3d at 529.
44 "The First Amendment: Where America Stands, 2023 Update," Freedom Forum, https://www.freedomforum.org/where-america-stands/2023-update/.
45 Waller, 763 F. Supp. at 1150.
46 Davidson, 1997 WL 405907, at *22.
47 Torries, 111 F. Supp. 2d at 810.
48 Davidson, 1997 WL 405907, at *22 (internal quotation omitted).
49 Davidson, 1997 WL 405907, *21.
50 Kasper, "Explicit Lyrics," 239; Robert Corn-Revere, *The Mind of the Censor and the Eye of the Beholder* (Cambridge University Press, 2021), 146–47; Gair, *American Counterculture*, 32; Amy Absher, *The Black Musician and the White City: Race and Music in Chicago, 1900–1967* (University of Michigan Press, 2018), 101.

Chapter Seven

"Terrorism" and Arguments to Disregard *Brandenburg*'s Incitement Test

Christina E. Wells

Brandenburg v. Ohio's incitement standard prohibits government officials from punishing advocacy of illegal activity unless it is directed and likely to incite imminent activity.[1] *Brandenburg*'s standard is a pillar of free speech law because it allows government officials to punish only truly dangerous speech while preventing them from suppressing speech simply because they dislike it. In recent years, however, terrorist advocacy urging or glorifying violence, spreading propaganda, and recruiting individuals to terrorist causes has put pressure on the *Brandenburg* standard. Although most such advocacy does not meet *Brandenburg*'s strict requirements, observers have suggested altering or working around *Brandenburg*'s incitement standard to counter the dangerous influence of terrorist advocacy, especially advocacy occurring through online sources.

Although concerns over the potential harms resulting from terrorist advocacy are understandable, exempting terrorist advocacy from the *Brandenburg* standard — and specifically from the requirement of imminent harm — ignores the important role that imminence plays in preventing officials from using national security crises to suppress dissenting viewpoints. Indeed, *Brandenburg* was largely a response to an earlier, more lenient, "clear and present danger" test that allowed government officials to target and punish disfavored groups as "dangerous." Removing the imminence requirement raises the risk that such abuse could occur again.

This is especially true given the nebulous nature of the concept "terrorism." Arguments for changing *Brandenburg* tend to focus on the dangers of international jihadist terrorism. But nothing about the term *terrorism* is so limited. Terrorism is a malleable concept with dozens of different social and legal definitions. The malleable nature of the terms *terrorist* and *terrorism* make them susceptible to abuse, with officials casting disfavored groups as terrorists while not using the term against groups about whom they approve. As one observer noted, "the definition of terrorism seems to depend on point of view — it is what the 'bad guys' do."[2]

Rewriting *Brandenburg* to fight the subjective danger of "terrorism" begs officials to misuse the standard. For example, the tendency to equate terrorism with international jihadist terrorism ignores numerous domestic organizations within the United States whose activities potentially fall within definitions of terrorism. In fact, right-wing domestic organizations, like the National Socialist Movement or Vanguard America, have dominated these activities,[3] but, until recently, most people rarely discussed their activities as terrorism. Although right-wing groups engage in terrorist advocacy, the free speech discussion surrounding their activities is opaque and confusing. Courts occasionally subject right-wing organizations' speech to *Brandenburg*'s standard but only cautiously and after violence occurred.[4] More often, arguments focus on whether their speech amounts to "hate speech," which is broadly protected in the United States.[5]

In contrast, some government officials have been increasingly willing to use the term *terrorism* to describe groups advocating on behalf of racial minorities, such as the Black Lives Matter movement, antifa, and environmental organizations, despite lack of evidence linking them to significant violence.[6] This seemingly arbitrary application of the term *terrorism* is dangerous, as it is rooted in historic attempts to suppress the speech of labor groups, socialists, communists, and other marginalized groups.

The first main section of this chapter, "A Brief History of the Road to *Brandenburg*," sketches the legal and social history leading up to *Brandenburg*, focusing on the punishment of speakers during World War I, the Red Scare, and the Cold War. It locates *Brandenburg* as a response to earlier, less-protective tests allowing government officials to target and suppress disfavored groups' speech. The second main section, "A Terrorism Exception to *Brandenburg* and Its Historic Implications," discusses scholarly proposals to exempt terrorist advocacy from *Brandenburg* and examines how those proposals discount the historical importance of the imminence requirement in protecting the speech of disfavored groups. The third main section "The Amorphous Definition of *Terrorism* and Its Effect on an Exception to *Brandenburg*," examines definitions of terrorism, demonstrating that they are broad and malleable. With an understanding of the malleability of these definitions, this final section reexamines the impact of weakening *Brandenburg*'s strict requirements and concludes that any attempt to regulate terrorist advocacy under a weakened *Brandenburg* test will allow officials to arbitrarily punish speech.

A Brief History of the Road to *Brandenburg*

Brandenburg evolved from an earlier test — the "clear and present danger test" created during the World War I era and tweaked over the next fifty years. An examination of this test and its evolution reveals why the current version is so important.

World War I and the Birth of "Clear and Present Danger"

During World War I, government officials prosecuted antiwar protestors under the Espionage and Sedition Acts, which prohibited interference with the war effort and disloyal speech.[7] Officials argued that even generalized criticism of the war was dangerous because "any speech to a large group might reach draft-age men [or any] communications to women might be passed onto their sons, brothers, and sweethearts."[8] Prosecutions particularly aimed to destroy disfavored groups, such as the Socialist Party and labor groups. As one scholar noted, people or groups "who had assured economic and social status, did not question the basis of our economic system, accepted the war as a holy crusade and expressed their views in somewhat temperate language were allowed to criticize the government; those who suffered were those whose views on the war were derived from some objectionable economic or social doctrines."[9] Courts convicted nearly half of those prosecuted for criticizing the war relying on the prevailing "bad tendency" test, which allowed courts to assume that criticism of the war effort tended to violate the law (for example, by causing resistance to the draft) and that the speaker's criticism showed intent to cause harm regardless of whether other evidence existed to support the government's charges.[10]

In *Schenck v. United States* (1919), the Supreme Court upheld an Espionage Act conviction against a free speech challenge. *Schenck* involved the conviction of a Socialist Party official for conspiracy to cause insubordination in the military after distributing a leaflet attacking the draft to potential draftees. Justice Oliver Wendell Holmes Jr., writing for a unanimous Court, acknowledged that the case implicated the First Amendment but believed the appropriate constitutional test was whether words were "used in such circumstances and [were] of such a nature as to create a clear and present danger that they will bring about the substantive evils that Congress has a right to prevent."[11] Although the leaflet seemingly urged lawful resistance to the draft, Holmes found it presented a clear and present danger of draft obstruction given the wartime circumstances and the defendant's presumed intent to obstruct the draft by sending the leaflet to potential draftees.

Because *Schenck* never defined the parameters of the clear and present danger test, government officials had little trouble characterizing political advocacy as dangerous sedition. Soon after *Schenck*, the Court invoked the decision to uphold convictions of unpopular speakers critical of the government.[12] As a result, the clear and present danger test was essentially a reformulation of the bad tendency test and did little to protect the speech of disfavored groups.[13]

The Red Scare: Judicial Deference

After World War I, repression of unpopular speakers, especially labor groups and socialists, continued. Demand for progressive economic reform by such groups prompted antipathy from moderate business and labor organizations concerned with maintaining the economic status quo while a series of labor strikes and bombings in 1919 sparked fear and suspicion.[14] Opponents of these organizations engaged in "red-baiting" designed to raise fear of foreign influence in labor activity and distrust of unions. States targeted ostensibly radical expression with criminal syndicalism laws that prohibited advocacy of overthrow of the government. In 1919 to 1920, government officials rounded up and deported hundreds of suspected radicals, often based on fabricated or exaggerated charges under these laws.[15] In this sense, the term *radical* covered "the most innocent departure from conventional thought" as people, especially people with liberal orientations, were accused of radical leanings.[16]

The Red Scare also affected the Supreme Court, which heard two key cases involving speech rights during the 1920s. In *Gitlow v. New York* (1925), Benjamin Gitlow was convicted under the New York criminal syndicalism law, which prohibited advocacy of violent overthrow of the government. Gitlow's conviction rested on his publication and distribution of the *Left Wing Manifesto*, which advocated for the necessity of communist revolutionary change.[17] The Supreme Court rejected Gitlow's claim that the New York law violated his free speech rights. Rather than apply the clear and present danger test, however, the Court simply deferred to the state legislature's decision to outlaw radical speech. According to the Court, the *Left Wing Manifesto* was a "call to action," even if only a future call to action, and the New York legislature's belief that such speech posed a "danger of substantive evil" was neither arbitrary nor unreasonable.[18] Two years later, in *Whitney v. California* (1927), the Court upheld the conviction of another defendant under California's criminal syndicalism law — this time for organizing a group that advocated violent overthrow of the government. Relying on *Gitlow*'s deferential approach, the Court found the California law reasonable because "united and joint action [with others] involve[d] even greater danger to the public peace and security than the isolated utterances and acts of individuals."[19]

Dissenters in both cases argued the clear and present danger test applied. In *Gitlow*, Justice Holmes noted that advocacy of violent regime change, like all expressions of opinion, may cause people to change their minds but argued that the First Amendment protected such speech. Because the *Left Wing Manifesto* merely attempted to induce an uprising at "some indefinite time in the future," Holmes argued, it did not present a clear and present danger of harm.[20] Holmes's version of the clear and present danger test in *Gitlow* is more stringent than in *Schenck*. It derives from an earlier dissent in *Abrams v. United States*,[21] where Holmes apparently came to see the requirement of imminent harm as necessary to distinguish between dangerous speech and mere criticism of government actions. In *Abrams*, Holmes argued that "only the present danger of immediate evil or an intent to bring it about . . . warrants Congress in setting a limit to the expression of opinion where private rights are not concerned."[22]

In *Whitney*, Justice Louis Brandeis similarly favored a strong application of the clear and present danger test but acknowledged that the Court had set few definitive standards regarding that test. Brandeis argued that the value of free speech in protecting human dignity and shared and stable government justified stringent protection, concluding that "advocacy of [law] violation, however reprehensible morally, is not a justification for denying free speech where the advocacy falls short of incitement and there is nothing to indicate that the advocacy would be immediately acted on."[23]

The Cold War: Clear and Present Danger Redux

The Holmes–Brandeis version of the clear and present danger test took hold by the early 1940s,[24] but the Cold War led to repression of an unpopular group — communists. Although most of them rarely did more than teach communist doctrine, fear of domestic communists led states to pursue them under sedition laws that prohibited advocating overthrow of the government. The Truman administration publicly equated domestic communists with Soviet aggression, making domestic communism an issue of national security; Herbert Hoover argued that "communists were infiltrating every aspect of life in the United States."[25] The House Un-American Activities Committee held hearings to expose communist sympathizers who allegedly threatened the American way of life. By the end of the 1940s, Americans held a pervasive fear that domestic communists posed a threat to the nation despite the lack of evidence to support this belief.[26]

In this atmosphere, federal officials charged leaders of the Communist Party USA (CPUSA) under the Smith Act, which prohibited knowingly or willfully advocating or teaching the duty, necessity, desirability or propriety of forcible overthrow of the government.[27] The government charged the defendants with conspiracy to advocate overthrow of the government, rather than advocacy of overthrow, due to the lack of evidence to support the latter charge.[28] The conspiracy charge allowed the government to argue that "by virtue of its adherence to Marxist-Leninist principles . . . the CPUSA was itself a conspiracy to advocate overthrow of the government."²⁹ The defendants were easily convicted given the prevailing atmosphere of fear.

The defendants appealed, claiming their convictions violated the First Amendment. Chief Justice Fred Vinson's plurality opinion in *Dennis v. United States* (1951) explicitly rejected the earlier deference of *Gitlow* and *Whitney* and acknowledged that the First Amendment only allowed punishment of speech presenting a clear and present danger of harm. According to Vinson, however, the test required courts to "ask whether the gravity of the 'evil,' discounted by its improbability, justifies such invasion of free speech as is necessary to avoid the danger." Unlike the Holmes–Brandeis version of the test, Vinson's version operated on a sliding scale, allowing punishment of speech causing less imminent or less probable harm if the harm was serious. Vinson and other justices in the plurality found that the communist conspiracy easily met this version of the test because it was highly organized, rigidly disciplined, and waiting for instructions to act when the time was right, which posed a danger that far outweighed the admittedly nonimminent potential overthrow of the government.³⁰

The dissenting justices in *Dennis* accused their colleagues of sacrificing the clear and present danger test to the fear permeating the times. Justice Hugo Black argued that the plurality had implicitly repudiated the test and that defendants were convicted of conspiring to do nothing more than organize the Communist Party and use legal publications to discuss the overthrow of the government.³¹ Justice William Douglas similarly argued that "[n]either prejudice nor hate nor senseless fear should be the basis" of a conviction and that free speech "should not be sacrificed on anything less than plain and objective proof of danger that the evil advocated is imminent."³²

Brandenburg: the Culmination of "Clear and Present Danger"

The hysteria of the early Cold War eventually waned, and in 1969 the Court revisited the clear and present danger test in *Brandenburg v. Ohio*. *Brandenburg* involved a Ku Klux Klan leader charged under an Ohio criminal syndicalism law prohibiting advocacy of government overthrow similar to those in *Whitney* and *Dennis*. For nearly a hundred years, the Klan had terrorized Black and Jewish citizens, among others. The *Brandenburg* charges, however, were based on speech occurring at an isolated, rural rally involving approximately twelve armed and hooded individuals. At the rally, the participants used racial epithets and made derogatory statements. In a speech to those present, the defendant said: "We're not a revengent organization, but if our President, our Congress, our Supreme Court, continues to suppress the white, Caucasian race, it's possible that there might have to be some revengeance taken."³³

The lower court convicted the defendant of violating the Ohio law; the Supreme Court reversed. According to the Court, "the mere abstract teaching . . . of the moral propriety or even moral necessity for a resort to force and violence is not the same as preparing a group for violent action and steeling it to such action." Thus, the First Amendment does "not permit a State to forbid or proscribe advocacy of the use of force or of law violation except where such advocacy is directed to inciting or producing imminent lawless action and is likely to incite or produce such action." Because the Ohio law did not distinguish between advocacy and incitement, it violated the defendant's freedom of speech.[34]

The *Brandenburg* standard is difficult to satisfy. It is designed to protect even the ugliest political advocacy while allowing punishment of speech intended and likely to cause imminent harm.[35] *Brandenburg* thus is a significant change from earlier standards. By requiring proof that a speaker intend to cause harm and that this harm will likely result from speech, the test builds on the Holmes–Brandeis speech protective tradition by prohibiting government officials from claiming that political advocacy is dangerous based on unwarranted causal inferences or unreasonably magnified harm.[36] The imminence requirement adds to this protection of political rhetoric. Under *Brandenburg*: "[it is] permissible to stir up opposition to government policy even with the specific intent that members of the audience be favorably disposed to lawless action at some future time. And it is permissible to expressly advocate lawless action if no one is likely to act on the advice, a principal that protects much emotionally fulfilling radical rhetoric about imaginary resistance."[37] In this sense, *Brandenburg* is the Court's response to previous tests that allowed persecution of unpopular speakers.[38]

A Terrorism Exception to *Brandenburg* and Its Historic Implications

Scholars' Arguments to Change the *Brandenburg* Standard

Terrorist advocacy arguably puts pressure on *Brandenburg*'s standard. Terrorist organizations increasingly spread propaganda, glorify violence, or urge others "to go to war with perceived enemies of Islam."[39] Many organizations use sophisticated electronic media campaigns, allowing them to recruit and influence potential followers: "The broad reach of the internet has made it easier than ever to establish terrorist contacts; groups that were formerly so geographically dispersed that communications between them were either impractical or impossible now have the means to collaborate, share membership lists, recruit new members, and advise each other. . . . Technically adept terrorist organizations and their devotees exploit social networking sites to spread ideologies, disseminate instructional videos, consolidate power, and threaten enemies."[40] These increased internet activities also correspond with violence. For example, internet distribution of the teachings and lectures of radical Muslim cleric, Anwar Al-Awlaki, arguably influenced several terrorists who attacked within the United States.[41]

Fearing the radicalization of those exposed to terrorist advocacy, some observers urge us to rethink *Brandenburg*'s role in the regulation of terrorist advocacy. Professor Cass Sunstein, for example, argues that "terrorism, and . . . [the] Islamic State in particular, pose a fresh challenge to the greatest American contribution to the theory and practice of free speech: the clear and present danger test." He acknowledges that regulating terrorist recruitment and propaganda does not meet *Brandenburg*'s requirements because most terrorist advocacy does not present an imminent threat of harm; he further notes that "there may be value in even the most extreme and hateful forms of speech," if for no other reason than that we "can learn what other people believe." However, Sunstein argues that the *Brandenburg* standard is relatively new and "might not be so well-suited" to terrorist advocacy. Asking whether the benefit of terrorist advocacy outweighs "the genuine risk[s] of large numbers of deaths," Sunstein proposes that we allow punishment if an individual explicitly incites violence that produces a genuine risk to public safety, regardless of whether the harm is imminent.[42]

Professor Eric Posner argues that "[n]ever before in our history have enemies outside the United States been able to propagate genuinely dangerous ideas on American territory in such an effective way . . . [i.e.,] ideas that lead directly to terrorist attacks that kill people." Posner suggests criminal penalties for those who "access websites that glorify, express support for, or provide encouragement for ISIS or support recruitment by ISIS," or who distribute or encourage access to links to such websites. His proposal is designed to deter innocent yet curious readers from accessing websites to prevent their radicalization. Posner acknowledges *Brandenburg* as an obstacle to his proposal, but argues that the standard should be considered in light of the numerous pre-*Brandenburg* cases allowing punishment of "dangerous" speech regardless of imminent harm. "[A]nti-propaganda laws," Posner argues, may be warranted "because of the unique challenge posed by ISIS's sophisticated exploitation of modern technology."[43]

Professor Alexander Tsesis maintains that *Brandenburg* does not prevent criminalizing terrorist advocacy, but instead applies only to situations involving imminently dangerous statements. Recognizing that most terrorist advocacy instead seeks indoctrination, mentoring, and recruitment, Tsesis argues that *Dennis* is a more appropriate precedent to apply to terrorist speech that falls short of imminent incitement. *Dennis*, he reasons, recognized the dangers of slow communist indoctrination and revised the clear and present danger test to address the difference between those circumstances and the typical case involving advocacy of imminent violence. *Dennis* thus distinguishes between "agitating for change," which the First Amendment protects, and speech that incites or directly supports violence through the use of propaganda or recruitment efforts, which the First Amendment does not protect. Because *Brandenburg* did not expressly overrule *Dennis*, Tsesis argues both cases address different situations.[44]

Locating Scholars' Arguments in *Brandenburg*'s History

Although concern about terrorism advocacy is understandable, proposals to alter or work around *Brandenburg* are misguided because they ignore the social and legal history leading up to *Brandenburg*. The idea that terrorist advocacy is uniquely dangerous ignores that the nearly identical arguments were made about the speech of socialists and communists during the Red Scare and Cold War. During the Red Scare officials described Russian Bolshevism as the "greatest danger" facing the country."[45] Cold War officials argued communism was "a far greater threat to our existence than any other threat," and if the United States "does not successfully cope with the communist threat, then it need not worry about any other threat to the internal security of this nation, because it is not impossible that there will be no nation."[46]

Fears about the ease with which the internet allows terrorists to influence others are also similar to earlier eras. Even without the internet, officials during World War I and the Cold War warned of foreign actors who had created sophisticated networks of operatives willing to do their work (sometimes unwittingly) to undermine the country. In *Dennis*, for example, the Court called the CPUSA "a highly organized conspiracy, with rigidly disciplined members subject to call when the leaders . . . felt that the time had come for action."[47] Similarly, during World War I, President Wilson, cited the "military masters of Germany" who filled "our unsuspecting communities with vicious spies and conspirators."[48]

Furthermore, while the internet is a new and powerful communication tool, the research is unclear as to whether it, and social media in particular, leads to increased radicalization (as opposed to reflecting a demand that already exists).[49] A great deal of outreach, discussion, and planning can occur on the internet as the Supreme Court recently noted, even as it unanimously rejected imposing aiding and abetting liability on social media platforms for terrorist activity. As Justice Clarence Thomas wrote, "bad actors" could just as easily use cell phones and email for their "illegal — and sometimes terrible — ends."[50] We should closely scrutinize the argument that online terrorism advocacy is somehow exceptional and a reason to alter *Brandenburg*.

Arguments that the imminence requirement is unnecessary because terrorists seek long-term indoctrination also ignore that identical arguments supported *Dennis*'s extraordinarily deferential approach, which is criticized for distorting the Holmes–Brandeis version on which it purported to rely.[51] Abandoning the imminence requirement ignores its role in helping judges and juries determine the presence of intent, causation, and actual harm resulting from speech.[52] Courts cannot dispense with that requirement without ill effects. Rather, history shows that its removal subjects speakers to a wide variety of abuses at the hands of the government.

Arguments for changing or working around *Brandenburg* are especially problematic because such change may be unnecessary. According to Professor Alan Chen, the government often satisfies *Brandenburg*'s requirements in terrorism prosecutions and most serious dangers posed by terrorists' speech are "direct, step-by-step incitement and hand-holding" that clearly subject individuals to prosecution. After examining prosecutions involving international terrorism activities, he noted that courts willing to consider First Amendment defenses rejected them because the actions of the groups easily satisfied *Brandenburg*'s requirements and "far exceed[ed] the general type of advocacy that *Brandenburg* protects." Chen concluded: "[I]f there are grave concerns about national security and the internet leading to tangible social harms that cannot be addressed in any way other than relaxing the *Brandenburg* standard, the evidence of such a problem has yet to emerge in any concrete way."[53]

The Amorphous Definition of *Terrorism* and Its Effect on an Exception to *Brandenburg*

If removing the imminence requirement in the name of terrorism renders *Brandenburg* subject to abuse, the nebulous nature of the term *terrorism* further exacerbates the problem. In the above examples, advocates for change focused on the unique and potentially catastrophic harm international jihadist terrorism poses. Yet nothing limits the definition of terrorism to jihadist terrorists. Terrorism is a malleable concept susceptible to abuse as officials use the term to cast certain groups in a disfavored light while refraining from using it against groups about whom they approve. The arbitrariness associated with punishing terrorist advocacy parallels the demonization of labor, socialist, and communist groups of the early twentieth century.

The Difficulty with Defining *Terrorism*

One can generally define *terrorism* as intentionally violent action against innocents that is politically or ideologically motivated and designed to intimidate or coerce.[54] Yet even here there exists disagreement. For example, almost everyone agrees that violence and political or ideological motivation are necessary aspects of terrorism.[55] But there is widespread disagreement over the necessity of various other elements — for example, must terrorist activity target innocents or must it involve group activity?[56] As a result, there is no single definition of *terrorism*. Rather, commentators have cataloged hundreds of definitions of that term.[57]

The plethora and generality of definitions make labeling acts of violence as terrorism a subjective and pejorative exercise. Use of the term *terrorism* "assigns a moral judgment to the act and the actor, a moral judgment, which is nearly universally negative."[58] It is thus tempting to use the term against those one wants to degrade socially, while not applying it to perpetrators of violence with which one sympathizes. Not surprisingly, governments use the terms *terrorism* or *terrorist* against opponents to maintain power: "To label a person, group, or activity 'terrorist' serves not just as a shorthand description, nor even simply as a statement of moral indignation, but primarily as a call to action — a demand for elimination."[59]

Arguably, we could avoid the subjectivity associated with the term terrorism by using an appropriately specific legal definition. For example, Section 2331 of the federal criminal code defines "international terrorism" as activities that:

> involve violent acts or acts dangerous to human life that are [or would be] a violation of the criminal laws of the United States or of any State [if committed in that jurisdiction];
> appear to be intended —
> to intimidate or coerce a civilian population;
> to influence the policy of a government by intimidation or coercion; or
> to affect the conduct of a government by mass destruction, assassination, or kidnapping; and
> occur primarily outside the territorial jurisdiction of the United States, or transcend national boundaries in terms of the means by which they are accomplished, the persons they appear intended to intimidate or coerce, or the locale in which their perpetrators operate or seek asylum.[60]

Yet Section 2331's definition, although more structured than the general definition discussed earlier, is strikingly similar to it. At its core, the law simply prohibits ideologically motivated actions outside of the United States designed to coerce individuals, groups, or the government into action. The statutory definition is not much narrower than the general definition and still leaves much discretion to officials. The few guardrails associated with the legal definition are relatively feeble. Various provisions of federal law incorporate Section 2331, which arguably give additional guidance as to its use; but federal law also contains at least nineteen different legal definitions of *terrorism*, all with their own approach.[61] The multiple and overlapping definitions of *terrorism* cause confusion about when actions amount to terrorism, since actions considered terrorism under one provision may not be terrorism under another.[62] Furthermore, the multitude of definitions fuels long-standing criticism that government officials selectively apply the term *terrorism* only to disfavored criminal defendants.[63] The legal definitions, then, provide little more protection from inconsistent application than the general definitions.

Arbitrary Applications of Terrorism Definitions to Regulate Speech: Domestic Organizations

The United States' treatment of domestic groups reflects the arbitrary nature of the term *terrorism* and its potential for great mischief when speech is involved. Numerous groups within the United States arguably engage in activities fitting within the definition of "domestic terrorism," which federal law defines nearly identically to "international terrorism," except that the actions must occur within (instead of outside of) US jurisdiction.[64] The Department of Justice has identified domestic terrorism threats to encompass criminal activity by left-wing groups (for example, animal rights extremists, ecoterrorists, anarchists, and Black separatists) and right-wing groups (for example, antigovernment extremists, white supremacists, and anti-abortion extremists).[65] A report in 2020 noted that attacks by right-wing groups (defined as white nationalists, antigovernment and incel organizations) "account[ed] for the majority of all terrorist incidents in the United States since 1994" and the "total number of right-wing attacks and plots has grown substantially during the past six years."[66] In 2019, FBI officials noted that white supremacists were responsible "for the most lethal incidents among domestic terrorists in recent years."[67]

Nevertheless, scholars have highlighted officials' reluctance to label violence by such groups as terrorism.[68] To be sure, after the mass shootings in El Paso, Texas, and Buffalo, New York, in 2019 and 2022, members of the public and officials are increasingly willing to use the term *domestic terrorism* when discussing atrocities motivated by white supremacist ideology.[69] Yet, this orientation is recent and stands against a long history of officials tolerating white violence against minorities and leftist groups even as officials pursued actions against outsider (largely immigrant) groups such as those discussed in the first section of this chapter. As far back as the nineteenth century, "bombings attributed to anarchists or labor activists often served to justify widespread campaigns of suppression against radical movements" while "[l]ynchings and race riots, by contrast, generally met with inaction, even approval, in official circles. . . . Normative judgments, not simply law enforcement strategy, have long shaped how and if acts of terrorism become national emergencies."[70] Our current discussion of terrorism continues this racialized narrative in which terrorism is committed by Muslims, rather than white people, and where "far-right violence . . . is severely under-addressed as a matter of Justice Department policy and practice."[71]

Arbitrary treatment of the terrorism label extends to speech as well. The online speech activities of white supremacist organizations, for example, are similar, if not identical, to those of international jihadist organizations. Such organizations use social media to make and post plans about future violence, to boast of past violence at rallies, and to recruit potential members.[72] Finally, noting that "extremist groups are able to quickly normalize their messages by delivering a never-ending stream of hateful propaganda to the masses," observers have cataloged acts of violence perpetrated by individuals exposed to this propaganda online.[73]

But few people label this speech "terrorist advocacy" or suggest regulating it under a modified *Brandenburg* standard.[74] Rather, many often label it as "hate speech" because it involves derogation of or calls to act against racial or religious minorities.[75] Regulation of "hateful" speech is controversial since the Supreme Court has long protected incendiary and offensive speech.[76] As the Court has observed, "[s]peech that demeans on the basis of race, ethnicity, gender, religion, age, disability, or any other similar ground is hateful; but the proudest boast of our free speech jurisprudence is that we protect the freedom to express 'the thought that we hate.'"[77] Thus, calls to regulate terrorist advocacy of white nationalist organizations are frequently characterized as censorial and prohibitively difficult because of the inherent subjectivity in determining whether speech falls into that category.[78]

After the May 2022 Buffalo supermarket shootings, authorities discovered the shooter's online radicalization after reading about "replacement theory," a conspiracy theory about a plan to replace white voters with an inundation of immigrant voters in the United States.[79] Although such internet activity is similar to jihadist terrorist radicalization, observers rarely referred to the Buffalo incident as involving terrorist advocacy or incitement. Instead, most demanded greater accountability for online hate speech, noting that "[t]here's got to be a recognition of the role that . . . social media companies can play in ferreting out the use of technology to promote hate."[80] That demand for greater accountability in turn engendered pushback from others. News personality Tucker Carlson, for example, argued to his audience that hate speech is merely "speech that our leaders hate. So because a mentally ill teenager murdered strangers, you cannot be allowed to express your political views out loud."[81]

In *Sines v. Kessler*, a federal district court rejected the First Amendment defense of white nationalist organizations (for example, National Socialist Movement, Identity Evropa) that planned and executed the August 2017 violent protests in Charlottesville, Virginia. Instead, the court found their speech unprotected under *Brandenburg* due to the groups' extensive planning and intent to incite violence at the protests. *Sines* involved an attempt to impose civil liability under a Reconstruction-era terrorism law. The case arguably recognized the terrorist aspects associated with the protests. Yet the overall discussion of the groups' actions largely flitted around the role of hate speech and whether it should be outlawed. At the very least, we remain unsure of the appropriate lens with which to discuss this issue, highlighting how easy it is to manipulate.[82]

In contrast to white supremacist groups, some federal officials during the first Trump administration were increasingly willing to use the term *terrorist* to describe leftist activists within the United States. The Federal Bureau of Investigation's (FBI's) Domestic Terrorism Analysis Unit concluded that the "Black Identity Extremist" movement posed a "violent threat" because "black activists' grievances about racialized police violence and inequities in the criminal justice system have spurred retaliatory violence against law enforcement officers."[83] The FBI's statement referred only to isolated incidents of violence and contained no reference to an African American organization committing violence against a police officer. The lack of evidence to support the existence of a "Black Identity Extremist" movement prompted one expert to declare that the term primarily referred to "black people who scare [the FBI]."[84]

President Trump similarly announced that he was considering designating antifa, a militant left-wing movement that sometimes clashes violently with white supremacist organizations at rallies, as a terrorist organization.[85] Reports also suggested that the FBI opened domestic terrorism investigations into environmental protestors that the FBI referred to as extremists.[86] After January 6, 2021, President Trump and supporters continued to label leftist movements, especially antifa and Black Lives Matter, as terrorist or violent organizations in an attempt to diminish the violence that occurred at the US Capitol.[87] In May 2023, Representative Dan Bishop, chair of the House Homeland Security Subcommittee on Oversight, Investigations, and Accountability, announced a hearing on "left-wing violence," which noted that *"[t]he left-wing lawlessness Americans experienced during the summer of 2020 was, unfortunately, only the beginning of a long season of political violence and intimidation."*[88]

Despite these officials' statements, studies suggest that the overwhelming number of Black Lives Matter protests were peaceful and that violence by left-leaning organizations is low, especially compared to right-wing organizations.[89] Furthermore, when violence or property damage has occurred at rallies or other events, it is often a by-product of the protest rather than the purpose of it.[90] Lack of purposeful violence or damage places these groups' actions beyond the realm of terrorism since politically or ideologically motivated violence is the linchpin of *terrorism*'s definition. The decision to call leftist groups terrorists absent supporting evidence is deliberately stigmatizing. Such uses of the term *terrorism* delegitimize protestors, much as officials attempted to delegitimize dissent of marginalized groups in earlier eras. If these actions occur while the *Brandenburg* rule remains intact, creating an exception to *Brandenburg* for terrorist advocacy would give officials considerably greater ability to manipulate the label, quell dissent, and marginalize groups as they see fit.

Conclusion

Acts of terrorism are, and should be, the subject of our concern and condemnation. But focusing on terrorism as a reason to alter *Brandenburg*'s incitement standard is unwise. That standard protects against arbitrary repression of unpopular political advocacy, especially of outsider organizations. Even with *Brandenburg*, officials manipulate the terrorism label to stigmatize some activists while protecting others. Without *Brandenburg*'s imminence requirement making officials prove actual incitement of violence, the law would provide no protection at all against arbitrary designations and return us to the abuses of the first half of the twentieth century.

Notes

1. Brandenburg v. Ohio, 395 U.S. 444, 447 (1969) (per curiam).
2. Brian M. Jenkins, *International Terrorism: A New Kind of Warfare* (Rand, 1974), 1, https://www.rand.org/pubs/papers/P5261.html.
3. Seth G. Jones, Catrina Doxsee and Nicholas Harrington, "The Escalating Terrorism Problem in the United States," CSIS Briefs (June 2020): 2, https://csis-website-prod.s3.amazonaws.com/s3fs-public/publication/200612_Jones_DomesticTerrorism_v6.pdf.
4. Sines v. Kessler, 324 F. Supp. 3d 765, 802-04 (W.D. Va. 2018).
5. R.A.V. v. City of St. Paul, 505 U.S. 377 (1992).
6. Khaled A. Beydoun and Justin Hansford, "The FBI's Dangerous Crackdown on 'Black Identity Extremists,'" *New York Times*, Nov. 15, 2017, https://www.nytimes.com/2017/11/15/opinion/black-identity-extremism-fbi-trump.html; Adam Federman, "Revealed: How the FBI Targeted Environmental Activists in Domestic Terror Investigations," *Guardian*, September 24, 2019, https://www.theguardian.com/us-news/2019/sep/23/revealed-how-the-fbi-targeted-environmental-activists-in-domestic-terror-investigations.
7. Espionage Act of 1917, ch. 30, 40 Stat. 217; Sedition Act of 1918, ch. 75, 40 Stat. 553.
8. Douglas Laycock, "The Clear and Present Danger Test," *Journal of Supreme Court History* 25, no. 2 (2000): 163–64.
9. Robert Justin Goldstein, *Political Repression in Modern America* (University of Illinois Press, 2001), 115; Laycock, "Clear and Present Danger," 164.
10. Shaffer v. United States, 255 F. 886, 887 (9th Cir. 1919).
11. Schenck v. United States, 249 U.S. 47, 52 (1919).
12. Frohwerk v. United States, 249 U.S. 204 (1919); Debs v. United States, 249 U.S. 211 (1919); Abrams v. United States, 250 U.S. 616 (1919).
13. Geoffrey R. Stone, *Perilous Times: Free Speech in Wartime from the Sedition Act of 1798 to the War on Terrorism* (W. W. Norton, 2004), 195; David M. Rabban, "The First Amendment in Its Forgotten Years," *Yale Law Journal* 90:3 (1981): 585–86.
14. Goldstein, *Political Repression*, 139–46; Stone, *Perilous Times*, 221–22.
15. Goldstein, *Political Repression*, 147–50; Stone, *Perilous Times*, 222–23.
16. Robert K. Murray, *Red Scare: A Study in National Hysteria* (University of Minnesota Press, 1955), 17; Goldstein, *Political Repression*, 154.
17. Gitlow v. New York, 268 U.S. 652, 655–57 (1925).
18. Gitlow, 268 U.S. at 665–71.
19. Whitney v. California, 274 U.S. 357, 372 (1927), overruled in part by Brandenburg v. Ohio, 395 U.S. 444 (1969).
20. Gitlow, 268 U.S. at 672, 673 (Holmes, J. dissenting).
21. Abrams v. United States, 250 U.S. 616 (1919).

22 Abrams, 250 U.S. at 628 (Holmes, J., dissenting).
23 Whitney, 274 U.S. at 374, 375–76 (Brandeis, J., concurring).
24 Bridges v. California, 314 U.S. 252, 263 (1941); Cantwell v. Connecticut, 310 U.S. 296, 308–9 (1940); Thornhill v. Alabama, 310 U.S. 88, 105 (1940).
25 Christina E. Wells, "Fear and Loathing in Constitutional Decision-Making," *Wisconsin Law Review* (2005): 128.
26 Wells, "Fear and Loathing," 131–44.
27 18 U.S.C. § 2385.
28 Wells, "Fear and Loathing," 142; Peter L. Steinberg, *The Great "Red Menace": United States Prosecution of American Communists, 1947–52* (Praeger, 1984), 108.
29 Wells, "Fear and Loathing," 143.
30 Dennis v. United States, 341 U.S. 494, 505–8, 510, 510–11 (1951).
31 Dennis, 341 U.S. at 579 (Black, J., dissenting).
32 Dennis, 341 U.S. at 589–90 (Douglas, J., dissenting).
33 Brandenburg v. Ohio, 395 U.S. 444, 445–46 (1969) (per curiam).
34 Brandenburg, 395 U.S. at 447.
35 Vincent Blasi, "Reading Holmes Through the Lens of Schauer: The Abrams Dissent," Notre Dame Law Review 72:5 (1997): 1358–59; Thomas Healy, "Brandenburg in a Time of Terror," *Notre Dame Law Review* 84, no. 2 (2009): 664.
36 Blasi, "Reading Holmes," 1358–59; Bernard Schwarz, "Holmes versus Hand: Clear and Present Danger or Advocacy of Unlawful Action," *Supreme Court Review* (1994): 240.
37 Laycock, "Clear and Present Danger," 181.
38 Christina E. Wells, "Discussing the First Amendment," *Michigan Law Review* 101, no. 6 (2003): 2577; Stone, *Perilous Times*, 524.
39 David S. Han, "Terrorist Advocacy and Exceptional Circumstances," *Fordham Law Review* 86, no. 2 (2017): 490.
40 Alexander Tsesis, "Terrorist Speech on Social Media," *Vanderbilt Law Review* 70, no. 2 (2017): 654–55.
41 Han, "Terrorist Advocacy," 490–91; Tsesis, "Terrorist Speech," 657.
42 Cass R. Sunstein, "Islamic State's Challenge to Free Speech," *Bloomberg*, Nov. 23, 2015, http://www.bloombergview.com/articles/2015-11-23/islamic-state-s-challenge-to-free-speech.
43 Eric Posner, "ISIS Gives Us No Choice but to Consider Limits on Speech," *Slate*, Dec. 15, 2015, http://www.slate.com/articles/news_and_politics/view_from_chicago/2015/12/isis_s_online_radicalization_efforts_present_an_unprecedented_danger.single.html.
44 Tsesis, "Terrorist Speech," 667, 663, 675. Professor Tsesis also argues that officials can punish terrorist advocacy using the federal material support statute after Holder v. Humanitarian Law Project, 561 U.S. 1, 39 (2010). This chapter focuses on arguments involving Brandenburg's incitement

standard. For fuller treatment of the material support aspect of Tsesis's argument, see Christina E. Wells, "Assumptions About Terrorism and the Brandenburg Incitement Test," *Brooklyn Law Review* 85, no. 1 (2019): 129. Brandenburg interpreted Dennis to support its holding. Brandenburg v. Ohio, 395 U.S. 444, 447n2 (1969). As discussed below, most scholars believe the Court effectively undermined Dennis with its Brandenburg ruling.

45 Stone, *Perilous Times*, 221–22.
46 Ellen Schrecker, *Many Are the Crimes: McCarthyism in America* (Princeton University Press, 1998), 48.
47 Dennis, 341, U.S. at 510.
48 Christina E. Wells, "Questioning Deference," *Missouri Law Review* 69:4 (2004): 914–15.
49 Mathew Ingram, "Have the Dangers of Social Media Been Overstated?" *Columbia Journalism Review*, June 9, 2022, https://www.cjr.org/the_media_today/have-the-dangers-of-social-media-been-overstated.php.
50 Twitter v. Taamneh, 598 U.S. 471, 499 (2023).
51 Wells, "Fear and Loathing," 201–2.
52 Paul Horwitz, "Free Speech as Risk Analysis: Heuristics, Biases, and Institutions in the First Amendment," *Temple Law Review* 76, no. 1 (2003): 45; Frederick M. Lawrence, "The Collision of Rights in Violence-Conducive Speech," *Cardozo Law Review* 19, no. 4 (1998): 1347.
53 Alan K. Chen, "Free Speech and the Confluence of National Security and Internet Exceptionalism," *Fordham Law Review* 86, no. 2 (2017): 398, 387.
54 Sudha Setty, "Country Report on Counterterrorism: United States of America," *American Journal of Comparative Law* 62: supp. 1 (2014): 644–45. Jenkins, *International Terrorism*, 1–2.
55 Nicholas J. Perry, "The Numerous Federal Legal Definitions of Terrorism: The Problem of Too Many Grails," *Journal of Legislation* 30, no. 2 (2004): 251.
56 Jenkins, *International Terrorism*, 2; Theodore P. Seto, "The Morality of Terrorism," *Loyola of Los Angeles Law Review* 35 (2002): 1236–39; Perry, "Definitions of Terrorism," 251.
57 Perry, "Definitions of Terrorism," 249.
58 Perry, "Definitions of Terrorism," 252; Jenkins, International Terrorism, 1.
59 Ileana M. Porras, "On Terrorism: Reflections on Violence and the Outlaw," *Utah Law Review* 1 (1994): 122.
60 18 U.S.C. § 2331(1).
61 Perry, "Definitions of Terrorism," 255–61.
62 Perry, "Definitions of Terrorism," 270; Setty, "Country Report," 645–46.

63 Perry, "Definitions of Terrorism," 270; Shirin Sinnar, "Separate and Unequal" The Law of 'Domestic' and "International' Terrorism," *Michigan Law Review* 117, no. 7 (2019): 1335–36, 1343–66.
64 18 U.S.C. § 2331(5); 28 C.F.R. § 0.85.
65 Domestic Terrorism: An Overview," Congressional Research Service, R44921 (August 21, 2017): 10, https://crsreports.congress.gov/product/pdf/R/R44921.
66 Jones, Doxsee, and Harrington, "Escalating Terrorism Problem," 2.
67 Confronting White Supremacy Before the House Oversight and Reform Committee, Subcommittee on Civil Rights and Civil Liberties, 116th Congress (2019) (statement of Michael C. McGarrity, assistant director, Counterterrorism Division, and Calvin A. Shivers, deputy assistant director Criminal Investigative Division).
68 Ed Pilkington, "FBI Failing to Address White Supremacist Violence Warns Former Agent," *Guardian*, May 20, 2022, https://www.theguardian.com/us-news/2022/may/20/fbi-white-supremacist-violence-michael-german; Michael German and Sara Robinson, "Wrong Priorities on Fighting Terrorism," Brennan Center for Justice, 2018, 2, https://www.brennancenter.org/media/120/download; Caroline Mala Corbin, "Terrorists Are Always Muslim but Never White: At the Intersection of Critical Race Theory and Propaganda," *Fordham Law Review* 86, no. 2 (2017): 466–72.
69 Robert Moore and Mark Berman, "Officials Call El Paso Shooting a Domestic Terrorism Case, Weigh Hate Crime Charges," *Washington Post*, August 4, 2019, https://www.washingtonpost.com/nation/2019/08/04/investigators-search-answers-after-gunman-kills-el-paso/; Mark Berman and Meryl Kornfield, "Buffalo Shooting Suspect Charged with Murder as A Hate Crime, Domestic Terrorism," *Washington Post*, June 1, 2022, https://www.washingtonpost.com/nation/2022/06/01/buffalo-shooting-indictment/.
70 Beverly Gage, "Terrorism and the American Experience: A State of the Field," *Journal of American History* 98 (2011): 88.
71 German and Robinson, 1.
72 "Domestic Terrorism: An Overview," 48; See Order Granting Defendants Robert Rundo, Robert Boman, and Aaron Eason's Joint Motion to Dismiss the Indictment, Slip Op. at 3, Case No.: CR 18-00759-CJC (C.D. Cal. June 3, 2019); Jesselyn Cook, "Far Right Activists Are Taking Their Message to Gen Z on TikTok, *HuffPost*, Apr. 16 2019, https://www.huffpost.com/entry/far-right-tiktok-gen-z_n_5cb63040e4b082aab08da0d3.
73 Rachel Hatzipanagos, "How Online Hate Turns into Real Life Violence," *Washington Post*, November 30, 2018, https://www.washingtonpost.com/nation/2018/11/30/how-online-hate-speech-is-fueling-real-life-violence/.
74 Professor Sunstein has recently discussed in the context of a broader discussion that his argument for an exception to Brandenburg could extend to domestic terrorism, rather than simply jihadist terrorism. Cass R.

Sunstein, "Does the Clear and Present Danger Test Survive Cost Benefit Analysis," *Cornell Law Review* 104, no. 7 (2019): 1781–82.
75   Cook, "Far Right Activitists"; Hatzipanagos, "Online Hate."
76   Snyder v. Phelps, 562 U.S. 443 (2011); Texas v. Johnson, 491 U.S. 397 (1989); Hustler Magazine v. Falwell, 485 U.S. 46 (1988); Cantwell v. Connecticut, 310 U.S. 296 (1940).
77   Matal v. Tam, 137 S. Ct. 1744, 1764 (2017) (quoting United States v. Schwimmer, 279 U.S. 644, 655 (1929) [Holmes, J., dissenting]).
78   "Hate Speech," *FIRE*, Mar. 28, 2019, https://www.thefire.org/issues/hate-speech/.
79   Rob Garver, "In the Wake of Buffalo Shooting, Calls for Accountability for Online Platforms," *VOA*, May 17, 2022, https://www.voanews.com/a/in-wake-of-buffalo-shooting-calls-for-accountability-for-online-platforms-/6576886.html.
80   Garver, "Buffalo Shooting" (quoting Marc H. Morial, president of National Urban League); Will Oremus, "What a Racist Massacre Tells Us About Free Speech Online," *Washington Post*, May 18, 2022, https://www.washingtonpost.com/technology/2022/05/18/buffalo-shooting-video-elon-musk-free-speech-twitter/.
81   Garver, "Buffalo Shooting."
82   Sines v. Kessler, 324 F. Supp. 3d 765, 802-04, 773 (W.D. Va. 2018); Dara Lind, "Why the ACLU Is Adjusting Its Approach to Free Speech After Charlottesville," *Vox*, Aug. 21, 2017, https://www.vox.com/2017/8/20/16167870/aclu-hate-speech-nazis-charlottesville; Joseph Goldstein, After Backing Alt-Right In Charlottesville, A.C.L.U. Wrestles with Its Role, *New York Times*, Aug. 17, 2017, https://www.nytimes.com/2017/08/17/nyregion/aclu-free-speech-rights-charlottesville-skokie-rally.html.
83   Beydoun and Hansford, "FBI's Dangerous Crackdown." See also Counterterrorism Division, FBI, "Black Identity Extremists Likely Motivated to Target Law Enforcement Officers" (2017): 3, https://s3.documentcloud.org/documents/4067711/BIE-Redacted.pdf.
84   Beydoun and Hansford, "FBI's Dangerous Crackdown" (quoting former FBI agent Michael German).
85   Zeeshan Aleem, "Ahead of a Far-Right Rally in Portland, Trump Tweets a Warning to Antifa," *Vox*, Aug. 17, 2019, https://www.vox.com/policy-and-politics/2019/8/17/20810221/portland-rally-donald-trump-alt-right-proud-boys-antifa-terror-organization.
86   Federman, "FBI Targeted Environmental Activists in Domestic Terror Investigations."
87   Julie Watson, "Comparison Between Capitol Siege, BLM Protests Denounced," *AP News*, January 14, 2021, https://apnews.com/article/donald-trump-capitol-siege-race-and-ethnicity-violence-racial-injustice-afd7dc2165f355a3e6dc4e9418019eb5.

88 Media Advisory, "Bishop Announces Sub-Committee Hearing on Left-Wing Violence," May 10, 2023, https://homeland.house.gov/media-advisory-bishop-announces-subcommittee-hearing-on-left-wing-violence/.
89 Sinnar, "Separate and Unequal," 1389n309; Jones, Doxsee, and Harrington, "Escalating Terrorism Problem," 3 (figure 1).Watson, "Comparison Denounced"; Erica Chenoweth and Jeremy Pressman, "This Summer's Black Lives Matter Protestors Were Overwhelmingly Peaceful, Our Research Finds," *Washington Post*, October 16, 2020, https://www.washingtonpost.com/politics/2020/10/16/this-summers-black-lives-matter-protesters-were-overwhelming-peaceful-our-research-finds/.
90 Mary Papenfuss, "As Far-Right Violence Surges, Ted Cruz Seeks to Brand Antifa a Terrorist Organization," *HuffPost*, July 21, 2019, https://www.huffpost.com/entry/antifa-right-wing-violence-ted-cruz-bill-cassidy-resolution_n_5d33c982e4b0419fd32de46b; Watson, "Comparison Denounced."

PART III:
BRANDENBURG IN THE CONTEMPORARY ERA

Chapter Eight

Incitement on the Internet

Rethinking First Amendment Standards in Cyberspace

Howard Schweber and Rebecca J. Anderson

On January 6, 2021, President Donald Trump gave a speech at the Ellipse in which he called on his supporters to march to the Capitol to "to try and give [lawmakers] the kind of pride and boldness that they need to take back our country." Earlier in the rally, his personal lawyer Rudolph W. Giuliani argued that the election should end in "trial by combat." The result of these words was that the thousands of people they had gathered in Washington, DC for the rally did, in fact, march to the Capitol and, after engaging in an all-out battle with the US Capitol Police, physically breached the building and halted the counting of electoral votes for a time. Lawmakers were evacuated from the building and one rioter was shot by Capitol Police while attempting to enter the Speaker's Lobby through a broken window. After several hours of general mayhem, including calls to hang Vice President Mike Pence, Trump finally issued a plea for the rioters to return home, telling them they were "very special" and "We love you." By the end of the day, five people died in the chaos.[1]

The above telling neglects the weeks of online discourse regarding "[stopping] the steal" that permeated all forms of social media prior to the electoral vote count. In the period between the election and the official recording of electoral votes in Congress, "Stop the Steal" discourse swamped some portions of social media. On Facebook, while some of the major "Stop the Steal" groups were eventually removed others flourished with their meteoric rise fueled by relatively few highly involved users.[2] Similar posts promoting the idea that President-elect Joe Biden was stealing the election and must be stopped also appeared with some regularity on other major social networks like Twitter (now "X") and TikTok.

Explicit calls for violence were also featured in less well-known corners of the internet such as thedonald.win[3] and Parler, a "free speech" themed social network popular with conservatives.[4] Yet, despite the role of social media in hosting the discourse that served as fuel for the riot, what consequences have they faced? For both the posters and the service providers the answer is, surprisingly few. Trump himself was banned for a time from essentially all major social media platforms including Facebook (and its subsidiary Instagram), Twitter, and YouTube, forcing him to start his own platform. Google, Meta, and Twitter were served subpoenas to retain information related to the riot for the use of the congressional inquiry into the events of the day.[5] The companies have clearly placed the blame on the individual actors who stormed the Capitol,[6] while on the individual level, we are unaware of any attempts to bring criminal charges or civil suits against individuals who posted inflammatory messages in the days leading up to January 6, 2021.

The entire enterprise of holding individuals or social media companies accountable is complicated by Section 230 of the Communications Decency Act, which provides immunity to internet service providers for materials posted by third parties.[7] Even without the effect of that statute, however, establishing liability for online incitement is difficult because existing First Amendment doctrine holds that "mere advocacy" of violence is protected speech. To constitute unprotected incitement, expression has to be "directed to inciting or producing imminent lawless action and [be] likely to incite or produce such action." *Brandenburg v Ohio* (1969).[8] It is the difference between saying "Something must be done!" at a meeting of local activists and "Throw a brick through his window now!" to an angry crowd holding bricks. In this chapter we argue that the *Brandenburg* test is not well suited to deal with the type of incitements to violence that are prevalent on the internet today. We suggest that it ought to be reshaped in a number of ways in order to better meet contemporary challenges.

The idea that a new medium of communication calls for new developments in First Amendment doctrine is not new. For example, the rise of broadcast media (in the form of radio) led the Supreme Court to develop new rules about the regulation of content that was "indecent" but not "obscene," meaning that it was inappropriate for children but protected against regulation with respect to adults. The Court ruled that the FCC could ban indecent materials from being broadcast during daylight hours on the grounds that the radio was an "intrusive" medium that could reach children, in *FCC v. Pacifica Foundation* (1978).[9] Thus far, however, the Court has not yet dealt with the peculiar characteristics of the internet and the adjustments to traditional doctrines that are called for as a result.[10]

In what follows, we describe first the requirements of the *Brandenburg* test, then why it is ill-suited to deal with inciting speech on the internet. Finally, we offer suggestions for modifications to the *Brandenburg* standard that would allow for better regulation of potentially inciting speech occurring on the internet.

The *Brandenburg* Test

Brandenburg involved a rally conducted in a field in Ohio away from observers, which was filmed by a reporter.[11] Based on consideration of this scenario, the *Brandenburg* test adopted a new definition of punishable incitement: "The constitutional guarantees of free speech and free press do not permit a state to forbid or proscribe advocacy of the use of force or of law violation except where such advocacy is directed to inciting or producing imminent lawless action and is likely to incite or produce such action."[12] The facts of the case present what we will refer to as the "ideal *Brandenburg* scenario": a physically defined space with a delimited body of observers — that is, potential subjects of incitement — isolated from any larger community, expression that is spoken and heard at the same instant, a speaker who is aware of his listeners and intends them to be moved to action, and reference to long-recognized categories of "lawless action." President Trump's statements to his supporters could fit that model; calls for violence posted on the internet cannot.

In fact, the problem of incitement never limited itself neatly to that ideal scenario. In 1952 in *Beauharnais v. Illinois* the US Supreme Court had ruled that states had the constitutional authority to punish "group libel." The category of unprotected speech at issue was libel, not incitement, but concerns with incitement suffused Justice Frankfurter's majority opinion. "From the murder of the abolitionist Lovejoy in 1837 to the Cicero riots of 1951, Illinois has been the scene of exacerbated tension between races, often flaring into violence and destruction. In many of these outbreaks, utterances of the character here in question, so the Illinois legislature could conclude, played a significant part."[13] Thus "group libel" was defined in terms of incitement, but in a way that does not fit into the *Brandenburg* definition of the category. A later case points to another way in which "incitement" has been stretched to cover situations that do not fit the ideal *Brandenburg* scenario. In 1997 in *Rice v. Paladin Press*, the Fourth Circuit Court of Appeals upheld the conviction of a publisher who produced a book entitled *Hit Man: A Technical Manual for Independent Contractors* on the grounds that it contained instruction rather than mere advocacy.[14] In a 2002 case, the instruction theory was applied to uphold the conviction of a gang leader. Writing in support of the Court's decision to deny *certiorari* in the case, Justice Stevens wrote, "[w]hile the requirement that the consequence be 'imminent' is justified with respect to mere advocacy, the same justification does not necessarily adhere to some speech that performs a teaching function."[15] Similarly, the court ruled in 2023 in *United States v Hansen* that "purposeful solicitation and facilitation" of acts that violate federal law is can be criminalized.[16]

The invention of new categories such as "group libel" or "instruction" were ways to deal with the inadequacies of *Brandenburg* by the ad hoc creation of new rules to fit specific cases. One problem with this approach is that in 2010 the Supreme Court held that no new categories of unprotected expression would be recognized, calling into question the continuing validity of the *Rice* principle.[17] Another problem is that often things that observers would readily recognize as incitement simply did not fit the ideal *Brandenburg* scenario. For example, Southern newspapers had for decades printed stories and editorials that led directly to race riots.[18]

Nonetheless, in 1969 it seemed that the loss of the government's ability to suppress incitements to violence was a cost worth paying to avoid the tendency of security officials, in particular, to find ways to criminalize political opinions. But whatever the merits of the balance struck in 1969, in the context of online incitement to violence, the reliance on an ideal scenario involving physical proximity, immediacy, and an imagined speaker-listener relationship is deeply problematic.

Problems of Applying *Brandenburg* to the Internet: Space, Time, Interaction, and Lawless Action

To repeat, the ideal *Brandenburg* scenario involves a speaker addressing identifiable listeners at a particular location at a particular time with the intention and expectation of causing them to engage in lawless conduct on the spot. None of these elements applies to inciting communication that occurs in cyberspace. In turn, the particular characteristics of online communications that make the application of *Brandenburg* problematic point to an alternative approach.

Internet communications occur everywhere all at once, last forever, are accessible without any effort, and in most cases completely lack editorial control. Internet incitement can be "intended" in a way that does not involve any specific expectation of a relationship between speaker and listener. Search algorithms add an additional element. Not only is it not necessary for a speaker to seek out listeners, internet users do not even have to seek inciting speech: it seeks them out. Taken one at a time, none of these characteristics necessarily requires new First Amendment principles. After all, film recording of the event in *Brandenburg*, like recordings of broadcasts and printed volumes, are also permanent. But unless those recordings or printed texts are uploaded into cyberspace, they do not share other characteristics that mark internet communications. It is the combination of these elements that makes the internet in its present form such a problematic context for the application of the *Brandenburg* test.

Physical Proximity: The Problem of Space

One difference between the ideal *Brandenburg* scenario and the internet is that in the latter case the "space" of communication is universal: anyone in the world can access the expression and hear or view its content. Some sites do have restricted membership that at least partly delimits the immediately affected audience of a communication, but these are often large and unselective (as in the case of listservs). Meanwhile, blogs, discussion boards, Twitter, and other platforms are precisely based on the model of broadcast media that seeks to reach a maximally large, unknown and unidentifiable population without any of the limitations of licensing or the barriers to the distribution and receipt of recordings that apply to broadcasts — unless they are preserved on the internet.

Yet at the same time, the users of the internet do each occupy physical spaces where incitement to lawlessness may occur. The problem of incitement is that what happens on the internet neither begins nor remains on the internet. In 1993, in the very early days of the internet an event occurred that raised questions to which legal categories still have no response. The event was a virtual assault that occurred in LambdaMOO. "MOOs" were early forms of virtual communities (the term stands for multiuser domain, object oriented). LambdaMOO was one of the largest and most important of these early online communities. A user calling himself "Mr. Bungle" was able to introduce a malicious program that allowed him to take control of virtual characters, and he used this power to make characters perform violent sex acts on other characters. As described by journalist and participant Julian Dibbel, the users of LambdaMOO gathered in virtual space to discuss what to do. "Could Bungle's university administrators punish him for sexual harassment? Could he be prosecuted under California state laws against obscene phone calls?" In the end the "wizards" (administrators) of LambdaMOO introduced a form of online self-government for the community that provided for the expulsion of bad actors. But when Dibbel later researched the case for an article and a book, he discovered something even more disturbing. "[T]he Bungle account had been the more or less communal property of an entire NYU dorm floor, that the young man at the keyboard on the evening of the rape had acted not alone but surrounded by fellow students calling out suggestions and encouragement."[19] The virtual reality crime, in other words, had real life antecedents.

In more recent years, the connections between vicious online and real-life interactions have become increasingly evident. "Gamergate" was an ongoing program of misogynistic online harassment directed at three specific female game programmers. The campaign was organized on 4Chan, Reddit, and Twitter, platforms uniquely suited to the purpose.[20] These kinds of attacks have very sadly become increasingly commonplace, frequently featuring racist, misogynistic, and generally viciously insulting and threatening campaigns of harassment, incited by users through calls to action organized on platforms essentially devoted to that purpose.

In some instances, courts have taken cognizance of these kinds of events. In 2017 neo-Nazi Andrew Anglin encouraged readers of his site, *Daily Stormer*, to harass Tanya Gersh, a Jewish real estate agent in Montana, apparently because of a dispute she had with the mother of another white nationalist. Anglin put out a call to his readers to harass Gersh by a "troll storm." Anglin's readers then targeted Gersh's voicemail with recordings of gunshots, filled her email inboxes with death threats, and found and targeted her children online in more than 700 messages. Gersh sued Anglin under the Montana Anti-Intimidation Act. During the suit Anglin claimed that his conduct was protected by the First Amendment, a claim the court rejected. The *Gersh* court did not consider the question of incitement, because it had not been raised in the pleadings. If it had done so, would incitement have been found? Judge Christensen seemed to suggest the answer might be yes but did not present an analysis.[21]

In the LambdaMOO cast the students in the New York University dorm were physically in each others' presence; to the extent that the law in 1993 recognized a crime of online harassment there could have been an argument for finding incitement consistent "with *Brandenburg*. But that reasoning falls apart when we get to Gamergate. That involved interactions among a limited group of people, but not all in the same "place." Access to 4Chan is both unlimited and anonymous. It is literally not possible for a poster to know who is "there" at any given time. Administrators could access that information within the limits of guarantees of anonymity; if the only legal issue were incitement, would *Brandenburg* permit a law requiring them to keep a record of users online so that the reach of an alleged incitement could be determined? Perhaps an analogy between physical and online space would be constitutionally permissible, but that would not solve the problem of defining spatial proximity.

Even the limited analogy to an Ohio field available in the Gamergate case evaporates in the face of the Andrew Anglin's troll storm attack against Tanya Gersh. Mr. Anglin was never in the same physical space as his listeners, nor did he occupy the same virtual space at the same time. Instead, his approach was closer akin to sending a radio message into the ether and hoping for a response, but unlike a radio message the contents of his site were available permanently and could reach the entire globe.[22] This is not an isolated issue: while this chapter was being written news reports broke the story of a long-standing, organized series of online campaigns of threats and harassment organized and led by an individual in federal custody and carried out by his online followers.[23] If the category of incitement does not cover that case, it is not clear that there is any possibility of a legal response to what is increasingly becoming a plague in the American polity.

Imminent Action: The Problem of Time

Even outside the context of cyberspace, the requirement of "imminent" lawless action has always been one of the trickiest elements of *Brandenburg* to define with any precision. In 1979 a California Court considered the question in the context of a radio broadcast. When the American Nazi Party announced its intention to hold a march in Skokie, Illinois, the national director of the Jewish Defense League offered $500 to anyone who "kills, maims, or seriously injures a member of the American Nazi Party. . . . And if they bring us the ears, we'll make it a thousand dollars. The fact of the matter is, that we're deadly serious. This is not said in jest, we are deadly serious."[24] The march was still five weeks away, but the California Court of Appeals ruled that this expression constituted punishable incitement on the theory that the likely lawless action was still imminent. The judge in the case (Herndon, J. pro tem.) observed that "imminence" may be a relative term. "Time is a relative dimension and imminence a relative term, and the imminence of an event is related to its nature. A total eclipse of the sun next year is said to be imminent. An April shower thirty minutes away is not."[25] Applied to internet incitement to lawless action, what is the scope of "imminence"? A website is available the second it is produced and remains available into the indefinite future. In that situation, what is the point in time from which "imminence" is to be measured: the posting of the material or the moment a reader sees it?

Again, it is important to recognize that the way these questions arise in the context of the internet is different from the way the same questions arise in the context of printed material or broadcasts. Even if one wants to argue that elements of the question of imminence appear across all three cases, internet postings raise these issues to a far higher degree. Unlike an oral address or a broadcast, a web site lasts (potentially) forever. At the same time, unlike a book, the website comes into existence instantaneously in real time. The combination of instant creation plus lasting influence simply does not fit into the *Brandenburg* framework.[26]

The Speaker-Listener Interaction: "Stochastic Incitement"

The ideal *Brandenburg* scenario posits a particular kind of interaction between speaker and incited listener. The speaker addresses an identifiable listener directly, with the intent or expectation of motivating that listener (or group of listeners) to violence, based on some awareness of how the listener got there (for example, chose to attend a demonstration, was part of an angry crowd, was already engaged in conversation with the speaker) and is aware of the speaker addressing him. But none of that has to be true for incitement to occur on the internet. This was the problem that was raised in the case involving the infamous anti-abortion site "The Nuremburg Files." The site provided names, addresses, photos, and personal information about doctors known to perform abortions. When doctors on the list were killed, their names were crossed out in red; when they were merely injured in attacks by anti-abortion activists, their names were marked in gray. A civil suit found the owner of the site liable for engaging in true threats; as in the *Anglin* case the question of incitement was not specifically reached.[27] The reason is simple. Despite the facts that pointed clearly to incitement as the logical legal category of analysis, a webpage is incapable by its nature of satisfying the imminence requirement of the *Brandenburg* ideal scenario.[28]

But substituting threat for incitement is a weak and unreliable strategy. A federal court in Alabama found that a website that displayed a "wanted" poster of a government witness was protected speech because it did not qualify as a "true threat" under the Eleventh Circuit standard, under which a true threat requires "sufficient evidence to prove beyond a reasonable doubt that the defendant intentionally made the statement under such circumstances that a reasonable person would construe them as a serious expression of an intention to inflict bodily harm."[29] Did the provision of information on the Nuremburg Files site or the doxing campaign that was directed at Gersh constitute unprotected "true threats"?[30] Furthermore, the threat standard requires the kind of interaction between speaker and listener that exists in the ideal *Brandenburg* scenario. Internet incitement does not always work that way. As the Nuremburg Files illustrates, the more common scenario is an inciting message broadcast to the world, available to everyone forever without any need to seek it out (see discussion of algorithms, below). The communication is frictionless: there is no effort required by speaker or listener to connect.

In the context of security studies this has been recognized as a new phenomenon: "stochastic terrorism," in which there is no need for traditional forms of recruitment, training, and preparation. Instead, one can use the internet to distribute a call for violence to the world and hope that among the millions upon millions of potential viewers some will be motivated to perform terroristic acts.[31] The concept of stochastic terrorism clarifies the crucial differences between online incitement and the kind of incitement to action that might occur in a printed book or a television broadcast. In the case of a book, federal courts have held that while printed material cannot satisfy the *Brandenburg* test of incitement to *imminent* lawless action, where materials cross a line into instruction — explaining to readers how to commit lawless acts — the expression is unprotected under a separate category of "instruction."[32] But to experience that incitement a reader has to go to the effort of finding the book and obtaining a printed copy, of which there are a limited number. Post the same material to the internet and its reach becomes infinite. And what is true of instruction in bomb-making is equally true of incitement to make bombs. Similarly, as noted previously, the difference between the internet and broadcasts appears on the dimension of time, as the permanence of internet postings creates an ongoing danger of incitement — imminent with respect to the viewer, perhaps, but potentially years removed from the act of posting — that has no parallel in the case of broadcast media.

Consider again the issue of what constitutes a threat. In 2023 the Court heard a case involving a criminal conviction for online harassment and stalking for sending more than 2,000 unwelcome messages to a folk singer over a period of six years. Writing for the majority, Justice Kagan ruled that a finding of a true threat requires a subjective state of at least recklessness.[33] As a result, even an egregious campaign of online harassment remains protected by the First Amendment unless the harasser is subjectively reckless about the possibility that they will be understood to be threatening bodily harm. And applying any similar intent standard to online incitement demonstrates the obvious problem that the stochastic version of incitement does not require any particular level of intent at all.

Yet a different problem arises when we consider the role of algorithms, as mentioned earlier. In order to maintain maximum engagement, platforms use these algorithms to direct users toward material consistent with their apparent preferences based on prior searches and retrievals. The result, as has been well documented, is to create a "feed" that pushes users further and further in extreme directions through a process of continuing preference reinforcement. Moreover, there is substantial evidence that platforms are aware of this phenomenon of radicalization and choose to encourage it in order to maximize engagement and hence profitability.[34] Internet incitement often involves a three-way interaction among speaker, algorithm, and listener. The phenomenon occurs even in unexpected places such as YouTube, whose selection/preference-reinforcement algorithms have been connected to political radicalization among users.[35]

Search algorithms are not the only technological intervention that exacerbates the problem of online incitement for First Amendment analysis. If portions of the internet sometimes seem like cesspools of misinformation, trolling, and abuse now, just wait: things may be about to get much worse. Artificial Intelligence (AI) researcher Yannic Kilchner has created an automated internet presence (a "bot") that produces abusive messages based on analyzing and re-creating the style of communication of 4Chan. The bot produced 30,000 posts in one day, all featuring the misogyny, racism, insults, and provocations for which the site is infamous.[36]

The emergence of AI in one sense is merely the logical next step from "troll farms," organized projects aimed at disseminating provocation, misinformation, and especially incitement across the internet. In other words, even without the intervention of AI technology, the relationship between a speaker and a listener that is modeled on the *Brandenburg* ideal scenario simply need not exist and usually does not exist in the context of the internet. Thus, on the internet, incitement can occur without any identifiable speaker, by a speaker who has no knowledge of the effect of his words on a listener, and without any identifiable listener at all. Once uttered, the inciting statements will be amplified and strategically distributed by search algorithms to those most likely to be susceptible. And with the addition of AI, an infinite volume of inciting expression can be created with zero effort and minimal cost. Yet as recent experience has shown, the inciting effects and their consequences are at least as dangerous as those posed by old-time Klan rallies.

Lawless Action

The discussions thus far have showcased various problems with the application of *Brandenburg* to cyberspace, focusing on spatial proximity, imminence, and the nature of the speaker-listener interaction. A separate problem arises in connection with the meaning of "lawless action." Consider the phenomena of "doxing" and "trolling." "Doxing is the kind of action that occurred on the Nuremburg Files site, in which personal information is publicly displayed in the anticipation that it will lead others to harass the target. "Trolling" is merely the deliberate attempt to provoke a negative reaction by making outrageous statements, but in its weaponized form, as in *Gersh v. Anglin*, this becomes a "troll storm." Under the *Counterman* standard these are not "true threats," yet the harms they cause are enormous. Do they qualify as "lawless action"? Even if, as in *Gersh*, the act of participating in online harassment may be punished, does the law reach incitement to such participation? The problem is particularly acute since in the case of stochastic incitement a "speaker" may have no actual knowledge at all of the effect of his expression on any identifiable listener.

In 2022 Netflix produced a three-part documentary about Hunter Moore titled *The Most Hated Man on the Internet*. Mr. Moore's specialty was posting hacked or stolen revealing photos of women, many supplied to him as "revenge porn," others simply stolen. States have found ways to use theories of invasion of privacy to criminalize revenge porn but is there no way to reach a site operator who deliberately sets out to facilitate and encourage — in other words, to "incite" — such postings? At present, Mr. Moore's practices are protected federal statute,[37] but does the First Amendment preclude creating laws to reach such blatantly destructive behavior? So long as we are bound by the *Brandenburg* ideal scenario, the category of incitement is unavailable to lawmakers in this context, as well.[38]

A New Approach to Incitement as a First Amendment Category of Expression

In response to the problems with current incitement standards described in the previous section, a number of approaches have been recommended. One recent article essentially recommends abandoning traditional institutions of law and governance. Kate Klonick suggests that the only possible approach is to appeal to the CEOs of Facebook, Twitter, and other platforms — referred to as New Governors — to adopt First Amendment norms and apply them through voluntarily adopted policies. Any regulatory policies, by this approach, should be shaped around existing voluntary systems of self-regulation.[39] Klonick suggests that we can be confident that platform operators will be motivated to adopt and implement First Amendment norms in the operation of their businesses, at the cost of reduced profits, because of a combination of "a foundation in American free speech norms, corporate responsibility, and the economic necessity of creating an environment that reflects the expectations of their users."[40] Klonick's approach seems wildly optimistic about the willingness of CEOs to become guardians of constitutional norms. But regardless, essentially declaring the internet a law-free zone is not an outcome that should be tolerable to anyone concerned with the First Amendment in cyberspace. Most of all, when it comes to the problem of incitement the motivation to "incentivize engagement" within a system of "voluntary self-regulation" is precisely the problem, and the name of the problem is "algorithm."

We therefore present the following proposal for revisions to the *Brandenburg* standard for defining incitement in the context of the internet. We should note that we are not asking for the abandonment of the basic categorical approach to speech protection, nor are we requesting the creation of new speech categories specific to the internet.[41] In our view "incitement" perfectly captures one of the most important and most dangerous phenomena in internet expression, and with changes to the specific terms of the *Brandenburg* approach, a new internet-specific incitement standard would provide legal authorities with sufficient room to respond effectively to threats without abandoning basic commitments to freedom of expression, privacy, and "technological due process."[42]

Content: The Definition of Internet Incitement

Space

Begin with the question of space and the implication of physical proximity in the archetypal *Brandenburg* scenario with its implication of face-to-face interaction. The "space" in which expression occurs should be understood in terms of the specific context in which it occurs. A posting to a listserv or discussion board should be understood to be expression that occurs in the "presence" of subscribers. A posting to the web should be understood to be expression made available to search results. And a posting on a system driven by selection algorithms — again, designed with the motivation of maximizing user engagement and hence profitability — presents yet a third situation. Recognizing these differences means that to some extent the evaluation of incitement will require a case-by-case evaluation, making the test for incitement context specific.[43] This should not be any more startling than the observation that publishing newspapers, broadcasting television broadcasts, and shouting from the rooftops are different kinds of expressive activity with different kinds of potentials for incitement.

In addition, algorithms do not so much operate in a space as they *shape* the discursive space in which communication occurs, a process that goes beyond mere amplification of the sort familiar from earlier technologies. The result is that extreme minority views become not only visible but inescapable, reaching viewers who did not seek out such materials at all, a phenomenon that is exacerbated when the fact of online presence itself becomes the subject of media reporting about "trending topics," thus bringing the inciting content to the attention of millions of additional potential viewers. The very first requirement of a meaningful incitement standard is that it takes account of the inappropriateness of using physical proximity occurring in a neutral preexisting space as the basic model for conceiving of internet communications. Instead, the focus needs to be on the content and effects of the message itself. We therefore call for abandonment of any requirement of physical proximity in the context of internet incitement.

Time: Imminence

An internet posting is always in the present and remains so forever. In that context the requirement of imminent lawless conduct seems inapposite. On the other hand, to simply get rid of the imminence requirement is to open the door to the punishment of mere advocacy, an outcome that should be unacceptable to everyone. Our solution is to shift the focus of the inquiry away from the moment at which material is posted to the moment when it is encountered. In other words, the imminence requirement becomes an analysis of content rather than circumstances: Is the posted content the kind of thing that evinces an intention to incite lawless action and, if experienced immediately, would be likely to lead to imminent lawless action? We view this as a further development in the historical shift from a circumstances-based "clear and present danger" approach of earlier eras to the categorical approach — focusing on carefully defined categories of unprotected expression — that began in the 1940s. *Brandenburg*'s test for incitement preserves an element of treating otherwise protected expression as unprotected because of the circumstances in which it occurred based on the ideal scenario. Courts would do well to continue the development of free speech doctrine away from a focus on circumstances in the context of internet incitement.

Speaker-listener interactions

While we agree with current doctrine that evidence of an intent to incite lawless action is a key element of any incitement test, the question of the identification of speakers and their motivations is more complicated in the internet context. To return to an example that was discussed previously, as a constitutional matter, there should be no problem in holding the creator of an AI program liable for the content that it produces; this is the flip side of a human individual taking credit for producing intellectual property using technology. Where the case becomes more complicated is in the consideration of service providers. Even if the First Amendment does not require the kind of absolute immunity currently provided for in the statutes, there is nothing unusual about an argument that says the First Amendment implies a requirement of a certain degree of intentionality before unprotected expression may be punished, as in the case of the "true threat" standard discussed earlier or the holding of the Supreme Court in 1974 that strict liability standards for libel are unconstitutional.[44] We share the concerns of others that a standard that makes the risk of liability for unintended consequences could have a chilling effect on expression. As a result, while we propose that service providers should be considered "speakers" for purposes of incitement analysis, we propose a constitutional standard for incitement that says that a speaker who intentionally *or recklessly* engages in expression likely to result in lawless action may be held criminally liable under an otherwise properly drafted statute. Such a speaker may constitutionally be subject to civil liability for *negligently* inspiring lawless action.

It is important to note that the standard for incitement is an objective one. Applied to the internet this would mean that a posting contains incitement if a reasonable person would perceive an intentional call to commit lawless acts. This is precisely the First Amendment space that is occupied by incitement: something more than encouragement, something less than instruction. As a result of the application of this objective standard for evaluation of content, neither the fact that someone was motivated to violence, nor the absence of that outcome should be dispositive.

Most important, the focus of the intent inquiry must be shifted away from a traditional recruitment model to the stochastic model of incitement described above. That is, if the speaker's intent is to launch an incitement in the expectation that it will reach some unspecifiable and unknown recipient, that should be sufficient for both civil and criminal liability. In our view, launching an incitement into cyberspace is analogous to dropping rocks from a highway overpass or deliberately introducing pollutants into a water system, a form of conduct so dangerous that the lack of a specific intent to produce a specific harmful outcome should not preclude criminal punishment.

Lawless activity

Finally, there is the question of what kind of "lawless action" is an appropriate basis for a finding of incitement? We call on lawmakers to engage in a careful consideration of the implications of practices such as doxing: these activities need to be defined as crimes so that incitement to their performance can itself become the basis for liability. Specifically, we call on lawmakers to enact laws providing civil or criminal liability for organized online harassment campaigns, defined as conduct that would constitute unprotected harassment that creates an objectively hostile environment if it occurred in real time in the workplace. Proving the "organized" character of a campaign may present evidentiary difficulties, and in some instances may be impossible to show, but for the many, many instances — indeed the routinization — of easily identifiable organized online harassment campaigns at present the availability of protection from state agencies would be a major and critical step.

Algorithms

As we noted above, the internet phenomena of frictionless and instantaneous communication are joined to mechanisms for maximizing engagement that have the known effects of increasing tendencies toward violence. We argue that these algorithms present a new category of activity without any obvious precedent in earlier technologies. In a very real sense, platform operators are not just allowing incitement, they are *engaging in* incitement. It is a form of incitement that is contentless — incitement for the sake of incitement, the internet descendant of the "if it bleeds it leads" school of yellow journalism to the modern "enrage to engage" model of algorithm design which is much more dangerous, not least because it is entirely outside the control of its designers.

One issue that appears to be of concern to members of the Roberts Court based on recent oral argument is that it is difficult to ban harmful uses of preference-reinforcing algorithms without interfering with their legitimate business purpose of maximizing "clicks." The problem, in our view, is a fundamental mischaracterization of algorithms and what they do. Search algorithms are not s form of expression, they are a means of *amplifying* expression. There is no constitutional right to the use of a bullhorn in a setting where that may cause harms to the peace and tranquility of a public space regardless of the business advantages that might accrue.

However, while in our view the Constitution would permit an outright ban on algorithms, that does not mean that there are no other plausible approaches. Therefore, rather than a ban we call for the imposition of liability on ISPs who knowingly operate search algorithm programs that have been shown to exacerbate incitement. That is, if there is evidence that a platform operator has been informed that their algorithms are resulting in incitement, they should be required to shut down the algorithm's operation until the problem can be solved or face civil liability for harms that result from their failure to do so. As always, liability standards can vary depending on the degree of intentionality — negligence, recklessness, deliberate action — that is involved.

Application of the Model to Technology Companies

Posters and platform operators are not the whole story. While it is tempting to focus attention on Facebook and Google, a great deal of the most extreme incitement on the internet occurs on sites such as 8Chan (a successor to 4Chan). Those sites, in turn, cannot operate without the assistance of technology companies. To see how this plays out, consider the case of Cloudflare and Kiwi Farms. Cloudflare is a company that provides a range of services, serving as a hosting company but also providing a range of security services to approximately 20 percent of web hosts worldwide. Kiwi Farms is an extreme right-wing site that identifies targets — primarily persons in the trans community — and targets them for harassment. The site maintains "a massive archive of sensitive information on their targets" often featuring "social media pictures of their targets' friends and family, along with contact information of their employers. The information is used in an effort to get their targets fired or socially isolated by spreading rumors that they are pedophiles or criminals."[45]

Cloudflare had previously insisted it would not deny services to anyone based on content. Nonetheless, in September 2022 the company blocked Kiwi Farms from its hosting services, citing "imminent and emergency threat to human life." What makes this interesting is that Cloudflare has a robust system of internal moderation of the sort Klonick admires with respect to its hosting services. Cloudflare will shut down sites that feature objectionable material across a range of categories. On the other hand, it is Cloudflare's policy never to deny its security services on the basis of objectionable content. "Just as the telephone company doesn't terminate your line if you say awful, racist, bigoted things, we have concluded in consultation with politicians, policy makers, and experts that turning off security services because we think what you publish is despicable is the wrong policy."[46]

With respect to its provision of security services, we believe that Cloudflare's analogizing itself to a utility is valid. Private companies that operate communications should neither have the responsibility nor the authority to determine the meaning of the First Amendment and turn that understanding into legislation: In a constitutional democracy that is precisely the province of government.

Hosting Liability and Section 230

A fourth question is how First Amendment principles should apply to site operators who provide platforms or services that enable the presentation of incitement to violence. Here, too, the question begins as one of First Amendment rules to determine the scope of possible regulation, but then quickly becomes a question about what lawmakers will choose to do with the authority that the First Amendment grants them. As noted earlier, at present platform operators have near-total immunity from liability for anything that is posted on their sites by virtue of Section 230 of the Communications Decency Act. For our purposes, the question is what kinds of liability would simultaneously preserve First Amendment principles and diminish the harms of internet incitement?

A particularly concerning element of the problem concerns anonymity. The opportunity for anonymous expression is baked into the architecture of the internet, but it is also a feature of many sites. Certainly, insisting that every internet posting be traceable to a sender would clamp down on incitement, but it would also have a profound chilling effect on many kinds of valuable discourse as well as providing oppressive governments with tools to track and locate their critics. On the other hand, the immunity that ISPs are granted under Section 230 has played a role in the rise of online incitement to violence. In particular, when anonymity is combined with the stochastic model of incitement, the results can be far reaching, as in the case of the QAnon conspiracy theory and the violent acts it has inspired.[47]

We propose that an ISP that chooses to permit anonymous content should lose its Section 230 immunity with respect to incitement. That is, we do not argue that there should be a general duty of curation for all sites, only for those that choose to publish materials anonymously. In that situation the only party in a position to limit inciting expression is the ISP, since government authorities have no way to reach the poster. Again, we recognize the likely loss of opportunity for anonymous discourse as ISPs (and their liability insurers) contemplate the potential costs of the ever-ubiquitous comment sections. But in the special context of the internet, the invitation to consequence-free incitement has proven to be too irresistible and its consequence too damaging for lawmakers to continue to ignore the problems.

Conclusion

From AI bots posting messages to an "internet of things" capable of acting as a platform for incitement, there is a profound need to reconceive First Amendment principles regarding incitement. Our proposed standard is, in fact, a very modest redrafting of the *Brandenburg* test that takes account of the transformative effects of internet communications.

Notes

1. Philip Rucker, "Trump's Presidency Finishes in 'American Carnage' as Rioters Storm the Capitol," *Washington Post*, January 7, 2021, https://www.proquest.com/docview/2475622106/citation/952C0F620AF7467FPQ/1.
2. Timberg, Craig, Elizabeth Dwoskin, and Reed Albergotti. "Inside Facebook, Jan. 6 Violence Fueled Anger, Regret over Missed Warning Signs," *Washington Post*, Oct. 24, 2021, https://www.proquest.com/newspapers/inside-facebook-jan-6-violence-fueled-anger/docview/2584854825/se-2.
3. James Purtill, "Weeks of Rhetoric Online Made the January 6 Storming of the Capitol 'Entirely Predictable,' Experts Say," *ABC Science Online*, January 7, 2021, http://www.proquest.com/docview/2498487628/abstract/6D0ABEF7070647EFPQ/1.
4. Luke Munn, "More than a Mob: Parler as Preparatory Media for the U.S. Capitol Storming," *First Monday*, February 7, 2021, https://doi.org/10.5210/fm.v26i3.11574.
5. Hugo Lowell, "Capitol Attack Panel Subpoenas Google, Facebook and Twitter for Digital Records," *Guardian* (Online) (London (UK), United Kingdom: Guardian News & Media Limited, January 13, 2022), https://www.proquest.com/docview/2619342184/citation/FFA4B256673C4E51PQ/1.
6. Timberg, Dwoskin, and Albergotti, "Inside Facebook, Jan. 6 Violence Fueled Anger, Regret over Missed Warning Signs."
7. 47 U.S.C. sec. 230.
8. 395 U.S. 444, per curiam.
9. 438 U.S. 726.
10. In Reno v. ACLU, 521 U.S. 844 (1997) and Packingham v. North Carolina, 582 U.S. 98, No. 15-1194 (2017), the majority opinions indicated that expression on the internet would be treated the same as expression occurring in other spaces.
11. 395 U.S. at 445–46.
12. 395 U.S. at 447.
13. Beauharnais v. Illinois, 343 U.S. 250, 258–59 (1952). The continuing validity of the ruling in Beauharnais has been called into question due to the ruling in R.A.V. v. City of St. Paul, 505 U.S. 377 (1992) that regulation of even unprotected expression such as libel has to be neutral as to both viewpoint and content. Nonetheless, the case has never been overruled, and has been cited as an example of the treatment of libel as unprotected speech as recently as United States v. Stevens, 559 U.S. 460, 468 (2010) (Roberts, C.J.).
14. Rice v. Paladin Enterprises 128 F.3d 233 (4th Cir. 1997).
15. Stewart v. McCoy, 537 U.S. 993, 994 (2002).
16. United States v. Hansen, 599 U.S. 762 (2023).
17. United States v. Stevens, 559 U.S. 460 (2010).

18   Timothy Tyson, "The Ghosts of 1898: Wilmington's Race Riot and the Rise of White Supremacy," *Wilmington News and Observer*, http://media2.newsobserver.com/content/media/2010/5/3/ghostsof1898.pdf.
19   Julian Dibbel, "A Rape in Cyberspace," available at http://www.juliandibbell.com/articles/a-rape-in-cyberspace/.
20   Nick Wingfield, Feminist Critics of Video Games Facing Threats in 'GamerGate' Campaign," *New York Times*, Oct. 24, 2014, available at https://www.nytimes.com/2014/10/16/technology/gamergate-women-video-game-threats-anita-sarkeesian.html.
21   Gersh, at 15–17.
22   We are not aware of any practice akin to doxing that occurred during the Radio Age. The question why not is fascinating, since radio broadcasts have certainly been used to incite violence, for example during the genocide in Rwanda.
23   Will Carliss, "How one man pushed harassment 'raids,' sold racist paraphernalia online, while in federal custody," *USA Today* online, May 3, 2023, available at https://www.usatoday.com/story/news/nation/2023/05/03/paul-nicholas-miller-gypsy-crusader-online-raids/70170754007/.
24   People v. Rubin, 96 Cal. App. 3d 968, 982 (Cal. Ct. App. 1979).
25   People v. Rubin, 978.
26   Nadine McSpadden, "Slow and Steady Does Not Always Win the Race: The Nuremburg Files Website and What It Should Teach Us About the Internet," *Indiana Law Journal* 76 (2001).
27   Planned Parenthood v. American Coalition for Life, 290 F.3d 1058 (9th Cir. en banc, 2002).
28   McSpadden, "Slow and Steady Does Not Always Win the Race."
29   United States v Alaboud, 347 F.3d 1293 (11th Cir. 2003).
30   Jennifer L. Brenner, "True Threats: A More Appropriate Standard for Analyzing First Amendment Protection and Free Speech When Violence Is Perpetrated over the Internet Note," *Notre Dame Law Review* 78, 753–84 (2002).
31   Molly Amman and J. Reid Meloy, Stochastic Terrorism: A Linguistic and Psychological Analysis," *Perspectives on Terrorism* 15 (2022), available at https://www.universiteitleiden.nl/binaries/content/assets/customsites/perspectives-on-terrorism/2021/issue-5/amman-and-meloy.pdf.
32   Rice v. Paladin Enterprises, supra. n.xiv.
33   Counterman v. Colorado, 600 U.S. 66 (2023).
34   Brandy Zadrozny, "'Carol's Journey,' What Facebook Knew About How It Radicalized Users," *NBC News*, Oct. 22, 2021, available at https://www.nbcnews.com/tech/tech-news/facebook-knew-radicalized-users-rcna3581. For a discussion of proposed regulations of the use of these algorithms, see Amb. (retired) Karen Kornbluth, "Disinformation, Radicalization, and Algorithmic Amplification: What Steps Can Congress Take?," Just Security Feb. 7, 2022, available at https://www.justsecurity.

org/79995/disinformation-radicalization-and-algorithmic-amplification-what-steps-can-congress-take/.
35 See Twitter v. Taamneh, 598 U.S. 471 (2023) and Gonzales v. Google, LLC, 598 US 617 (2023), holding that operators of social media sites that employ algorithms do not meet the definition of "knowingly providing substantial assistance" to terrorists under the Anti-Terrorism Act.
36 Matt Murphy, "The Dawn of A.I. Mischief Models." *Slate*, Aug. 3, 2022, available at https://slate.com/technology/2022/08/4chan-ai-open-source-trolling.html.
37 Section 230 of the Communications Decency Act, see endnote xiii, supra.
38 Moore was convicted of participating in computer hacking and identity theft. Louis Chilton, "The Most Hated Man on the Internet: Netflix Viewers horrified by 'vile details' in revenge porn documentary," *Independent*, Aug. 1, 2022, available at https://www.independent.co.uk/arts-entertainment/tv/news/most-hated-man-internet-hunter-moore-is-anyone-up-website-b2135394.html.
39 Kate Klonick, "The New Governors: The People, Rules, and Processes Governing Online Speech," *Harvard Law Review* 131, no. 6 (April 2018): 1598–670, 1670.
40 Klonick, "The New Governors," 1602.
41 See, for example, Scott Hammack, "The Internet Loophole: Why Threatening Speech On-line Requires a Modification of the Courts' Approach to True Threats and Incitement," *Columbia Journal of Law and Social Problems* 36, no. 65 (2002) (proposing a new "incitement-threat hybrid" category).
42 See John P. Cronan, "The Next Challenge for the First Amendment: The Framework for an Internet Incitement Standard," *Catholic University Law Review* 51, no. 425 (2002).
43 For a similar approach to this problem, see Russell Weaver, "Brandenburg and Incitement in a Digital Era," *Mississippi Law Journal.* 80, no. 1263 (2010–2011).
44 Gertz v. Robert Welch, 419 U.S. 323.
45 Ben Collins and Kat Tefarge, "Anti Trans Stalkers at Kiwi Farms Are Chasing One Victim Around the World. Their List of Targets Is Growing." *NBC News*, Sept. 2, 2022, https://www.nbcnews.com/tech/internet/cloudflare-kiwi-farms-keffals-anti-trans-rcna44834.
46 Matthew Prince and Alissa Starzak, "Cloudflare's Abuse Policies & Approach," *The Cloudflare Blog*, Oct. 31, 2022, available at: https://blog.cloudflare.com/cloudflares-abuse-policies-and-approach/.
47 Lois Beckett. "QAnon: A Timeline of Violence Linked to the Conspiracy Theory," *Guardian online*, October 16, 2020, available at https://www.theguardian.com/us-news/2020/oct/15/qanon-violence-crimes-timeline.

Chapter Nine

Incitement in Context

JoAnne Sweeny

The aftermath of the January 6, 2021, insurrection is still being felt today. On January 6, 2021, 150 police and security officers were injured and at least four were killed.[1] As a result of the FBI's investigation, at least 919 people have been charged so far, mostly with criminal trespass.[2] The House of Representatives also reacted swiftly, first by impeaching Donald Trump for incitement,[3] and then by creating the Select Committee to Investigate the January 6th Attack on the United States Capitol to further investigate Trump's ties to the insurrection.[4] The Committee issued its report on December 22, 2022, which laid out a compelling case of incitement against Trump and called for his indictment.[5] Eleven members of the House of Representatives and two Capitol police officers have also sued Trump and his allies for incitement.[6]

That litigation is still ongoing, but the District Court has already denied Trump's motion to dismiss by holding that it is plausible that Trump did incite his audience that day. The judge did so by looking at Trump's words in the context of Trump's speech, including the audience and the timing of his speech.

> The "import" of the President's words must be viewed within the broader context in which the Speech was made and against the Speech as a whole. Before January 6th, the President and others had created an air of distrust and anger among his supporters by creating the false narrative that the election literally was stolen from underneath their preferred candidate by fraud and corruption. Some of his supporters' beliefs turned to action. . . . Against this backdrop, the President invited his followers to Washington, D.C., on January 6th. It is reasonable to infer that the President would have known that some supporters viewed his invitation as a call to action.[7]

Likewise, the articles of impeachment are not limited to Trump's speech on the day, but place that speech in a larger context of months of "false claims of election fraud" and Trump's phone call to Georgia Secretary of State Brad Raffensperger where Trump asked him to "find" votes to overturn the election and threatened him if he failed to do so.[8]

This attention to context is a significant departure from Trump's last incitement case, which was focused on his command to his audience at a Louisville, Kentucky rally to "get [protestors] out of here!" Trump's speech in that case was held by the US Court of Appeals for the Sixth Circuit to not be incitement, and the court's decision was limited to examination of Trump's words alone.[9] In making its decision, the Sixth Circuit explicitly ignored audience's reaction and any other evidence that could have placed Trump's words in context.[10]

Although it is unclear whether Trump will ever be criminally prosecuted for the January 6, 2021, insurrection, the question still remains: did he actually commit incitement? Looking at his words that day in isolation — "We fight like hell. And if you don't fight like hell, you're not going to have a country anymore" — is his most explicit call for violence. Those words alone do not seem to be sufficient. But when the context of his speech is considered, the picture changes. Trump's speech was only the last words that his audience heard, the final match to light a gasoline-soaked pile of kindling. Even that day, the audience had been primed with multiple speakers whose words were far more explicitly violent.[11] And before January 6, Trump had used media appearances and Twitter to prime his base to take action.[12] All of this context paints a much clearer picture of what was in his audience's minds that day and how he put it there.

Incitement is a long-standing doctrine that has been defined and redefined by the Supreme Court, with lower courts filling in the gaps.[13] Long dormant, Trump and the alt-right resurrected the doctrine in the courts, and the legal system is now grappling with how to view incitement in light of modern communication. This chapter posits that the only way to bring incitement into the twenty-first century is to allow context to have a larger role in determining what a speaker's intention was and how their speech was reasonably received by their audience.

Defining Incitement with Context

Incitement has a unique place in American law because it is both a crime and a counterargument to claims of First Amendment protection. As with many First Amendment concepts, incitement is a murky concept that has evolved as a legal doctrine during conflicting political movements. It was originally used against World War I protestors who were being prosecuted under the Espionage Act,[14] but was later redefined by *Brandenburg v. Ohio* (1969),[15] *Hess v. Indiana* (1973),[16] and *NAACP v. Claiborne Hardware* (1982)[17] in reaction to the civil rights movement. Since 1982, the Supreme Court has not attempted to further explain or define incitement and lower courts have struggled to fill the gaps created by more modern technologies. The most recent cases that have attempted to do just that are *Sines v. Kessler* (2018), which involves the Unite the Right rally in Charlottesville and *Nwanguma v. Trump* (2016), the Sixth Circuit case that decided that Trump did not incite his audience at a Louisville rally.

In 2016, Trump was sued for incitement by three activists who were injured at his March 1, 2016 rally in Louisville, Kentucky.[18] The activists alleged that they were punched and shoved by Trump supporters who were acting on Trump's command to "get them outta here." Although a Kentucky district court judge ruled that Trump's words were not protected by the First Amendment, the Sixth Circuit reversed that decision.[19]

Despite the violence that erupted at Trump's rally in response to his speech, the Sixth Circuit in *Nwanguma* found there was no incitement by keeping its focus squarely on Trump's words themselves. In doing so, the Sixth Circuit heavily relied on a 2015 Sixth Circuit case, *Bible Believers v. Wayne County*, which found no incitement when a group of fundamentalist Christians were escorted out of a Muslim festival by police after their anti-Muslim words and signs caused the festivalgoers to react violently. However, *Bible Believers* is easily distinguishable (discussed at length in chapter 1) because the speech there was merely (though offensively) critical of Islam and did not include any commands to act. In fact, because the speaker's words were likely to anger the audience because the speaker was in opposition to his audience, *Bible Believers* more akin to a "fighting words" than an incitement case. Because of the animosity between the speaker and his audience, even if he had made a call to action, it is unlikely that the audience would obey him. Instead, his intentional offensiveness caused his audience to react with violence. This is not incitement because there was no commonality of intent or purpose between the speaker and his audience.[20]

The Sixth Circuit also relied on the Supreme Court's decision *Hess v. Indiana* to hold that the audience's reaction to a speech does not transform words into incitement; "the subjective reaction of any particular listener cannot dictate whether the speaker's words enjoy constitutional protection." Even though, as the Sixth Circuit conceded in *Nwanguma*, Trump's "words may *arguably* have had a tendency to encourage unlawful use of force, but they did not specifically advocate for listeners to take unlawful action and are therefore protected."[21]

However, the Sixth Circuit in *Nwanguma* did acknowledge that it should consider context under the Supreme Court case *Snyder v. Phelps* (2011) but limited what context could be considered to "the content, form, and context of the *speech*: what was *said*, where it was *said*, and how it was *said*." This analysis was limited to Trump's speech to his audience that day: the words were said to his unnamed audience who were "not sympathetic to the protestors," did not "specifically advocate" violence, and included the disclaimer "don't hurt 'em." However, the Sixth Circuit did not fully consider *how* the disclaimer was said, including the tone or any nonverbal cues Trump may have given at the time to indicate that he was being sarcastic. Considering that there was video evidence of the event that the Sixth Circuit could have watched to ascertain this context, the court's failure to do so is problematic.[22]

More problematic is the Sixth Circuit's comparison of the "disclaimer" *Nwanguma* to the efforts made by the defendants in *Bible Believers* to ensure that their words did not result in violence. Specifically, the defendants in *Bible Believers* had previously approached local law enforcement to ensure that any angry members of the public would be "ke[pt] at bay."[23] What the Sixth Circuit in *Nwanguma* failed to acknowledge, however, is that the words relied on in *Bible Believers* took place before the day of the rally, which means that the Sixth Circuit in that case was willing to look at the speaker's prior communications to find a context that would protect their speech. However, despite ample evidence of prior and later communications by Trump condoning violence at his other rallies,[24] the Sixth Circuit refused to consider it in *Nwanguma* (this case is discussed in greater detail in chapter 10).

Sines v. Kessler presents another way to consider context in modern incitement cases. In 2018, a Virginia district court denied the defendants' motion to dismiss claims of a civil conspiracy under the First Amendment for activity related to the 2017 Charlottesville Unite the Right rally. In its decision, the district court focused on the allegations that the defendants had given "specific instructions to carry out violent acts or threats."[25] These instructions mainly took place several days before the violent protest and included instructions to "wear good fighting uniforms" and bring "self-defense implements which can be turned from a free speech tool to a self-defense weapon should things turn ugly."[26] These instructions were also apparently followed; during the rally, when fighting broke out between the alt-right and antifascist groups, both sides used makeshift weapons, including flagpoles.[27] In its decision, the district court noted that these statements taken alone may appear to be protected speech but when considered in the context of the plaintiffs' other allegations,[28] they "can serve as evidence of an agreement to commit violence." After losing their motion to dismiss, the case ultimately went to trial and the jury awarded the plaintiffs over $25 million in damages.[29]

More recently, the Supreme Court of Colorado explicitly examined context when deciding if Trump committed incitement on January 6.[30] The Colorado Supreme Court quoted the Supreme Court case *Schenck v. United States*[31] to hold that context is relevant in incitement cases because "the character of every act depends upon the circumstances in which it is done."

The Sixth Circuit's refusal in *Nwanguma* to fully consider context is deeply problematic and, as existing case law and scholarly commentary shows, inconsistent with the purpose of the doctrine. Context does belong at every point in an incitement inquiry. As noted by the Sixth Circuit, the *Brandenburg* incitement test has three requirements: (1) a call to action that is (2) likely to produce imminent lawlessness or violence, and (3) the intent to produce such a result.[32] The question that remains is what contextual evidence courts should consider when examining each of these requirements.

Call to Action

Perhaps the most important requirement for incitement is that the speaker does more than merely advocate for violence or illegal acts; they must instead convince their audience to commit these acts.[33] One of the key distinctions between advocacy and incitement is that, for incitement, the speaker does not use conditional language.[34] Similarly, merely using offensive language[35] or describing violence[36] is not enough of a command to be incitement. As noted by the Supreme Court of California, there is a difference between advocating for the death of all criminals and encouraging an audience to lynch a prisoner currently being held in the jail nearby.[37]

However, other than these boundaries, courts have struggled with how to interpret the word spoken by an alleged inciter. As noted above, the Sixth Circuit has recently limited its examination of incitement's call to action requirement to only the words uttered by the speaker.[38] The Sixth Circuit cases are not the latest word on the matter. The DC district court in *Thompson v. Trump* held that, as recognized by the Supreme Court in *Hess*, "words can *implicitly* encourage violence or lawlessness"[39] This recognition of implied or indirect incitement prevents "the strategic speaker" from hiding behind the First Amendment if their words "advocate for imminent violence or lawlessness . . . through unmistakable suggestion and persuasion."

Multiple scholars have likewise advocated for the consideration of indirect incitement.[40] Indirect incitement also contemplates the use of coded language to express the speaker's command, much like solicitation where the jury is permitted to look at the defendant's words and infer their meaning even if he did not request criminal activity outright. For example, organized criminals have a variety of words they use instead of the word *murder*, such as *pop*, *clip*, *hit*, and *burn*.[41] Without an understanding of this code, the literal words used by an organized crime boss might not appear to be a direct call to violence.

As one scholar has noted, language is flexible and "context can determine the meaning" of a particular word or phrase.[42] However, allowing for indirect incitement begs the question of how to determine whether a statement has the necessary meaning for the audience. Scholars have used phrases such as "sufficiently likely to cause immediate harm" and when "listeners' reactions are easily predictable,"[43] as well as "inferences the hearer would rationally make from the utterance."[44] One way to determine the meaning an audience will infer is to look at the speaker's past communications, the medium of the speech, the surrounding communications at the time, and the audience susceptibility to violent reactions.[45] If these factors are considered, the implications of Trump's speech on January 6, 2021 takes on an entirely new meaning.

Prior Communications

Trump has a history of encouraging his followers to be violent and issuing commands to them at rallies. Trump used the phrase "get him out of here" in several rallies during his presidential campaign, which often led to violence.[46] He also stated that he wanted to fight the protestors at his rallies and stated that anyone who did not fight them was weak.[47] When violence did occur, Trump seemed to enjoy it and often defended his violent followers in the media. This pattern of behavior, going back to 2016, was essential background to the Colorado Supreme Court when it determined that Trump's encouragement to "fight," though perhaps metaphorical when spoken by others, was, effectively, "coded language," that was understood by his audience as an explicit call do violence on January 6.[48]

At the very least, on January 6, Trump knew that the audience might react to his words violently because they had in the past. In the months leading up to the January 6 rally, Trump and his allies made repeated statements with a few key themes: the election was fraudulently stolen from Trump, Congress and "weak" Republicans could stop this theft but were too cowardly to do so, and that his followers by "fighting," could right this wrong.

As part of their messaging, Trump and his allies used violent imagery, exhortations, and several repeated catchphrases or hashtags. The most prominent hashtag was "Stop the Steal." The phrase was first popularized on social media after the 2016 election and resurrected in 2020 by Trump and his allies to mobilize his followers. From election night until January 6, it was used in social media, fundraising solicitations, and as the name of rallies. The repeated use of this phrase created and then gave access to a world of conspiracy theories and increasingly violent rhetoric.[49]

Even before election day, Trump and his allies began spreading stories about the election being rigged against him, which has been referred to as the Big Lie, a reference to *Mein Kampf*.[50] A flurry of lawsuits were initiated to stop the votes from being confirmed and sent to Congress.[51]

Throughout the month of December 2020, Trump's team began losing their court cases and the rhetoric surrounding "Stop the Steal" became increasingly violent. Trump and his allies also began explicitly targeting their enemies. On December 2, Trump ally Lin Wood made a statement at a Stop the Steal Rally in Georgia where he threatened to "slay" liberals and promised that "Joe Biden will never set foot in the Oval Office of this country. It will not happen on our watch. Never gonna happen."[52]

Trump's allies also began reaching out to his followers for their help to keep Trump in the White House. These pleas typically were pleas for fundraising to pay for Trump's legal battles but, as January 6 neared, Trump's allies began to make a different kind of request. On December 8, the official Twitter account of the Arizona Republican Party made several Tweets that effectively asked their followers if they were willing to give their lives to Stop the Steal.[53] On Twitter,

Powell suggested that Trump followers who want to "rise up" could "swarm the state capital, Congress." Former National Security Director Michael Flynn, another Trump ally who would later argue for martial law to stop Biden taking office, retweeted that Tweet.[54]

At a December Washington, DC rally, Trump senior campaign adviser Katrina Pierson stated that if using the system did not work "we will take our country back." [55] Trump Tweeted his support of the rally, mentioning "Stop the Steal."[56] On December 30, Wood asked on Parler "Will you sit quietly & allow Communists & Globalists to control every aspect of your lives? Or will you stand tall & #FightBack for your freedom? The choice is yours to make. Choose wisely." Several other Trump allies also used the word *fight*: Flynn Tweeted on January 2, "We are not going away and #WeThePeople will continue to #FightForTrump" and Donald Trump Jr. told a January 4 rally audience in Georgia "We need to fight." At a January 5 rally, Trump himself stated, "They're not taking this White House. We're going to fight like hell."[57]

In December, both Wood and attorney Sidney Powell, another Trump ally, gave interviews that threatened future violence on a massive scale. Powell stated on the Fox Business Network that "This is essentially a new American revolution. And anyone who wants this country to remain free needs to step up right now." Wood was even more explicit, saying in an interview on the pro-Trump TV station called New Tang Dynasty Television, "I believe there will be violence in our streets soon." Also during this time, Trump's allies continued to imply that a violent confrontation was imminent. On December 18, Wood said in a podcast interview that Americans should keep extra provisions on hand in case of unrest. At no point did Trump distance himself from Wood and Powell despite this rhetoric and was retweeting their "stop the steal" tweets as late as January 3, 2021.[58]

Not only was violence threatened, it actually occurred. On the evening of the December Washington, DC rally, the rally turned violent as pro and anti-Trump groups clashed: four people were stabbed and thirty-three people were arrested.[59] Several of those injured were police officers. Once Joe Biden's Electoral College victory was formalized on December 14,[60] Trump and his allies began pushing for his followers to attend the January 6 rally.

Also in December, along with the promises that his followers could be part of "stopping the steal," Trump and his followers set the date for the ultimate confrontation: January 6. On December 19, Trump tweeted "Big protest in D.C. on January 6th. Be there, will be wild!"[61] On December 27, December 30, and January 1, Trump repeatedly encouraged his followers to attend the rally.[62] His January 1 Tweet included the phrase "Stop the Steal." Trump also retweeted a rally organizer's tweet that the "calvary [*sic*] is coming."

On January 5, Eric Trump Tweeted another plea for Trump's followers to attend the January 6 rally: "Patriots — Who's coming to Washington D.C. tomorrow!!! Let's #StopTheSteal." At a January 5 rally, Flynn warned Congress that "tomorrow we the people will be here."[63] By the time January 6 arrived, these communications had Trump's followers primed for a conflict.

Surrounding Communications

The communications that took place just before Trump's speech on January 6 also provide context for his words. On the face of it, Trump's repeated call for the audience to "fight like hell" was mitigated by his command to go to the Capitol to have their voices heard "peacefully and patriotically."[64] However, just before that speech, his audience heard Trump's son, Donald Trump Jr. threaten Republican lawmakers who did not support Trump's efforts to overturn the election with the words "we're coming for you and we're going to have a good time doing it." Although that phrase could mean that Trump and his allies would be "coming for" Republicans by unseating them in the next election, a more violent interpretation of that phrase was certainly possible, particularly because it was followed by personal lawyer, Rudy Giuliani's, speech that advocated for "trial by combat."

The morning of January 6 included Tweets from Trump and Wood again riling up Trump's followers. Trump's Tweet included the phrase "BE STRONG!" and Wood stated, "The time has come Patriots. This is our time. Time to take back our country. Time to fight for our freedom. Pledge your lives, your fortunes, & your sacred honor . . . TODAY IS OUR DAY."[65] That line, which references the Declaration of Independence, was echoed on January 5 by pro-Trump politicians such as Marjorie Taylor Green who stated to far-right publication *NewsMax*, "this is our 1776 moment." Some have argued that "1776 moment," which references the American Revolution, is a coded phrase calling for violence.[66]

Trump's Twitter messages that day also give context to his speech. Shortly before taking the stage, Trump accused Mike Pence of not having "the courage to do what should have been done to protect our Country and our Constitution" on Twitter.[67] These surrounding speeches give new meaning to Trump's own speech that day: Congress and Mike Pence, all of whom were currently in the Capitol, were to blame for not protecting the country. Although Trump said his followers should march to the Capitol "peacefully," he also said "patriotically." That word, along with the more violent phrasing of his son and lawyer, arguably gave his followers a very specific message: go to the Capitol and stop the wrongdoers by any means necessary. When looking at Trump's speech not in isolation but as the culmination of months — if not years — of communications to his followers via his and his allies' media appearances, as well as his escalating communications on Twitter, Trump's command to "fight like hell" and march on the Capitol, even with the caveat that the march should be peaceful, takes on a different meaning.

Medium of Communication

The medium of Trump's speech was twofold: he spoke in person to the crowd of followers and journalists that had gathered and his speech was also being live streamed. Not only was the speech live, it took place in Washington, DC, on a stage with sound and video equipment. This was a well-funded and planned affair that had been organized and sponsored by PACs such as the Save America PAC, which was created specifically to try to overturn the 2020 election.[68] That it was in person only made the speech more likely to spawn immediate reactions from the audience. Indeed, the audience actively participated by chanting and later marching and some of them were armed with baseball bats, pepper spray, and stun guns.[69]

Moreover, the location of the speech heightened the meaning of Trump's words and commands to march to the Capitol, which was only blocks away. The timing of the speech, on the day that Biden would be certified by Congress as the next President also lent a sense of purpose and urgency to Trump's speech: the theft of the election was almost complete, and the thieves were a short walk away.

Susceptibility to Violence

Trump and his allies had been priming his followers not for a march or protest, but a revolution. As the December rally showed, Trump's followers, many of whom were members of fascist or alt-right groups such as the Proud Boys, were willing to do violence. Messages from his followers on social media and chatrooms such as Parler showed that, even before the election, they were prepared to stop Biden's election with violence.[70] After election night, his followers rallied around voting stations in several swing states in an attempt to stop the counting of mail-in ballots. These attempts included chanting outside of or even trying to break into vote-counting centers.[71] Some of these protestors were armed with loaded handguns.[72]

As noted by the district court in *Thompson v. Trump*, Trump and his advisers "actively monitored" pro-Trump websites and social media and saw that these "forums lit up in response to the rally announcement." Some of Trump's supporters threatened violence that day or targeted the people certifying the election, and these online messages were widely reported and so well-known that one of Trump's former aides predicted violence that day. As the district court aptly put it, due to these prior communications, "when the President stepped to the podium on January 6th, it is reasonable to infer that he would have known that some in the audience were prepared for violence. Yet, the President delivered a speech he understood would only aggravate an already volatile situation."[73]

As the district court also noted, because his followers were already primed for violence, Trump's pleas for his audience to "not concede," and "show strength" so they could "take back their country," took on a very specific meaning that day. All in all, it is clear that Trump's followers were more than willing to put action to their words in an effort to keep him in office and his speech arguably gave them an explicit command to do just that. Moreover, as the Colorado Supreme Court noted, Trump's supporters "listen to him like no one else" and through his yearslong pattern of encouraging violence at his rallies and then refusing to condemn that violence after the fact, Trump's exhortation to "fight" on January 6 read like a command.[74]

Perhaps the strongest evidence for incitement is that Trump's followers understood his words to be a call to violence. In the aftermath of January 6, dozens of insurrectionists were arrested and faced criminal charges.[75] Several blamed Trump for their actions, saying that his words to "fight like hell" meant that they should storm the capital. As one insurrectionist stated on the witness stand, "[i]f the president's giving you almost an order to do something," you feel "felt obligated to do that."[76] The January 6 Committee report contains several similar statements by insurrectionists: that they came to Washington DC on Trump's orders so they could help him stop the election from being stolen from him. One insurrectionist, who brought a gun with him to Washington, stated "I was in Washington, D.C. on January 6, 2021, because I believed I was following the instructions of former President Trump and he was my president and the commander-in-chief. His statements also had me believing the election was stolen from him."[77]

Considering everything that preceded and surrounded Trump's January 6, 2021 speech, it is easy to see why they felt that way. Indeed, the DC District Court perhaps put it most elegantly: Trump's speech was "an implicit call for imminent violence or lawlessness" because he "called for thousands 'to fight like hell' immediately before directing an unpermitted march to the Capitol, where the targets of their ire were at work, knowing that militia groups and others among the crowd were prone to violence."[78] His position of president and commander-in-chief could only strengthen his influence over his followers. This call was the culmination of months of incendiary language and lies. Any one of the statements made by Trump or his allies could perhaps be explained away but when all of them are combined, the picture is quite clear: the violence was exactly what Trump asked for.

Imminence

The second requirement for incitement is imminence, which means that the speaker must call for violence or illegal acts to happen immediately, not at a later time or based on the satisfaction of a condition.[79] The Supreme Court has never fully defined imminence, though its most obvious definition is "closeness in time between the offending speech and the intended responsive action."[80] At the very least, imminence means that call for the violence or illegal acts cannot mean that those actions should happen "at some indefinite future time."[81]

The imminence standard becomes more complicated for speech that takes place online where it is difficult to know when it was "heard" by its audience. In such situations, courts have interpreted imminence to not just mean a short amount of time but that violence or illegal acts were likely to result.[82] When using likelihood as a proxy for imminence, context again comes into play. One scholar has identified several factors to use when determining the foreseeability of violence: "the likely make-up of the target audience, whether there was a prior history of violence by members of that audience, and whether the violence took place with little delay upon receiving the inciting speech."[83]

Of the three elements for incitement, imminence is the easiest to prove here. Violence was certainly likely to occur. As noted above, the audience was made up of die-hard Trump supporters and neofascist groups that had already shown themselves to be violent in their support of Trump. Moreover, just looking at the timing of the speech, Trump's statements were made in person, and directly after his speech was finished the audience marched to the Capitol and, thirty-five minutes later, broke inside.[84] There was no pause in the action or a chance to reflect; even the walk to the Capitol was done with the crowd urging each other on both online and in person.[85]

Intent

Although not specifically mentioned in *Brandenburg*, courts and legal scholars have added an intent requirement into incitement. As noted by the California Supreme Court, "incited violence . . . must be a specifically intended consequence of the speaker's plea and not a result of unreasonable reactions by hostile onlookers or overly zealous supporters."[86] Intent also presumes knowledge of the likely outcome.

When looking at intent, context again matters. As noted by a California Court of Appeals, courts should look at "words and circumstances" of the speech to determine the speaker's intent. Use of jokes, conditional language, or disclaimers can show that the speaker did not intend to incite their audience.[87] In contrast, positive reference to prior acts of violence likewise can show a speaker's intent to incite a crowd. Intent can also be inferred from a speaker's prior statements and the amount of the speaker's influence over the crowd.[88] The Colorado Supreme Court likewise analyzed Trump's intent on January 6 by looking at the circumstances of his speech, which included Trump's words and actions regarding the 2020 election before the insurrection and after it had begun.[89]

Trump's statements before and during the insurrection clearly show his intent. Trump's political rallies were known for being rowdy and even violent and he repeatedly defended his violent audiences and stated that he would like be physically violent with protestors. Even after he was elected, Trump's rhetoric did not become any more moderate. He initially turned his ire toward the press, calling them dishonest and the enemy of the people. He maintained his stance even after journalists began to be physically attacked. In fact, he praised Republican Representative Greg Gianforte after Gianforte body-slammed a reporter. Similarly, Trump encouraged the police to be more violent with suspects. Trump also refused to disavow the neofascist groups that supported him, famously telling the Proud Boys to "Stand Down and Stand By," a phrase that the Proud Boys later used as a slogan.[90]

In his speech on January 6, 2021, Trump did say that his audience should march "peacefully," which could be seen as a disclaimer, much like his "don't hurt 'em" statement at his Louisville rally, which heavily influenced the Sixth Circuit. Before the DC District Court, however, Trump's "passing reference to "peaceful and patriotic protest" did not "inoculate him against the conclusion that his exhortation, made nearly an hour later, to "fight like hell" immediately before sending rally-goers to the Capitol, within the context of the larger Speech and circumstances, was not protected expression." Similarly, the Colorado Supreme Court found this passing reference to be part of Trump's pattern of saying inflammatory words and then throwing in a moderating phrase with a figurative wink to his audience, who knew he was doing so just to maintain plausible deniability in front of the cameras.[91]

Moreover, unlike in the Sixth Circuit case, there is ample evidence that Trump approved of the violence at the Capitol once it occurred. Fifteen minutes after the riot had begun at the Capitol, Trump tweeted again, calling out Mike Pence for his lack of courage, which the rioters at the Capitol repeated over megaphones.[92] His continuing criticism of Pence, after he knew that his followers were storming the Capitol, shows his approval of their actions. A few minutes later, Trump was informed that Pence was being evacuated for his safety and was then entreated by House Leader Kevin McCarthy, who had just been evacuated from his office, to call off the rioters; Trump refused, first blaming antifa and then telling McCarthy "maybe these people are just more angry about this than you are."[93] Trump's reticence to call off his supporters is not surprising. Several Trump employees and former allies have made statements that Trump was "delighted" when he saw the violence erupt on his television[94] and initially refused to intercede either by making a statement[95] or calling the national guard.[96] All in all, Trump waited thirty minutes after the riot began before asking his supporters to be peaceful and ninety minutes to record a video asking them to go home after reminding them that the election had indeed been stolen.[97] These statements were made at the urging of his staff, children, and allies.[98]

Taking all of Trump's statements, the repeated violence at his rallies, and the general moblike atmosphere he encouraged, his positive reaction to the violence once it began, and his reluctance to call it off, it is likely that these contextual clues will be sufficient to show Trump's intent to incite the crowd.

Conclusion

January 6, 2021, was a pivotal moment in our nation's history, and one we are still grappling with today. An incitement case being brought against a former president who is running for office again is an incredibly unique case and one that brings a lot of the *Brandenberg* standard's deficiencies to light. In today's highly charged political climate, more and more potential incitement cases are being brought to court. It seems that it is only a matter of time before the Supreme Court will have to weigh in on what incitement means in today's society and with today's modern means of communication. Any attempt to redefined incitement in the modern era will necessarily involve an examination of the role context should play in determining what a speaker's words meant and what the speaker intended them to mean. Considering the purpose of the incitement doctrine, one can only hope that the Supreme Court will eschew the narrow definition created by the Sixth Circuit and allow for context to provide a richer understanding of the speech at issue.

Notes

1. Chris Cameron, "These Are the People Who Died in Connection with the Capitol Riot," *New York Times*, January 5, 2022, https://www.nytimes.com/2022/01/05/us/politics/jan-6-capitol-deaths.html.
2. Madison Hall, et al., "At least 919 people have been charged in the Capitol insurrection so far. This searchable table shows them all," *Insider*, September 21, 2022, https://www.insider.com/all-the-us-capitol-pro-trump-riot-arrests-charges-names-2021-1.
3. Lisa Mascaro et al., "Donald Trump Becomes the First U.S. President to Be Impeached Twice," PBS, January 13, 2021, https://www.pbs.org/newshour/politics/majority-of-house-members-vote-for-2nd-impeachment-of-trump.
4. Rachel Looker et al., "January 6 Hearing Recap: Panel Subpoenas Trump, Shows New Video of Pelosi as Mob Attacked," *USA Today*, October 13, 2022, https://www.usatoday.com/story/news/politics/2022/10/13/january-6-committee-hearing-live-updates/10441093002/.
5. Final Report: Select Committee to Investigate the January 6th Attack on the United States Capitol, December 22, 2022, https://www.jan-6.com/_files/ugd/acac13_ffa28ed6c2694272a265860e447122c7.pdf.
6. Thompson v. Trump, 590 F. Supp. 3d 46 (D.D.C. 2022), aff'd sub nom. Blassingame v. Trump, 87 F.4th 1 (D.C. Cir. 2023).
7. Thompson, 590 F. Supp. 3d at 115.
8. Brian Naylor, "Article of Impeachment Cites Trump's 'Incitement' of Capitol Insurrection," NPR, February 9, 2021, https://www.npr.org/sections/trump-impeachment-effort-live-updates/2021/01/11/955631105/impeachment-resolution-cites-trumps-incitement-of-capitol-insurrection.
9. Jonathan Stempel, "Trump Wins Dismissal of 'Inciting to Riot' Lawsuit over 2016 Rally," Reuters, September 11, 2018, https://www.reuters.com/article/us-usa-trump-kentucky-lawsuit/trump-wins-dismissal-of-inciting-to-riot-lawsuit-over-2016-rally-idUSKCN1LR22B.
10. Nwanguma v. Trump, 903 F.3d 604, 613 (6th Cir. 2018).
11. Ed Pilkington, "Incitement: A Timeline of Trump's Inflammatory Rhetoric Before the Capitol Riot," *Guardian*, January 7, 2021, https://www.theguardian.com/us-news/2021/jan/07/trump-incitement-inflammatory-rhetoric-capitol-riot.
12. Pilkington, "Incitement: A Timeline of Trump's Inflammatory Rhetoric Before the Capitol Riot."
13. Dr. JoAnne Sweeny, "Incitement in the Era of Trump and Charlottesville," *Capital University Law Review* 47 (2019): 594.
14. Mark Strasser, "Incitement, Threats, and Constitutional Guarantees: First Amendment Protections Pre- and Post-Elonis," *University of New Hampshire Law Review* 14 (2015): 164–71.
15. Brandenburg v. Ohio, 395 U.S. 444, 446 (1969).

16 Hess v. Indiana, 414 U.S. 105 (1973).
17 NAACP v. Claiborne Hardware Co., 458 U.S. 886 (1982).
18 Eliott C. McLaughlin, "It's Plausible Trump Incited Violence, Federal Judge Rules in OK'ing Lawsuit," CNN, April 3, 2017, https://www.cnn.com/2017/04/02/politics/donald-trump-lawsuit-incite-violence-kentucky-rally/index.html.
19 Nwanguma, 903 F.3d at 613.
20 Bible Believers v. Wayne County, Mich., 805 F.3d 228, 244 (6th Cir. 2015).
21 Nwanguma, 903 F.3d at 613, 610 (emphasis in original).
22 Nwanguma, 903 F.3d at 611, 612 (emphasis in original).
23 Bible Believers, 805 F.3d at 244.
24 Ben Mathis-Lilley, "A Continually Growing List of Violent Incidents at Trump Events," *Slate*, April 25, 2016, http://www.slate.com/blogs/the_slatest/2016/03/02/a_list_of_violent_incidents_at_donald_trump_rallies_and_events.html.
25 Sines v. Kessler, 324 F. Supp. 3d 765, 803 (W.D. Va. 2018).
26 Sines, 324 F. Supp. 3d at 803.
27 Hawes Spencer, "A Far-Right Gathering Bursts into Brawls," *New York Times*, August 13, 2017, https://www.nytimes.com/2017/08/13/us/charlottesville-protests-unite-the-right.html.
28 According to the court, the plaintiffs also alleged that the Defendants encouraged the throwing of torches at counterprotesters and ordered others to "charge!" *Sines*, 324 F. Supp. 3d at 803.
29 Neil MacFarquhar, "Jury Finds Rally Organizers Responsible for Charlottesville Violence," *New York Times*, November 23, 2021, https://www.nytimes.com/2021/11/23/us/charlottesville-rally-verdict.html.
30 Anderson v. Griswold, 543 P.3d 283, 337 (Colo. 2023), cert. granted sub nom. Trump v. Anderson, 144 S. Ct. 539 (2024), and rev'd sub nom. on other grounds Trump v. Anderson, 601 U.S. 100 (2024), and cert. dismissed sub nom. Co Republican State Cent. Comm. v. Anderson, No. 23-696, 2024 WL 1143820 (U.S. Mar. 18, 2024).
31 249 U.S. 47, 52 (1919).
32 Nwanguma, 903 F.3d at 609.
33 S. Elizabeth Wilborn Malloy and Ronald J. Krotoszynski Jr., "Recalibrating the Cost of Harm Advocacy: Getting Beyond Brandenburg," *William and Mary Law Review* 41 (2000): 1197. "Brandenburg addresses speech activity designed to persuade someone to commit an unlawful act, not speech designed to facilitate the commission of an unlawful act by a person who has already decided to act." See also United States v. Buttorff, 572 F.2d 619, 624 (8th Cir. 1978) (statement must go beyond "mere advocacy").
34 Brandenburg, 395 U.S. at 446 (revengance" was "possible" and "might" be needed); Hess, 414 U.S. at 107 ("We'll take the fucking street again" or "We'll take the fucking street later"); McCoy, 282 F.3d at

631–32 (advocacy of future gang violence was deemed "very general" and "abstract" because his advice was "not aimed at any particular person or any particular time").

35 Bible Believers, 805 F.3d at 244.
36 Yakubowicz v. Paramount Pictures Corp., 536 N.E.2d 1067, 1071 (Mass. 1989); McCollum v. CBS, Inc., 249 Cal. Rptr. 187, 194 (Cal. App. 2d Dist. 1988).
37 People v. Bohmer, 120 Cal. Rptr. 136, 145 (Cal. App. 4th Dist. 1975).
38 Nwanguma, 903 F.3d at 610.
39 Thompson, 590 F. Supp. 3d at 117.
40 Joseph Jaconelli, "Incitement: A Study in Language Crime," *Criminal Law and Philosophy* 12 (2017): 248; David Crump, "Camouflaged Incitement: Freedom of Speech, Communicative Torts, and the Borderland of the Brandenburg Test," *Georgia Law Review* 29 (1994): 67; Gregory S. Gordon, "Music and Genocide: Harmonizing Coherence, Freedom and Nonviolence in Incitement Law," *Santa Clara Law Review* 50 (2010): 623–24; Kent Greenawalt, *Speech, Crime and the Uses of Language* (Oxford University Press 1992): 267–68.
41 "The Ultimate Mafia Glossary," *National Crime Syndicate*, https://www.nationalcrimesyndicate.com/ultimate-mafia-glossary/ (last accessed April 22, 2023).
42 Greenawalt, *Speech, Crime and the Uses of Language*, 267–68.
43 Martin H. Redish, "Advocacy of Unlawful Conduct and the First Amendment: In Defense of Clear and Present Danger," *California Law Review* 70 (1982): 1179.
44 Bradley J. Pew, "Comment, How to Incite Crime with Words: Clarifying Brandenburg's Incitement Test with Speech Act Theory," *Brigham Young University Law Review* (2015): 1098.
45 Greenawalt, *Speech, Crime and the Uses of Language* at 274.
46 Ben Mathis-Lilley, "A Continually Growing List of Violent Incidents at Trump Events," *Slate*, April 25, 2016, http://www.slate.com/blogs/the_slatest/2016/03/02/a_list_of_violent_incidents_at_donald_trump_rallies_and_events.html.
47 Eric Bradner, "Trump: Sanders "Showed Such Weakness" with #BlackLivesMatter protesters," CNN, August 12, 2015, https://www.cnn.com/2015/08/11/politics/donald-trump-2016/index.html.
48 Anderson, 543 P.3d 283 at paras. 239–44.
49 Michael Edison Hayden, "Far Right Resurrects Roger Stone's #StopTheSteal During Vote Count," *Southern Poverty Law Center*, November 6, 2020, https://www.splcenter.org/hatewatch/2020/11/06/far-right-resurrects-roger-stones-stopthesteal-during-vote-count.
50 Melissa Block, "The Clear and Present Danger of Trump's Enduring 'Big Lie,'" NPR, December 23, 2021, https://www.npr.org/2021/12/23/1065277246/trump-big-lie-jan-6-election. Trump later

promised to appropriate the phrase "the Big Lie" to refer to the "lie" that he had lost the election. Andrew Solender, "Trump Says He'll Appropriate 'The Big Lie' to Refer to His Election Loss," *Forbes*, May 3, 2021, https://www.forbes.com/sites/andrewsolender/2021/05/03/ trump-says-hell-appropriate-the-big-lie-to-refer-to-his-election-loss/?sh=4426156a5584.

51 William Cummings et al., "By the Numbers: President Donald Trump's Failed Efforts to Overturn the Election," *USA Today*, January 6, 2021, https://www.usatoday.com/in-depth/news/politics/elections/2021/01/06/trumps-failed-efforts-overturn-election-numbers/4130307001/.

52 *Washington Examiner*, Twitter Post, December 2, 2020, https://twitter.com/dcexaminer/status/ 1334228469832531968?lang=en.

53 Sophie Lewis, "Arizona Republican Party Asks followers If They're Willing to Die to Overturn Election Results," CBS News, December 10, 2020, https://www.cbsnews.com/news/arizona-republican-party-overturn-election-results-death/. After criticism, those tweets were deleted.

54 Rebecca Ballhaus et al., "Trump and His Allies Set the Stage for Riot Well Before January 6," *Wall Street Journal*, January 8, 2021, https://www.wsj.com/articles/trump-and-his-allies-set-the-stage-for-riot-well-before-january-6-11610156283.

55 Nathalie Baptiste, "Newly Pardoned Michael Flynn Was a Crowd Favorite Among the Extremists at Trump's Latest Rally," *Mother Jones*, December 12, 2020, https://www.motherjones.com/politics/2020/12/march-for-trump-dc-michael-flynn/.

56 Ryan Goodman et al., "Incitement Timeline: Year of Trump's Actions Leading to the Attack on the Capitol," *Just Security*, January 11, 2021, https://www.justsecurity.org/74138/incitement-timeline-year-of-trumps-actions-leading-to-the-attack-on-the-capitol/.

57 Ballhaus et al., "Trump and His Allies Set the Stage for Riot Well Before January 6."

58 Ballhaus et al., "Trump and His Allies Set the Stage for Riot Well Before January 6"; see also Trump Twitter Archive, https://www.thetrumparchive.com/ (last accessed April 22, 2023).

59 Lauren Koenig, "Several People Stabbed and 33 Arrested as 'Stop the Steal' Protesters and Counterprotesters Clash in Washington, DC," CNN, December 13, 2020, https://www.cnn.com/2020/12/12/us/stop-the-steal-protest-washington-dc-trnd/index.html.

60 Mark Sherman, "Electoral College Makes It Official: Biden Won, Trump Lost," Associated Press, December 14, 2020, https://apnews.com/article/joe-biden-270-electoral-college-vote-d429ef97af2bf574d16463384dc7cc1e.

61 Tom Dreisbach, "How Trump's 'Will Be Wild!' Tweet Drew Rioters to the Capitol on Jan. 6," *New York Times*, July 13, 2022, https://www.nytimes.com/2021/01/06/us/politics/capitol-mob-trump-supporters.html.

62 Dreisbach, "How Trump's 'Will Be Wild!' Tweet Drew Rioters to the Capitol on Jan. 6."
63 Greg Miller et al., "A Mob Insurrection Stoked by False Claims of Election Fraud and Promises of Violent Restoration," *Washington Post*, January 9, 2021, https://www.washingtonpost.com/national-security/trump-capitol-mob-attack-origins/2021/01/09/0cb2cf5e-51d4-11eb-83e3-322644d82356_story.html.
64 Pilkington, "Incitement: A Timeline of Trump's Inflammatory Rhetoric Before the Capitol Riot." He also said he would march with them but instead returned to the White House.
65 Ballhaus et al., "Trump and His Allies Set the Stage for Riot Well Before January 6."
66 Nathan Place, "Lawyer Fighting to Disqualify Marjorie Taylor Greene Says She Used 'Codeword' to Encourage Capitol Riot," *Independent*, April 21, 2022, https://www.independent.co.uk/news/world/americas/us-politics/marjorie-taylor-greene-codeword-1776-b2062673.html.
67 Trump Twitter Archive, last accessed October 21, 2022, https://www.thetrumparchive.com/.
68 Rachel Looker, "Trump's 'Save America' PAC Raised Millions After the Election. Here's What You Need to Know About It," *USA Today*, August 11, 2022, https://www.usatoday.com/story/news/politics/2022/08/11/jan-6-committee-trump-campaign-spending/10265619002/?gnt-cfr=1.
69 Tom Dreisbach and Tim Mak, "Yes, Capitol Rioters Were Armed. Here Are the Weapons Prosecutors Say They Used," NPR, March 19, 2021, https://www.npr.org/2021/03/19/977879589/yes-capitol-rioters-were-armed-here-are-the-weapons-prosecutors-say-they-used.
70 Goodman et al., "Incitement Timeline: Year of Trump's Actions Leading to the Attack on the Capitol."
71 Annalise Frank, "Chaos at TCF Center as Crowds of Election Challengers Shout 'Stop the Vote,'" *Crain's Detroit Business*, November 4, 2020, https://www.crainsdetroit.com/elections/chaos-tcf-center-crowds-election-challengers-shout-stop-vote; Christian Boone, "Pro-Trump protesters convinced the fix is in," *Atlanta Journal-Constitution*, November 5, 2020, https://www.ajc.com/politics/election/pro-trump-protesters-convinced-the-fix-is-in/FL44ZCNCCFGIPEL5UEEWSLO6DI/.
72 "Armed Men Arrested Near Philadelphia Vote Counting Location," Associated Press, November 6, 2020, https://apnews.com/article/philadelphia-men-guns-arrested-near-vote-d9f8fa1f3d556f3ee014769c543abd0d.
73 Thompson, 590 F. Supp. 3d at 115, 116.
74 Anderson, 543 P.3d 283 at paras. 247, 253.
75 Alan Feuer and Nicole Hong, "'I Answered the Call of My President': Rioters Say Trump Urged Them On," *New York Times*, January 17, 2021, https://www.nytimes.com/2021/01/17/nyregion/protesters-blaming-trump-pardon.html.

76 Alan Feuer, "Blaming Trump, Jan. 6 Suspect Says He Fell Down a 'Rabbit Hole' of Lies," *New York Times*, April 13, 2022, https://www.nytimes.com/2022/04/13/us/politics/jan-6-suspect-trump.html.
77 Final Report: Select Committee to Investigate the January 6th Attack on the United States Capitol at 3.
78 Thompson, 590 F. Supp. 3d at 117.
79 A recent example of conditional speech is the Walking Dead fan–created slogan "If Darryl dies, we riot." Henry Hanks, "'Walking Dead' Finale: If Daryl Dies, We Riot," CNN, December 1, 2013, https://www.cnn.com/2013/11/29/showbiz/walking-dead-norman-reedus/index.html.
80 Mark Rohr, "Grand Illusion? The Brandenburg Test and Speech That Encourages or Facilitates Criminal Acts," *Willamette Law Review* 38 (2002): 17 (citing Martin H. Redish, *Freedom of Expression: A Critical Analysis* 190 [Lexis Publishing, 1984]).
81 Hess, 414 U.S. at 108–9.
82 People v. Rubin, 158 Cal. Rptr. 488, 493 (Cal. App. 2d Dist. 1979).
83 Lyrissa Barnett Lidsky, "Incendiary Speech and Social Media," *Texas Tech Law Review* 44 (2011): 162.
84 "Capitol Riots Timeline: What Happened on 6 January 2021?" BBC, June 10, 2021, https://www.bbc.com/news/ world-us-canada-56004916. In contrast, and as the DC District Court noted, Giuliani's statement "let's have trial by combat" is more akin to "'advocacy of illegal action at some indefinite future time'" because there was no sense of immediacy to his words. Thompson, 590 F. Supp. 3d at 118 (quoting Hess, 414 U.S. at 108).
85 Final Report: Select Committee to Investigate the January 6th Attack on the United States Capitol at 647–48.
86 Braxton v. Mun. Ct., 514 P.2d 697, 703 (Cal. 1973).
87 People v. Rubin, 158 Cal. Rptr. at 493.
88 Greenawalt, *Speech, Crime and the Uses of Language* at 274.
89 Anderson, 543 P.3d 283 at paras. 233–25.
90 Mathis-Lilley, "A Continually Growing List of Violent Incidents at Trump Events;" Jenna Johnson and Mary Jordan, "Trump on Rally Protester: 'Maybe He Should Have Been Roughed Up,'" *Washington Post*, November 22, 2015, https://www.washingtonpost.com/news/post-politics/wp/2015/11/22/black-activist-punched-at-donald-trump-rally-in-birmingham/?noredirect=on&utm_term=.7fb2066f63e7; Fabiola Cineas, "Donald Trump Is the Accelerant," *Vox*, January 9, 2021, https://www.vox.com/21506029/trump-violence-tweets-racist-hate-speech; Ben Collins and Brandy Zadrozny, "Proud Boys Celebrate After Trump's Debate Callout," NBC, September 29, 2020, https://www.nbcnews.com/tech/tech-news/proud-boys-celebrate-after-trump-s-debate-call-out-n1241512.
91 Anderson, 543 P.3d 283 at para. 240.
92 Thompson, 590 F. Supp. 3d at 101.

93   Final Report: Select Committee to Investigate the January 6th Attack on the United States Capitol at 84.
94   Hugh Hewitt, "Senator Ben Sasse on Impeachment and Transition, the GOP in Minority," Hugh Hewitt, January 8, 2021, https://hughhewitt.com/senator-ben-sasse-on-impeachment-and-transition-the-gop-in-minority/.
95   Rosalind S. Helderman and Josh Dawsey, "Trump's Lawyers Say He Was Immediately 'Horrified' by the Capitol Attack: Here's What His Allies and Aides Said Really Happened That Day," *Washington Post*, February 9, 2021, https://www.washingtonpost.com/politics/trump-actions-capitol-attacks/2021/02/09/6dada250-6a3b-11eb-9ead-673168d5b874_story.html.
96   Helene Cooper et al., "As the D.C. Police Clear the Capitol Grounds, the Mayor Extends a Public Emergency," *New York Times*, January 6, 2021, https://www.nytimes.com/2021/01/06/us/politics/national-guard-capitol-army.html.
97   Kevin Liptak, "Trump's Presidency Ends with American Carnage," CNN, January 6, 2021, https://www.cnn.com/2021/01/06/politics/donald-trump-capitol-mob/index.html.
98   Domenico Montanaro, "Trump Didn't Act and Didn't Want to, Plus 4 Other Takeaways from the Jan. 6 Hearings," NPR, July 22, 2022, https://www.npr.org/2022/07/22/1112324462/jan-6-hearing-takeaways; Anumita Kaur, "Trump Didn't Stick to Script Asking Supporters to Leave Capitol, Jan. 6 Panel Says," *Los Angeles Times*, July 21, 2022, https://www.latimes.com/politics/story/2022-07-21/jan-6-hearing-trump-rose-garden-video.

Chapter Ten

We Told You So

Why Courts Won't Hold Trump Accountable for Incitement

Daniel J. Canon

At the core of all the confusion resulting from the January 6, 2021 insurrection lies one irrefutable truth: a new era of American election violence has begun. Despite numerous opportunities to slow this moment's arrival, the courts repeatedly declined to do so. Why? In this chapter, I begin to explore possible answers by examining my own attempt to sue Donald Trump and his campaign for election-related violence. I then discuss other failed attempts to use the courts to hold Trump responsible for similar instances of violence, and how those cases served to enable the January 6 attacks. Finally, using prior federal case law and models of judicial decision-making, I argue that the courts' reluctance to restrain Trump's incitement of violence has little to do with First Amendment precedent, but was instead driven by external political factors.

Nwanguma v. Trump

On March 1, 2016, then–candidate Donald Trump held a campaign rally in downtown Louisville, Kentucky. Kashiya Nwanguma, a twenty-one-year-old Black college student, attended that rally. As Trump began speaking, Nwanguma quietly made her way to the front of the crowd and held up a poster depicting Trump's head on a pig's body. When Trump spotted Nwanguma, he ordered the crowd to eject her. That was just one of five times Trump stopped his half-hour speech to point out protesters and to command his crowd of supporters to "get 'em out of here."[1] Upon Trump's orders, the crowd attacked three people who would later become my clients: Nwanguma; Henry Brousseau, a seventeen-year-old white high school student; and Molly Shah, a thirty-six-year-old white mother and special education teacher.

The crowd punched and shoved Brousseau and Shah, but Nwanguma received the worst of the crowd's wrath. Matthew Heimbach, an outspoken white nationalist, repeatedly shoved Nwanguma toward the exit while shouting "leftist scum."[2] Then Nwanguma was passed off to Alvin Bamberger, a seventy-five-year-old white military veteran, who also shoved her as she was exiting.[3] Others groped her and shouted racial epithets. As my clients were being manhandled, Trump stated: "Don't hurt 'em. If I say 'go get 'em,' I get in trouble with the press, the most dishonest human beings in the world." Trump went on to say: "In the old days, which isn't so long ago, when we were less politically correct, that kinda stuff wouldn't have happened. Today we have to be so nice, so nice."[4]

The Trial Court

The 2016 Louisville rally was the sort of howling nightmare commonly seen at subsequent Trump events, but at the time it was novel enough to garner national attention. Although political violence has always existed in one form or another in the United States, there had been no recorded incidents of violence at major party presidential campaign rallies before Trump, and certainly no record of a presidential candidate asking supporters to attack protesters. Legal analysts asked: "Is Donald Trump Inciting Violence?"[5]

My colleagues and I tried to answer that question with a lawsuit against Trump, the Trump Campaign, Heimbach, and Bamberger. In our complaint, we argued that while this type of violence was unprecedented in a general sense, it was the same type of havoc Trump was deliberately trying to wreak in the months before the Louisville rally. On November 21, 2015, a protester was attacked at an Alabama rally. Trump responded that "maybe he should have been roughed up."[6] On February 1, 2016, Trump instructed an Iowa crowd to "knock the crap out of" anyone who was "getting ready to throw a tomato." Trump followed this instruction by saying, "Seriously. Okay? Just knock the hell . . ." Trump assured the crowd, "I will pay for the legal fees. I promise. I promise."[7] Just a week before the Louisville rally, Trump responded to a protester in Las Vegas by alluding to the fact that protesters had it too easy in present times. "I love the old days. You know what they used to do to guys like that when they were in a place like this? They'd be carried out on a stretcher, folks." Trump told his supporters that he would like "to punch [the protester] in the face."[8] All of these prior incidents, which were highly publicized at the time, were collected and described in detail in our complaint.

We also warned the court that the violence in Louisville was indicative of a dangerous trend; one that would get much worse if the courts did not end it. As evidence, we laid out six more incidents of campaign rally violence that happened between the Louisville rally (March 1, 2016) and when we filed our complaint (March 31, 2016). Specifically, on March 4, 2016, at a rally in Michigan, Trump instructed the crowd to remove a protester, promising "If you [hurt him], I'll defend you in court. Don't worry about it."[9] Then on March 8, 2016, a reporter was thrown to the ground at a press conference in Florida by Trump's campaign manager, who was later arrested for assault.[10] The next day at a rally in North Carolina, Trump again spoke of the "good old days" when protesters were treated "very, very rough." Trump asserted that such treatment deterred the protesters from doing it "again so easily."[11] Two days later, at a rally in St. Louis, Trump claimed that "part of the problem and part of the reason it takes so long" to remove protesters was that people are too averse to hurting each other.[12] On March 19, 2016, at a rally in Arizona, a protester was punched and kicked repeatedly after being pointed out and described as "disgusting" by Trump from the stage. Finally, on March 29, 2016, at a rally in Janesville, Wisconsin, a fifteen-year-old protester was pepper sprayed and sexually assaulted by two unidentified Trump supporters. As the protester left the rally, Trump's supporters erupted with name-calling (for example, "goddamn communist, n***** lover"), cries of victory, and an echo of Trump's usual response to protesters: "Get 'em out of here!"[13] Again, these incidents took place in the thirty days it took us to draft and file our complaint.

The Trump defendants immediately filed motions to dismiss the lawsuit, claiming that we had failed to state a claim on which relief could be granted. The centerpiece of their argument was that Trump was merely exercising his right to free speech, and "[p]olitical speech at a political rally lies at the core of the First Amendment."[14] We argued that Trump knew exactly what he was doing. By barking commands at a crowd that was already primed for violence, Trump knew by March 1, 2016, that the crowd would treat protesters, in his words, "very, very rough." Not only did Trump know what he meant by "get 'em out of here," but his intended audience knew it too and acted accordingly. In fact, Heimbach and Bamberger explicitly said so. In cross-claims against Trump and the Trump campaign, both assaulters claimed they were acting on Trump's orders.[15] Surely, we said, the First Amendment cannot shield someone who is deliberately stirring up violence at rallies all over the country, especially when the violence-doers themselves say they were following instructions.

For a while, it seemed we were right. A year to the day after we filed our complaint, US District Judge David Hale issued an opinion allowing most of the suit to go forward, including an incitement claim against Trump.[16] According to Judge Hale, "Plaintiffs allege throughout the complaint that Trump knew or should have known that his statements would result in violence, and they describe a prior Trump rally at which a protestor was attacked. The Court finds these allegations to be sufficient [to overcome a First Amendment defense]."[17]

But the case did not proceed to discovery. Four months and two rounds of briefing later, Judge Hale reversed himself and dismissed our negligence claim against the Trump defendants as "incompatible with the First Amendment."[18] Still, Hale permitted the incitement claim to survive. He rejected the argument that "that Trump's statement [should] be considered in a vacuum," and held that "the cases cited by the Trump Defendants demonstrate that whether speech constitutes incitement is a fact-specific inquiry."[19] Under Hale's analysis of a long line of cases including *Hess v. Indiana*,[20] *Cohen v. California*,[21] *NAACP v. Claiborne Hardware*,[22] and *Connick v. Myers*,[23] the court concluded that "context matters; 'the character of every act depends upon the circumstances in which it is done.'" Hale underscored the issue of discovery, explaining that nearly all of the aforementioned speech cases "were fully litigated prior to appeal, and the Supreme Court's decisions in those cases were based on the evidence of record."[24] "For example, the exclamation "Shoot!" might constitute incitement if directed to a crowd of angry armed individuals, but shouted by a basketball fan or muttered in disappointment, it has no violent connotations. . . . [T]he mere absence of overtly violent language in Trump's statement does not appear fatal to Plaintiffs' incitement claim."[25] Indeed, the dismissal of the negligence claim was partially premised on the survival of the incitement claim. Hale wrote, "The purported negligence was ordering audience members to remove protestors — an intentional act, and one subsumed by Plaintiffs' incitement claim, the appropriate vehicle for challenging Trump's statement."[26] Thus, the entirety of Nwanguma's case hung on whether Trump could be held liable for incitement.

At Trump's urging, Hale certified for immediate appeal whether the First Amendment protected him from the incitement claim. And so, before any documents could be exchanged or testimony taken, Judge Hale's ruling was heard by the Sixth Circuit Court of Appeals.

The Sixth Circuit

The appellate court issued its ruling on September 11, 2018. By then, it had been more than two years since the Louisville rally. There had been many incidences of violence at Trump events, and anyone who was paying attention knew that Trump had become the first major party candidate — and the first president — in American history to openly encourage election-related violence. We were hopeful that the Sixth Circuit would act to stop it. They did not.

In a published opinion styled *Nwanguma v. Trump*, authored by Judge David McKeague, the Court of Appeals sharply diverged from Hale's opinion by focusing exclusively on the literal content of Trump's words: "In the ears of some supporters, Trump's words may have had a tendency to elicit a physical response, in the event a disruptive protester refused to leave, but they did not specifically advocate such a response."[27] McKeague explained as folllows:

> It is the words used by the speaker that must be at the focus of the incitement inquiry, not how they may be heard by a listener. This, of course, is sensible and plaintiffs have not rebutted this

understanding by reference to any contrary authority. The bottom line is that the analysis employed in [prior cases] evidences an unmistakable and consistent focus on the actual words used by the speaker in determining whether speech was protected. Following these authorities, we hold that Trump's speech, too, is protected and therefore not actionable as an incitement to riot.[28]

Additionally, the court seemed to treat Trump saying "don't hurt 'em" as something to be taken seriously enough to be legally significant, even after months of Trump saying, in essence, "hurt 'em." McKeague wrote: "That this undercuts the alleged violence-inciting sense of Trump's words can hardly be denied."

McKeague's opinion acknowledged the need to evaluate the context of a statement, and even quoted *Snyder v. Phelps* for the proposition that "it is necessary to evaluate all the circumstances of the speech, including what was said, where it was said, and how it was said."[29] But these "circumstances" were ultimately unimportant to the Sixth Circuit, which held: "So, yes, in addition to the content and form of the words, we are obliged to consider the context, based on the whole record. Here, of course, the '"whole record' consists of the complaint."[30] In its reliance on *Snyder*, *Hess*, and its own *en banc* opinion in the case of *Bible Believers v. Wayne County*,[31] the appellate court disregarded Hale's emphasis on record development, collapsing the case into a facile analysis of the literal meaning of a speaker's words and reframing the high court's emphasis in *Snyder* to be primarily about "what was *said*, where it was *said*, and how it was *said*."[32]

Our request for *en banc* review to the full Sixth Circuit Court of Appeals was denied in November of 2018. By that time, two Trump-appointed justices were on the Supreme Court. We decided a petition for certiorari would likely do more harm than good, and so the case of *Nwanguma v. Trump* came to an end.

Aftermath

What has happened in the years since the Sixth Circuit's opinion? Violence at Trump rallies did not abate, and Trump himself has become more brazen about encouraging it every chance he gets. Worse, his embrace of brutality-*cum*-politics has demonstrably spread. One source notes that episodes of political violence "skyrocketed" from 2016 to 2021, and identifies political speech as a factor driving the increase in such violence.[33] As a society, it seems the very idea no longer bothers us quite so much; according to a 2021 *Washington Post/University of Maryland* poll, only 62 percent of Americans now believe violence is never justified, down from 90 percent in the 1990s,[34] and another poll shows that a majority of Republicans agree that they "may have to use force to save" the "traditional American way of life."[35] Seven years after the Louisville rally, the Select Committee to Investigate the January 6th Attack on the United States Capitol issued a voluminous report aimed at establishing the same basic issue we posited in *Nwanguma*, that is, that Trump was not-so-slyly asking his supporters to engage in violence, and that some of those supporters complied.[36]

The Courts' Repeated Failures to Act

Long before attending law school, I understood that courts are supposed to stop bad things from happening. This idea reverberates throughout any theoretical framework we apply. Classical deterrence theory "posits that if the probability of being caught and suffering negative consequences is high enough, people will choose not to engage in conduct that results in sanctions."[37] Theoretical models focused on individual recompense rather than general welfare still take basic social cohesion into account: if the state will not allow aggrieved parties to take the law into their own hands, the courts must therefore offer meaningful relief or the stability of society is at risk.[38] Even under cold, calculating economic theories of justice, the courts are charged with ensuring the safety of the public (so long as it does not cost too much).[39] Most of us believe in one or more of these models for understanding the role of the courts, or at least the ideals they are supposedly based on. Under any of these theories, the Sixth Circuit should have taken decisive action to protect American democracy from those who have shown themselves to be its chief assailants, but it did not.

Similarly, one might reasonably expect that courts might use the First Amendment as a tool for stopping, rather than allowing, political violence at presidential campaign rallies. One can find a lot of waxing patriotic about free speech used to further the best interests of democracy,[40] but few commentators would likely argue that an imperative given to a seething mob of white supremacists after months of explicit calls for violence should be entitled to sacrosanct-speech status (especially when violence actually results). And yet that is apparently what the Sixth Circuit did in the *Nwanguma* opinion.

The tendency to absolve Trump for deeply troubling conduct is not confined to one conservative circuit court. Nearly every other court to weigh in on Trump's brand of political violence has ended up advancing a similar interpretation of the law. In another suit brought by victims of rally violence, the trial court held that despite Trump's calls for violence and a prior incidence of rally violence, Trump could not have foreseen "violence against *these particular* plaintiffs."[41] That case, like *Nwanguma*, was dismissed and no discovery was ever conducted. Another protester claimed he was roughed up by police at the behest of the Trump campaign at an event one month after the Louisville rally, but that was not enough to survive a motion to dismiss in the trial court.[42] The appellate court did not want to hear oral argument on appeal, and its unpublished opinion was only a paragraph long.[43]

There are only a few cases regarding Trump's involvement in election-related violence in which plaintiffs have been able to get past the motion to dismiss stage. The earliest of these cases involved an assault by hired security against protesters outside of Trump Tower in September 2015, but did not apparently involve contemporaneous orders given by Trump himself.[44] After six years of litigation in New York, Trump finally gave his first and only deposition in any protester-violence case in October of 2021.[45] The case quietly settled on the eve of trial, more than seven years after the rally in question, and nearly two years after the events of January 6th.[46] Only one other campaign-violence case has produced any tangible consequences to Trump. In that case, the district court stripped out all the claims against Trump himself, leaving only claims against individual police officers and a campaign official who tossed pro se plaintiff Roderick Webber into a table in October 2015.[47] This case also did not involve any contemporaneous commands by Trump. The Trump campaign finally settled the case for $20,000 on December 23, 2020 — a little more than one month after Trump lost the 2020 election.[48]

Despite years of plaintiffs and their attorneys sounding the alarm, the courts took no real action to stop Trump's increasingly bold calls for campaign violence before the events of January 6, 2021. And even *after* the fact, the federal judiciary has been unwilling to impose consequences one might expect following a failed coup d'état. High-profile members of Congress filed suit against Trump and other high-level insurrectionists in a case called *Thompson v. Trump*.[49] US District Court Judge Amit P. Mehta allowed most of the claims against Trump to proceed past the motion to dismiss stage, but not without some hand-wringing. Judge Mehta went further than many district courts by looking at the broader context of Trump's January 6 rally to hold that his speech "plausibly" constituted "words of incitement."[50] But Mehta, like McKeague, reasoned that Trump's winks and nods to heavily armed protesters tended to absolve him. Taking Trump's exhortation to march "peacefully and patriotically" at face value, Judge Mehta cited the Sixth Circuit's opinion in *Nwanguma* to conclude: "Those words are a factor favoring the President."[51] This, in a context in which the president had been actively fomenting inauguration-related violence for days and violence in general for years.

To Mehta's credit, he does not apply the First Amendment quite as pedantically as McKeague. Had *Thompson* followed the Sixth Circuit's ruling in *Nwanguma*, Trump would almost certainly bear no liability for January 6th. Sure, he said "fight like hell," but the word "fight" can mean many things. One can "fight" over children in a custody battle, and no physical violence need occur. The "Fight for 15" campaign presumably does not mean you get into fisticuffs with your boss to raise your wage. Trump did not specifically say "march down to the Capitol building, break the doors down, beat a police officer to death, and ransack congressional offices," so he could not have incited violence under the Sixth Circuit's expansive view. And what does "like hell" mean? According to the *Cambridge English Dictionary*, it could be used to mean "certainly not," in which case he was telling people not to fight at all.[52] Besides, after all the violence at the Capitol, Trump said "We don't want anybody hurt," which is a lot like saying "don't hurt 'em," and therefore immunizing. So perhaps *Thompson* is a signal that the judiciary is finally moving in the right direction.

However, given the overall context (that is, "[t]he first ever presidential transfer of power marred by violence"),[53] Judge Mehta extends Trump the benefit of the doubt to an unsettling degree at the pleading stage. The *Thompson* opinion cannot be read as a full-throated denunciation of an attempt to provoke a violent overthrow of an election. It is essentially fifty pages of analyzing Trump's insincere arguments to determine that only a few claims may proceed past the initial filing stage. Critically, the court summarily denied the plaintiffs' request that the judge order Trump not to engage in similar misconduct pending the outcome of the litigation, holding that the plaintiffs "have not plausibly pleaded at this stage any likelihood of future injury."[54] As of this writing, almost three years after the January 6th insurrection, discovery in *Thompson* is just beginning, and Trump is back on the campaign trail.

Pretending for a moment that the courts are a monolith, what can be said about their treatment of Trump's incitement of election violence? No court in any jurisdiction has been willing to impose meaningful civil consequences on Trump for what amounts to an unprecedented, brutal subversion of American democracy. Most will not even allow incitement-type claims to proceed beyond a motion to dismiss. Of the courts that have allowed claims to proceed, none have acted with urgency; no injunctions or meaningful sanctions have been issued, and Trump has been ordered to give only a single deposition in nearly a decade of incitement litigation that spans the entire country. Stacked up against other courts, the opinion of the DC district court looks positively brave. In the aggregate, it seems the only way the courts can assign liability to someone trying to foment election-related violence is if they come very close to actually overthrowing the government — and this extreme scenario might only get a plaintiff to the discovery phase. When the courts fail to prevent, or even hinder, obviously bad actors from their attempts to openly and violently disrupt democratic processes, we should ask why.

Why Do Courts Do What They Do?

First Amendment Jurisprudence and the Legal Decision-Making Model

At the outset, I should acknowledge that readers have likely been *Brandenburg*'d nearly to death by this point in the volume, and I have no intention of hastening their demise. There is nothing I can add to the analysis of incitement jurisprudence that has not been said (and said better) by my colleagues in the preceding chapters. What I propose here is that the courts' recent incitement decisions may have little to do with *Brandenburg*, the First Amendment, or anything we would call "law" at all.

First, free speech jurisprudence does not demand the degree of absolutism given to Trump in *Nwanguma* or the other incitement cases discussed above. Professor James Weinstein has described a "large range of speech regulated on account of its content, all without a hint of interference from the First Amendment," concluding that "a more accurate snapshot of First Amendment protection is almost the photonegative of the all-inclusive approach: highly protected speech is the exception, with most other speech being regulable... with no discernible First Amendment constraint."[55] This assertion is true for incitement-type cases specifically.[56]

Take the courts' near-universal approach to solicitation crimes. Courts have not been shy about prosecuting those who suggest that other people engage in bad actions, even when the suggestion is vague. The US Court of Appeals for the Seventh Circuit in *United States v. White* (2010) found that a member of the "American National Socialist Workers Party," could be tried for posting on a website that unnamed individuals "deserved assassination for a long time," and then subsequently posting the personal information of a juror in a different case.[57] Judge Richard Posner et al., in a *per curiam* opinion, held "that a request for criminal action is coded or implicit" does not entitle it to First Amendment protection. Indeed, the defendant did not give any command to anyone — he simply posted some cryptic language, followed by a posting of jurors' personal information three years later. In *United States v. Hale* (2006), an appellate court held there was sufficient evidence to uphold a solicitation conviction where the defendant never explicitly asked his chief enforcer to do anything but locate a judge's home address, and made statements such as, "that information's been pro, provided. If you wish to, ah, do anything yourself, you can, you know?" The defendant went so far as to say, "I can't take any steps to further anything illegal," but this was not enough to overturn his solicitation conviction.[58]

The willingness to overlook the supposed requirement that speech explicitly advocate violence extends to civil cases. In *Doe v. Mckesson* (2019), an unidentified police officer-plaintiff sued for injuries he sustained at a Black Lives Matter rally in 2016. According to the complaint, demonstrators stole water bottles from a convenience store and threw them at police. When those "ran out" an unidentified person threw a "rock-like" object that hit the plaintiff. The complaint alleged that "activist[s] began pumping up the crowd." DeRay Mckesson, an organizer and media personality, was one of those activists. The plaintiff did not allege that Mckesson himself threw anything, nor that he told anyone to throw anything, nor even that he suggested any violent action. Yet the US Court of Appeals for the Fifth Circuit saw the First Amendment as "no bar" to foreseeability-based liability for the unlawful acts of others, a ruling contrary to the district court's relatively lenient holding in *Nwanguma*. The US Supreme Court vacated the ruling due to a provision of state law but declined to hear the First Amendment issue.[59]

None of these courts — indeed, few judges in US history — would say that speech could only be actionable in the unlikely event that a speaker explicitly said, "do a violent thing right this very second." To do so would subvert the entire idea that words may *implicitly* encourage violence, which has long been the accepted standard.[60] In fact, neither the Sixth Circuit nor Judge McKeague himself has ever been so hawkish on the First Amendment before Trump's campaign shenanigans. Judge McKeague has joined opinions holding, for example, that the Free Speech Clause does not keep a court from telling a third party nonlitigant that it cannot contact class members if it thinks those communications were "misleading,"[61] and that it is constitutionally permissible to order an incarcerated person be subject to a permanent visitation restriction in retaliation for complaints of abuse by guards.[62] Even judges thought of as "liberals" do not seem fazed by, say, an eight-level sentence enhancement for making suggestive Facebook comments.[63] Such issues are decided under different legal standards, to be sure, but tend to controvert any notion of free-speech absolutism as a guiding judicial philosophy.

Furthermore, it is apparent that courts nearly always delve into an extensive set of circumstances beyond the face of a complaint or indictment to determine the context in which certain comments were made. This is true of the Supreme Court's most famous speech cases, including *Brandenburg*, *Hess*, and *Snyder*, all of which were decided on appeals from trials, and in the high court's most recent speech cases, too.[64] Even the Sixth Circuit's *en banc* opinion in *Bible Believers*, relied heavily on by McKeague in the *Nwanguma* opinion, was issued on appeal from a ruling on cross motions for summary judgment (in which both parties asserted that no material facts were in dispute). The *Nwanguma* court's out-of-hand dismissal of the need for any discovery at all must therefore be seen as an outlier, or at the very least as a deliberate decision to buck ordinary procedural conventions by the Sixth Circuit. *Nwanguma*'s myopic focus on the specific words of a speaker, to the point that the opportunity to determine the context in which those words were used is precluded, is not consistent with Supreme Court precedent or the Sixth Circuit's prior rulings.

The bottom line is to analyze Trump-era incitement cases as "normal" First Amendment cases, or as jurisprudentially informed at all, is to invite madness. It is natural for litigators to want to make sense of the inconsistencies and absurdities resulting from these decisions under a standard legal decision-making model,[65] in which rules from one opinion are followed or distinguished in the next, but to do so bends the imagination to the point of breaking. How, then, are we to understand the courts' laissez-faire response to election violence?

The Attitudinal Model

One way is to assume the courts are fundamentally antidemocratic and agree with Trump's agenda, and/or that they generally believe right-wing politicians should be able to use violence to influence elections. Scholars might call this the "attitudinal model" of decision-making. Under that theory, judges "decide cases based on their individual political preferences and are not constrained in that ideological pursuit by congressional or presidential intent, nor even by the dictates of the law."[66] In other words, judges do whatever they want and dress up their personal biases in fancy constitutional clothes.

If the legal decision-making model is too naive, perhaps the attitudinal model is too cynical. Thus far, neither the First Amendment nor any other doctrine has presented a barrier to prosecuting the hundreds of Trump acolytes who stormed the Capitol on January 6th.[67] In the civil realm, the courts have allowed suits to go forward against other officials — even police officers[68] — who contributed in various ways to campaign rally acts of violence, and in 2021 a federal court in Virginia issued the biggest judgment against right-wing provocateurs in the history of the country.[69] It is true that the judges who issued the decisions that were most deferential to Trump were white, male, and appointed by Republican presidents. But the judges who did not fall into that demographic gave him a pass, too, and even when they did not, their responses were hardly resolute.[70]

The Strategic Decision-Making Model

Perhaps the best way to analyze the behavior of the courts vis-á-vis Trump's incitement is by reference to the strategic decision-making model sometimes referred to as "rational choice" or "positive political" theory. Professors Daniel Rodriguez and Matthew McCubbins explain: "Because judges act in the middle of a political process and are *not* the end point, they must act strategically to get what they want. That is, judges must anticipate how other political actors will react and must take these reactions into account."[71] Under some interpretations of this model, commentators suggest that judges trick themselves into believing their own hackneyed rationales. Judge Richard Posner once asserted that "[j]udges have a terrible anxiety about being thought to base their opinions on guesses or their personal views. To allay that anxiety, they rely on the apparatus of precedent and history, much of it extremely phony."[72]

Under this theory, the First Amendment becomes a tool that can be used to handily dispose of difficult cases. A court faced with the uncomfortable task of involving itself in a heated political battle where the stakes are high may instead hide behind the illusion of unrestrained "free speech." Taking down bad actors is one thing, but if that bad actor happens to be the president of the United States, the power dynamics change — especially where the president has a social media pulpit that is often used to call out judges by name. Courts make "strategic" choices to account for that change, based on "constraining and incentivizing factors."[73] In a separate article, I discuss why this theoretical framework best explains why jurists might cautiously microparse Trump's language and conduct, even when it is clearly designed to result in violence.[74] But the evidence suggests that First Amendment jurisprudence had less bearing on the outcome of Trump's incitement cases than we might like to think.[75]

Conclusion

This chapter is meant to introduce the idea that we must look beyond the First Amendment to explain the courts' failure to stop Trump's incitement. But this modest conclusion raises a slew of follow-up questions: Could the courts really have stopped January 6th or any other incidence of election-related violence? What factors led to the judiciary's "strategic decision" not to act? Why do courts apparently possess the political will to allow Trump's criminal prosecutions now, when they were unwilling to impose civil liability before? Can the courts be useful in preventing more political violence from occurring in the future? If so, how? I have explored these questions at length elsewhere, but they are by no means resolved.[76] For now, though we know little about the extent of the judiciary's effectiveness in this new era of election violence, we know that independent, courageous courts are critical to the success of any democracy.[77] If we want to keep ours, we need courts that will act to preserve it. But if they won't, then at least I can say *we told them so*.

Notes

Assistant professor and director of externships, University of Louisville, Louis D. Brandeis School of Law. The author is deeply indebted to Farrah Alexander, Courtney Arthur, Brian Fields, Krista Sutherland, and Frank Bencomo-Suarez for their time and energy on this project, as well as to colleagues Sarah Ochs, Shavonnie Carthens, Ariana Levinson, C. J. Ryan, Marcia Ziegler, and Kelly Meurer for suggestions. This chapter is dedicated to the memory of Henry Brousseau.

1. "Complete Speech: Donald Trump in Louisville." WLKY News Louisville, YouTube, March 1, 2016, https://www.youtube.com/watch?v=dp-M9siqfvY.
2. Joe Heim, "This White Nationalist Who Shoved a Trump Protester May Be the Next David Duke," *Washington Post*, April 12, 2016, https://www.washingtonpost.com/local/this-white-nationalist-who-shoved-a-trump-protester-may-be-the-next-david-duke/2016/04/12/7e71f750-f2cf-11e5-89c3-a647fcce95e0_story.html.
3. "Video Goes Viral of Trump Supporters Pushing Woman out of Rally," WLKY News Louisville, YouTube, March 2, 2016, https://www.youtube.com/watch?v=lb-KFVv4XEs.
4. "Complete Speech: Donald Trump in Louisville," WLKY News Louisville, YouTube, March 1, 2016, https://www.youtube.com/watch?v=dp-M9siqfvY, 27:00.
5. Dahlia Lithwick, "Is Donald Trump Inciting Violence?," *Slate*, March 15, 2016. https://slate.com/news-and-politics/2016/03/is-donald-trump-inciting-violence-he-might-be.html.
6. Jenna Johnson and Mary Jordan, "Trump on Rally Protestor: 'Maybe He Should Have Been Roughed Up,'" *Washington Post*, November 22, 2015, https://www.washingtonpost.com/news/post-politics/wp/2015/11/22/black-activist-punched-at-donald-trump-rally-in-birmingham.
7. Nolan D. McCaskill, "Trump Urges Crowd to 'Knock the Crap out of' Anyone with Tomatoes," *Politico*, February 1, 2016, https://www.politico.com/blogs/iowa-caucus-2016-live-updates/2016/02/donald-trump-iowa-rally-tomatoes-218546.
8. Michael E. Miller, "Donald Trump on a Protester: 'I'd Like to Punch Him in the Face,'" *Washington Post*, February 23, 2016, https://www.washingtonpost.com/news/morning-mix/wp/2016/02/23/donald-trump-on-protester-id-like-to-punch-him-in-the-face/.
9. Libby Cathey and Meghan Keneally, "A Look Back at Trump Comments Perceived by Some as Inciting Violence," ABC News, May 30, 2020, https://abcnews.go.com/Politics/back-trump-comments-perceived-encouraging-violence/story?id=48415766.

10 Hadas Gold, "Trump Campaign Manager Gets Rough with Breitbart Reporter," *Politico*, May 9, 2016, https://www.politico.com/blogs/on-media/2016/03/trump-campaign-manager-breitbart-reporter-220472?lo=ap_c3.

11 Robert Mackey, "Trump Concerned His Rallies Are Not Violent Enough" *Intercept*, March 11, 2016, https://theintercept.com/2016/03/11/trumps-good-old-days-when-battering-protesters-was-celebrated-in-the-white-house.

12 Nick Gass, "Trump: 'There Used to Be Consequences' for Protesting," *Politico*, May 3, 2016, https://www.politico.com/blogs/2016-gop-primary-live-updates-and-results/2016/03/trump-defends-protest-violence-220638.

13 "Wisconsin Police: Teen Girl Sexually Assaulted, Pepper-Sprayed Outside Trump Rally," CBS New York, March 29, 2016, https://www.cbsnews.com/newyork/news/donald-trump-wisconsin-rally/.

14 Nwanguma v. Trump, Defendants' Motion to Dismiss, Case 3:16-cv-00247-DJH (W.D. Ky., filed May 20, 2016), https://www.politico.com/f/?id=00000159-ddf2-d10a-abf9-ddf79e210002.

15 Kenneth P. Vogel, "White Nationalist Claims Trump Directed Rally Violence," Politico, April 17, 2017, https://www.politico.com/story/2017/04/donald-trump-rally-violence-237302.

16 Nwanguma v. Trump, 273 F. Supp. 3d 719 (W.D. Ky. 2017).

17 Nwanguma v. Trump, 727.

18 Nwanguma v. Trump, 3:16-CV-247-DJH-HBB, 2017 WL 3430514, at *4 (W.D. Ky. Aug. 9, 2017).

19 Nwanguma v. Trump, *2.

20 414 U.S. 105 (1973).

21 403 U.S. 15 (1971).

22 458 U.S. 886 (1982).

23 461 U.S. 138 (1983).

24 Nwanguma v. Trump, 3:16-CV-247-DJH-HBB, 2017 WL 3430514, at *2 (W.D. Ky. Aug. 9, 2017).

25 Nwanguma v. Trump, *3.

26 Nwanguma v. Trump, *4.

27 Nwanguma v. Trump, 903 F.3d 604, 612 (6th Cir. 2018).

28 Nwanguma v. Trump, 613.

29 Snyder v. Phelps, 562 U.S. 443 (2011).

30 Nwanguma v. Trump, 903 F.3d 604, 611 (6th Cir. 2018).

31 Bible Believers v. Wayne Cnty., 805 F.3d 228, 246 (6th Cir. 2015) (en banc).

32 Nwanguma v. Trump, 903 F.3d 604, 611 (6th Cir. 2018) (quoting Snyder v. Phelps, emphasis added by Nwanguma court).

33 Rachel Kleinfeld, "The Rise of Political Violence in the United States," *Journal of Democracy* 32, no. 4 (October 2021): 160–76.

34 Ivana Saric, "Poll: Americans Increasingly Justifying Political Violence," Axios, January 2, 2022, https://www.axios.com/2022/01/02/poll-america-violence-against-government.
35 Rachel Kleinfeld, "The Rise of Political Violence in the United States," *Journal of Democracy* 32, no. 4 (2021): 162. https://www.journalofdemocracy.org/articles/the-rise-of-political-violence-in-the-united-states.
36 U.S. Congress, Select Committee to Investigate the January 6th Attack on the United States Capitol, Final Report, 117th Cong., 2d sess., 2022, H. Rep. 117-663, https://www.govinfo.gov/content/pkg/GPO-J6-REPORT/pdf/GPO-J6-REPORT.pdf.
37 Deana A. Pollard, "Sex Torts," *Minnesota Law Review* 91, (2007): 769–824.
38 Benjamin C. Zipursky and John C. P. Goldberg, *Recognizing Wrongs* (Harvard University Press, 2020).
39 Richard A. Posner, *Economic Analysis of Law* (Little, Brown, 1972).
40 See, for example, Ashutosh Bhagwat, "The Democratic First Amendment, *Northwestern University Law Review* 110 (2016): 1097, 1102; James Weinstein, "Participatory Democracy as the Central Value of American Free Speech Doctrine," *Virginia Law Review* 97, no. 491 (2011).
41 Southall v. Birmingham Jefferson Conv. Ctr. Auth., 2:16-CV-01687-LSC, 2017 WL 4155100, at *4 (N.D. Ala. Sept. 19, 2017).
42 Thaler v. Donald J. Trump for President, Inc., 304 F. Supp. 3d 473, 480 (D. Md. 2018), aff'd, 730 Fed. Appx. 177 (4th Cir. 2018) (unpublished).
43 Thaler v. Donald J. Trump for President, Inc., No. 18-1194 (4th Cir. Jul. 13, 2018) (unpublished).
44 Galicia v. Trump, First Amended Complaint, Supreme Court of the State of NY, Bronx Co. No. 24973/2015E, filed November 11, 2015, https://www.politico.com/f/?id=00000159-05ef-d6f8-af7f-1fffc8750000.
45 Laura Italiano, "Meet the Only Lawyer Who's Managed to Sit Donald Trump down for a Deposition since the 2016 Election," *Insider*, March 4, 2022. https://www.businessinsider.com/deposing-trump-persistence-works-says-only-lawyer-to-win-2022-3.
46 Chloe Atkins and Tom Winter. "Protestors' NYC Civil Assault Suit Against Trump Reaches Settlement," NBC 4, New York, November 2, 2022, https://www.nbcnewyork.com/news/local/crime-and-courts/protestors-nyc-civil-assault-suit-against-trump-reaches-settlement/3935285/.
47 Webber v. Deck, 433 F. Supp. 3d 237 (D.N.H. 2020).
48 "The Trump Campaign Agrees to Pay $20,000 to Settle 2015 Assault Claim," *Document Cloud*, December 28, 2020, https://www.documentcloud.org/documents/20437951-the-trump-campaign-agrees-to-pay-20000-to-settle-2015-assault-claim.
49 Thompson v. Trump, 590 F. Supp. 3d 46 (D.D.C. Feb. 18, 2022).
50 Thompson v. Trump, 115.
51 Thompson v. Trump, 117.

52   "Definition of 'Like Hell,'" *Cambridge Dictionary*, September 22, 2022, https://dictionary.cambridge.org/us/dictionary/english/like-hell).
53   Thompson v. Trump, 46.
54   Hadas Gold, "Trump Campaign Manager Gets Rough with Breitbart Reporter," Politico, March 9, 2016, https://www.politico.com/blogs/on-media/2016/03/trump-campaign-manager-breitbart-reporter-220472.
55   James Weinstein, "Participatory Democracy as the Basis of American Free Speech Doctrine: A Reply," *Virginia Law Review* 97, no. 3 (2011): 633–79, http://www.jstor.org/stable/41261527.
56   JoAnne Sweeny, "Incitement in the Era of Trump and Charlottesville," *Capital University Law Review* 47 (2019): 594.
57   U.S. v. White, 610 F.3d 956, 960 (7th Cir. 2010).
58   United States v. Hale, 448 F.3d 971, 979 (7th Cir. 2006).
59   Doe v. Mckesson, 945 F.3d 818 (5th Cir. 2019), cert. granted, judgment vacated, 592 U.S., 1, 141 S.Ct. 48, 208 L.Ed.2d 158 (2020). On remand, the Fifth Circuit again rejected the argument that the First Amendment prevented Doe's claims. 71 F.4th 278 (5th Cir. 2023).
60   Hess v. Indiana, 414 U.S. 105 (1973).
61   Fox v. Saginaw County, Michigan, 35 F.4th 1042, 1048 (6th Cir. 2022).
62   Haertel v. Mich. Dep't of Corr., No. 20-1904, 2021 U.S. App. LEXIS 14047, at *9 (6th Cir. May 11, 2021).
63   U.S. v. Adams, 598 Fed. Appx. 425, 427 (6th Cir. 2015) (Opinion of Martha Craig Daughtrey, a Clinton appointee and former Vanderbilt professor noted for being the first woman to serve on the Tennessee Supreme Court, among other accomplishments).
64   (See, for example, Counterman v. Colorado, 143 S. Ct. 2106, 2111 [2023], "True threat" analysis requires proof of the "subjective understanding of the threatening nature of his statements," and if that proof is lacking, even the plain meaning of the speech may be negated); United States v. Hansen, 143 S. Ct. 1932, 1942 (2023) ("When words have several plausible definitions, context differentiates among them").
65   Kate Webber, "It Is Political: Using the Models of Judicial Decision Making to Explain the Ideological History of Title VII," *St. John's Law Review* 89 (2015): 841.
66   Kate Webber, "It Is Political," 841.
67   Martin Pengelly, "Republican Party Calls January 6 Attack 'Legitimate Political Discourse,'" *Guardia*n, February 4, 2022, https://www.theguardian.com/us-news/2022/feb/04/republicans-capitol-attack-legitimate-political-discourse-cheney-kinzinger-pence.
68   See Puente v. City of Phoenix, CV-18-02778-PHX-JJT, 2022 WL 357351 (D. Ariz. Feb. 7, 2022).
69   See also Sines v. Kessler, 324 F. Supp. 3d 765, 803 (W.D. Va. 2018) (referenced in chapter 9), where nearly all claims were allowed to proceed against all defendants based on the pleadings, save for a few that were

dismissed not on First Amendment principles but on Iqbal plausibility grounds.
70 Nwanguma v. Trump, 903 F.3d 604, 614 (6th Cir. 2018) (concurrence of Helene N. White).
71 Daniel B. Rodriguez and Mathew D. McCubbins, "The Judiciary and the Role of Law," in *The Oxford Handbook of Political Economy*, ed. Barry R. Weingast and Donald A. Wittman (2006), 274 (emphasis in original).
72 Nancy Scherer, "Viewing the Supreme Court's Marriage Cases Through the Lens of Political Science," *Case Western Reserve Law Review* 64 (2014): 1131.
73 Interview with Dr. Meshack Simati (on file with author).
74 Daniel J. Canon, "The Trump Exception to the Constitution: Assessing the Role of Judicial Attitudes in a New Era of American Election Violence," *Rutgers University Law Review* (forthcoming).
75 I say "had" here because cases like Nwanguma have created a sort of self-fulfilling prophecy. Courts treat the First Amendment as Trump's impenetrable armor, and it has become so. The civil opinions discussed in this chapter undoubtedly factored into Special Counsel Jack Smith's decision not to include incitement crimes in his indictment of Trump. (See J. D. Capelouto, "Why Jack Smith Didn't Charge Trump with Inciting an Insurrection," Semafor, August 2, 2023, https://www.semafor.com/article/08/02/2023/donald-trump-indictment-jack-smith-insurrection-charge.) If Smith thinks it too risky to charge him for January 6th, it is unlikely that any other prosecutor will charge him for lesser incitements in the future, and few plaintiff's lawyers will seek redress on behalf of protesters injured at future rallies. The First Amendment, as applied to Trump, has become too robust a defense.
76 Canon, "The Trump Exception to the Constitution," 101.
77 See, for example, Stephanie M. Burchard and Meshack Simati, "The Role of the Courts in Mitigating Election Violence in Nigeria," *Cadernos de Estudos Africanos* 38 (2019): 123–44.

Conclusion

The Future of *Brandenburg*, Incitement, and the First Amendment

Eric T. Kasper and JoAnne Sweeny

Now that you more fully understand the US Supreme Court's progression of cases on advocacy and incitement, and now that you have seen various defenses of, objections to, and proposed modifications to the *Brandenburg* test, we return to *Brandenburg* itself and ask about its future. Hopefully, after reading the preceding chapters, you understand that under the current test for incitement, context matters. Recall the Supreme Court's test under *Brandenburg*: "The constitutional guarantees of free speech and free press do not permit a State to forbid or proscribe advocacy of the use of force or of law violation except where such advocacy is directed to inciting or producing imminent lawless action and is likely to incite or produce such action."[1] This requires consideration of three elements, compelling courts to determine if (1) the speaker intended to, and (2) the speech is likely to, (3) incite imminent lawless action.

These elements help explain what was constitutionally protected, or proscribable, in expression cited in the introduction, including that by President Trump, President Biden, Senator Josh Hawley, Senator Chuck Schumer, Representative Louie Gohmert, Representative Maxine Waters, and Ben Ehrenreich. *Claiborne Hardware*, emphasizing the protection of "emotionally charged rhetoric,"[2] demonstrates that the speech by Waters, Schumer, and Ehrenreich was protected, as it did not result in any violence, and it was unlikely to do so; even if some of those statements were unadvisable, they were shielded by the First Amendment. The same is true for Hawley's gesture and Gohmert's comments, which lacked evidence of intent and likelihood of lawlessness, with Gohmert's statements also lacking imminence; again, these communications may have been imprudent, but they were protected. Similarly, President Biden's "bull's-eye" comment, while using a poor analogy, was not incitement, as it was apparently intended to focus attention away from concerns about his age, and said to donors several days before the attempted assassination of Donald Trump, with no evidence that the shooter ever even heard the language.

Regarding the speech from January 6, 2021, reasonable people can disagree over whether *Brandenburg* was met. We present possible arguments for both a theoretical prosecution and defense if a case were to go to trial.[3]

On the one hand, a prosecutor could argue that the First Amendment does not protect President Trump's speech because there was evidence of intent, likelihood, and imminent lawlessness (as multiple courts have found).[4] President Trump tweeted to his followers in the days leading up to the speech that they should "be there" in Washington, DC, because it "will be wild!" During his January 6 speech at times President Trump used violent imagery, warning listeners, "If you don't fight like hell, you're not going to have a country anymore." He excited his supporters by exclaiming that the election was rigged: "We won in a landslide. . . . This [is] the most corrupt election in the history, maybe of the world." He told listeners to blame the vice president and members of Congress for inaction at the Capitol, thus intentionally specifying targets to the crowd: "If Mike Pence does the right thing, we win the election. . . . We have come to demand that Congress do the right thing." Some of the rioters later chanted "Hang Mike Pence" and yelled, "Where's Nancy [Pelosi]?" at the Capitol. Evidence of intent can also be argued based on President Trump's actions after the speech, when he declined to take any action to stop the Capitol riot for hours after he was informed about it.

Regarding the likelihood of violence, it was a large crowd of strong Trump supporters (some of whom were known to possess weapons), whom he had encouraged to gather there. Lawyers for some rioters facing criminal charges have argued that their clients thought the commander-in-chief was directing them to act at the Capitol, meaning the likelihood of action was high, given the status of the speaker. Finally, as to imminence, violence was occurring almost simultaneous with Trump finishing his speech, at the Capitol, where he told his supporters to go. As explored elsewhere in this volume, the greater context in which a speech occurs matters in determining if incitement has taken place, meaning in particular that tweets and statements Trump gave before and after his speech — as well as his initial inaction after he was aware that violence was occurring at the Capitol — can be evidence of intent or likelihood of incitement.[5]

As far as Supreme Court cases with similar language used on January 6, 2021, there are parallels to *Feiner v. New York* (1951). Irving Feiner advised his listeners that their rights were being violated and that they needed to "rise up in arms and fight." The Supreme Court upheld Feiner's disorderly conduct conviction, reasoning that although "the police cannot be used as an instrument for the suppression of unpopular views," Feiner's speech was not protected where "the speaker passes the bounds of argument or persuasion and undertakes incitement to riot." Thus, one could argue that the *Feiner* decision made a pronouncement that is relevant today: "When clear and present danger of riot, disorder . . . or other immediate threat to public safety, peace, or order, appears, the power of the State to prevent or punish is obvious."[6]

On the other hand, a defense attorney could show significant First Amendment problems with prosecuting President Trump for what he said at the Ellipse on January 6, 2021, as incitement. Unlike *Feiner*, any prosecution for incitement today must strictly adhere to the imminent lawless action test established by *Brandenburg*, not the now discredited clear and present danger test. Applying *Brandenburg*, at various points in the speech Trump proclaimed to his audience what can be argued is intent *not* to engage in violence but instead to be loud and boisterous enough at an outdoor protest that members of Congress will take notice and possibly change their votes: "I know that everyone here will soon be marching over to the Capitol building to peacefully and patriotically make your voices heard." Like Trump's December 2020 tweet advising his supporters to attend the rally ("Big protest in D.C. on January 6th. Be there, will be wild!"), one reasonable interpretation of Trump's statements is that they were ill-advised, even reckless, attempts to promote raucousness, not intentional incitement of violence. Given the many thousands of peaceful protestors who remained outside and did not engage in disruptive or violent behavior that day, one can argue that the most likely result of that expression was peaceful protest.

Even the more aggressive language ("fight like hell") pales in comparison to the "emotionally charged rhetoric" that the Supreme Court protected in *Claiborne Hardware* (for example, "We're gonna break your damn neck"). If *Hess* informs the meaning of imminence, there are concerns about the distance from the Ellipse to the Capitol, as any rioters present at Trump's speech had to walk approximately one mile to engage in violence; that walk gave them time to cool off, or, conversely, to be incited by others walking with them (although that argument would not apply to any rioters already at the Capitol if they were livestreaming Trump's speech on their phones). These concerns are especially problematic if the speaker in question is a presidential candidate who is being prosecuted by a Justice Department headed by an appointee of the current president, who was the speaker's opponent in either the last election or an upcoming election. Above all, the First Amendment must be interpreted to protect against the government censoring criticism of itself. Indeed, the freedom of speech must shield us against criminal laws that may be wielded the same way Thomas I. Emerson characterized the Alien and Sedition Acts in 1798: "a major weapon [used] to wipe out all political opposition." And yet, if one does engage in incitement, that speaker cannot shield oneself from prosecution by running for office.[7]

Regarding those First Amendment concerns, Special Council Jack Smith did not indict President Trump for the crime of solicitation to commit violence solely for the speech he gave that day, giving a wide birth to the protection of the words uttered during the speech at the Ellipse, and focusing instead on the acts and statements by Trump leading up to, and including, that fateful day. In short, President Trump's political advocacy in his January 6, 2021, speech was protected by the First Amendment; this includes accusations in his speech about election integrity, "fake news," and "Big tech." Smith's indictment conceded as much, stating that Trump "had a right, like every American, to speak publicly about the election and even to claim, falsely, that there had been outcome-determinative fraud during the election and that he had won." Citing a litany of alleged events, communications, and actions from November 2020 to January 2021, the special counsel charged Trump with conspiracy to defraud the United States, conspiracy to obstruct an official proceeding, obstruction of an official proceeding, and conspiracy against rights. Although Trump's words on January 6 were cited in the indictment, the speech at the Ellipse constituted a very small portion of the facts alleged in Jack Smith's forty-five-page charging document, which focused on allegations of attempting to pressure Mike Pence in his role as president of the Senate to reject certification of Electoral College votes and interacting with state officials to subvert election results.[8]

If a speaker is charged not for incitement but for engaging in a larger criminal conspiracy, *Giboney v. Empire Storage & Ice Co.* (1949) is instructive, as in that case the Supreme Court "reject[ed] the contention" that "the constitutional freedom for speech and press extends its immunity to speech or writing used as an integral part of conduct in violation of a valid criminal statute," ruling that "it has never been deemed an abridgement of freedom of speech or press to make a course of conduct illegal merely because the conduct was in part initiated, evidenced, or carried out by means of language, either spoken, written, or printed." Put another way, if the expression at that Ellipse that day was protected by the First Amendment, there is a difference between a speech alone that advocates illegality and a criminal conspiracy that is orchestrated to cause acts of violence (although presidential immunity presents other obstacles to prosecution here after *Trump v. United States* [2024]). Furthermore, there is a difference between speech that could not be criminally prosecuted because it is constitutionally protected, and speech that may be so unbecoming for an elected leader to make that Congress may find that it constitutes an impeachable offense.[9]

But these considerations are only the beginning of the ultimate inquiry as we conclude this volume. Questions arise whether the Supreme Court should, or will, continue to adhere to *Brandenburg*. There are good reasons to continue that very high level of protection, particularly if the advocacy is on matters of public concern. There is a special need to guard political speech — especially speech by political leaders — to avoid those in power trumping up charges to effectively criminalize the speech of their rivals. But *Brandenburg* as currently constructed certainly has its detractors (including in some chapters of this volume), because of how much it protects advocacy of illegality, including among those who are intolerant and wish to turn our country toward utter chaos, authoritarianism, or totalitarianism. Karl Popper, in *The Open Society and Its Enemies*, argued that there is a "paradox of tolerance," whereby tolerance of intolerance permits the intolerant to spread their hate and get elected to office, then using their power to end tolerance altogether.[10] For this reason, there are countries and international agreements that protect less expression than *Brandenburg* protects in the United States.[11]

In that regard, when speech is followed by violence, one might wonder if that violence could have been prevented if the speech had not been made. For example, mass shootings in the United States have led to calls from politicians and others for gun control reforms and better mental health care. Investigations occurring after these incidents sometimes reveal that mass shooters have been motivated by racist, anti-Semitic, anti-Muslim, and anti-LGBTQ rhetoric.[12] Similar concerns arise with the hateful rhetoric that motivated the terrorists who orchestrated the attacks on September 11, 2001,[13] and the Boston Marathon bombing in 2013,[14] as well as those who attempted to exploit the George Floyd protests in 2020 by advocating that people engage in violence.[15] This connection between loose rhetoric and subsequent violent acts is one reason why some have advocated that the Supreme Court reduce how much speech is protected by *Brandenburg*.

Nevertheless, questions arise whether a shooter or terrorist would have become violent anyway, and clinging to a hateful philosophy simply gave them an easy excuse for their violence. Can reading hateful statements online or watching videos of hate-filled speeches really create violence in a person? And, if so, should the speakers or writers behind the expression be held legally responsible? Put another way, when people are violent, should we stop our criminal prosecution at those who actually commit the violent acts, or do we go after a purported "ringleader"? And are the people who write or record hateful statements really ringleaders at all?

When thinking about the continuing validity of *Brandenburg*, returning to January 6 is again instructive. There have now been over 1,000 arrests, prosecutions, and sentencing of people who engaged in criminal conduct at the Capitol building that day. These are the persons who committed acts of violence, damaged property, and injured police officers, and many of them have gone to jail or prison. If those who engaged in violence and property damage are competent adults who can make their own decisions, and should have known better, one can ask why Donald Trump or any other speaker should be legally responsible, even if they did encourage illegal acts. There is a distinction we tend to draw between conduct and speech, particularly political speech. As the Supreme Court explained in *Wisconsin v. Mitchell* (1993), unlike pure speech, "a physical assault is not by any stretch of the imagination expressive conduct protected by the First Amendment."[16]

One response is the unavoidable import of what happened that day: the country witnessed, shockingly, as a mob of people broke into the US Capitol to stop the certification of an election and the peaceful transfer of political power. An attempt to violently overthrow the government may have succeeded if not for the intervention of security and police. The prospect of something that significant — striking at the very heart of our representative democracy — makes us want to make sure it never happens again. If a speaker arguably provokes frenzied crowds at speeches where attendees have a history of violence, one could argue that the speaker's words are as much the cause of violence and destruction as the fists of his followers. The same concerns exist if an assassin is motivated by irresponsible rhetoric to attempt to kill a presidential candidate, as an assassination not only murders that politician but also strikes at the heart of democracy by using a bullet to remove a candidate choice from voters' ballots. If incitement is meant to prevent such dangerous political violence, is *Brandenberg*, as currently structured, up to the challenge?

Speakers with these motives are not a new phenomenon in the twenty-first century, however. In *Terminiello v. Chicago* (1949), the Supreme Court overturned the conviction of suspended Priest Arthur Terminiello for an inflammatory speech he gave to a crowd of an estimated 1,500 people. Terminiello's hate-filled, anticommunist speech was teeming with racism and anti-Semitism, tagging those who opposed him as "slimy scum" and "bedbugs." Yet, Terminiello also stated in his speech, "I don't want you to go from this hall with hatred in your heart for any person." Nevertheless, the crowd listening to Terminiello's speech was recounted as a "surging, howling mob hurling epithets at those [protestors] who would enter and tried to tear their clothes off." Audience members made their own racist and anti-Semitic statements after Teminiello's speech, including hateful comments that people of color and Jewish persons "would have to be gotten rid of." Hundreds of protestors outside the hall where Terminiello gave his speech were so incensed by his rhetoric that they blocked entrances, broke windows, and damaged a door.[17]

In *Terminiello*, Justice Robert Jackson warned of the dangers of speakers like Terminiello. Jackson famously said, "[t]his Court has gone far toward accepting the doctrine that civil liberty means the removal of all restraints from these crowds and that all local attempts to maintain order are impairments of the liberty of the citizen. The choice is not between order and liberty. It is between liberty with order and anarchy without either. There is danger that, if the Court does not temper its doctrinaire logic with a little practical wisdom, it will convert the constitutional Bill of Rights into a suicide pact."[18] It is this type of concern with *Brandenburg* turning the Constitution into a suicide pact by protecting speakers who channel rage in both their supporters and detractors that can cause one to question the validity of that precedent.

Nevertheless, Jackson dissented in *Terminiello*. The opinion of the Court, written by Justice William Douglas, adhered to the clear and present danger test then in force, with Douglas applying the test in a way that reflected the values of *Brandenburg*. Douglas explained the importance of protecting even irate speakers who gin up crowds with hateful rhetoric.

> The vitality of civil and political institutions in our society depends on free discussion. . . . It is only through free debate and free exchange of ideas that government remains responsive to the will of the people and peaceful change is effected. The

right to speak freely and to promote diversity of ideas and programs is therefore one of the chief distinctions that sets us apart from totalitarian regimes.

Accordingly a function of free speech under our system of government is to invite dispute. It may indeed best serve its high purpose when it induces a condition of unrest, creates dissatisfaction with conditions as they are, or even stirs people to anger. Speech is often provocative and challenging. It may strike at prejudices and preconceptions and have profound unsettling effects as it presses for acceptance of an idea. That is why freedom of speech, though not absolute, is nevertheless protected against censorship or punishment, [for causing] public inconvenience, annoyance, or unrest. There is no room under our Constitution for a more restrictive view. For the alternative would lead to standardization of ideas either by legislatures, courts, or dominant political or community groups.[19]

Douglas articulated concerns with expanding the definition of advocacy that can be proscribed as incitement. Using more of Jackson's approach, just two years after *Terminiello* the Supreme Court in *Dennis v. United States* upheld criminal convictions for political dissenters, sending them to prison for years. Enlarging the definition of incitement makes it easier for those in power to silence political rivals and dissidents, and it thus threatens the very foundations of our democracy. *Brandenburg* as presently constituted thwarts such efforts, ensuring that ideas across the ideological spectrum are protected. *Brandenburg* has been in force for more than half a century, and it has not turned our Constitution into the "suicide pact" that Jackson feared.

Still, an additional consideration with *Brandenburg* — as a long-standing precedent — is that it was issued by the Supreme Court before humans walked on the Moon. While that is, for reasons we revisit below, good in the sense that it has provided stability in what the First Amendment protects, it also means that one might question if the test still reflects the most common ways that we communicate. The rise of the internet, and social media in particular, has created a large shift in how we speak. The justices in 1969 were not thinking about Facebook, X (formerly known as Twitter), Snapchat, Instagram, TikTok, YouTube, and the other platforms that host a tremendous amount of speech today. Those justices were also not thinking about blogs, viral videos, email, text messages, or the notion that a person could carry a telephone/computer/camcorder/publisher in one's pocket. For the *Brandenburg* legal regime to survive and remain relevant, questions about these considerations are certainly worth asking.

Empirically, on the Supreme Court today a majority of justices have explained that original meaning is the most suitable way to interpret the Constitution, including protections in the Bill of Rights. Although there are certainly other viable methods of constitutional interpretation, and originalism is not free from concerns, the Court recently stated the following in a Second Amendment case, *New York State Rifle & Pistol Association v. Bruen* (2022): "Post-ratification adoption or acceptance of laws that are *inconsistent* with the original meaning of the constitutional text obviously cannot overcome or alter that text."[20]

Some lower courts have read decisions like *Bruen* to indicate that original meaning should be used to interpret the First Amendment as well. The Fifth Circuit Court of Appeals stated the following in *NetChoice v. Paxton* (2022) when reviewing a Texas law prohibiting social media companies from restricting speech based on viewpoint: "We turn now to the merits of the Platforms' First Amendment claim. As always, we start with the original public meaning of the Constitution's text."[21] On the Supreme Court, individual justices have concluded that long-standing First Amendment precedents should be reconsidered if they do not reflect original meaning. In a 2019 defamation case denying a writ of *certiorari*, Justice Clarence Thomas questioned the "actual malice" standard from *New York Times v. Sullivan* (1964), writing that "we should carefully examine the original meaning of the First and Fourteenth Amendments. If the Constitution does not require public figures to satisfy an actual-malice standard in state-law defamation suits, then neither should we."[22] In a 2021 case denying a writ of *certiorari*, Justice Neil Gorsuch indicated that he may agree with Justice Thomas, writing, "[d]epartures from the Constitution's original public meaning are usually the product of good intentions. But less clear is how well *Sullivan* and all its various extensions serve its intended goals."[23]

Thus, if the Supreme Court reconsiders *Brandenburg* soon, it would likely replace it with a standard the majority of justices concludes reflects the original meaning of the First Amendment. Is *Brandenburg* originalist? The intellectual origins of the test rest with Justices Holmes and Brandeis in the 1910s and 1920s. In his *Brandenburg* concurrence, Justice Douglas recalled how Holmes in his *Abrams* dissent rejected the clear and present danger test for something that would protect speech short of imminent harm.[24] Indeed, Holmes stated in *Abrams* that the "expression of opinions that we loathe and believe to be fraught with death" should be protected "unless they so imminently threaten immediate interference with the lawful and pressing purposes of the law that an immediate check is required to save the country."[25] This bears strong resemblance to what the Supreme Court later adopted in *Brandenburg*. How did Holmes arrive at it? In a letter to his friend Harold Laski in 1919, Holmes indicated that he had recently "reread Mill on *Liberty*" and referred to John Stuart Mill as a "fine old sportsman."[26] In *On Liberty*, one finds a passage that likely inspired Holmes: "An opinion that corn dealers are starvers of the poor, or that private property is robbery, ought to be unmolested when simply circulated through the press, but may justly incur punishment when delivered orally to an excited mob assembled before the house of a corn dealer, or when handed about among the same mob in the form of a placard."[27] Notice key elements of *Brandenburg* present in Mill's "corn dealer" example, including protecting speech short of a setting likely to result in immediate lawlessness.

If *Brandenburg* reflects a standard devised by Holmes that he built off of a nineteenth-century British philosopher's tract (*On Liberty* was first published in 1859), it is not a direct reflection of the original public meaning of the First Amendment, which was adopted in 1791. However, by rejecting the majority's standard in *Whitney v. California* (and overturning that decision), the Court in *Brandenburg* demonstrated some commitment to Brandeis's concurrence in *Whitney*. Brandeis's standard in *Whitney* reads even closer to what the Court pronounced in *Brandenburg* than Holmes's *Abrams* test. Brandeis argued that restrictions on speech are unconstitutional "unless speech would produce, or is intended to produce, a clear and imminent danger of some substantive evil which the state constitutionally may seek to prevent."[28] This reflects both the intent and imminence prongs of *Brandenburg*, and Brandeis's emphasis on producing lawlessness trends close to what the Court eventually adopted regarding likelihood.

Brandeis in *Whitney* claimed to be using what one could characterize as a form of originalism, referring to the founding generation: "Those who won our independence by revolution were not cowards. They did not fear political change. They did not exalt order at the cost of liberty. To courageous, self-reliant men, with confidence in the power of free and fearless reasoning applied through the processes of popular government, no danger flowing from speech can be deemed clear and present, unless the incidence of the evil apprehended is so imminent that it may befall before there is opportunity for full discussion."[29] Thus, if the Supreme Court wanted to emphasize originalism, there is at least an argument that *Brandenburg* reflects the views of the Founders, if we take Brandeis to be our guide on their meaning.

Of course, there is nothing talismanic about originalist interpretations of the Constitution. History is a valid and important constitutional consideration, but a historical analysis of the meaning of free speech and incitement at the time of the founding raises several questions. If the historical record is incomplete, are we biasing what we might conclude today is the original meaning of the First Amendment? What if there were competing views about the First Amendment's meaning when it was adopted, rather than there being a monolithic point of view that everyone held about it? What if the original meaning of the First Amendment was that the founding generation of Americans did not want us today to be held to whatever their beliefs were at that time? Which voices were systematically excluded from participating, or at the very least were marginalized from fully taking part, in the original public discussions of the First Amendment because of their race, sex, or economic class? Why is this method more (or less) valid than other ones, such as textualism, structuralism, pragmatism, living constitutionalism, or reliance on Supreme Court precedent (*stare decisis*)?

Regarding *stare decisis*, *Janus v. AFSCME* (2018) indicated the Supreme Court's willingness to overrule free expression precedents that are unworkable: "*stare decisis* applies with perhaps least force of all to decisions that wrongly denied First Amendment rights: 'This Court has not hesitated to overrule decisions offensive to the First Amendment (a fixed star in our constitutional constellation, if there is one).'"[30] However, *Janus* demonstrates an inclination to overrule past First Amendment precedents that *denied* free expression rights. Any attempts to change *Brandenburg* to be less protective of expression are unlikely to succeed on the current Supreme Court, even if there is an originalist argument suggesting support for another standard.

The Supreme Court's adherence to *Brandenburg* in recent years is evident in two cases not directly about incitement: *Counterman v. Colorado* (2023) and *United States v. Hansen* (2023). In *Counterman*, the Supreme Court reviewed a stalking conviction of Billy Counterman for his posts to a woman on Facebook, which included statements indicating he was surveilling her, telling her to "fuck off permanently," that "staying in cyber life is going to kill you," and that she should "die." *Counterman* outlined the meaning of a true threat — which, like incitement is *not* protected by the First Amendment — with the Supreme Court holding that "the First Amendment . . . requires proof that the defendant had some subjective understanding of the threatening nature of his statements," including having the mental state of recklessness.[31]

To help explain why the government must show that one has this mental state to prove that one made a true threat, the Supreme Court in *Counterman* turned to its incitement standard in *Brandenburg*: "Like threats, incitement inheres in particular words used in particular contexts: Its harm can arise even when a clueless speaker fails to grasp his expression's nature and consequence. But still, the First Amendment precludes punishment, whether civil or criminal, unless the speaker's words were 'intended' (not just likely) to produce imminent disorder. That rule helps prevent a law from deterring 'mere advocacy' of illegal acts — a kind of speech falling within the First Amendment's core." The *Counterman* decision reflected on concerns with prosecuting those advocating political violence unless there is clear and specific intent, rightly reasoning that since *Brandenburg*, the Supreme Court has "recognized that incitement to disorder is commonly a hair's-breadth away from political 'advocacy' — and particularly from strong protests against the government and prevailing social order. . . . A strong intent requirement was, and remains, one way . . . to ensure that efforts to prosecute incitement would not bleed over, either directly or through a chilling effect, to dissenting political speech at the First Amendment's core."[32]

Similar to *Counterman*, *Hansen* was a First Amendment case not about incitement, but it still has important implications for incitement. The Supreme Court in *Hansen* ruled that a federal statute that bans encouraging or inducing unlawful immigration is not overbroad, and therefore is constitutional. Focusing again on intent, the Supreme Court found that the relevant statute prohibited only "the intentional solicitation or facilitation of certain unlawful acts." Exhibiting *Giboney*'s distinction between advocacy and criminal conspiracy, *Hansen* affirmed that the law may prohibit "speech integral to unlawful conduct," because "[s]peech intended to bring about a particular unlawful act has no social value; therefore, it is unprotected."[33]

Cases like *Counterman* and *Hansen* demonstrate the contemporary Supreme Court's commitment to *Brandenburg* as well as the justices' continuing concerns with the mistakes of the pre-*Brandenburg* era, when too many speakers were wrongly sent to prison for mere political advocacy. They are cautionary decisions for anyone advocating legal action for expression on January 6, 2021, although they do not preclude court findings of liability if the facts show that a speaker intentionally induced illegality in a timely manner, in a speech and even more so through a larger conspiracy.

This is not to say that the *Brandenburg* test is perfect. But it is to say that history suggests other standards would be rife with their own problems. Thus, any changes — including ones like those contemplated by some chapters in this volume — must be carefully considered, and they must not be major changes. There are dangers with the Supreme Court modifying *Brandenburg* or crafting a completely different test. *Brandenburg* was a unanimous decision, and it has been the law of the land for over fifty years. Replacing that stability with something that would likely be pronounced by a divided Supreme Court could return this area of the law to the same state it was in for the fifty years before *Brandenburg*: one of constant reformulation and instability, too often resulting in speakers being imprisoned because the government disfavored the viewpoints they advocated, not because of any serious threat of violence. As discussed in this volume, *Brandenberg* did not create the concept of incitement; it was the culmination of decades of various tests trying to define incitement, through trial and error. *Brandenberg* sought to rebalance the concerns of safety with the right to speak, regardless of the viewpoint being expressed, even if that speech is offensive or advocates violence. The safeguards put in place by *Brandenberg* have protected the speech of the KKK and civil rights activists alike.

Changing *Brandenburg* to a standard less protective of speech risks creating something that completely devalues the importance of free expression (like *Gitlow* and *Whitney*'s bad tendency test), or something so malleable like the clear and present danger test that its level of protection could swing wildly from one case to the next, depending on the speaker's identity or who is serving on the Supreme Court, even to the point where it might criminalize something like merely "falsely" shouting fire in a crowded theater like the Supreme Court suggested in *Schenck*. Those scenarios are fraught with problems, and the Supreme Court's fifty-year journey from 1919 to 1969 should not be repeated; we can learn from those mistakes of the past.

This book has presented many facets of the *Brandenberg* test and contains chapters that both criticize it and defend it. The primary critiques of *Brandenberg* — like those by Feldman, VanLandingham, Schweber and Anderson, Sweeny, and Canon — have focused on its vagueness, particularly considering modern modes of communication, and concerns about whom the test empirically protects or does not protect. Proponents of maintaining *Brandenberg* in its current form and more narrowly defining incitement — like those by Kunz, Shiell, Carthens, Kasper, and Wells — have focused on the test's emphasis on protecting speech, fearing that any attempts to water it down, or refusing to fully apply it, will chill the expression of important, thought-provoking ideas and could easily lead to the criminalization of dissent.

As the back-and-forth reflections in this conclusion — presenting arguments in favor of, and against, maintaining *Brandenburg* in its current form — have probably already revealed, the editors of this volume have differing views on this subject, with one of us strongly wishing *Brandenburg* to be maintained as it stands and the other vigorously advocating that the Court make some clarifications to reflect changes in our society since 1969. We hope that our contemplations here — and in Downs's introduction and the substantive chapters throughout this volume — have helped you think deeply about the profound questions raised today by incitement and how it is defined by the Supreme Court. In the spirit of the free inquiry protected by the First Amendment, we, as the editors of this volume, are not here to dictate to you that *Brandenburg* must be maintained or specifically changed in some way, or what the First Amendment protected (or did not protect) on January 6, 2021; we ask that you draw your own conclusions on these matters after carefully considering what is written throughout this book.

Whatever you conclude about these matters, we suggest that in your own advocacy you *not* try to test that line between "mere advocacy" and incitement. There is good reason, given the state of American politics today, to counsel one to speak civilly, respectfully, and with moderation, even if one has the right to use more emotionally charged rhetoric. Relevant here are President Abraham Lincoln's words from his second inaugural address, given shortly before his death, in the closing days of the Civil War, where he counseled that we act, "with malice toward none" and "charity for all." His speech reminds us that we should choose our words considering that we all share this country together, and all human beings are worthy of dignity and grace.

We all possess First Amendment rights to oppose, condemn, and criticize extremism and hate. We also have the free speech rights to promote equality, justice, and truth. As the Supreme Court reasoned in *United States v. Alvarez* (2012), in a free society this type of counterspeech is a powerful remedy to expression we find to be disagreeable and even abhorrent: "The response to the unreasoned is the rational; to the uninformed, the enlightened; to the straightout lie, the simple truth."[34] Whatever courts decide in cases raising issues of incitement under *Brandenburg*, that reasoning from *Alvarez* lies at the core of the First Amendment's meaning. We have the choice of how to use that freedom, or decline to use it, as we see fit, to promote the common good.

Notes

1. Brandenburg v. Ohio, 395 U.S. 444, 447 (1969).
2. NAACP v. Claiborne Hardware Co., 458 U.S. 886, 928 (1982).
3. These issues were relevant to Special Counsel Jack Smith's indictment of President Trump, but that legal proceeding was wound down after Trump's reelection in November 2024, as it is Department of Justice policy not to prosecute a sitting president. Carrie Johnson, "Special Counsel Jack Smith Taking Steps to Wind Down Federal Cases Against Trump," NPR, November 6, 2024, https://www.npr.org/2024/11/06/g-s1-33021/trump-trials-jack-smith-election-2024.
4. Anderson v. Griswold, 543 P.3d 283, 299 (Colo. 2023), cert. granted sub nom; Trump v. Anderson, 144 S. Ct. 539 (2024), and rev'd sub nom; Trump v. Anderson, 601 U.S. 100 (2024), and cert. dismissed sub nom; Colorado Republican State C. Comm. v. Anderson, 144 S. Ct. 1085 (2024); Thompson v. Trump, 21-CV-00400 (APM), 2022 WL 503384 (D.D.C. Feb. 18, 2022).
5. Naylor, "Read Trump's Jan. 6 Speech"; BBC, "Capitol Riots Timeline: What Happened on 6 January 2021?"; Kyle Cheney and Josh Gerstein, "How Trump's Renewed Election Rhetoric Is Complicating Capitol Rioters' Legal Fight," *Politico*, April 27, 2021, https://www.politico.com/news/2021/04/27/trump-rhetoric-capitol-rioters-legal-fight-484787; Kevin A. Johnson and Craig R. Smith, *Fear and the First Amendment: Controversial Cases of the Roberts Court* (University of Alabama Press, 2024), 2–5. For more on events before and after the speech, see Final Report of the Select Committee to Investigate the January 6th Attack on the United States Capitol, H.R. Rep. No. 117-663 (2022), https://www.govinfo.gov/content/pkg/GPO-J6-REPORT/pdf/GPO-J6-REPORT.pdf.
6. Feiner v. New York, 340 U.S. 315, 324, 321, 320 (1951).
7. Naylor, "Read Trump's Jan. 6 Speech, a Key Part of Impeachment Trial"; H.R. Rep. No. 117-663, at 499 (2022); Colleen Long, "Trump's 8-Hour Gap: Minute-by-Minute During Jan. 6 Riot," Associated Press, March 31, 2022, https://apnews.com/article/capitol-siege-elections-donald-trump-presidential-elections-election-2020-3315609c4152b4429930a17191b5a217; Thomas I. Emerson, *Toward a General Theory of the First Amendment* (Random House, 1966), 23; see Trump v. United States, 603 U.S. 593 (2024) on constitutional limits on prosecuting a former president.
8. Naylor, "Read Trump's Jan. 6 Speech, a Key Part of Impeachment Trial"; Jaclyn Diaz, "The Charges Facing Trump in the Jan. 6 Investigation, Explained," NPR, August 2, 2023, https://www.npr.org/2023/08/01/1191493880/trump-january-6-charges-indictment-counts; United States v. Donald J. Trump, Indictment, U.S. District Court for the District of Columbia, August 1, 2023, https://www.justice.gov/storage/US_v_Trump_23_cr_257.pdf.

9 Giboney v. Empire Storage & Ice Co., 336 U.S. 490, 498, 502 (1949); Anthony D. Romero, "We Can Uphold Free Speech and Hold President Trump Accountable," American Civil Liberties Union, January 11, 2021, https://www.aclu.org/news/civil-liberties/we-can-uphold-free-speech-and-hold-president-trump-accountable.

10 Karl R. Popper, *The Open Society and Its Enemies* (Princeton University Press, 1994), 723.

11 Rebecca Meyer, "Pursuing a Universal Threshold for Regulating Incitement to Discrimination, Hostility or Violence," *Brooklyn Journal of International Law* 44 (2018): 310–44.

12 Anti-Defamation League, "Murder and Extremism in the United States in 2022," February 22, 2023, https://www.adl.org/resources/report/murder-and-extremism-united-states-2022 ("Of particular concern in recent years are shootings inspired by white supremacist 'accelerationist' propaganda urging such attacks. . . . For the near to medium future, the main threat of extremist-related mass killings seems to be white supremacist shooters attacking targets such as people of color, Jews and Muslims and the LGBTQ+ community").

13 See National Commission on Terrorist Attacks, *The 9/11 Commission Report* (Norton, 2004), 47 (in 1998, Osama Bin Laden and Ayman al Zawahiri issued a fatwa calling for the murder of any American anywhere in the world).

14 See Richard Valdmanis, "Boston Bomb Suspect Influenced by Al Qaeda: Expert Witness," *Reuters*, March 23, 2015, https://www.reuters.com/article/boston-bombings-trial/boston-bomb-suspect-influenced-by-al-qaeda-expert-witness-idINKBN0MJ29H20150323.

15 See Mia Bloom, "Far-Right Infiltrators and Agitators in George Floyd Protests: Indicators of White Supremacists," *Just Security*, May 30, 2020, https://www.justsecurity.org/70497/far-right-infiltrators-and-agitators-in-george-floyd-protests-indicators-of-white-supremacists/ (examples of "accelerationists" who encouraged followers to attend protests to engage in violence).

16 Wisconsin v. Mitchell, 508 U.S. 476, 484 (1993).

17 Terminiello v. Chicago, 337 U.S. 1, 14-26 (1949) (Jackson, J., dissenting).

18 Terminiello, 337 U.S. at 37.

19 Terminiello, 337 U.S. at 4–5 (internal citations omitted).

20 N.Y. State Rifle & Pistol Ass'n, Inc. v. Bruen, 597 U.S. 1, 36 (2022) (emphasis in original).

21 NetChoice, L.L.C. v. Paxton, 49 F.4th 439, 453 (5th Cir. 2022), cert. granted and vacated and remanded Moody v. NetChoice, LLC, No. 22-277, 2024 WL 3237685 (U.S. July 1, 2024).

22 McKee v. Cosby, 139 S. Ct. 675, 676 (2019) (Thomas, J., concurring in denial of cert.).

23 Berisha v. Lawson, 141 S. Ct. 2424, 2429 (2021) (Gorsuch, J., dissenting from denial of cert.).
24 Brandenburg, 395 U.S. at 452 (Douglas, J., concurring).
25 Abrams v. United States, 250 U.S. 616, 630 (1919) (Holmes J., dissenting).
26 Letter from Oliver Wendell Holmes Jr. to Harold Laski (Feb. 28, 1919), in *The Essential Holmes*, ed. Richard A. Posner (University of Chicago Press, 1992), 143.
27 John Stuart Mill, *On Liberty*, ed. Elizabeth Rapaport (Hackett, 1978), 53.
28 Whitney v. California, 274 U.S. 357, 373 (1927) (Brandeis, J., concurring).
29 Whitney, 274 U.S. at 377.
30 Janus v. American Federation of State, County, & Municipal Employees, 138 S. Ct. 2448, 2478 (2018) (quoting Federal Election Commission v. Wisconsin Right to Life, Inc., 551 U.S. 449, 500 [2007] [Scalia, J., concurring in part and concurring in judgment]).
31 Counterman v. Colorado, 600 U.S. 66, 70, 69 (2023).
32 Counterman, 600 U.S. at 76, 81.
33 United States v. Hansen, 599 U.S. 762, 766, 783 (2023).
34 United States v. Alvarez, 567 U.S. 709, 727 (2012).

Appendix A

Brandenburg v. Ohio, 395 U.S. 444 (1969) [unabridged]

PER CURIAM

The appellant, a leader of a Ku Klux Klan group, was convicted under the Ohio Criminal Syndicalism statute for "advocat[ing] . . . the duty, necessity, or propriety of crime, sabotage, violence, or unlawful methods of terrorism as a means of accomplishing industrial or political reform" and for "voluntarily assembl[ing] with any society, group, or assemblage of persons formed to teach or advocate the doctrines of criminal syndicalism." Ohio Rev. Code Ann. s 2923.13. He was fined $1,000 and sentenced to one to 10 years' imprisonment. The appellant challenged the constitutionality of the criminal syndicalism statute under the First and Fourteenth Amendments to the United States Constitution, but the intermediate appellate court of Ohio affirmed his conviction without opinion. The Supreme Court of Ohio dismissed his appeal, sua sponte, "for the reason that no substantial constitutional question exists herein." It did not file an opinion or explain its conclusions. Appeal was taken to this Court, and we noted probable jurisdiction. 393 U.S. 948, 89 S. Ct. 377, 21 L. Ed. 2d 360 (1968). We reverse.

The record shows that a man, identified at trial as the appellant, telephoned an announcer-reporter on the staff of a Cincinnati television station and invited him to come to a Ku Klux Klan "rally" to be held at a farm in Hamilton County. With the cooperation of the organizers, the reporter and a cameraman attended the meeting and filmed the events. Portions of the films were later broadcast on the local station and on a national network.

The prosecution's case rested on the films and on testimony identifying the appellant as the person who communicated with the reporter and who spoke at the rally. The State also introduced into evidence several articles appearing in the film, including a pistol, a rifle, a shotgun, ammunition, a Bible, and a red hood worn by the speaker in the films.

One film showed 12 hooded figures, some of whom carried firearms. They were gathered around a large wooden cross, which they burned. No one was present other than the participants and the newsmen who made the film. Most of the words uttered during the scene were incomprehensible when the film was projected, but scattered phrases could be understood that were derogatory of Negroes and, in one instance, of Jews.[1] Another scene on the same film showed the appellant, in Klan regalia, making a speech. The speech, in full, was as follows:

> This is an organizers' meeting. We have had quite a few members here today which are — we have hundreds, hundreds of members throughout the State of Ohio. I can quote from a newspaper clipping from the Columbus, Ohio Dispatch, five weeks ago Sunday morning. The Klan has more members in the State of Ohio than does any other organization. We're not a revengent organization, but if our President, our Congress, our Supreme Court, continues to suppress the white, Caucasian race, it's possible that there might have to be some revengeance taken.
>
> We are marching on Congress July the Fourth, four hundred thousand strong. From there we are dividing into two groups, one group to march on St. Augustine, Florida, the other group to march into Mississippi. Thank you.

The second film showed six hooded figures one of whom, later identified as the appellant, repeated a speech very similar to that recorded on the first film. The reference to the possibility of "revengeance" was omitted, and one sentence was added: "Personally, I believe the nigger should be returned to Africa, the Jew returned to Israel." Though some of the figures in the films carried weapons, the speaker did not.

The Ohio Criminal Syndicalism Statute was enacted in 1919. From 1917 to 1920, identical or quite similar laws were adopted by 20 States and two territories. E. Dowell, *A History of Criminal Syndicalism Legislation in the United States* 21 (1939). In 1927, this Court sustained the constitutionality of California's Criminal Syndicalism Act, Cal. Penal Code ss 11400–11402, the text of which is quite similar to that of the laws of Ohio. *Whitney v. California*, 274 U.S. 357, 47 S. Ct. 641, 71 L. Ed. 1095 (1927). The Court upheld the statute on the ground that, without more, "advocating" violent means to effect political and economic change involves such danger to the security of the State that the State may outlaw it. Cf. *Fiske v. Kansas*, 274 U.S. 380, 47 S. Ct. 655, 71 L. Ed. 1108 (1927). But Whitney has been thoroughly discredited by later decisions. See *Dennis v. United States*, 341 U.S. 494, at 507, 71 S. Ct. 857, at 866, 95 L. Ed. 1137 (1951). These later decisions have fashioned the principle that the constitutional guarantees of free speech and free press do not permit a State to forbid or proscribe advocacy of the use of force or of law violation except where such advocacy is directed to inciting or producing imminent lawless action and is likely to incite or produce such action.[2] As we said in *Noto v. United States*, 367 U.S. 290, 297–298, 81 S. Ct. 1517, 1520–1521, 6 L. Ed. 2d

836 (1961), "the mere abstract teaching... of the moral propriety or even moral necessity for a resort to force and violence, is not the same as preparing a group for violent action and steeling it to such action." See also *Herndon v. Lowry*, 301 U.S. 242, 259–261, 57 S. Ct. 732, 739–740, 81 L. Ed. 1066 (1937); *Bond v. Floyd*, 385 U.S. 116, 134, 87 S. Ct. 339, 348, 17 L. Ed. 2d 235 (1966). A statute which fails to draw this distinction impermissibly intrudes upon the freedoms guaranteed by the First and Fourteenth Amendments. It sweeps within its condemnation speech which our Constitution has immunized from governmental control. Cf. *Yates v. United States*, 354 U.S. 298, 77 S. Ct. 1064, 1 L. Ed. 2d 1356 (1957); *De Jonge v. Oregon*, 299 U.S. 353, 57 S. Ct. 255, 81 L. Ed. 278 (1937); *Stromberg v. California*, 283 U.S. 359, 51 S. Ct. 532, 75 L. Ed. 1117 (1931). See also *United States v. Robel*, 389 U.S. 258, 88 S. Ct. 419, 19 L. Ed. 2d 508 (1967); *Keyishian v. Board of Regents*, 385 U.S. 589, 87 S. Ct. 675, 17 L. Ed. 2d 629 (1967); *Elfbrandt v. Russell*, 384 U.S. 11, 86 S. Ct. 1238, 16 L. Ed. 2d 321 (1966); *Aptheker v. Secretary of State*, 378 U.S. 500, 84 S. Ct. 1659, 12 L. Ed. 2d 992 (1964); *Baggett v. Bullitt*, 377 U.S. 360, 84 S. Ct. 1316, 12 L. Ed. 2d 377 (1964).

Measured by this test, Ohio's Criminal Syndicalism Act cannot be sustained. The Act punishes persons who "advocate or teach the duty, necessity, or propriety" of violence "as a means of accomplishing industrial or political reform"; or who publish or circulate or display any book or paper containing such advocacy; or who "justify" the commission of violent acts "with intent to exemplify, spread or advocate the propriety of the doctrines of criminal syndicalism"; or who "voluntarily assemble" with a group formed "to teach or advocate the doctrines of criminal syndicalism." Neither the indictment nor the trial judge's instructions to the jury in any way refined the statute's bald definition of the crime in terms of mere advocacy not distinguished from incitement to imminent lawless action.[3]

Accordingly, we are here confronted with a statute which, by its own words and as applied, purports to punish mere advocacy and to forbid, on pain of criminal punishment, assembly with others merely to advocate the described type of action.[4] Such a statute falls within the condemnation of the First and Fourteenth Amendments. The contrary teaching of *Whitney v. California*, supra, cannot be supported, and that decision is therefore overruled.

Notes

1. The significant portions that could be understood were:
"How far is the nigger going to — yeah."
"This is what we are going to do to the niggers."
"A dirty nigger."
"Send the Jews back to Israel."
"Let's give them back to the dark garden."
"Save America."
"Let's go back to constitutional betterment."
"Bury the niggers."
"We intend to do our part."
"Give us our state rights."
"Freedom for the whites."
"Nigger will have to fight for every inch he gets from now on."

2. It was on the theory that the Smith Act, 54 Stat. 670, 18 U.S.C. s 2385, embodied such a principle and that it had been applied only in conformity with it that this Court sustained the Act's constitutionality. Dennis v. United States, 341 U.S. 494, 71 S. Ct. 857, 95 L. Ed. 1137 (1951). That this was the basis for Dennis was emphasized in Yates v. United States, 354 U.S. 298, 320–324, 77 S. Ct. 1064, 1077–1079, 1 L. Ed. 2d 1356 (1957), in which the Court overturned convictions for advocacy of the forcible overthrow of the Government under the Smith Act, because the trial judge's instructions had allowed conviction for mere advocacy, unrelated to its tendency to produce forcible action.

3. The first count of the indictment charged that appellant "did unlawfully by word of mouth advocate the necessity, or propriety of crime, violence, or unlawful methods of terrorism as a means of accomplishing political reform. . . ." The second count charged that appellant "did unlawfully voluntarily assemble with a group or assemblage of persons formed to advocate the doctrines of criminal syndicalism. . . ." The trial judge's charge merely followed the language of the indictment. No construction of the statute by the Ohio courts has brought it within constitutionally permissible limits. The Ohio Supreme Court has considered the statute in only one previous case, State v. Kassay, 126 Ohio St. 177, 184 N.E. 521 (1932), where the constitutionality of the statute was sustained.

4. Statutes affecting the right of assembly, like those touching on freedom of speech, must observe the established distinctions between mere advocacy and incitement to imminent lawless action, for as Chief Justice Hughes wrote in De Jonge v. Oregon, supra, 299 U.S. at 364, 57 S. Ct. at 260: "The right of peaceable assembly is a right cognate to those of free

speech and free press and is equally fundamental." See also United States v. Cruikshank, 92 U.S. 542, 552, 23 L. Ed. 588 (1876); Hague v. CIO, 307 U.S. 496, 513, 519, 59 S. Ct. 954, 963, 965, 83 L. Ed. 1423 (1939); NAACP v. Alabama ex rel. Patterson, 357 U.S. 449, 460–461, 78 S. Ct. 1163, 1170–1171, 2 L. Ed. 2d 1488 (1958).

Appendix B

Relevant US Supreme Court Rulings

- *Abrams v. United States*, 250 U.S. 616 (1919): Upheld Espionage Act convictions for distributing leaflets advocating a general strike during World War I. Dissent by Justice Oliver Wendell Holmes advocated protecting "free trade in ideas" in "the competition of the market," including for "opinions that we loathe and believe to be fraught with death, unless they so imminently threaten immediate interference with . . . the law."
- *Beauharnais v. Illinois*, 343 U.S. 250 (1952): Upheld a state law that criminalized racial and religious group libel. Any precedential value of the decision has been significantly called into question by *R.A.V. v. St. Paul* (1992) and *Snyder v. Phelps* (2011).
- *Brandenburg v. Ohio*, 395 U.S. 444 (1969): Overturned syndicalism conviction and established the imminent lawless action test for incitement: "the constitutional guarantees of free speech and free press do not permit a State to forbid or proscribe advocacy of the use of force or of law violation except where such advocacy is directed to inciting or producing imminent lawless action and is likely to incite or produce such action." Overruled *Whitney v. California* (1927) and replaced clear and present danger test.
- *Chaplinsky v. New Hampshire,* 315 U.S. 568 (1942): Upheld a breach of the peace conviction, establishing that "fighting words" are not protected by the First Amendment. Significantly limited by *Cohen v. California* (1971), which found protection for offensive speech.
- *Cohen v. California*, 403 U.S. 15 (1971): Overturned a breach of the peace conviction for wearing a jacket bearing the words "Fuck the Draft." Established that offensive speech, including the use of profanity, is generally protected in public

forums.
- *Counterman v. Colorado*, 600 U.S. 66 (2023): Overturned a stalking conviction, holding that for speech to constitute an unprotected "true threat," the government must prove the speaker had some subjective understanding of the statements' threatening nature.
- *Debs v. United States*, 249 U.S. 211 (1919): Upheld an Espionage Act conviction against a socialist leader who gave a speech critical of US involvement in World War I. The decision relied on *Schenck v. United States* (1919), which was decided one week earlier.
- *Dennis v. United States*, 341 U.S. 494 (1951): Upheld Smith Act convictions against Communist Party members who taught and advocated for communism, finding that when applying the clear and present danger test courts "must ask whether the gravity of the 'evil,' discounted by its improbability, justifies such invasion of free speech as is necessary to avoid the danger." This test was replaced in *Brandenburg v. Ohio* (1969).
- *Feiner v. New York*, 340 U.S. 315 (1951): Upheld a breach of the peace conviction against a speaker urging the audience to fight for equal rights, finding that with the clear and present danger test, the government has an interest "in maintaining peace and order on its streets."
- *Frohwerk v. United States*, 249 U.S. 204 (1919): Upheld an Espionage Act conviction for publishing newspaper articles critical of US involvement in World War I, applying the clear and present danger test used in *Schenck v. United States* (1919).
- *Giboney v. Empire Storage & Ice Co.*, 336 U.S. 490 (1949): Upheld an injunction against a conspiracy in restraint of trade, finding no constitutional protection for "speech or writing used as an integral part of conduct in violation of a valid criminal statute."
- *Gitlow v. New York*, 268 U.S. 652 (1925): Upheld an anarchy conviction for publishing a pamphlet advocating for strikes and mass action to achieve socialism, using a bad tendency test to conclude that government "may punish utterances endangering the foundations of government and threatening its overthrow by unlawful means." In dissent, Justice Oliver Wendell

Holmes argued the publication did not pose a clear and present danger.
- *Hess v. Indiana*, 414 U.S. 105 (1973): Overturned a disorderly conduct conviction for war protestor who yelled, "We'll take the fucking street again [or later]," finding the statement did not advocate for imminent lawlessness under the test from *Brandenburg v. Ohio* (1969).
- *Holder v. Humanitarian Law Project*, 561 U.S. 1 (2010): Upheld a federal prohibition on knowingly providing material support to foreign terrorist organizations, including if the support includes training to help groups resolve disputes peacefully.
- *NAACP v. Claiborne Hardware Co.*, 458 U.S. 886 (1982): Applied the *Brandenburg v. Ohio* (1969) test, finding nonviolent elements of a boycott are protected. Statements advocating violence were protected, when acts of violence "occurred weeks or months after" the speech in question.
- *Patterson v. Colorado*, 205 U.S. 454 (1907): Upheld a contempt conviction against a newspaper publisher on the theory that the First Amendment primarily prohibits prior restraints. Subsequent decisions have greatly expanded First Amendment protections.
- *R.A.V. v. City of St. Paul*, 505 U.S. 377 (1992): Struck down a bias-motivated crime ordinance, applied to a case involving a burning cross, as a content-based restriction on expression.
- *Schenck v. United States*, 249 U.S. 47 (1919): Upheld an Espionage Act conviction for distributing leaflets claiming the military draft was unconstitutional. The case established the clear and present danger test, which was replaced in *Brandenburg v. Ohio* (1969).
- *Snyder v. Phelps*, 562 U.S. 443 (2011): Overturned a jury award of monetary damages against funeral protesters for inflicting emotional distress on family of the deceased, holding speech in a public place on matters of public concern is protected by the First Amendment.
- *Terminiello v. City of Chicago*, 337 U.S. 1 (1949): Struck down a breach of the peace ordinance that prohibited stirring people to anger or inviting dispute as violating the First Amendment as measured by the clear and present danger test.

- *Thomas v. Collins*, 323 U.S. 516 (1945): Used the clear and present danger test to overturn a law that required labor organizers to obtain a government-issued permit before soliciting members, finding that there is a "preferred place" for First Amendment rights.
- *Thornhill v. Alabama*, 310 U.S. 88 (1940): Applied the clear and present danger test to strike down a law prohibiting labor picketing of businesses.
- *Whitney California*, 274 U.S. 357 (1927): Applied the bad tendency test to uphold a syndicalism conviction of a Communist Labor Party officer. Concurrence by Justice Louis Brandeis argued speech should be protected "unless speech would produce, or is intended to produce, a clear and imminent danger" the government may prohibit. The decision was overruled by *Brandenburg v. Ohio* (1969), which reflected arguments in Brandeis's opinion.
- *United States v. Hansen*, 599 U.S. 762 (2023): Upheld a federal law that bans encouraging or inducing illegal immigration for commercial advantage or financial gain.
- *United States v. Schwimmer*, 279 U.S. 644 (1929): Upheld government decision to deny naturalized citizenship to a pacifist immigrant. In dissent, Justice Oliver Wendell Holmes Jr. argued that that First Amendment protects "freedom for the thought we hate."
- *United States v. Stevens*, 559 U.S. 460 (2010): Struck down a ban on depictions of animal cruelty, finding such expression is not categorically excluded from constitutional protection.
- *Yates v. United States*, 354 U.S. 298 (1957): Held that the Smith Act prohibited only "advocacy of action for the overthrow of government by force and violence," not "advocacy and teaching of forcible overthrow as an abstract principle." The decision began calling into question the continued validity of the clear and present danger test.

Contributors

Rebecca J. Anderson is a dual JD/PhD candidate at the University of Wisconsin–Madison Department of Political Science and University of Wisconsin Law School. Her research and scholarly interests include constitutionalism and the intersection of feminist legal studies and political thought. She received her JD in 2021 and is a member of the Wisconsin State Bar Association.

Daniel J. Canon is an assistant professor of law and director of Externships at the University of Louisville, Louis D. Brandeis School of Law. He served as lead counsel for the Kentucky plaintiffs in the case of *Obergefell v. Hodges*, which established marriage equality in all fifty states, and has been involved in many other high-profile cases. He writes on civil and criminal justice issues for a variety of regional and national publications. His book titled *Pleading Out: How Plea Bargaining Creates a Permanent Criminal Class* is now available.

Shavonnie R. Carthens is an assistant professor of law in the J. David Rosenberg College of Law at the University of Kentucky. Her scholarly interests examine issues of public health law, environmental health law, and health equity, with a focus on how legal interventions might improve access to healthy living environments for marginalized communities. She also researches and writes at the intersection of legal literacy, patient protections, and health disparities among incarcerated populations.

Donald A. Downs is the Alexander Meiklejohn emeritus professor of political science, and emeritus professor of law and journalism at the University of Wisconsin–Madison. He has written about several topics, including books on free speech and liberal education, and has been involved in academic freedom movements at Wisconsin and nationally. He is currently a member of the Academic Committee of the Academic Freedom Alliance, centered at Princeton University.

Stephen M. Feldman is the Jerry W. Housel/Carl F. Arnold Distinguished Professor of Law and adjunct professor of political science at the University of Wyoming. He has published seven nonfiction books, including *Free Expression and Democracy in America: A History* (2008), and *Please Don't Wish Me a Merry Christmas: A Critical History of the Separation of Church and State* (1997). His latest book is *Pack the Court! A Defense of Supreme Court Expansion* (2021). He also writes fiction and has published several short stories.

Eric T. Kasper is a professor of political science at the University of Wisconsin–Eau Claire, where he serves as the director of the Menard Center for Constitutional Studies. His research is focused on the US Supreme Court and the US Constitution, particularly the First Amendment. He has authored or edited nine books, and he has authored twenty-four articles and book chapters. His books include *The Supreme Court and the Philosopher: How John Stuart Mill Shaped US Free Speech Protections* (with Troy A. Kozma) (2024) and *James Madison's Constitution: A Double Security and a Parchment Barrier* (with Howard Schweber) (2025).

Adam Kunz is an assistant professor of political science at the University of Wisconsin–Eau Claire where he teaches classes on political theory and constitutional law. His research focuses on egalitarian theories of justice, civil discourse and tolerance, and freedom for and from religion. His latest book, *To Hell with Heaven: An Introduction to Apatheism* (2024), draws from his experience leaving Mormonism to argue that when it comes to religious extremism, rather than "fight fire with fire," moderates should embrace passive resistance.

Howard Schweber is a professor emeritus in the Department of Political Science and was an affiliate faculty member in the law school, legal studies, and integrated liberal studies programs at University of Wisconsin–Madison. Schweber was a practicing lawyer before receiving his PhD in political science. He has taught various courses on constitutional law, the Supreme Court, and constitutional and democratic theory. He is the author of four books and coeditor of a fifth, as well as the author of more than forty articles and book chapters.

Timothy C. Shiell is professor emeritus of philosophy at the University of Wisconsin–Stout. Founder and past director of the university's Center for Applied Ethics and Menard Center for the Study of Institutions and Innovation, he has given over 200 scholarly and public presentations, workshops, panels, and guest lectures on free expression, academic freedom, and applied ethics. He is author of *Campus Hate Speech on Trial* (1998 and 2009) and *African Americans and the First Amendment* (2019), and editor of *Legal Philosophy: Selected Readings* (1993) and *Civil Liberties in Real Life: Seven Studies* (2020).

JoAnne Sweeny is professor of law at the University of Louisville, Louis D. Brandeis School of Law. She holds a PhD from the University of London and a JD from the University of Southern California Law School. She has taught courses on freedom of expression, comparative constitutional law, and comparative human rights law. She has also published several articles on various First Amendment topics, including incitement, the captive audience doctrine, and the right to petition.

Rachel E. VanLandingham is the Irwin R. Buchalter Professor of Law and associate dean for research at Southwestern Law School, where she was appointed to the faculty in 2014 after having served in the US Air Force for over twenty years. She teaches criminal law, criminal procedure, national security law, and the law of armed conflict, and has authored numerous law review articles, book chapters and op-eds. While on active duty, Professor VanLandingham served as a military prosecutor and defense counsel, and as the legal adviser for international law at Headquarters, U.S. Central Command. She is president emerita and current director of the National Institute of Military Justice, the leading nonprofit dedicated to improving military justice.

Christina E. Wells is the Enoch H. Crowder Professor Emeritus at the University of Missouri School of Law. Professor Wells's research focuses on the First Amendment, specifically on protests, access to information, and national security. She was coauthor of several editions of a casebook, *The First Amendment: Cases and Theory* by Ronald J. Krotoszynski et al., and has written Supreme Court amicus briefs and published numerous articles and book chapters appearing in such venues as the *Columbia Law Review*, *Michigan Law Review*, *Wisconsin Law Review*, *North Carolina Law Review*, *Harvard Civil Rights and Civil Liberties Law Review*, and *Constitutional Commentary*.

Index

abortion
  "The Nuremburg Files" anti-abortion internet site, 173–174
  Schumer comments on, 5
Abrams, Jacob, 8–9, 67, 147
Abrams v. United States (1919)
  advocacy and, 8–9
  Espionage Act conviction, 8–9, 67, 247
  Holmes and Brandeis dissent in, 9–10, 147, 232
abstract advocacy of violence incitement category, 53, *53*
  Brandenburg v. Ohio protection of, 55
accomplice liability, 86, 88, 94, 101n28
ACLED. *See* Armed Conflict Location & Event Data Project
actual malice standard, 232
actus reus harm spectrum, criminal solicitation on, 94
Adderly v. Florida (1966), 73, 74
Adler v. Board of Education of the City of New York (1952), 68–69
administrative overreach, prison
  in book censorship, 111–113, 115–116
  in incitement, 105–116
Administrative Procedure Act, 108
advocacy, 98
  Abrams v. United States, 8–9
  Bridges v. California, 13
  De Jonge v. Oregon, 12
  Dennis v. United States convictions sustained, 15
  First Amendment protections for, 2–3, 6–7, 51–56
  Fox v. Washington and, 7
  Gilbert v. Minnesota, 10
  Gitlow v. New York, 10–11

  Hartzel v. United States, 14
  Herndon v. Lowry clear and present danger test, 12–13
  incitement compared to, 191
  for lawless action, *Brandenburg* and, 40
  New York Times v. Sullivan on civil rights, 48
  Noto v. United States overturn of Smith Act conviction, 16, 54–55
  Pierce v. United States, 9–10
  political, 14–15
  protective approach and World War II, 14
  Schenck v. United States, 7–8
  Supreme Court approach during Cold War, 14–15
  Thornhill v. Alabama clear and present danger test, 13, 250
  United States ex rel. Turner v. Williams, 6
  Warren and Brennan and test revision, 16
  Whitney v. California, 11–12
  Yates v. United States, 16
AFL. *See* American Federation of Labor
AI. *See* Artificial Intelligence
Alexander, Michelle, 105
algorithms, internet and, 174, 175, 177, 180
American Communication Association v. Douds (1950), 68
American Federation of Labor (AFL), growth of, 62n32
Anglin, Andrew, 171–172
anti-egalitarian expressive rights, 50–51, 58
antimony within liberal egalitarianism, 31–33
anti-orthodoxy and inclusion

Douglas opinion on, 56–57
for expressive rights relationship, 47–51, 55
Hunter on inclusion values and, 47–48
Supreme Court case decisions on, 55–58
Armed Conflict Location & Event Data Project (ACLED), 64n58
Artificial Intelligence (AI), internet incitement and, 175
attitudinal decision-making model, 217
autonomy, 49, 50

bad tendency test, 145
  Brandenburg rejection of, 55
  described, 66
  freedom of expression and, 51, 66
  Gitlow v. New York use of, 10–11, 53–54, 67, 235
  MacKinnon proposal of revival of, 64n56
  Whitney v. California and, 11–12, 17, 51, 67, 235, 250
Baggett v. Bullitt (1964), 56
Bamberger, Alvin, 208, 209
Barron v. Baltimore (1833), 51
Battersby, James, 105
Beard v. Banks (2006), 81n111
Beauharnais v. Illinois (1952), 63n41, 169, 183n13, 247
Bell v. Wolfish (1979), 109
Berger v. United States (1921), 62n29
Bible Believers v. Wayne County, Michigan (2015), 36–37, 39–40, 189, 190, 211, 216
Biden, Joe, 5–6, 225
Bill of Rights (1791), 51, 230, 231
Black, Hugo, 17
  on *Adderly v. Florida*, 74
  on *Bridges v. California*, 13
  on clear and present danger test., 55

Dennis v. United States dissent, 15–16, 148
Black Identity Extremists designation, 58, 156
Black Lives Matter (BLM), 144, 156, 216
  protests in 2020, 58, 64n59
Blackmon, Douglas, 105
Blizzard of Ozz album, of Osbourne, 128, 130
BLM. *See* Black Lives Matter
The Bluest Eye (Morrison), 105
Body Count, 131, 132
Bond, Julian, 56
Bond v. Floyd (1966), 56
book censorship, in prisons
  administrative overreach of, 111–113, 115–116
  Bell v. Wolfish, 109
  categorical limitation on expression, 113
  Counterman v. Colorado, 113–114
  detrimental impacts of, 106–107, 115–116
  examples of, 105–106
  federal and state prison censorship commissions on, 114–115
  First Amendment rights to receive and read information, 107–110
  inconsistency of, 114
  lack of transparency barrier in, 115
  potential solutions and procedural safeguards, 113–115
  prior restraints and, 112–113
  Thornburgh v. Abbott, 109–110
  Turner v. Safley, 109–110, 112, 113
Brandeis, Louis, x–xi, 14, 52
  Abrams v. United States dissent, 9–10, 147, 232
  clear and present danger test and, 68, 232

dissenting in Espionage Act cases, 67
Gitlow v. New York dissent, 11, 67
Pierce v. United States dissent, 10
Whitney v. California concurrence, 11–12, 17, 147, 233
Brandenburg, Clarence, 17, 55, 70–71, 127
Brandenburg test
  Beauharnais v. Illinois on group libel punishment, 169
  fulfillment of obligation regarding dangerous speech, xi, 17
  illustrations of, 36–40
  on imminent lawless action, ix, 17, 41, 93, 227
  on incitement, x–xi, 2–3, 47, 97, 168–170
  liberal egalitarian justifications for, 27–43
  liberal egalitarian tolerance in, 34–35
  as most protective free speech test in world, ix, 65
  musical expression safeguards, 123–137
  Rice v. Paladin Press instruction theory and, 169, 170
  specific to constitutional law and protection against state action, 35
  on speech directed at inciting or producing action, ix, 2–3, 17, 34, 47, 69–72
  terrorism and arguments to disregard, 143–157
  theoretical left and right on, 30, 41–42
  three-part, ix, 17, 225
  Trump January 6, 2021 illustration, 38–40, 226–227, 229
  United States v. Hansen and, 169, 234, 235, 250

Brandenburg v. Ohio (1969), 123
  anti-orthodoxy, inclusion and, 56–59
  aspirations and possibilities beyond, 40–43
  bad tendency test rejection, 55
  continuing significance of, 19, 229
  critics of, xi–xii
  distinguishing criminal solicitation and incitement, 96–97
  doctrine to shield expression attacking outsiders and minorities, 65
  on expressive rights commitment, 57–58, 59
  First Amendment, incitement and future of, 225–236
  as First Amendment landmark, 65
  free speech, social justice and, 65–76
  on incitement, 97, 127, 168, 188
  Ku Klux Klan demonstration and, x, 47, 70–71, 148–149
  narrowing advocacy for state punishment, ix
  normative case for, x–xi
  overturn of *Whitney v. California*, 17, 247
  practical argument for, xi
  protection for abstract advocacy of violence, 55
  on S-M-R placement, x
  speech in criminal conspiracy and solicitation lack of protection in, xiiin12
  syndicalism conviction against Brandenburg and KKK rally, 17
  Tsesis on terrorism and, 150–151, 159n44
  unabridged presentation of, 241–243
  use in *McCollum*, 129
Braun, Stefan, 58
Brennan, William, 16, 70

Breyer, Stephen, 74
Bridges v. California (1941), 13, 78n37
Brousseau, Henry, 207–208
Brown v. Louisiana (1965), 48
Brown v. Socialist Workers '74 Campaign Committee (1982), 60n8
Burstyn v. Wilson (1952), 55–56

California Communist Labor Party, Whitney establishment of, 11
call to action
  Hess v. Indiana, 191
  prior communication in January 6, 2021 US Capitol attack, 192–194
  surrounding communication for January 6, 2021 US Capitol attack, 194
  susceptibility to violence and January 6, 2021 US Capitol Attack, 195–196
  Thompson v. Trump, 191
Campus Hate Speech on Trial (Shiell), 57
Cantwell v. Connecticut (1937), 48, 71
Carlson, Tucker, 155
Chaplinsky v. New Hampshire (1942), 247
Charlottesville Unite the Right rally (2017), 51, 61n21, 189, 190
Chauvin, Derek, 5
Chen, Alan, 152
child pornography, 2, 90
  United States v. Williams, 97
China, music censorship in, 125
Church of Lukumi Babalu Ave., Inc. v. City of Hialeah, 41
Citizens United v. Federal Election Commission (2010), 80n108
civil rights movement, 2, 73
  NAACP v. Claiborne Hardware and, 58, 75, 188

New York Times v. Sullivan on advocacy protection, 48
  Supreme Court cases on, 48
Clarke, John H., 67
classical deterrence theory, 212
classical liberalism, liberal egalitarianism compared to, 30
clear and present danger test, 67
  Black on, 55
  of Brandeis, 68, 232
  of *Brandenburg*, 143, 148–149
  Brandenburg not addressing of, 55
  Bridges v. California, 13
  Cold War and reconsideration of, 15, 147–148
  Douglas on, 17, 55–57, 230–231
  Hartzel v. United States, 14
  Herndon v. Lowry, 12–13, 48, 52
  of Holmes, 52, 68, 232
  incitement test replacement of, 55, 56–57
  Milk Wagon Drivers Union v. Meadowmoor Dairies, 13
  in prisons, 108
  punishment of speech and unlawful action, ix
  Schenck v. United States and, 8, 13, 14, 52, 54, 66, 145–146, 248
  Sunstein on, 64n56
  Thomas v. Collins, 14, 250
  Thornhill v. Alabama, 13, 250
  World War I and birth of, 145–146
  Yates and *Noto* lack of use of, 16
clear and probable danger test, Vinson and, 15, 69
Cloudfare, Kiwi Farms and, 181
Cohen, Paul Robert, 56
Cohen v. California (1971), 247–248
  on citizenry trusted to deal with less direct harms, x
  on Cohen "Fuck the Draft" protected expression, 56
  on incitement in context, 210
Cold War, 54, 68

clear and present danger test
  reconsideration and, 15, 147–148
  House Un-American Activities Committee and, 147
  Supreme Court approach to advocacy during, 14–15
  terrorism and, 147–148
Collins, Mike, 5–6
Communications Decency Act, on social media immunity, 168
Communist Party USA (CPUSA)
  Dennis v. United States and, 15, 54, 69, 147–148, 151, 248
  Herndon advocating for, 12
  Noto and Yates of, 16
  Yates v. United States involving, ix, 16
Comstock Laws, 56
Connick v. Myers (1983), 210
Conrad, Robert, 135–136
conspiracy, true threat compared to, 93
Constitution, US. *See also specific Amendment*
  free speech and, 1, 66, 123
  originalist interpretations of, 232–233
Constitutional law, on state action and dangerous speech, ix
contraband
  common sources of, 111
  prison evidence of books as, 110–111
  prisons and, 105
"Cop Killer," of Body Count, 131
Counterman, Billy, 234
Counterman v. Colorado (2023), 113–114, 176, 234, 235, 248
court decision-making models
  attitudinal decision-making model, 217
  legal decision-making model, 215–217
  strategic decision-making model, 217–218
CPUSA. *See* Communist Party USA
Criminal Law Cases and Materials (Dressler and Harvey), 101n27
criminal law self-defense doctrine, imminence test compared with, xiiin14, xi
criminal solicitation, 93
  on *actus reus* harm spectrum, 94
  as inchoate crime, 94
  incitement compared to, 96–99
  law enforcement and, 88–89, 94
  Model Penal Code on, 94–95, 96
  required elements of, 96–97
  Robbins on, 94
  Scott on, 102n44
  specificity factor in, 98–99
  suppression harmfulness and, 89–90
  thought crime and, 95–96
  Volokh on, 98
criminal solicitation and incitement
  accomplice liability and, 86, 88, 94, 101n28
  Brandenburg distinguishing, 96–97
  common law and, 93–94, 96
  as criminal speech, 85–99
  described, 85–87
  different crimes of, 96–99
  murder example, 86, 89, 99
criminal speech
  complicated arena of, 85–90
  criminal solicitation, 93–96, 101n35
  criminal solicitation and incitement as, 85–99
  First Amendment landscape of, 90–93
criminal syndicalism laws, 146
  labor strife and, 53
  states passage World War I, 67
Cruz, Ted, 3

Dakota Rural Action v. Noem (2019), 58
dangerous speech
　Brandenburg test fulfillment to obligation on, xi
　direct S-R trigger to action, x
　state prohibition to prevent imminent lawless action, xi
　tools for combatting, xii
Davidson, Bill, 131, 132
Davidson v. Time Warner (1997), 136–137
　Ward, Brandenburg, Hess use in, 131–132
De Jonge v. Oregon (1937), 12, 48, 56, 244n4
Debs v. United States (1919), 67, 77n21, 248
defamation, 2, 90
democracy
　of Athens, *isegoria* and *porrhesia* in, 49
　pluralist, 68
Dennis v. United States (1951), 56, 231
　Black dissent in, 15–16, 148
　convictions of CPUSA leaders upheld under, 15, 54, 69, 147–148, 151, 248
　Douglas dissent in, 16, 148
　prosecution against political dissenters and, 15
　Tsesis on, 150–151
　Vinson opinion in, 148
Department of Justice, on domestic organizations terrorism, 154
Dibbel, Julian, 171
Doe v. Mckesson (2019), 215–216
domestic terrorism, 144
　antifa as, 156
　BLM and, 144, 156
　Department of Justice on, 154
　hate speech, 155
　replacement theory and, 155
　Sines v. Kessler, 155, 188–189, 190
　Trump on antifa and leftist activists as, 156
　white supremacists and, 154
Douglas, William O.
　anti-orthodoxy and inclusion opinion by, 56–57
　on clear and present danger test, 17, 56–57, 230–231
　Dennis v. United States dissent, 16, 148
doxing, 174, 176, 179, 184n22
Dressler, Joshua, 101n27
Due Process Clause, of Fourteenth Amendment, 6, 23n26, 23n43
Dworkin, Ronald, 29

egalitarian expression, law enforcement use of, 58, 156
egalitarian theories, equity above other values in, 31
Ehrenreich, Barbara, 4
Ehrenreich, Ben, 4
Elfbrandt v. Russell (1966), 56
Emergence of a Free Press (Levy), 57
Emerson, Thomas I., 227
equal right of citizens to participate in public debate. *See isegoria*
equality, LGBT community expressive rights and, 47–48
equity, in egalitarian theories, 31
Espionage Act (1917)
　Abrams violation of, 8–9, 67, 247
　Debs v. United States, 67, 77n21, 248
　First Amendment concerns and, 52
　Frohwerk v. United States, 67, 248
　Hartzel v. United States conviction reversal for, 14
　incitement cases dissent by Holmes and Brandeis, 67

incitement cases prosecutions, 66–67
incitement defining and, 188
Schenck v. United States case, 8, 55, 66, 145, 248, 249
Supreme Court upholding conviction of, 52, 62n28
Evers, Charles, 18, 72–73
expressive rights. *See also* free speech; freedom of expression
anti-egalitarian, 50–51, 58
anti-orthodoxy and inclusion to, 47–51, 55
Brandenburg on commitment to, 57–58, 59
Forsyth County v. Nationalist Movement, 51
Holmes and Brandeis support of, 52
justifications for, 49–50
LGBT community equality and, 47–48
partisan attacks on, 57
progress in equality and, 47
R.A.V. v St. Paul, 51
in Supreme Court decisions, 48–49, 55
Terminiello v. Chicago, 50–51
white supremacists Charlottesville Unite the Right march in 2017, 51, 61n21

falsely shouting fire in crowded theater, 8, 235
FBI. *See* Federal Bureau of Investigation
FBI Counter-Intelligence Program from 1956 to 1971, 58
FCC. *See* Federal Communication Commission
FCC v. Pacifica Foundation (1978), 168

federal and state prison censorship commissions, proposal for, 114–115
Federal Bureau of Investigation (FBI) Domestic Terrorism Analysis Unit, on Black Identity Extremist movement, 156
Federal Communication Commission (FCC)
government censorship of music, 126–127
Supreme Court on broadcast ban of indecent material, 168
federal criminal code, terrorism defined by, 153
Feiner v. New York (1951), 71–72, 226, 248
fight like hell statement, by Trump, 3, 4, 38, 188, 193, 194, 196, 198, 213, 226
films, First Amendment protection of, 52, 55–56
FIRE. *See* Foundation for Individual Rights and Expression
First Amendment, xiiin2
anti-orthodoxy and advocacy of violence decisions, 51–56
Douglas and Black statement on clear and present danger test and, 55
Espionage Act and concerns for, 52
film protection, 52, 55–56
Fortas as expert on, 70
four-part test for prison challenges, 109, 110
Free Speech Clause and, 6, 11, 38, 48
on freedom of speech or press, 6
Holmes on lack of application to state, 52
internet and new approach to incitement, 176–182

landscape for criminal speech, 90–93
music protection from, 136
Mutual Film Corp v. Ohio on film not as speech, 52
prevention of government restrictions on music, 123
protection of emotionally charged rhetoric, 225
protection to SDS, 48, 55
rights to public school students, 48–49
rights to receive and read information in prisons, 107–110
state legal prohibition of speech, ix
for stopping political violence at presidential campaign rallies, 212–213
Supreme Court address on free expression until 1919, 66
Supreme Court incorporation of clauses in, 55–56
First Amendment, protection outside of
child pornography, 2, 90, 97
defamation, 2, 90
fraud, 2, 90
obscenity, 2, 6, 90, 100n16
speech integral to criminal conduct, 2
true threats, 2, 92
First Amendment jurisprudence, 215–218
Doe v. Mckesson, 215–216
United States v. Hale, 215
United States v. White, 215
Weinstein on, 215
Fiske v. Kansas (1927), 54, 56
Fitzpatrick, Duross, 130
Floyd, George, 5, 229
Flynn, Michael, 193
FOIA. *See* Freedom of Information Act

Forsyth County v. Nationalist Movement (1992), 31
Fortas, Abe, 70
Foundation for Individual Rights and Expression (FIRE), 58
4Chan, 171–172, 175, 181
Fourteenth Amendment, 232
Due Process Clause of, 6, 23n26, 23n43
Patterson v. Colorado and free-expression principles, 66
Fox v. Washington (1915), 7, 52
Frankfurter, Felix, 13
fraud, 2, 90
Free Exercise Clause, 41, 48
free speech, ix, x, 48–51. *See also* expressive rights; freedom of expression
Brandenburg test as most productive test, ix, 65
executive and legislative branches engaging in subversion of, 57
IWW fights for, 62n37
liberal egalitarianism tolerance through, 28
public school student rights to, 2
Schauer on, 99
U.S. Constitution and Supreme Court on, 1
free speech and social justice
Brandenburg and, 65–76
Supreme Court depiction as defender of outsiders and minorities, 65
victories at expense of outsiders and minorities, 71, 75
Free Speech Clause, of First Amendment, 216
Gitlow v. New York and, 6, 11, 48
Trump claim under, 38
Free Speech for Me (Hentoff), 57
Free Speech in Its Forgotten Years (Rabban), 57
freedom of conscience, 32–34, 40–41

freedom of expression. *See also* expressive rights; free speech
  bad tendency test and, 51, 66
  Bill of Rights privilege of, 51, 230, 231
  states right to censor, 51–52
  World War I and hostility toward, 51
freedom of expressive association, *NAACP v. Alabama* and, 48
Freedom of Information Act (FOIA), 114
Frohwerk v. United States, 67, 248

Gamergate case, incitement not addressed in, 171, 172, 174
Gersh v. Anglin (2017), 171–172, 176
Gertz v. Robert Welch, Inc. (1974), 1
Giboney v. Empire Storage & Ice Co., 248
  distinction between advocacy and criminal conspiracy, 228, 234
Gilbert v. Minnesota (1920), 10
Ginsburg, Ruth Bader, 74
Gitlow, Benjamin, 48
  The Left Wing Manifesto, 10, 67, 146–147
Gitlow v. New York (1925), 248–249
  bad tendency test use in, 10–11, 53–54, 67, 235
  First Amendment freedom of speech protection in, 6, 11, 48
  Holmes and Brandeis dissent in, 11, 67
  incitement categories and, 53–54
  Red Scare and, 67, 146–147
Giuliani, Rudy, 3, 205n84
Gohmert, Louie, 4–5
Gorsuch, Neil, 232
government censorship, of music
  FCC and, 126–127
  historical examples of, 124–125
group libel punishment, *Beauharnais v. Illinois* and, 63n41, 169, 247

Hague v. CIO (1939), 55
Hale, David, 209–210
Hart v. State (2024), 132–133
Hartzel v. United States (1944), 14
Harvey, Stephen P., 101n27
hate groups, x
  social media facilitation of, xii
hate speech, 57, 71, 155
Hawley, Josh, 4
Healy v. James (1972), 48, 55
Heimbach, Matthew, 208, 209
Hentoff, Nat, 57
Herndon, Angelo, 12
Herndon v. Lowry (1937), 54, 56
  clear and present danger test, 12–13, 48, 52
Hess, Gregory, 17–18
Hess v. Indiana (1973), 98, 189, 191, 211, 249
  imminence clarification in, 17–18, 227
  on incitement in context, 210
  musical expression safeguards and, 123, 127
  use in *McCollum*, 129
Holder v. Humanitarian Law Project (2010), 72, 73, 249
  Breyer, Ginsburg, and Sotomayor on, 74
  foreign terrorist organizations concern, 74
  PKK and LTTE in, 74–75
Holmes, Oliver Wendell, Jr., 8, 14, 146, 247
  Abrams v. United States dissent, 9–10, 147, 232
  clear and present danger test, 52, 68, 232
  dissenting in Espionage Act cases, 67
  Gitlow v. New York dissent, 11, 67
  Pierce v. United States dissent, 10

264 | Index

on *Schenck v. United States*, 66, 145
The Holy Book of Adolf Hitler (Battersby), 105
hostile-audience cases
   Feiner v. New York, 71–72, 226, 248
   Terminiello v. Chicago, 71–72
House Un-American Activities Committee, Cold War and, 147
Howard, Ronald, 131, 132
Hughes, Charles Evans, 12
Hunter, Nan, 47–48

imminence
   criminal law self-defense doctrine compared to test of, xiiin14, xi
   defined, x
   Hess v. Indiana clarification of, 17–18
   incitement in context and, 196–197
   NAACP v. Claiborne Hardware Co. on, 18, 127, 227
imminent lawless action, 127
   Brandenburg test on, ix, 17, 41, 93, 227
   dangerous speech prohibition by state to prevent, xi
   Holmes on *Abrams v. United States* and, 9
   incitement to, 2–3
   internet and, 172–173, 176, 179–180
   standard for incitement, 19, 53, 70, 93, 127, 168–169, 225
impeachment, Trump and, 187–188
inchoate crimes, 101n27, 101n29
   criminal solicitation as, 95
incitement
   advocacy compared to, 191
   Biden comments and Trump assassination attempt, 5–6, 225
   Brandenburg test on, x–xi, 47, 97, 168–170
   cases with Espionage Act prosecutions, 66–67
   categories of, *53*, 53–55
   contemporary examples of, 3–6
   criminal solicitation compared to, 96–99
   defined, 2
   to imminent lawless action, 2–3, 47, 174
   January 6, 2021 US Capitol attack and, 3–5
   prison administrative overreach and, 105–116
   Schumer comments on Supreme Court abortion case, 5
   Supreme Court test for, 2–3, 56–57, 70, 93, 127, 168–169, 225
   test replacement of clear and present danger test, 55, 56–57
   Waters comment on Chauvin criminal trial, 5
incitement, Courts reluctance to constrain Trump and
   external political factors for, 207–218
   Nwanguma v. Trump, 207–212, 216
incitement and social justice
   Brandenburg v. Ohio and, 69–72
   New York Times v. Sullivan, 69
   Tinker v. Des Moines Independent Community School District, 69
incitement cases
   first Red Scare and, 66, 67–68, 146–147
   second Red Scare and, 66, 68–69, 146–147
   before World War I era, 6–7, 66–67
incitement cases, after *Brandenburg*
   Hess v. Indiana, 17–18, 98, 127
   Holder v. Humanitarian Law Project, 72, 73–74

NAACP v. Claiborne Hardware Co., 18–19, 72
incitement in context, January 6, 2021 US Capitol attack
  Bible Believers v. Wayne County, 189, 190, 211, 216
  Brandenburg redefining of, 188
  call to action, 191–196
  defining, 188–189
  Espionage Act use, 188
  imminence and, 196–197
  intent, 197–199
  Nwanguma v. Trump, 189, 190
  Schenck v. United States, 190
  Sines v. Kessler and, 155, 188–189, 190
  Snyder v. Phelps, 189
indirect incitement, 191
Industrial Workers of the World (IWW), free speech fights of, 62n37
instruction theory, *Rice v. Paladin Press* and, 169, 170
intent, January 6, 2021 US Capitol attack incitement in context, 197–199
intentional incitement category, 53, 53
international jihadist terrorism, 144, 161n74
internet. *See also* social media
  AI and incitement, 175
  algorithms use, 174, 175, 177, 180
  Brandenburg test not suited to deal with incitement of violence of, 168–170
  doxing or trolling on, 176
  8Chan, 181
  FCC v. Pacifica Foundation and, 168
  4Chan, 171–172, 175, 181
  Gersh v. Anglin, 171–172, 176
  imminent action problem of time, 172–173, 178

  incitement on, 167–182
  Klonick on incitement approach, 176–177
  liability and Section 230 of Communications Decency Act, 181–182
  "The Nuremburg Files" anti-abortion site, 173–174
  online discourse prior to January 6, 2021 US Capitol attack, 167–168
  online harassment, 175
  physical proximity problem of space, 170–172
  problems of *Brandenburg* application to, 170–176
  speaker-listener interaction and stochastic terrorism, 173–175, 178–179, 182
isegoria (equal right of citizen to participate in public debate), 49
IWW. *See* Industrial Workers of the World

Jackson, Robert, 230
  at Nuremburg trials, 15
January 6, 2021 US Capitol attack
  criminal convictions for, 3
  First Amendment arguments on, 226–228
  five deaths from injuries at, 3, 167
  Gohmert and, 4–5
  Hawley gesture at, 4
  incitement doctrine and, 3–5
  litigation on determination of Trump incitement, 187–188
  online discourse prior to, 167–168
  Pence and, 3, 4, 167, 194, 198, 226, 228
  Trump and *Brandenburg* test example, 38–40, 229
  Trump calls for campaign violence before, 212–213

Trump claim of protected speech under First Amendment Free Speech Clause, 38
Trump fight like hell statement, 3, 4, 38, 188, 193, 194, 196, 198, 213, 226
Trump incitement rhetoric on, 3–4, 87–88
Trump sued under Ku Klux Klan Act, 38
Janus v. American Federation of State, City & Municipal Employees (AFSCME) (2018), 81n112, 233–234
Jehovah's Witnesses, Supreme Court cases on, 48, 55, 71, 81n114
justice
　Brandenburg test commitment to liberal egalitarian metavalue of, 34–36, 39, 43
　expression in liberal egalitarianism, 33

Kant, Immanuel, 29
Keyishian v. Board of Regents (1967), 56
Kilchner, Yannic, 175
Kiwi Farms, Cloudfare and, 181
Klonick, Kate, 176–177
Knox v. Service Employees International Union (2012), 81n112
Ku Klux Klan Act (1871), 38
Ku Klux Klan demonstration, *Brandenburg* and, x, 47, 70–71, 148–149

labor activism and unions, 13, 52, 68, 78n37, 145, 146, 154
　AFL growth and, 63n32
　IWW free speech fights, 62n37
　postmaster denial of labor publications mailing, 62n33
　Supreme Court on employer rights for employee promise not to join, 62n33
labor strife, 2, 13, 144, 250
　criminal syndicalism laws and, 53
　from mid-1880s into twentieth century, 51
　Supreme Court cases on, 48
LambdaMOO event, 171, 172
law enforcement
　criminal solicitation and, 88–89, 94
　use of egalitarian expression, 58, 156
lawless action. *See also* imminent lawless action
　Brandenburg and advocacy for, 40, 85, 98
　internet and, 172–173, 176, 179–180
The Left Wing Manifesto (Gitlow), 10, 67, 146–147
Legacy of Suppression (Levy), 57
legal decision-making model, 215–216
Levy, Leonard, 57
LGBT community, expressive right and equality, 47–48
liberal democracies
　public forum and marketplace of ideas to variety of voices, ix–x
　on racial incitement to include advocacy and rhetoric, ix
liberal egalitarian metavalue, 31–33
　Brandenberg test commitment to justice, 34–36, 39, 43
liberal egalitarian tolerance, 28, 41
　in *Brandenburg* test, 34–35
　broader speaking context and, 39
　deferential to liberty use, 35
liberal egalitarianism
　action space of citizens to pursue good, 29, 33, 35, 39, 40

American law and politics framework, 33
antimony within, 31–33
antinomy and metavalue within, 31–33
background on, 28–40
Bible Believers case illustration and, 36–37, 39–40
Brandenburg defense through, 27–43
classical liberalism compared to, 30
criticism of, 30
Dworkin influence on, 29
freedom of conscience, 32–34, 40–41
fundamentals of, 29–31
law backed by state power to protect liberty, 30
liberalism form through public laws, 29
liberty consistent with equity, 29
multiculturalism compared to, 30
as political and social arrangement, 35
public order focus by, 35, 41
Rawls on, 31–32
Rousseau, Locke and Kant influence of, 29
similarity to social contractarian theories, 30
situating *Brandenburg* within, 33–36
speech for provocative and violent behavior for, 34–35
tenets of, 29
theory of equity, 29
Thompson case illustration and, 38–40
Liberation Tigers of Tamil Eelam (LTTE), 74–75
liberty, 29, 30, 32, 232–233
liberty of conscience. *See* freedom of conscience

Locke, John, 29
Loper Bright Enterprises v. Raimondo (2024), 108
Louisville, Kentucky campaign rally, of Trump
Nwanguma v. Trump and, 189–190, 207–212, 216
Trump violent rhetoric at, 208–209
LTTE. *See* Liberation Tigers of Tamil Eelam

MacKinnon, Catharine, 64n56
Mahanoy Area School District v. B.L. (2021), 1
Manhattan Community Access Corporation v. Halleck (2019), 81n109
Marsh v. Alabama (1946), 55
Marshall, Thurgood, 51
on autonomy and self-realization, 50
on strong equality and speech protection, 48
Martin v. City of Struthers (1943), 50, 81n114
Marx, Karl, 53
Masterpiece Cakeshop, Ltd. v. Colorado (2018), 80n108
Matal v. Tam (2017), 60n8
Matarazzo v. Aerosmith Productions (1989), 133–134
Matthews v. State (1978), xiiin16
McCollum v. CBS (1988), 128, 130
Brandenburg and *Hess* use in, 129
McConnell, Mitch, 3
McCutcheon v. FEC (2014), 2
McKeague, David, 210–211, 216
Mehta, Amit P., 213–214
Meiklejohn, Alexander, x, 50
Meredith, James, 56
metavalue, liberal egalitarian, 31–33
Brandenberg test commitment to justice, 34–36, 39, 43
Milk Wagon Drivers Union v. Meadowmoor Dairies (1941), 13

Mill, John Stuart, 49, 232–233
Miller, Christopher, 3
Miller v. California (1973), 100n16
Mineshima-Lowe, Dale, 53
minorities. *See* societal outsiders and minorities
Model Penal Code, 102n42
  on criminal solicitation, 94–95, 96
Moore, Hunter, 176, 185n38
Morissette v. United States (1952), 102n40
Morrison, Toni, 105
Mosley, Earl, 56
The Most Hated Man on the Internet documentary, 176, 185n38
multiculturalism, liberal egalitarianism compared to, 30
Murdock v. Pennsylvania (1943), 71
Murphy, Frank, 13–15
Murray, Pauline, 51
music censorship
  in China, 125
  in Nazi Germany, 124
  in Russia, 124–125
  in United States, 125–127
musical expression safeguards
  Davidson v. Time Warner, 131–132
  Hart v. State, 132–133
  Hess v. Indiana and, 123, 127
  at live events, 133–134
  Matarazzo v. Aerosmith Productions, 133–134
  McCollum v. CBS, 128–129, 130
  Schad v. Mount Ephraim, 128, 130
  Southeastern Promotions, Ltd. v. Conrad, 123, 127–128
  Stricklin v. Stefani, 135–136
  Torries v. Hebert, 134, 136
  Vance v. Judas Priest, 129–130
  Waller v. Osborne, 130, 136
  Ward v. Rock against Racism, 123, 124, 128, 131
Mutual Film Corp v. Ohio (1915), 52

NAACP. *See* National Association for the Advancement of Colored People
NAACP v. Alabama (1958)
  freedom of expressive association in, 48
  on incitement in context, 210
NAACP v. Claiborne Hardware Co. (1982), 58, 60n8, 72–73, 97, 102n51, 127, 249
  Evers and boycott of white-owned businesses, 18, 72
  on imminence, 18, 127, 227
  incitement redefined by, 188
  on protected advocacy and unprotected incitement, 19
National Association for the Advancement of Colored People (NAACP), 18, 48
National Socialist Movement, 144
Nazi Germany, music censorship in, 124
Near v. Minnesota (1931), 52
NetChoice v. Paxton (2022), 232
The New Jim Crow Mass Incarceration in the Age of Colorblindness (Alexander), 105
New York State Rifle & Pistol Association v. Bruen (2022), 232
New York Times Co. v. Sullivan (1964), 1, 48, 69, 232
NLRB v. Jones and Laughlin Steel Corporation, 68
Norton, Eleanor Holmes, 51
Noto, John, 16
Noto v. United States (1961), 56
  overturn of Smith Act conviction, 16, 54–55
"The Nude and the Prudes" magazine article, *Fox v. Washington* and, 7, 52
"The Nuremburg Files" anti-abortion internet site, 173–174
Nuremburg trials, Jackson at, 15

N.W.A., 130–131, 132
Nwanguma, Kashiya, 207–208
Nwanguma v. Trump (2016), 189, 190
    Courts reluctance to constrain Trump and incitement, 207–212, 216
    Hale and incitement claim against Trump, 209–210
    physical attacks on rally protestors, 207–208
    Sixth Circuit court and, 210–211, 216
    trial court and, 208–210
    Trump Louisville, Kentucky campaign rally, 207–212, 216

obscenity, 2, 90
    laws passed in 1870s banning, 6
    Miller v. California and, 100n16
On Liberty (Mill), 232–233
The Open Society and Its Enemies (Popper), 238–239
originalist interpretations, of Constitution, 232–233
Osbourne, Ozzy, 128, 130, 137
outsiders. *See* societal outsiders and minorities

parrhesia (license to say what, how, and when one pleased), 49
Partiya Karkeran Kurdistan (PKK), 74–75
Patterson, Thomas, 7, 52
Patterson v. Colorado (1907), 249
    contempt citation against Patterson upheld, 52
    free-expression principles under Fourteenth Amendment, 66
    on Patterson publications and administration of justice, 7
PEN America
    defense of free expression by, 57
    on prisoner book possession denials, 110

Pence, Mike, 3, 4, 167, 194, 198, 226, 228
physical proximity problem of space, with internet, 177–178
    Gamergate and, 171, 172
    LambdaMOO event, 171, 172
Pierce v. United States (1920), 9
    Holmes and Brandeis dissent in, 10
Pierson, Katrina, 193
PKK. *See* Partiya Karkeran Kurdistan
Planned Parenthood v. American Coalition of Life Activists (2002), xiiin16
Pleasant Grove City v. Summum (2009), 81n110
PLRA. *See* Prison Litigation Reform Act
pluralist democracy, description of, 68
Police Department of Chicago v. Mosley (1972), 56
political advocacy, 14–15
Popper, Karl, 238–239
Posner, Eric, 150
precedent. *See stare decisis*
present/imminent violence, of incitement category, 53
Priest, Judas, 129, 137
prior communication, Trump call to action and, 192–194
Prison Litigation Reform Act (PLRA), on prisoner exhaustion of remedy prior to court, 112
prisons. *See also* book censorship, in prisons
    administrative overreach and incitement, 105–116
    censorship actions, 105
    contraband and, 105, 110–111
    four-part test of First Amendment challenges in, 109, 110
    incitement, prison security and precedent, 108–110

PLRA on prisoner exhaustion of remedy prior to court, 112
  protections for speech in, 107–108
  Supreme Court deference to prison wardens, 107–108
Procunier v. Martinez (1974), 108
public laws, liberal egalitarianism form of liberalism through, 29
public order
  Bible Believers and *Thompson* case on, 39
  liberal egalitarianism focus on, 35, 41
public school students, free speech rights of, 2
pursuit of truth, as expressive rights justification, 49

Rabban, David, 57
radical, defined, 146
Rainey, John, 131–132, 136–137
R.A.V. v. St. Paul (1992), 51, 183n13, 247, 249
Rawls, John, 29, 32
red flag ban, *Stromberg v. California* and, 52
Red Hot Chili Peppers, 133
Red Scare, first in 1919 and 1920
  Gitlow v. New York and *Whitney v. California* cases, 67, 146–147
  incitement cases, 67–68
Red Scare, second after World War II
  Abrams v. United States and, 147
  Adler v. Board of Education of the City of New York, 68–69
  American Communications Association v. Douds and, 68
  government restriction of free expression during, 68
  incitement cases, 68–69
  terrorism and, 146–147
replacement theory, domestic terrorism and, 155

Rice v. Paladin Press (1997), 169, 170
Roberts, John, 5
Roberts Court, 65, 75, 76, 80n108
Roth v. United States (1957), 56
Rousseau, Jean-Jacques, 29
Rucho v. Common Cause (2019), 81n113
Russia, music censorship in, 124–125
Rutledge, Wiley, 14, 15

Schad v. Mount Ephraim (1981), 128, 130
Schauer, Frederick, 99
Schenck, Charles, 7–8
Schenck v. United States (1919), 7, 15, 235
  clear and present danger test in, 8, 13, 14, 52, 54, 66, 145–146, 248
  Espionage Act conviction in, 8, 55, 66, 145, 248, 249
  Holmes on, 66, 145
  incitement in context and, 190
Schneider v. New Jersey (1939), 55
Schumer, Chuck, 5
Scott, I. R., 102n44
SDS. *See* Students for a Democratic Society
Second Amendment, *New York State Rifle & Pistol Association v. Bruen* case, 232
Section 230, of Communications Decency Act, 181–182
Sedition Act (1798), 6, 51, 61n23, 145, 227
self-realization, 49, 50
Senn v. Tile Layers Protection Union (1937), 55
Shah, Molly, 207–208
Shakur, Tupac, 131–132, 136, 137
Shaw v. Murphy (2001), 110
Shiell, Timothy C., 57
Shuttlesworth, Fred, 51

Sines v. Kessler (2017), 155, 188–189, 190
Sixth Circuit Court of Appeals, on *Nwanguma v. Trump*
  aftermath of, 211
  Bible Believers and, 216
  McKeague on, 210–211
  Snyder, Hess, and Bible Believers reliance on, 211
Slavery by Another Name (Blackmon), 105
Smith, Jack, 223n76, 227–228, 237n3
Smith Act, 244n2
  Dennis v. United States and conviction of CPUSA leaders under, 15, 54, 69, 147–148, 151, 248
  Noto v. United States conviction overturn for, 16, 54–55
  Yates v. United States conviction under, 16, 54, 250
S-M-R. *See* stimulus-mind-response
Snyder v. Phelps (2011), 189, 211, 247, 249
  on hurtful speech protection for public debate, 1–2
social contractarian theories, liberal egalitarianism similarity to, 30
social justice. *See also* free speech and social justice; incitement and social justice
  described, 65
  for societal outsiders and minorities, 65, 71, 75
social media, 57–58, 167–168, 195
  abusers use of, xii
  Communications Decency Act on immunity of, 168
  hate groups facilitated by, xii
  terrorism and, 149–150, 151, 155
societal outsiders and minorities
  free-speech victories at expense of, 71, 75
  punishment of dissident, 69
  social justice for, 65, 71, 75

Supreme Court depiction of defender of, 65
Sotomayor, Sonia, 74
Southeastern Promotions, Ltd v. Conrad (1975), 123, 127–128
speaker-listener internet interaction, stochastic terrorism and, 173–175, 178–179, 182
specificity factor, in criminal solicitation, 98–99
speech. *See also* criminal speech; dangerous speech; free speech
  Brandenburg lack of protection for criminal conspiracy and solicitation, xiiin12
  Brandenburg test on inciting or producing action, ix, 2–3, 17, 34, 47, 69–72
  followed by violence, 229
  hate, 155
  integral to criminal conduct, 2, 90
  prisons and protections for, 107–108
speech, modern doctrine
  clear and present danger test and, ix
  government neutrality for content and viewpoint of, xi
  punishment allowance in, xii
S-R. *See* stimulus-response
Stained Class album, of Judas Priest, 129
Stanley v. Georgia (1969), 56
stare decisis (precedent), *Janus v. AFSCME*, 233–234
State v. Cotton (1990), 102n39
states
  Brandenburg test protection against action by, 35
  criminal syndicalism laws World War I, 67
  dangerous speech prohibition to prevent imminent lawless action, xi

First Amendment and legal prohibition of speech by, ix
freedom to censor expression, 51–52
Patterson v. Colorado on censorship by, 52
prohibition of ideas being heard or read, x
Stefani, Gwen, 135
stimulus-mind-response (S-M-R), *Brandenburg* placement of mind in, x
stimulus-response (S-R), dangerous speech as trigger to action in, x
stochastic terrorism, 173–175, 178–179, 182
Stop the Steal discourse, of Trump, 167, 192–194
Straight Outta Compton album, of N.W.A., 130–131
strategic decision-making model, 217–218
Street v. New York (1969), 56
Stricklin v. Stefani (2018), 135–136
Stromberg v. California (1931), 56, 78n32
red flag ban and, 52
on state restriction on free speech, 48
Students for a Democratic Society (SDS), First Amendment protection for, 48, 55
Sunstein, Cass, 64, 150, 161n74
Supreme Court, 1
adherence to *Brandenburg*, 234
anti-orthodoxy and inclusion case decisions, 55–58
cases on Jehovah's Witnesses, 48, 55, 71, 81n114
Congress in 1870s on federal question jurisdiction, 6
deference to prison warden decisions, 107–108
as depiction of defender of outsiders and minorities, 65
expressive rights in decisions of, 48–49, 55
on FCC ban of broadcasting indecent materials, 168
First Amendment clauses incorporation, 6, 48, 55–56
identified categories of unprotected speech, 63n41
Roberts Court, 65, 75, 76, 80n108
stare decisis precedent, 233–234
test for incitement, 2–3, 56–57
transition from republican to pluralist democracy acceptance, 68
surrounding communication, Trump call to action and, 194
susceptibility to violence, Trump call to action, 195–196
Sweezy v. New Hampshire (1957), 48
Sykes, Emerson, 58–59
syndicalism law, as unconstitutional, 17, 247

Terminiello, Arthur, 230
Terminiello v. Chicago (1949), 71–72, 249
Douglas on clear and present danger test, 230–231
on expressive rights, 50–51
Jackson on, 230
terrorism
amorphous definition of, 152–156
arbitrary treatment of label of, 155
arguments to change *Brandenburg* standard, 149–151
BLM movement and, 144, 156
Brandenburg and clear and present danger, 148–149
Brandenburg test and disregard of, 143–157
Chen on *Brandenburg* and, 152
Cold War and, 147–148

of domestic organizations, 144, 154–156
federal criminal code definition of, 153
international jihadist terrorism and, 144, 161n74
locating scholar arguments in *Brandenburg* history, 151–152
malleable nature of term of, 143–144
Posner on *Brandenburg* and, 140
Red Scare, second and judicial deference, 146–147
social media and, 149–150, 151
Sunstein on *Brandenburg* and, 150, 161n74
Tsesis on *Brandenburg* and, 150–151, 159n44
World War I and birth of clear and present danger test, 145–146
Texas v. Johnson (1989), 1, 60n8
theory of equity, liberal egalitarianism and, 29
Thirteenth Amendment, *Schenck v. United States* and, 8
Thomas, Clarence, 232
Thomas, Shawn, 131
Thomas v. Collins (1945), 50, 250
 clear and present danger test, 14
 Rutledge on, 14
Thompson v. Trump (2022), 38–40
 Mehta on broader context of January 6, 2021, 213–214
Thornburgh v. Abbott (1989), 109–110
Thornhill v. Alabama (1940), 13, 250
thought crime, criminal solicitation and, 95–96
Tinker v. Des Moines (1960), 48–49, 69
de Tocqueville, Alexis, 75
tolerance
 liberal egalitarianism through free speech, 28
 violence and, 28

Tolley v. California (1960), 56
Torries v. Hebert (2000), 134, 136
true threats, 179
 conspiracy compared to, 93
 Counterman v. Colorado and, 234
 First Amendment protections outside of, 2, 92
 2023 Supreme Court on, 92
Trump, Donald. *See also* January 6, 2021 US Capitol attack; Louisville, Kentucky campaign rally; *Nwanguma v. Trump*
 on antifa and leftist activists as domestic terrorism, 156
 Biden comments and assassination attempt on, 5–6, 225
 cases regarding Trump involvement in election-related violence, 213
 claim under First Amendment Free Speech Clause, 38
 denial to dismiss on *Brandenburg* grounds, 39
 impeachment and, 187–188
 medium of communication and, 195
 prior communications considerations, 192–194
 Smith indictment of, 223n76, 227–228, 237n3
 Stop the Steal discourse, 167, 192–194
 susceptibility to violence and, 195–196
 violent rhetoric at rallies of, 208–209, 212
Trump v. United States (2024), 228
truth, Mill on expressive rights and search for, 49
Tsesis, Alexander, 150–151, 159n44
Turner, John, 6
Turner v. Safley (1987), 109–110, 112, 113

2Pacalypse Now album, of Shakur, 131–132, 136, 137

Unite the Right rally. *See* Charlottesville Unite the Right rally (2017)
United States ex rel. Turner v. Williams (1904), 6
United States v. Hale (2006), 215
United States v. Hansen (2023), 169, 234, 235, 250
United States v. Robel (1967), 56
United States v. Schwimmer (1929), 250
United States v. Stevens (2010), 250
United States v. White (2010), 215
United States v. Williams (2008), 97
Updegraph v. Commonwealth (1824), 66

Vallandigham, Clement Llaird, 87–88, 89
Vance, James, 129
Vance v. Judas Priest (1990), 129–130
Vinson, Frederick M., 148
  clear and probable danger test and, 15, 69
violence
  anti-orthodoxy and First Amendment decisions on advocacy of, 51–56
  liberal egalitarianism for speech for, 34–35
  speech followed by, 229
  tolerance and, 28
  Trump call to action and susceptibility to, 195–196
  Trump January 6, 2021 US Capitol attack and calls for campaign, 212–213
Virginia State Board of Pharmacy v. Virginia Citizens Consumer Council (1976), 50
Volokh, Eugene, 98

Waller v. Osborne (1991), 130, 136
Ward v. Rock against Racism (1989), 123, 124, 128, 131
Warren, Earl, 16, 70
Waters, Maxine, 5
Weinstein, James, 215
West Virginia v. Barnette (1943), 48
white supremacists, 238n12
  Charlottesville Unite the Right march in 2017, 51, 61n21, 189, 190
  domestic terrorism and, 154
Whitney, Charlotte, 11, 67–68
Whitney v. California (1927), 56
  bad tendency test and, 11–12, 17, 51, 67, 235, 250
  Brandeis concurrence in, 11–12, 147, 233
  Brandenburg v. Ohio overturn of, 17, 247
  incitement categories and, 54
  Red Scare, first and, 67, 146–147
Wisconsin v. Mitchell (1993), 229
Wood, Lin, 192–193
Wooley v. Maynard (1977), 1
World War I
  clear and present danger birth and, 145–146
  hostility toward freedom of expression, 51
  incitement cases and Espionage Act prosecutions, 66–67
World War II
  advocacy protective approach during, 14
  second Red Scare after, 68–69, 146–147

Yates v. United States (1957), 56
  clear and present danger test and, 16
  involving CPUSA, ix, 16
  Smith Act convictions upheld in, 16, 54, 250